Technology, Outsourcing and Transforming HR

Technology, Outsourcing and Transforming HR

Edited by
Grame Martin
Martin Reddington
Heather Alexander

AMSTERDAM • BOSTON • HEIDELBERG • LONDON • NEW YORK • OXFORD
PARIS • SAN DIEGO • SAN FRANCISCO • SINGAPORE • SYDNEY • TOKYO
BUTTERWORTH-HEINEMANN IS AN IMPRINT OF ELSEVIER

Butterworth-Heinemann is an imprint of Elsevier
Linacre House, Jordan Hill, Oxford OX2 8DP, UK
30 Corporate Drive, Suite 400, Burlington, MA 01803, USA

First edition 2008

British Library Cataloguing in Publication Data
A catalogue record for this book is available from the British Library

Library of Congress Cataloging-in-Publication Data
A catalog record for this book is availabe from the Library of Congress

ISBN: 978-0-75-068645-7

Printed and bound in Hungary
08 09 10 11 12   10 9 8 7 6 5 4 3 2

To Vanessa, Chris, Roz, Rhiannon, Alayna, Callum and Andrew
— *Graeme*

To Nicola, Alexander, Matthew, Lynda, James and Sybil
— *Martin*

To my mother
— *Heather*

Contents

Notes on Contributors

Graeme Martin is Professor of Human Resources (HR) and Director of the Centre for Reputation Management through People (CRMP) at the University of Glasgow's School of Business and Management, where he leads an advanced practice Masters in Strategic HR and Organizational Change. Graeme also holds visiting appointments in the USA, Sweden, Italy and France. After an early career in personnel and industrial relations management, he began teaching, researching and consulting in HR management (HRM) in 1978. He has published widely in the fields of international HRM, organizational change, HR development, HRM and, more recently, e-Learning and e-HR. Currently, he is editing a book series for Butterworth Heinemann on Advanced HRM Practice, having written or co-authored recent books on corporate reputations, branding and HR, managing people and organizations, and HR in Sino-foreign joint ventures. Graeme is also on the Advisory Board on Human Capital for the Scottish Government, current advises the NHS in Scotland, government departments and private sector firms on strategic HR and works with a leading firm of consultants in the field.

Martin Reddington is Director of Martin Reddington Associates and Visiting Research Fellow of Roffey Park Institute and School of Management, University of Glasgow. In January 2000, Martin was appointed Programme Director of e-HR Transformation at Cable & Wireless PLC. This global programme received acclaim at the National Business Awards and HR Excellence Awards in 2002. Since leaving Cable & Wireless in October 2002, Martin has blended academic research with consultancy. He has just submitted his doctoral thesis for examination on the topic of the perceived impacts of e-HR on both HR and line managers.

Martin has his own consulting business, Martin Reddington Associates, and provides a range of consultancy services for companies on HR transformation. He is a member of the CIPD's National Advisory Group on Technology and HR and was a judge for the Personnel Today HR Excellence Awards 2006. He is also a special adviser to the PPMA HR Transformation Policy Group. His most recent book *Transforming HR: Creating Value Through People* was published in 2005 by Butterworth Heinemann.

Martin is currently undertaking leading edge research with Professor Graeme Martin into the impact of e-HR in organizations, in particular how it affects the creation of value. Some of this work was presented at the first European academic conference on e-HR in October 2006.

Heather Alexander has been in business for over 30 years, mostly working for large FTSE100 companies such as BT, and is now running a small consultancy practice. Her background is in information technology, focused at the strategic level, looking at how businesses can best exploit technology to their advantage and then making the chosen strategy a reality. While in BT, she led or contributed to a number of company-wide projects, including the Directory Enablement project that supported BT's e-HR endeavours. In her own business, she now applies her experience to the needs of smaller businesses and other organizations. Outside of work, Heather has been involved in a variety of not-for-profit organizations, including serving as a director on the board of a Glasgow regeneration company, and she was a founding director of Central Easterhouse Credit Union. Heather has a PhD in human–computer interaction, has authored two books in the field and is an honorary professor in the Department of Computing Science at the University of Glasgow.

Douglas K Macbeth is Professor of Purchasing and Supply Management in the School of Management, University of Southampton. His research interests include supply chain management and strategy, applications of change management and

chaos theory to supply chains and logistics and the globalization of supply chains. He is also Associate Editor of *European Management Journal.* Douglas had decade of experience
in operations management roles in industry before he began
his academic career, which has taken in four UK Universities
and visiting roles in GSBA Zurich, SUNY at Albany, USA and
IESEG, Lille.

Anna Comacchio, PhD in Management, University Ca' Foscari
Venice, Italy, is full professor of Organization and manage-
ment at the Department of Business Economics and Manage-
ment University Ca' Foscari, Venice, Italy. She has been visiting
Scholar, Centre of Corporate Strategy and Change, Warwick
Business School, University of Warwick, GB. She is the coordi-
nator of the master in tourism economics and management,
University Ca' Foscari Venice, Italy.

The areas of interests are organizational design and people
management. Main focuses are organization and people management for innovation and internationalization, technology
transfer and development and innovation of small and medium
enterprises (SMEs), people management and e-HRM.

She has published in Italy and abroad. Her recent publications are Comacchio A., Scapolan A., (2005), "E-learning strategies of Italian companies", in Torres-Coronas T. and Arias-Oliva
M., ed., *e-Human Resources Management: Managing Knowledge
People*, Idea Group Inc. book, Hershey, pp. 171–204; Comacchio A., Scapolan A., Bonesso S., (2007), "Innovation, complementarities and performance in micro/small enterprises",
in *International Journal Entrepreneurship and Innovation Management*, Vol. 7, No. 1, pp. 5–28; Camuffo A., Comacchio A.,
(2005), "Linking intellectual capital and competitive advantage: a cross-firm competence model for North-East Italian
SMEs in the manufacturing sector", in *Human Resource Development International*; Comacchio A., Scapolan A., (2004), "The
adoption process of corporate e-learning in Italy", *Education
and training*, Special issue – International developments in
e-Learning, Vol. 46, No. 6–7, pp. 315–325.

Fabrizio Gerli, adjunct professor of Organizational Behavior
and Organizational Design at the Ca' Foscari University of
Venice, holds a PhD in Management from the Ca' Foscari

University. His research areas are competency-based HRM, innovation management and supply network management. He has published essays on competency-based HRM and articles in *Industrial Relations* and *International Journal of Training and Development*. He is director of the Master in Innovation Management at CUOA Business School.

Annachiara Scapolan is Lecturer of Organizational Behaviour and HRM at the University of Modena and Reggio Emilia, Italy. She holds a degree and a PhD in Management from the Ca' Foscari University of Venice. Her research areas are e-HRM, high-performance work practices, HRM and innovation of SMEs, and organizational and strategic complementarities. Among her recent publications are Comacchio A., Scapolan A., Bonesso S. (2007), "Innovation, complementarities and performance in micro/small enterprises", *International Journal of Entrepreneurship and Innovation Management*, Vol. 7, No. 1, 5–28 and Comacchio A., Scapolan A., (2005), "E-learning strategies of Italian companies", in Torres-Coronas T. and Arias-Oliva M., eds, *e-Human Resources Management: Managing Knowledge People*, Idea Group Publishing, Hershey (USA).

Sara Bonesso holds a PhD in Management at Ca' Foscari University of Venice. Her research areas are organizational studies and HRM. She has working experience in different research fields including industrial clusters, innovation, entrepreneurship and small business. Her current research focuses on innovation management with specific regards to the technology sourcing and absorptive capacity issues.

Veronique Guilloux is a lecturer at Paris 12 university (LEA-IRG). She teaches international management and international logistics. She has written several articles on e-business (Intranet and HR, outsourcing and HRM, EDI and inter-organizational relationships) and is currently working on shared service centres in multinationals.

Michel Kalika is Professor at the University Paris Dauphine. He is the director of CREPA (Centre de Recherche en Management & Organisation). He has written several books and research articles in e-management and information systems (see http://www.crepa.dauphine.fr/)

Elaine Farndale (PhD Cranfield School of Management) is Assistant Professor in the Department of HR Studies at Tilburg University in the Netherlands and is a member of the *Change Management Consortium* at Cass Business School, City University, UK. Her research in the fields of international HRM, the HR department, and change management and HRM has been published in both academic and practitioner journals and books and presented at numerous international conferences.

Jaap Paauwe (PhD Erasmus University Rotterdam) is Professor of HR Studies at Tilburg University and also affiliated to Erasmus University Rotterdam, School of Economics. His main research interests are in the area of HRM, corporate strategy, organizational change and industrial relations. His latest book is *HRM and Performance: Achieving Long Term Viability* (Oxford University Press, June 2004), for which he received the Dutch HRM network Award in 2005.

Claire Hyde holds a first degree in Sociology with HRM and a Masters degree in HRM, including CIPD accreditation, and has experience working in a variety of HR roles in both the public and private sectors. Claire currently operates in an HR consultancy capacity, helping organizations understand the rate of progress and impact of their HR transformation agendas, including the deployment of e-HR. She has recently accepted the position of HR Executive with the Connexions service, based at Head Office in Dorchester, but her role extends across all operations in the county.

Huub Ruël works as an Assistant Professor of Strategic HRM at Kuwait Maastricht Business School. He holds a Master in Work and Organizational Psychology, and a PhD in Business Administration/HRM. His thesis focused on implementation of IT in office environments based upon Adaptive Structuration Theory ideas. After that his main research focus became e-HRM, combining IT and HRM knowledge. In 2004 he published a book *e-HRM: Innovation or Irration?*, together with T. Bondarouk and J. C. Looise, in which the results of e-HRM implementation in five large international companies were described. Articles derived from this e-HRM study have been published in academic and professional journals.

Tanya Bondarouk is an Assistant Professor of HRM at the University of Twente, The Netherlands. She holds her PhD's in the fields of Didactics and Business Administration. Her main teaching and research interests are in the area of social aspects of implementation of information technologies and HRM, with a special reference to the interpretive research methods. More recently, she is involved in the research into e-HRM, conducting research projects in different private and public sector organizations. In 2006 together with H. Ruël, she organized the First Academic European Workshop on e-HRM in The Netherlands.

T. Nichole Phillips, MBA is a doctoral candidate and is completing her dissertation on the relationship between employee acculturation experiences and work-related outcomes at the University of Central Florida. A recipient of the McKnight Doctoral Fellowship, she earned her MBA from Florida A&M University. She has presented papers at the meetings of the Academy of Management, the Society of Industrial and Organizational Psychology, and the Southern Management Association. Her research has been published in the *Journal of Applied Social Psychology*. Her research interests include organizational acculturation, organizational diversity and HR information systems.

Linda C. Isenhour received her PhD from the University of Central Florida and is currently an Assistant Professor of Management at Eastern Michigan University. Her research interests include recruitment, cultural values, HRM strategy and HR information systems. Dr. Isenhour has published book chapters on HRM and technology, recruitment, HRM and cultural values, and HRM and privacy. In addition she has presented scholarly papers to the Academy of Management, Society of Industrial and Organizational Psychology, Southern Management Association, and Western Business and Management Association. Dr. Isenhour is a member of the American Psychological Association, Academy of Management, Southern Management Association, and Society for HRM.

Dianna Stone received her PhD from Purdue University and is a Professor of Management at the University of Texas at San Antonio. Her research focuses on diversity in organizations, Hispanic work issues, the influence of culture on HR practices, e-HRM and information privacy. The results of her research have been published in such journals as the *Journal of Applied Psychology*, the *Academy of Management Review, Personnel Psychology, Organizational Behavior and Human Decision Processes, Human Resources Management Review*, and the *Journal of Management*. She has edited two books on e-HRM including one with Hal Gueutal titled *The Brave New World of eHR: Human Resource Management in the Digital age*. She is a Fellow of the American Psychological Association, the Society for Industrial and Organizational Psychology, and the Association for Psychological Science. She is also the Editor of the *Journal of Managerial Psychology* and Associate Editor of the *Business Journal of Hispanic Research*.

Miguel R. Olivas-Luján (PhD, University of Pittsburgh) is Professor of Management at Clarion University of Pennsylvania, 840 Wood St, Clarion, PA, USA 16214 [Tel: +1 814 393-2641; Fax: +1 814 393-1910; e-mail: molivas@clarion.edu] and a Faculty member at Tecnológico de Monterrey (Mexico). His research areas include Information Technologies in HR, Gender, Business Ethics and Culture. He serves on editorial boards for the *Business Journal of Hispanic Research*, the *Journal of e-Business* and the *Encyclopedia of Human Resources Information Systems: Challenges in e-HRM*. His work has been presented in conferences in four continents and published in three languages, in over a dozen international outlets. In 2007, the Brazilian Ministry of Education awarded his co-edited book *Successful Women of the Americas* the highest scores possible for a research book. He has been a member of Mexico's National Researcher's System since 2004.

Gary W. Florkowski is an Associate Professor of Business Administration at the Katz Graduate School of Business, where he has taught a wide variety of courses in HRM and international business at the MBA and executive-MBA levels. He graduated from Cornell University with a BS degree in Industrial & Labor Relations and received his PhD and JD degrees from Syracuse University. Dr. Florkowski's primary teaching and research interests focus on the infusion of information technology in HRM and industrial relations processes, international HRM and comparative law. He is presently conducting a joint study of the determinants and effects of automating HR services in large North American, European and Asian companies with Dr. Miguel Olivas-Lujan. His recently published book, *Managing Global Legal Systems: International Employment Regulation and Competitive Advantage,* assesses the extent to which private actors can influence the evolution of domestic and international labor standards.

Elke Schuessler is currently finishing her doctorate on path-dependent strategizing and organizing in the restructuring of the German clothing industry at the School of Business and Economics, Freie Universitaet Berlin. She previously worked for three years as a business consultant for a Berlin-based consultancy firm specialized on HR processes and technology, where she has been involved in several e-HRM projects in large German organizations. She holds a BA in Psychology from the University of Sussex and an MSc in Industrial Relations and Personnel Management from the London School of Economics.

Martyn Sloman is CIPD Adviser, Learning, Training and Development. From 1997 to 2000, he worked as Director of Management Education and Training for Ernst & Young.

His most recent book was *The Changing World of the Trainer* (Butterworth Heinemann), which was published in April 2007.

Martyn is Visiting Professor in HR Development at Caledonian Business School, Glasgow Caledonian University, a visiting Professor at Kingston Business School, Kingston University, and a Teaching Fellow in the Department of Management and Organizational Psychology Birkbeck College, University of London.

Margaret Savage's wide and deep experience in HR, Organizational Design and Operational Property Management roles in locations at home and abroad underpin worldwide recognition as a thought leader and guru on the design and introduction of HR Shared Service operations, global outsourcing and right shoring, amongst other things. She was the driving force behind the comprehensive programme that saw the introduction of a global standard operating environment involving HR Policy simplification, process re-engineering, functional cost restructuring and the successful deployment of a single, truly global people management and HR information management system for the dynamic BT Group. Margaret's visionary design and innovative augmentation of Oracle-Peoplesoft 8.8 created the BT Peoplesystem, which has e-enabled people management practices for over 27K line managers through their desk tops and expanded self-service activities for over 100K employees worldwide across the group. Accessed through a universal people portal, the outcome is a twenty-first century solution for a company committed to exploiting the benefits of a digitally networked economy.

Additionally, Margaret has held or still holds a variety of complementary roles:

BT's first award-winning Gender champion and member of Opportunity Now Leadership Council; Pensions Trustee; President of the BT International Twinning Federation and active twinner; Sponsor of the Internationally renowned BT Hot Air Balloon Team (Marketing & Team Building); a Fellow of the CIPD; Non-Executive Director with the MOD – People Pay & Pensions Agency.

She has two daughters, three grandchildren and homes in both UK and USA.

Andy Field currently works at the London Stock Exchange as the HR Operations Manager, with the responsibility for delivering HR services to the business. Previous experience has been as an HR generalist before specializing in HR project management, particularly in the field of change management and the practical application of technology to deliver high-value, low-cost HR services.

Andy is a fellow of the Chartered Institute of Personnel and Development and has worked in both the public and private sectors. He currently lives in Bedfordshire with his wife and three children.

Neville Clement has over 20 years experience in HR. He has written this chapter based upon his collective experiences within National Australia Bank as: HR Business Partner for the Technology function; General Manager of the global HR Shared Services function, within which he directly contributed to the strategic development and execution of the HR transformation journey; Program Director for the implementation of SAP HR for the Australian business, and General Manager of Service Delivery, where his responsibilities included functional Business Process ownership of the SAP HR system within Australia. Neville is now Global L&D Manager for WorleyParsons, a publicly listed engineering services company headquartered in Australia.

Graham White, in his current position as Head of HR and organizational Development for Surrey County Council, is responsible for delivering the entire HR remit for the Council's workforce of 33,000, including Strategic Human Capital Management, Career Succession Planning, Talent Management and Pay and Workforce Planning.

His breadth of experience and expertise in HR and Personnel Management covers both the public and private sectors with positions in a variety of commercial, public and financial institutions including manufacturing, service, banking, policing and both central and local government.

A fellow of the Chartered Institute of Personnel and Development, Graham is a devoted family man who is personally committed to the values of flexible working as he maintains a full family life in his home in Northern Ireland and a busy professional career in the county of Surrey.

Anne Keegan is Associate Professor of HRM and Director of the MSc (Business Studies) at the University of Amsterdam. She delivers courses in HRM, and her research interests include critical analyses of transformations in the HR function, managing employees in knowledge intensive and project based work, and leadership and change in project-based organizations. She has published a number of articles in leading journals including the *Journal of Management Studies, Journal of Applied Psychology, Long Range Planning, Management Learning* and the *Human Resource Management Journal.*

Helen Francis is programme director of the MSc (HRM) and director of research and knowledge transfer at the newly established Edinburgh HR Academy at Napier University Business School. Her teaching and research interests are located within HRM/development and management learning, including CPD and reflective practice, emotion management, the psychological contract and the changing roles of HRM/development practitioners. Helen has published a wide range of articles in leading management journals and has contributed to two textbooks on HRM.

Preface

This book is the second in a series primarily designed to help senior practitioners in human resource management (HRM) develop their knowledge and skills in the strategic issues facing them and their organizations. In mid-2007, we conducted two surveys of different groups of senior HR managers, asking them among other things about their agendas items over the next few years. Very high on both lists was the issue of e-HR, the application of new information and communications technologies to the HR function and the function of HR. And given the role that technology can play in addressing operational, service delivery and strategic issues in HR, this came as no surprise. It is clear from the research that e-HR has the potential to make substantial cost savings and headcount reductions. It is also clear that it has the potential to improve service quality to managers and staff, though as we shall see, this is not always the outcome of e-HR innovations. What is less clear is the capability of HR managers and the HR function to use new information and communications technologies (ICT) to change their 'business model' – their ways of working to deliver strategic advantage. This is sometimes known as the transformational dimension of e-HR and is only rarely a feature of current applications of technology to the HR function, but one that is slowly growing in importance.

To this end, we have been involved in a series of research projects, conferences and practical work concerned with the application of technology to HRM and HR development since the late 1990s – the first author as a practically-oriented academic, the second as an HR transformation practitioner, who has since turned to academic life and consulting, and the third as a senior ICT practitioner who has a background in practice, university research and consulting. Our collective experience in this field, coupled with involvement with the Chartered Institute and Development (CIPD) in the UK on this issue, has led us to produce this collaborative book, which is a joint venture between academics and senior practitioners. In doing so, it has anticipated one of the key proposals resulting from a debate in the November, 2007 edition of the *Academy of Management Journal*. In this discussion, generated by a further study revealing why practitioners do not read or use HR research, collaborative working was posed as a remedy – involving academics, practitioners and consultants. In generating useful knowledge, academics bring their frameworks, theories and rigorous research techniques to the table, practitioners bring experience, theories-in-use and, most importantly, the key questions still to be answered, while consultants bring their specialist knowledge and solutions from different cases and, often, different countries. Hopefully, the results of this collaboration are useful to all three parties and to the community at large.

Along the way, we have learned quite a few lessons and met a large number of extremely pleasant and capable colleagues who have made excellent contributions to this book. One of the early lessons we learned was that you cannot distinguish the study and practice of technology to HR without considering the related issues of outsourcing and the new architectures of the HR function. It is often through the process mapping exercises which accompany the introduction of e-HR systems that firms find themselves in a better position to simplify their work and/or identify what are core and non-core processes. This leaves them in a better position to retain in-house what is core and outsource what can be successfully and economically to others. Similarly, the introduction of HR technology is often associated with leaving time and space for HR to undertake work of greater strategic value, or to work more closely as partners with line managers on business matters.

Regarding our colleagues, we first began this project as a more tangible outcome of a conference we ran with the CIPD in Edinburgh during November 2005, when we were present at some excellent presentations, certainly deserving to be heard or read by a wider audience. Second, we have to thank Tanya Bondarouk and Huub Ruel for producing an even better event in Enschede, the Netherlands during October, 2006 – the first International Workshop on e-HRM. At that event we also met some new academic colleagues who had much to contribute to useful theory and practice. We are grateful that no one turned us down for a contribution from either of these events, thus forming the basis for much of this book. Add to this mixture some invited contributions from leading practitioners and academics in this emerging field, and the result is a text that embraces relevant theory and practice in e-HR from seven countries. To our knowledge, there is not another book in this field that touches these different bases – theory and practice in so many different international settings – but the game is one which we hope will be played again in the near future.

Following an introduction from us, the first section of the book focuses on the outsourcing agenda, with contributions from academics in the UK, France, Italy and the Netherlands. The second section provides something of a survey by academics and practitioners of key e-HR issues in the UK, North America, the Netherlands and Germany, sometimes drawing on large-scale surveys and sometimes on depth case work in companies. The third section is mainly given over to senior practitioners to describe and critically evaluate e-HR and HR transformation projects they have led, including BT, the London Stock Exchange, Surrey County Council and the National Australia Bank. Fittingly, the final piece is an evaluation of these changes on the nature of the HR function itself by colleagues from the UK and Netherlands.

We hope that the book achieves its main aim, which is to inform practice and practitioners in this new field of HR. We also hope that it achieves a no less important but secondary aim – to generate unresolved questions for HR academics, the answers to which will also result in informed and reflective practice.

Graeme Martin, Martin Reddington and Heather Alexander

Acknowledgements

Any book, especially a collaborative one, is the outcome of the efforts of numerous people, most importantly in this case the authors of the various chapters without whom this work would never have seen the light of day and our commissioning editor, Ailsa Marks of Elsevier, who has been equally supportive in the project. As noted in the Preface, the impetus for this book arose from links we had with the CIPD in the UK, which has seen e-HR as a major agenda item for their research programme. Graeme Martin and Martin Reddington have undertaken a number of pieces of research, speaking engagements and advisory work for them, but the CIPD has also helped us in very direct and indirect ways in our research and development. So, we would like to thank Martyn Sloman and Vanessa Robinson for their support in this work (and to Martyn for his chapter), also Linda Holbeche, the new CIPD Director of Research and Policy, for her support for our future work on e-HR. Also, as noted earlier, Tanya Bondarouk and Huub Ruel are deserving of special thanks for organizing the first e-HR network and making possible the opportunity for further network meetings, as are Bluefin Solutions for their sponsorship of our book launch in February, 2008.

We would like to thank other colleagues who have helped us in this project, including the people who have taken the time to endorse the book: George Bishop, Director of Personnel and General Services, The Royal Borough of Kensington and Chelsea; Vance Kearney, Vice-President HR, Oracle EMEA; John Gilkes, Chief Executive of Roffey Park; and Chris

Brewster, Henley Management College and the University of Reading.

We would also like to acknowledge and thank Julia Kiely at Bournemouth University for her continued support of Martin's efforts to bridge the academy/practice gap and colleagues in the Department of Management at the University of Glasgow for their support in this project, including Judy Pate, Phil Beaumont and Sheena Bell.

We would also like to acknowledge and thank the support of the many organizations that have allowed us and our co-authors to co-opt their sites, managers and employees in our research. Many of these organizations wish to remain anonymous, but we can name BT, National Australia Bank, London Stock Exchange and Surrey County Council.

Finally, we would like to thank the staff of Elsevier, who have been at their usual excellent best in helping us get this book out on time, especially Sunita Sundararajan, who led us through the production phase of the project so ably. Sunita is based in India, which helps prove the case that technology works.

The editors and publishers would also like to thank the following people and organizations for permission to reprint material:

Figure 10.2 adapted from Orlikowski (1992, p. 410) with permission. Copyright 2007, the Institute for Operations Research and the Management Sciences, 7240 Parkway Drive, Suite 310, Hanover, MD 21076 USA.

Every effort has been made to contact owners of copyright material, though we are not aware of omissions in this regard. However, the authors would like to hear from any copyright owners of material produced in this book who may feel that their copyright has been unwittingly infringed.

CHAPTER 1

Technology, Outsourcing, and HR Transformation: an Introduction

Graeme Martin, Martin Reddington, and Heather Alexander

Introduction

The contemporary human resource (HR) function in for-profit and not-for-profit organizations faces a number of competing challenges, so creating ambiguities and tensions in what it delivers, how it delivers, how effectively it delivers, and to whom it delivers (Ulrich and Brockbank, 2005; Huselid et al., 2005; Paauwe, 2004). The drivers of HR have traditionally been described in three-fold terms (Lepak and Snell, 1998):

- Making itself more cost effective by reducing transaction costs, headcount, and/or improving its efficiency of its services (*the operational driver*);
- Improving its transactional (e.g. payroll) and traditional services (e.g. advice on selection, legal matters, etc.) to increasingly demanding line managers,

employees, business partners, and contractors (*the relational driver*);

■ Addressing the strategic objectives of the business or organization.

However, for HR functions in developed economies, we can now add a fourth driver relevant to the technology and HR transformation debate. This is best summed up by John Kay (2004), a well-known British economist, who cogently argued it is not only knowledge for innovation but also brands and reputations that are the major sustainable bases on which modern organizations and modern nation states can compete with those in the developing world. This *reputational driver* means that the HR function is also faced with:

■ Meeting the longer-term demands placed on corporations in society at large for being *different* from the 'normal' in terms of reputations with key stakeholders (external and internal brands) while remaining *legitimate* (Boxall and Purcell, 2007; Martin and Hetrick, 2006). In this context, legitimacy is fast extending to reputations for ethical and sustainable practice, good governance and leadership, and for being a good employer in the eyes of regulatory institutions, the increasingly influential business press, existing and potential customers, clients and employees.

The tensions underlying these challenges reflect two distinctive and often divergent sets of pressures on organizations. The first set is the *external* versus *internal pulls* that exercise the minds of managers, often embedded in the distinction between operational and strategic management. The second set relate to the goals of strategic or operational activity inside an organization – whether these are principally aimed at satisfying unitary objectives, associated with the concept of shareholder value, or whether these are more plural in nature (Whittington, 2000), and associated with the notion of stakeholder management and with modern forms of networked organizations (Figure 1.1).

These dimensions, related orthogonally, produce a matrix which helps us understand how contemporary human resource

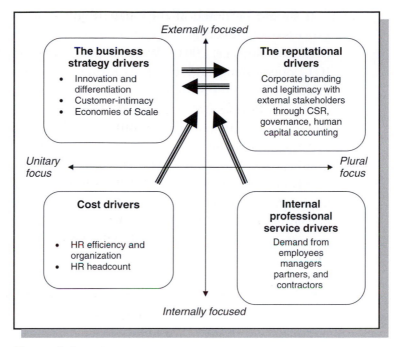

Figure 1.1
Competing claims on HR and their relationships.
Note: Corporate Social Responsibility.

management (HRM) teams in a number of organizations have developed a set of interrelated, *internal* delivery and professional service strategies to meet the *external* challenges set by the business strategies of modern organizations and the longer-term branding and reputational drivers (Reilly and Tamkin, 2006). The first of these internal strategies is the re-organization of the HR function itself, combining so-called *HR transformations* (new HR delivery models based on a tripartite model of shared services, centers of excellence, and strategic or business partnering) along the lines recommended by Ulrich and Brockbank (2005) with *outsourcing* and, in some cases, *off-shoring* of key services, especially shared service centres (CIPD, 2005; Cooke, 2006; Reddington et al., 2005). The second, like other business functions, is the turn to *information and communications technologies (ICT)*, often introduced in combination with HR transformations and outsourcing to rationalize or radically change HR's internal operations (Gueutal and Stone, 2005; Martin, 2005; Shrivastava and Shaw, 2004).

It should be noted at the outset that these organizational, process re-engineering and technological solutions are interdependent (Keebler, 2001). Without progressively sophisticated ICT, outsourcing and HR transformations would not be as effective: indeed it is the increased reach and richness of ICT-enabled information and organizational learning that have facilitated simultaneous centralization and delegation of decision making in HR, the single most important claimed distinctive capability of new HR transformation models (Ulrich and Brockbank, 2005). And, according to some academics and leading practitioners, one of the logical consequences of these developments is the potential 'virtualization' or, at least, significant 'leaning' of HR (Keebler, 2001; Reilly and Tamkin, 2006; Snell et al., 2001). This virtualization results from simultaneously reducing the numbers of specialists required to deliver HR services internally while improving the quality of these same services and developing new HR business models for innovative organizations (Taylor and LaBarre, 2006; see also Chapter 15: Using Technology to Transform HR at Surrey County Council for some case data).

The claims for new organizational solutions to HR and for the increased application of 'e' to HR seem to be much more acceptable as a novel, compelling, and credible message in the marketplace for management knowledge. In line with the predictions of the institutional theory and the 'bandwagon effect', which sheds light on the tendency of organizations to become similar in structure, often through mimicry of 'best practices' (Abrahamson, 1991; Lavie, 2006), there is strong peer pressure on organizations, including many in the public sector, to replace their integrated HR functions with the tripartite 'Ulrich' framework of shared services, centers of excellence, and business partnering. For example, a report by Mercer Consulting claimed that in response to a survey of client organizations 'nearly 80% of companies have completed or are in the process of undergoing HR transformation' (Theaker and Vernon, 2006). At the same time, in line with the predictions of agency theory, supply chain management thinking has been applied to HR, especially in the USA, in the form of increased contracting out of non-core and low-value added HR services such as payroll and partnering with other providers to provide other non-core but higher value-added services such as legal advice, recruitment, and training (Keebler, 2001). By 2004, academics were pointing out that outsourcing of HR services was on the minds of most global companies (Brewster et al., 2004), in part driven by the question asked by financial analysts not on whether companies have an outsourcing strategy but what it is.

Thus, the e-HR bandwagon seems to be growing at a rapid rate driven by some evidence of promising practices and positive evaluations of technology and outsourcing projects. As a result, both of the largest HR professional bodies in the world – the Chartered Institute of Personnel and Development (CIPD) and the US-based Society of Human Resource Management (SHRM) – have made this issue one of their key areas for research and for educating members. Furthermore, HR and information systems academics have also begun to see the application of ICT to HR as a key area of interest and the subject of specialist conferences in Europe and tracks in the Academy of Management Annual Conferences.

However, this bandwagon is also fuelled by some 'dangerous half truths' or 'total nonsense' (Pfeffer and Sutton, 2006), resulting in irrational forms of imitation fuelled by the persuasive powers of the growing number of consulting firms selling e-HR as part of a package of enterprise resource planning (ERP) solutions (Lengnick-Hall and Lengnick-Hall, 2006; Walker, 2001). Notwithstanding the rhetoric and groundswell of opinion among the HR community in support of e-HR, re-engineering the HR function and outsourcing, progress in the form of the more transformational benefits and pay-off in terms of cost reductions seems to have been more piecemeal and problematic (Caldwell, 2004; Reilly and Williams, 2006). Again to quote the Mercer Consulting report:

'Over half the survey respondents report that they are ineffective or very ineffective at realising the expected ROI [return on investment] from technology investments. HR people openly acknowledge that they frequently under-use technology and therefore do not gain full benefit' (Theaker and Vernon, 2006).

On HR transformations, Reilly and Tamkin (2006), in a report for the CIPD, claimed there was not much evidence of the adoption of Ulrich model (see also Chapter 16: Strategic Amplification of HR: New Forms of Organization or Social Disintegration?), at least in the UK where it had a lot of 'air time'. Finally, recent evidence suggests that the outsourcing bandwagon may have slowed down due to firms being unable to realize the claimed cost advantages or because of complications arising from contractual and governance arrangements (Hesketh, 2006; CIPD, 2007). Indeed, recent international survey evidence suggests that the global trends in outsourcing may have always been overstated (by consultants seeking to fuel demand for their own services?) (Brewster et al., 2007).

Such evidence raises important questions about e-HR, and the associated developments in HR transformations and outsourcing, which we attempt to address in this book. These are:

1 To what extent have the claims made by advocates of new forms of professional service delivery for improved cost effectiveness and reductions in HR headcount been realized without reducing service delivery, and what are the key impediments to realizing these cost benefits?

2 To what extent have the claims made for improved professional service delivery to managers and employees been realized and are there significant negative effects in moving from a face-to-face to a virtual and/or more distant relationship in HR and people management that have not been apparent to systems specifiers and developers? For example, how do significant injections of technology mediation influence the jobs of HR specialists, many of whom had entered the profession because they wanted to 'deal with people', and what new skills will they require? How are the jobs of line managers affected when they are progressively required to deal with their own HR problems as a consequence of the introduction of self-service e-HR systems and physical separation from HR specialists with whom they used to have face-to-face contact? And, how will employees, again used to face-to-face relationships

with HR staff, cope with technology mediation and the extra 'distance' imposed on them by the setting up of in-house or outsourced call or service centers?

3   To what extent have these forms of professional service delivery helped realize transformations in HR and new ways of people management, including freeing up HR staff to work on more strategic-level issues, such as the design and development of more sophisticated e-HRM systems and improved utilization. What is the potential for such developments in the near future, and how are they likely to change the nature of HR work, managerial work, and employee relationships?

4   Why is it that some organizations' HR departments are more effective at continuous innovation in the field of professional service delivery than others? Are those HR department and organizations that are best suited to innovation in e-HR also least suited to exploiting such learning?

5   To what extent are there innovative new HR business models beyond the inevitable mimicry of the Ulrich model, brought about by so-called best practice diffusion, and to what extent are we witnessing real innovations in HR practices?

To help provide some preliminary answers to these questions and to do some further scene-setting, we have developed a framework to show how internal HR delivery and professional service strategies, particularly e-HR, fit into overall HR strategies. This framework also helps show how the following chapters in this book relate to one another; in so doing it provides a rationale for the text. Thus we draw on some of our previous attempts to map out the territory of e-HR and HR service delivery that some academics and practitioners have been kind enough to suggest were useful in thinking about the subject (Martin et al., 2006; Reddington and Martin, 2006).

Introducing e-HR and associated forms of service delivery

e-HR, service delivery, and strategic HRM: a definition

As we have already claimed, e-HR is one of the most important recent developments in HRM (Gueutal and Stone, 2005; Lengnick-Hall and Lengnick Hall, 2003; Reilly and Tamkin, 2006; Snell et al., 2001). Yet, despite the growing body of literature devoted to e-HR, there is a dearth of useful frameworks to help our intended audience (HR practitioners, academics, consultants, and vendors) think about what might lead to successful implementation, or, indeed, what successful implementation might even look like. Given the potential for virtualization, a useful starting point is to see e-HR as a key element of e-business in the form of the 'virtual value chain', this time with a focus on the inside rather than outside of the firm (Rayport and Sviokla, 1995). By creating added value for managers and employees through more effective information flows in its 'marketspace', HR can claim to create competitive advantage and align the function more closely with business/corporate strategy and the longer-term branding and reputational aims of organizations.

The arguments for these claims are four-fold. First, e-HR can reduce HR transaction costs and headcount, for example, by supplying the same HR information to large numbers of people on a virtual rather than physical basis. Second, e-HR can substitute physical capability by leveraging the 'law of digital assets' to re-use information flexibly on an infinite number of occasions at little or no marginal cost. For example, this is most notable in the real time delivery of e-training and e-learning to large numbers of people across the globe. Third, e-HR can facilitate more effective virtual 'customer relationships' and internal labor markets by increasing the reach and richness of two-way information. Illustrations of such improved information flows are already evident in certain applications, including enabling internal/external recruitment and search by 'deep-web mining', online-career development and performance management, employee engagement surveys to tailor specific 'employee value propositions' to small groups of employees, more flexible working to attract people from non-traditional recruitment pools, and outsourcing of key HR services. Fourth, it can transform the traditional HR 'business model' by e-enabling HR to provide strategic value to organizations which it previously could not do, for example, by using the facilities of Web 2.0, including online learning to 'feed-forward' into organizational learning and organizational knowledge, thus creating international virtual communities of practice, capturing data for real-time human capital management, and facilitating more flexible organizational structures and ways of home-working. Recent data from a McKinsey survey shows how firms are beginning to use the interactive Web to transform their businesses generally (McKinsey Quarterly, 2007), so providing a roadmap for innovative HR departments to achieve greater credibility with business colleagues.

Though ICT has been widely used in human resource information systems (HRISs) since the 1980s, this application of technology has to be distinguished from e-HR. HRISs are focused on automating the systems used by the HR function itself: thus its main 'customer' has been HR staff rather than employees or managers. Moreover, HRISs have not been sufficient to create the type of internal virtual value chain discussed earlier. For example, HRISs have usually been applied to automating systems such as payroll and personal information, often with little or no attempt to make such data interactive or available to staff outside of HR; in contrast, e-HR is concerned with the application of the Internet, web-based systems, and mobile communications technologies to change the nature of interactions among HR staff, line managers, and employees from a pure face-to-face relationship to a technology-mediated relationship (Ruël et al., 2004). Through such technology mediation, e-HR has begun to replace or complement face-to-face relationships and HRIS with a 'smart self-service relationship', customized content, and greater individualization of services. By doing so, it creates a parallel internal HR virtual value chain, complementing the existing physical internal HR value chain.

Modeling e-HR and associated forms of service delivery

There have been few significant developments to-date to provide overall theoretical models for explaining e-HR adoption. Three notable exceptions are Shrivastava and Shaw's (2004) stage model, Florkowski and Olivas-Luján's (2006) survey-based model, and Ruël et al. (2004) who made use of the 'Harvard' model of HRM to link e-HR to HR outcomes. We have attempted to combine elements of these with our previous work (see Martin, 2005; Reddington et al., 2005) to explain the links between HR strategies, e-HR and service delivery drivers, e-HR technologies, and e-HR outcomes (see Figure 1.2). The basic elements of the framework are described in the following paragraphs.

HR strategies and polices

The HR strategies and policies of an organization interact with its strategic environment, corporate and business strategies,

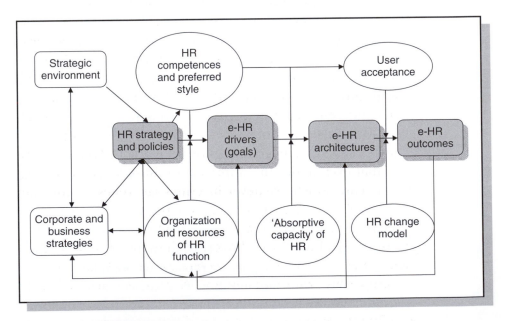

Figure 1.2
A model of e-HR.
Note: HR, human resources.

often in a complex, recursive relationship. Outside-in approaches to strategy stress the linear and hierarchical relationships in which HR strategies are deemed to flow from key corporate and business strategies as second- or even third-order strategies (Boxall and Purcell, 2007). In contrast, the resource-based view (RBV) of strategy stresses a more inside-out relationship, with HR and people management shaping or even driving key corporate and business strategies, especially in industries and sectors that trade on important intangible assets such as knowledge, reputations, and brands (Boxall and Purcell, 2007; Martin and Hetrick, 2006; Paauwe, 2004). Our perspective on HR strategies is summarized in Table 1.1, which is a simplified attempt to combine both perspectives in the form of a configuration framework.

Thus, we suggest that HR strategy can be related to three root sources of competitive advantage in the market sector, which we believe are also relevant to the public sector. These are (1) customer captivity/reputations for high levels of customer intimacy, (2) proprietary forms of disruptive technology and knowledge, and (3) economies of scale combined with exploitation of existing knowledge (Hagel III and Seely-Brown, 2005; Greenwald and Kahn, 2005a; Morris et al., 2005). These sources of advantage are either temporary or must be combined with one or both of the others to have any lasting advantage in global markets (Greenwald and Kahn, 2005b). Competition usually ensures that customers have plenty of options in the long run, while disruptive technology and knowledge becomes obsolete or widely available, and even economies of scale only provides a competitive advantage for restricted markets. One organization that exemplifies this approach to thinking about strategy is Wal-mart, which, whatever its critics say, relies on the combinative effects of all three sources of strategic advantage in its relentless drive to dominate world retailing markets (Fishman, 2006). In addition, like Wal-mart, how organizations think about their human resources in terms of fit with these sources of competitive advantage and how they manage people in practice enables them to create the necessary strategy-structure configurations and dynamic capabilities to sustain their advantage over longer periods of time (Hagel III and Seely Brown, 2005). For the purposes of illustrating these strategy-structure

Table 1.1
Archetypical configurations of business strategies and HR strategies.

Business strategy	High road/ disruptive innovation (prospector)	Low road/ low tech(defender)	Segmented architectural approach (analyzer)
Source of competitive advantage	Proprietary forms of knowledge/learning for disruptive innovation and/or customer captivity or intimacy	Focus on economies of large scale and exploitation of existing knowledge	Mixed - Proprietary forms of knowledge for disruptive innovation and/or reputations for high customer captivity or intimacy combined with and economies of large scale and exploitation of existing knowledge
Dominant workforce development, talent management and HR supply chain policy	ILM strategy. Workforce development for all. Inclusive view of talent. Limited outsourcing	ELM strategy. Workforce development focused on managers and key workersAutocratic fordism or traditional bureaucracy combined with high levels of market-based subcontracting	Mixed ILM/ELM strategy based on a segmented HR strategy. Segmentation based on potential of employees to add value and the level of investment in their firm specific training. Exclusive view of talent limited to core employee groups which are valuable and unique. Widespread partnering and outsourcing
Degree of investment in individual human capital stocks and flows	High investment in general and firm-specific skills. Accelerated development of high potentials	Relatively low, except for managers and certain core workers	High investment in internal workforce comprising core talent segment and traditional workforce. Low investment in external segments.
Associated form of Work Organization and Psychological Contracts	Flexible work design, temporary and cross-functional project teams, relational and ideological contracting	Bureaucratic organization and heavy reliance on transactional contracts	Flexible work design, networking and outsourcing. Mixture of ideological, relational and transactional contracts, segment dependent

Notes: ELM, External labor market; ILM, Internal labor market.

configurations, we have also highlighted three such archetypes, closely resembling the well-known and widely used prospector/defender/analyzer typology of Miles and Snow (2003). For example, Wal-mart, like IBM when it made computers rather than sold services, would best fit the analyzer model. Wal-mart is known for innovation not only in its famed logistics operations but also for putting pressure on its suppliers to innovate in product design and in ways in which they can shave costs. It is also well known for its customer captivity strategy by acting as their champion to deliver 'always low prices' through leveraging their scale economies and power with suppliers.

To achieve competitive advantage, however, firms also have to design appropriate HR strategies. (It is in this field that Wal-mart have had some well-publicised problems, including class actions taken out against them in the USA and their withdrawal from of Germany in 2006, in part caused by their inappropriate HR policies in that country, which fell foul of German labor laws and expectations.) These can be defined in terms of choices they exercise in four key areas of people management.

- The dominant strategy on *workforce development and talent management.* This includes the nature and levels of investments in individual human capital stocks and flows and in managing talented people (Morris et al., 2005). It also includes the choices exercised over *HR supply chains* (Swart and Kinnie, 2003). Options here embrace doing everything in-house, establishing business partnerships and joint ventures, and a range of different insourcing, outsourcing, and offshoring strategies (Keebler, 2001);

- The associated forms of *work organization* and *psychological contracts* with employees. Work organization design is principally shaped by the different forms of flexibility that organizations seek, including numerical, function, and financial flexibility (Atkinson, 1984). Similarly, choices can be exercised over the forms of psychological contracts entered into with different segments of employees. These can be a mixture of transactional, relational, and ideological and idiosyncratic contracts (Sparrow and Cooper, 2003);

■ The nature of *employer–employee independence*. This refers to the levels of investment in *social capital* (engagement and identification, trust, communications, networking, and knowledge sharing both inside and outside of the organization) and the degree of *job security* provided to employees in general (Adler and Kwon, 2002);

■ The extent to which decision making through *participation and involvement strategies* is delegated to individuals and/or collectives, and the dominant basis of rewards systems (Purcell, 2005; Whitely, 1999).

The strategic drivers of e-HR

The strategic drivers or goals of e-HR flow from the HR strategies and policies that we have just discussed. These drivers can address HR's *transactional* or *transformational* goals. The former focus on reducing the costs of HR services or improving its productivity, and improving service delivery to managers and employees; the latter focus on freeing up time for HR staff to address more strategic issues rather than basic administration, and by transforming the contributions that HR can provide to the organization (its 'business model'). The transformational goals have been alluded to earlier and involve extending HR's reach to more remote parts of the organization to create a sense of 'corporateness' or internal integration in extended enterprises (e.g. through HR portals); enabling more sophisticated recruitment searches (e.g. through deep-web mining to uncover people not actively seeking jobs) and (self) selection through online tools (Economist, 2006); facilitating deep learning in communities through online interactions; increasing the 'IQ' of the extended enterprise through organizational learning and knowledge; creating new forms of organizational community and methods of communications through new forms of social software, e.g. interactive employee engagement surveys, virtual communities of practice, 'blogging', 'wikis', etc.; and creating greater choice in how people work and in work–life balance through remote and virtual working (Florkowski and Olivas-Luján, 2006; Martin, 2005; Reddington et al., 2005). The transformational goals of e-HR are closely linked to the transformational re-organization of the HR function into a tripartite structure of shared services, centers of excellence, and strategic or business partners. e-HR makes such a re-organization more possible and more necessary since technology helps reduce the physical and hierarchical distance created by centralizing certain HR functions; at the same time, however, it helps create that distance by introducing technology mediation into previous face-to-face relationships.

e-HR architectures

The extent to which an organization focuses on any or all of these goals should, in theory, influence the types of e-HR architecture it adopts. We have borrowed the concept of technology architecture from the ideas of Galliers and Newell (2003), who used the term to describe how flexible socio-ICT systems can dynamically respond to changing information requirements during ICT implementation projects. Thus, an e-HR architecture is a broader notion than e-HR technologies because it incorporates not only what we would traditionally consider as e-HR, which typically mean *HR data, systems, and technologies*, but also how these are *sourced* and the accompanying *HR organization, infrastructure, and resources* . Sourcing refers to the internal/external choices discussed earlier but the HR organization, infrastructure, and resources is broader than the notion of HR transformational models also discussed earlier in that it also refers to the configuration of HR roles for providing e-HR services, how HR staff and the HR organization interacts with the new technologies, levels of e-HR skills and capabilities, HR's potential to adapt and develop the e-HR technologies, and the resources they are given to do their jobs, including the level of sponsorship from senior management. For example, some companies have set up in-house shared services centers and applied e-HR solutions to them but simultaneously outsourced major applications such as pay and pensions (CIPD, 2007; Cooke, 2006). The organization of roles in these new HR service centers can result in certain HR staff work almost exclusively through ICT-mediation, requiring them to work with and master new online and telephony relationships and skills quite different from the traditional face-to-face mode they have been used to working in. Often e-HR technologies determine how these people work leaving little room for them to adapt the systems, though certain of these systems are deliberately designed to be more flexible and amenable to user adaptation.

Thus, we can classify e-HR architectures according to the three dimensions discussed earlier in describing the e-HR value chainHR. The first dimension draws on the classification of e-HR goals, that is whether the architecture draws on *operational* technologies and operational skills demands of HR (e.g. HRIS and basic ICT skills); *relational technologies and HR skills* (e.g. manager self-service (MSS) and employee self-service systems (ESS) and HR portals, etc., accompanied by skills in using technology-mediated HR transactions); and *transformational technologies and HR skills* in areas such as sophisticated search technologies, online survey tools, career development tools, human capital management systems, social software, e-learning, and knowledge management platforms, virtual meetings software, etc.). The second dimension relates to how these technologies and skills are sourced. As we have discussed, there is an increasing level of discussion at least on the use of outsourcing of e-HR to contractors, often for reasons of cost and lack of internal expertise (CIPD, 2007; Cooke, 2006; Lawler and Mohrman, 2003). How such relationships are managed and experienced by both parties can have important consequences for the outcomes of e-HR implementation. The third dimension refers to how internal and external HR-related staff and organizations interact, formally and informally, with these technologies, and their levels of existing skills and potential for developing these socio-technical systems.

Moderating influences on the adoption of e-HR architectures

e-HR and broader service delivery adoption will be moderated by the *absorptive capacity of HR* to seek out knowledge about and exploit these architectures to the full (Zahra and George, 2002; Martin et al., 2003; 2006). It will also be moderated by levels of *HR competence* in ICT and business and management (Bell et al., 2006). The notion of absorptive capacity of the HR function is potentially very important in shaping internal service and e-HR adoption and exploitation (Martin et al., 2003;

2006). Absorptive capacity in this context can be defined as the *potential* for the HR function, supported by ICT specialists, to acquire and assimilate knowledge about e-HR technologies and its uses into their vision for a changed HR function (Zahra and George, 2002; Jansen et al., 2005). It can also be defined in terms of the capacity of the HR function to *realize* e-HR potential, the first stage of which is to transform e-HR technologies by developing them and fusing them with existing HR processes. Two important issues arise out of the application of absorptive capacity models to e-HR and HR more generally. The first is the perennial question of whether e-HR technologies should be adapted to existing or revised HR processes (customization) or whether HR processes should be adapted to fit usually bought in technologies (the 'vanilla' solution). Evidence to-date suggests that the vanilla solution is more prevalent because of the difficulties in changing existing e-HR technologies at reasonable cost (Shrivastava and Shaw, 2004). This realization phase is also marked by the ability of the HR function to combine face-to-face and technology-mediated HR approaches to produce a new business model for HR, i.e., e-HR's ability to transform what it can currently do with available knowledge and technology into a more strategically oriented function which addresses the key strategic drivers of the organization (Huselid, et al., 2005).

The second issue relates to a paradox noted in the innovation literature, which when translated into HR terms proposes that those HR departments strong on acquiring and assimilating knowledge on e-HR are probably least effective at exploiting it; conversely, those HR departments that are efficient at exploiting knowledge on e-HR are likely to be less able to acquire and assimilate new knowledge in the field, thus reducing the likelihood of future technological innovation. These apparent paradoxes arise because technological applications in general are most effective in mechanistic departments dominated by routine work systems and people skilled in administrative operations, whereas learning and innovation are best suited to departments with adaptive, organic firms employing people with related innovative and creative competences (Kogut and Zander, 1992; Lengnick-Hall and Lengnick-Hall, 2006; Martin et al., 2006). This paradox can explain why some HR departments are more likely to be continuous innovators in service delivery and, indeed, strategic HR more generally.

e-HR outcomes

Finally, the adoption of specific e-HR architectures should lead to specific *e-HR outcomes*. Drawing on the existing literature and our research findings from preliminary casework, we have set out these potential e-HR outcomes in Table 1.2. Note that e-HR outcomes can be both intended or unintended, and also positive or negative: much of the existing literature has focused on the benefits of e-HR adoption, but it becoming gradually recognized that there are potentially negative consequences from e-HR adoption for HR staff and their internal clients, especially if the issues connected with change management and technology acceptance are handled ineffectively (Ruël et al., 2004; Reddington et al., 2005; Martin et al., 2006). It should also be noted that the positive and negative classification will sometimes depend on where one stands; a good example of this is headcount reduction of HR, which is often used as a justification by the organization for e-HR but has potentially damaging consequences for organizational memories and knowledge retention as well as for those HR staff displaced by the reduction.

Moderating influences on e-HR outcomes

Again it should be noted that these outcomes will be moderated by the *change models* and approaches adopted. The change management literature is extensive, analyzing how different approaches to change produce better or worse results; controversy still exists over the merits of top-down versus bottom-up change, incrementalist approaches versus 'big-bang', and the pace at which change should be driven. Martin and Beaumont (2001) have developed a model of strategic HR change that focuses on a complex set of events, activities, linguistic practices, emotions, and reactions that help explain what would be needed for successful change to occur and why most such initiatives are less-than-successful in producing sustainable change. There is not sufficient space here to elaborate what is a complicated model. All that we can usefully say at this point is

Table 1.2
Classifying e-HR outcomes.

	Positive	Negative
Intended	**Transactional** Reduced costs of HR transactions and HR headcount reduction Greater responsiveness to needs of managers and employees' needs for (real-time) information and tailored HR solutions on demand Increased self-efficacy among managers and employees **Transformational** Greater accountability of managers for people management Increased acceptance of self-development by employees Improved talent management through self-selection, self-assessment, performance management, etc Improved two-way communications leading to higher levels of organizational engagement and satisfaction with HR/people management Greater access to individual learning Greater capability to feed forward individual learning into group and organizational learning across distributed organizations Greater sense of corporate identity through uniform HR portals More time for HR to focus on expert/strategic issues Greater ability to work flexibly from home and other workplaces	**Transactional** HR headcount reduction **Transformational** Lack of face-to-face contact and remoteness of HR staff from 'clients' Intellectual property and data ownership transferred to outsourcing partner

(continued)

Table 1.2

(*Continued*)

	Positive	Negative
Unintended	**Transactional** Spillover of information from HR into other areas of business **Transformational** Greater sense of organizational innovativeness/progress modeled through adoption of sophisticated e-HR	**Transactional** Displacement of existing HR staff and loss of organizational knowledge Lack of job satisfaction among HR staff working in shared service centres Manager/employee frustration over ease of use and value of information Resistance to new ways of working through 'benign neglect', opposition, or mild forms of sabotage. Increased levels of cynicism with HR/organizational change programs Increased perception by managers of 'doing HR's job' and work overload

Note: HR, human resources.

that there are no easy or one-best-way answers to strategic HR change, which also extends into e-HR implementations and HR transformations. Change is situationally bound, in which receptive contexts play an important part, especially in transferring practices across international boundaries or even corporate ones. Moreover, successful change seems to rest on the abilities of system designers and implementers to align compelling, credible, and novel strategic discourses at the various stages of the change process. These strategic narratives translate into making the case for changes in practice, attending to the politics of who wins and loses, gaining the buy-in from key opinion leaders, securing early wins, and measuring the penetration and durability of the changes at appropriate stages in conceiving, implementing, and embedding new working practices into the organizations. As we shall see in a number of the following chapters, some organizations have been sensitive to such issues, while others have been less so, paying a heavy price for their neglect. We shall also see how certain shibboleths of change management, including involving those most affected by the change in the system design, does not always produce the best results, even in circumstances which are most conducive to such consultation (see Chapter 10).

Nevertheless, one of the most important factors shaping the success of technological change is *user acceptance* (Fisher and Howell, 2004). Thus, important moderating factors that need to be considered are architectural systems design decisions, factors affecting employee and manager reactions to the e-HR technologies, including the nature of individual characteristics and situational characteristics, and intended or unintended user reactions to the systems architecture.

An Outline of the book

These frameworks are intended to help us bring together the diverse contributions from academics and reflective practitioners who are currently researching and/or implementing e-HR, outsourcing, and HR transformations in the USA, Europe, and Australia. The academics have been asked to provide lessons for practitioners and the practitioners have been asked to think about the wider implications of their cases for use with students and in developing useful frameworks and models to help others understand the problems involved in this field. Though some chapters have been specially invited, much of the material for the book was presented at two conferences in late 2005 and 2006 and has been subsequently revised and updated. (CIPD Scottish Partnership Annual Conference, Edinburgh Business School, 16 November, 2005 on e-HR and outsourcing and 1st International Workshop on e-HR, University of Twente, the Netherlands, 25–26 October, 2006.) All chapters attempt to get beyond the hype and to present a balanced picture in relation to the scale and consequences of developments (inevitably some are more polemical than others as a provocation to a debate). Though the idea for the book began with a focus on the applications of e-HR, we believe this topic cannot be examined without considering related developments in delivery and professional service strategies. Consequently, we have organized the book into three parts. Part one deals with outsourcing, shared services, and changing landscape of HR in four European countries. Part two presents a set of chapters on e-HR in different international settings, including the UK, North America, the Netherlands, and Germany. Some of these chapters are based on wide-scale survey data, others are based on in-depth case studies of company implementations of e-HR. Part three brings together e-HR, outsourcing, and HR transformations in a series of cases written by practitioners to give a view of life on the ground. In combination, we believe the three parts provide an in-depth, contemporary, and reflective account of new forms of HR service delivery internationally, one that will be of interest to both practitioners seeking to get beyond the hype and to academics interested in hard evidence and practical illustrations of what is going on internationally in this field.

Part one. Outsourcing and shared services

In Chapter 2: Lessons on Outsourcing from a Supply Chain Management Perspective, Douglas MacBeth from the UK was asked to provide some lessons for HR practitioners and academics on outsourcing from a supply chain management perspective, which he does with lucidity. Drawing on the insights of transaction cost economics and the more practitioner-oriented ideas of make or buy, MacBeth provides a framework for analyzing the benefits and costs of different types of outsourcing arrangements found in HR, including *soft-in/insourcing*, where a service provider (SP) takes over the activities previously provided internally; *hard-out/resource outsourcing*, where an SP takes over the HR functions, process, staff, and other assets previously owned in-house; *total-invest-out/enhanced service outsourcing*, which offers additional benefits beyond the previous on by agreeing to improve on service performance; *share-in/internal JV*, where the firm and a SP form an HR services joint venture; and *share-out/trading services*, where a firm invests in a new business entity to sell services to others.

In Chapter 3: HR Outsourcing in Italy, Anna Comacchio and her colleagues draw on transaction cost economics and the fashionable RBV of strategy to explain the drivers of HR outsourcing in northern Italy, which are broadly consistent with the lessons from the previous chapter. Drawing on case study and survey data of 33 firms, they find that strategic reasons associated with the need to bolster internal resources rather than purely cost considerations are the most important antecedents of HR outsourcing. Also consistent with this perspective, they find that the firms tend to keep those more strategic and higher added-value HR processes inside the organization, made all the more possible because of outsourcing labor-intensive, low added-value processes such as payroll administration and recruitment.

Veronique Guilloux and Michel Kalika have examined the theory and practice of HR outsourcing in France to address the question of whether it can resolve the tensions between the traditional administrative role of HR in French companies and the desire to make HR a strategic partner. In Chapter 4: Outsourcing HR in France: Theory and Practice they provide data on different types of HR outsourcing, which, they argue, is not as well developed in France as in Anglo-Saxon countries. They conclude that the HR outsourcing is often driven by the desire of chief executives for greater levels of business process outsourcing rather than by HR departments and also point out the important relationships between outsourcing and e-HR, one of the key messages of this opening chapter.

Elaine Farndale and Jaap Paauwe in Chapter 5: Restructuring the HR Function: HR Shared Service Centers in the Netherlands use survey data from Dutch HR consultants, Berenschot, to examine the motives underlying the phenomenon of HR shared service centers, the performance expectations created by their establishment, and the realized outcomes. Not unexpectedly, cost, standardization, and improved service delivery are primary motivations rather than more strategic reasons, but most of the companies studied lacked performance measurement systems to assess improvements. Farndale and Paauwe draw seven practical lessons from their research, including the need to standardize HR practices before developing shared services centers, developing performance measures, using an incremental change model whereby the most basic HR services are restructured first, and having realistic expectations of cost-savings as a long-term rather than short-term ambition.

Part two. The theory and practice of e-HR in different countries

In part two of the book, the international theme is continued with high-quality contributions from the UK, the Netherlands, the USA, and Germany on current practices in e-HR. In Chapter 6: The Impact of e-HR on Line Managers and Employees in the UK: Benefits, Problems, and Prospects, Martin Reddington and Claire Hyde use elements of the model introduced in Chapter 1 and on earlier work on HR transformations by Reddington et al. (2005) to set discuss the impact of e-HR on the cost-savings, HR communications, and the impact on HR and line managers. Drawing on focus group interviews and survey data from a case of the introduction of e-HR into a major UK-based international mobile telephone company, they highlight the benefits and problems created for HR managers and line managers. Their study:

'highlights a very mixed picture indeed when viewed from the perspective of line managers. In terms of the impact on improving employee communication and engagement it is apparent that technology can facilitate employee engagement... However, [the] research shows that unless the e-HR tools are intuitive to use and attractive in terms of relevance and personalisation, then problems concerning alienation of the user can result.'

Chapter 7: Exploring the Relationship between E-HRM and HRM Effectiveness: Lessons Learned from Three International Companies by Huub Ruël and Tanya Bondarouk, two Dutch researchers who, along with their colleague Jan Looise, produced one of the first academic books on e-HR, examine human resource management (HRM) and e-HR effectiveness in three cases of international companies from contrasting sectors in the Netherlands. They begin by outlining a model of the links between e-HR and HRM effectiveness, which has helped academics and practitioners (including ourselves) think more strategically about this issue. They use the model to organize their case study data from which they conclude that the content and the structure of e-HRM applications can have a positive effect on the 'technical' (administrative functions of HRM) and strategic HRM effectiveness. These authors also examine the link between e-HRM and the commitment of employees, which is an area that the CIPD are interested in and links to the work of Reddington and Hyde in Chapter 6. The tentatively conclude that:

'respondents sense that they get more attention in terms of receiving information and development opportunities, which may make them more committed to their organizations.'

Chapter 8: The Potential for Privacy Violations in Electronic Human Resource Practices is a welcome contribution from T. Nicole Phillips, Linda Isenhour, and Diana Stone from the USA. Stone co-authored a key American text on e-HR, which we have used in our studies; she has chosen, with Phillips and Isenhour, to focus on the relatively unexplored issue of the potential for privacy violations created by e-HR. As these authors point out, organizations now have greater access to a wide array of data about individuals that are beneficial to both the firms and employees. However, these data can be, and are being, disseminated to third parties, including credit agencies, potential employers, and government for a range of reasons, without the express agreement of employees and potential employees. Drawing on Stone's earlier work on organizational privacy, this chapter provides a number of propositions that are helpful to academics and practitioners in dealing with the issue of individual and organizational rights in the context of e-HR. They see:

'individual rights tak(ing) precedence over those of organizations, unless there is a bona fide reason for the opposite to occur.'

Miguel R. Olivas-Luján and Gary W. Florkowski use Chapter 9: Diffusion of HR-ICTs, an Innovations Perspective to provide a rather different contribution from the USA in exploring the diffusion of e-HR internationally, drawing on the ideas from the innovation literature and large-scale survey data. They analyze how e-HR (they call it human resource information and communication technologies, HR-ICT) can be described and classified according to researchers who examine the determinants of innovation. Following this analysis, they discuss some early results of a major study into HR-ICT innovation in several English-speaking countries. Finally, they provide some much needed advice to HR managers seeking to make a business case for e-HR investment in their organizations. This chapter is written very much in the tradition of evidence-based management, which is all too often neglected in HR more generally (see Pfeffer and Sutton, 2006) and is of particular relevance to readers concerned with the change management dimensions of e-HR.

The last contribution in this section, Chapter 10: Designing and Implementing e-HRM – a Structurational Approach to Investigating Technological and Organizational Change, has been written by Elke Schüßler, formerly a consultant working on e-HR transformations and now an academic. Schüßler has drawn on her first-hand insights and more objective research to tell a tale about the experiences of four German companies, each rather different, which have recently implemented e-HR programs. She has constructed a complex and highly insightful 'structuration model' of information technology and organizational change to answer the questions: how does the organizational context influence the design and implementation processes of e-HR initiatives and how does the design and implementation of e-HR initiatives influence organizational contexts? This study reminds us about the context-bound nature of HR changes more generally, how solutions to one set of problems are only temporary, and that today's solutions are often tomorrow's problems. Like other chapters, Schüßler's academic reflections have important lessons for practitioners as befits a former consultant, especially on how to work with consultants.

Part three. Practitioners forum

This section of the book is written by practitioners (with one exception) to get a perspective of 'life on the ground' and to provide some further practical advice from individuals who have been intimately involved with e-HR, outsourcing, and HR transformations. Martyn Sloman, a leading CIPD adviser on policy on HR development, writer on training and e-learning, and visiting professor at Glasgow Caledonian University, Glasgow, UK, makes one of the strongest statements on technology in Chapter 11: Going Forward With E-HR: What Have Learned and What Must We Become?, claiming:

> 'The brutal truth is that we have failed to secure an adequate understanding (let alone mastery) of the HR/technology interface. We cannot allow this to continue, because ultimately it will put the credibility of the HR profession at risk.'

This assertion reflects the CIPD's research agenda, which places technology/outsourcing/HR transformation center-stage. Sloman reviews the CIPD's work in this field to-date and supplements his arguments with four short case illustrations from the UK Department of Health, the Scottish Fire and Rescue Service, Penna, an outplacement consulting firm, and the British Broadcasting Corporation (BBC). He uses these cases to make two important points for practitioners: the first is the need for perceived relevance and consent among users; the second is getting the balance right between automation and face-to-face support, two messages that resonate with many of the chapters in this book.

Chapter 12: The e-Enablement of People Management in BT by Margaret Savage, former HR director of BT, and Heather Alexander, formerly a senior information manager with BT and now an independent consultant and visiting professor at the University of Glasgow, in the UK, is one of the most detailed cases of HR transformation and technology. The case is an insider, almost blow-by-blow account of BT's most recent overhaul of its people, HR, and HR systems strategy, focusing on the design and implementation phases. As such it provides an excellent platform for academics to understand what an HR transformation/e-HR program looks like in practice and provides a roadmap for HR practitioners contemplating such a journey. One of the most interesting aspects of the case is how BT spent almost as much time re-engineering and simplifying its HR processes as it did on systems design, development, and deployment. Learning from their past experience of having to engage in major customizations to software to fit the then existing BT HR processes, taught the company a bitter lesson about the need to keep e-HR systems design as 'vanilla' as possible. This technology-led approach seems to be one that many companies have followed, though recognizing that modifications in global systems will be needed to reflect country differences (Shrivastava and Shaw, 2004).

Chapter 13: Building a Road Map for e-HR at the London Stock Exchange by Andy Field, HR operations manager of the London Stock Exchange, is also written up as a roadmap for e-HR implementation. This case, however, focuses on the benefits that can be derived from e-HR in a relatively small organization. The study examines a number of issues, including linking e-HR with business and HR strategy, the drivers of e-HR, making a business case, choices over technology, designing the overall solution, and implementation. Of particular interest to practitioners should be the sections on option choices for e-HR architectures and their costs and benefits, and the framework for assessing the impact of e-HR services. One of the key lessons learned from this case is that the application of e-HR in small-to-medium enterprises (SMEs) can be just as valuable as in large organizations in achieving tangible benefits and cost reductions.

In Chapter 14: e-HR at the National Australia Bank, Neville Clement, formerly a senior HR executive for director of the National Australia Bank, provides another insider account of a major e-HR implementation project. Like the BT and London Stock Exchange cases, this account is rich in detail and insights into workings of e-HR projects, thus helping practitioners, academics, and students of HR understand the processes involved in a large-scale project. Also like the other cases, Clement has attempted to provide some lessons learned and an evaluation of costs and benefits. He concludes that cost savings have been a major feature of this project:

'process re-engineering, the removal of paper, and the implementation of e-enabled processes contributed an initial saving in transactional costs of around 20% . . . the introduction of [the e-HR modules, process re-engineering and reorganized HR work] has resulted in a reduction of core direct operating costs of around 40%.'

However, costs were not the only benefit; according to an internal survey, user satisfaction with HR services increased from 20% in 2001 to 90% in 2004.

The last case study in the book in Chapter 15: Using Technology to Transform HR at Surrey County Council takes the form of an interview conducted by Martin Reddington with Graham White, HR director of Surrey County Council, UK. White has been a long-time advocate of HR transformation, outsourcing, and the application of technology to HR and has applied his ideas to a major re-organization of the HR function in a large UK local government body. Like the BT case, where the HR function has been substantially slimmed down since the early 1990s, Surrey County Council's HR department has become almost virtual along the lines predicted by Lepak and Snell (1998). In this chapter, White explains his rationale, strategy, and organization for an HR function fit-for-purpose. This is an excellent case to conclude our practitioner contribution section since it provides one possible scenario for the HR function which serves as a warning to some and as a model for others. It also touches on many of the issues raised by the academic contributions to this book, including the links between strategy and e-HR and the changing nature of the HR function.

While Graham White's contribution presents a mixed picture of pessimism over the future of HR because of its lack of relevance and optimism if it manages to transform itself to become more strategic through e-HR and outsourcing, we give the final word in this practitioner forum to two practically minded academics, Anne Keegan of the University of Amsterdam, the Netherlands and Helen Francis of Napier University in Edinburgh, UK, on the effects of e-HR, outsourcing and HR transformations on HR professionals themselves, line managers, and employees. In Chapter 16 Keegan and Francis provide much needed evidence on the ground of HR professionals and new entrants into the profession. Their analysis points to the potential for 'social disintegration' of the function, exemplified by a displacement of the 'soft' version of HRM by the 'hard', strategic one, potential problems for people management created by overloading line managers with HR responsibilities, and the denigration/removal of the traditional 'employee champion' role of HR that had led many people to enter the occupation in the first place and was associated with a loss of employee trust and confidence in the new HR. This is a rather different criticism of the trajectory along which HR is proceeding, but one that provides a much need corrective to the advocates of a transformed HR function though technology and outsourcing and one that resonates with the experience of many HR practitioners.

We hope these chapters reveal some of the major tensions, paradoxes, and ambiguities facing the HR function of the future and shed some light on how they may be resolved. In our own minds as academic-practitioners, we hold a pluralist perspective on these issues. There will be simultaneous cause for optimism and pessimism with winners and losers in reorganized HR functions and in the organizations in which they operate precisely because we are dealing with a complex picture of interlocking and often divergent interests, regardless of the unitary sentiments expressed in much of the HRM literature and practice. Though we share the concerns of those contributors pointing to the 'dark-side' of e-HR, outsourcing, and new HR delivery models, there is enough in them to warrant a strong degree of optimism. However, we believe that the HR professionals of the not-to-distant future may be rather different from the traditional practitioners who have staffed the function. Consequently, we hope this book digs deep into what they need to know and what the need to become.

References

Abrahamson, E. (1996) Managerial fashion. *Acad. Manage. Rev.* 21, 254–85.

Adler, P.S. and Kwon, S. (2002) Social capital: prospects for a new concept. *Acad. Manage. Rev.* 27, 17–40.

Beatty, B.D. (2001) A framework for transforming your HR function. In *The Technologies and Trends that are Transforming HR: Web-Based Human Resources* (A.J. Walker, ed.) pp. 150–72. New York: McGraw Hill/Towers Perrin.

Bell, B.S., Lee, S.W., and Yeung, S.K. (2006) The impact of e-HR on professional competences in HRM: implications for the development of HR professionals. *Hum. Resource Manage.* 45, 295–308.

Boxall, P. and Purcell, J. (2007) *Strategy and Human Resource Management.* 2nd Edition London: Palgrave Macmillan.

Brewster, C., Sparrow, P., and Vernon, G. (2007) *International Human Resource Management.* (2nd edn.), London: CIPD.

Business Week (28 December, 2006) *Outsourcing Beyond Bangalore: Special Report.* BusinessWeek. Available online at www.business week.com/ globalbiz/newsletter/europe/index.html (last accessed 9 September 2007).

Caldwell, R. (2004). *In Search of Strategic Partners in Business Partnering: a New Direction for HR.* London: CIPD.

Chartered Institute of Personnel and Development. (2005) *HR outsourcing: the key decisions.* London: CIPD.

Chartered Institute of Personnel and Development. (2007) A guide to HR outsourcing. *People Manage.* 6 February 2007.

Cooke, F.L. (2006) Modeling an HR shared services center: experience of an MNC in the United Kingdom. *Hum. Resource Manage.* 45, 211–28.

Economist. *The Search for Talent: Why it's Getting Harder to Find.* 7 October 2006. London: Economist Newspapers.

Fisher, S.L. and Howell, A.W. (2004) Beyond user acceptance: an examination of employee reactions to information technology systems. *Hum. Resource Manage.* 43, 243–58.

Fishman, C. (2006) *The Wal-Mart Effect: How an Out-of-Town Superstore Became a Superpower.* London: Allen Lane.

Florkowski, G.W. and Olivas-Luján, H.R. (2006) The diffusion of human resource information technology innovations in US and non-US firms. *Pers. Rev.* 35, 684–710.

Galliers, R.D. and Newell, S. (2003) Strategy as Data + Sense Making. In *Images of Strategy* (S. Cummings and D.C. Wilson, eds.) pp. 164–96. Oxford: Blackwell.

Greenwald, B. and Kahn, J. (2005a) *Competition Demystified: a Radically Simplified Approach to Business Strategy.* New York: Portfolio/Penguin.

Greenwald, B. and Kahn, J. (2005b) All strategy is local. *Harvard Bus. Rev.* Sept–Oct, 94–107.

Gueutal, H.G. and Stone, D.L. (eds.) (2005) *The Brave New World of eHR: Human Resources in the Digital Age.* San Francisco: Josey Bass.

Hagel III, J. and Seely-Brown, J. (2005) *The Only Sustainable Edge. Why Business Strategy Depends on Productive Friction and Dynamic Specialization.* Boston: Harvard Business School Press.

Hesketh, A.J. (2006) *Outsourcing the HR Function: Possibilities and Pitfalls.* Corporate Research Forum.

Huselid, M.A., Becker, B.E., and Beatty, R.W. (2005) *The Workforce Scorecard: Managing Human Capital to Execute Strategy.* Boston, MA. Harvard Business School Press.

Jansen, J.J.P., Van Den Bosch, F.A.J., and Volberda, H.W. (2005) Managing potential and realized absorptive capacity: how do organizational antecedents matter? *Acad. Manage. Rev.* 48, 999–1015.

Kay, J. (2004) *The Truth About Markets: Why Some Nations are Rich but Most Remain Poor.* London: Penguin Books.

Keebler, T. (2001) HR outsourcing in the Internet era. In *The Technologies and Trends that are Transforming HR: Web-Based Human Resources* (A.J. Walker, ed.) pp. 259–76. New York: McGraw Hill/Towers Perrin.

Kogut, B. and Zander, U. (1992) Knowledge of combinative capabilities, and the replication of technology. *Organ. Sci.* 3, 383–97.

Lavie, D. (2006) The competitive advantage of interconnected firms: an extension of the resource-based view. *Acad. Manage. Rev.* 31, 638–58.

Lawler III, E.E. and Mohrman, S.A. (2003) HR as a strategic partner: what does it take to make it happen? *Hum. Resource Plann.* 26, 15–29.

Lengnick-Hall, C.A. and Lengnick-Hall, M.L. (2006) HR, ERP and knowledge for competitive advantage. *Hum. Resource Manage.* 45, 179–94.

Lengnick-Hall, M.L. and Lengnick-Hall, C.A. (eds.) (2003) Human resource management. In *The Knowledge Economy: New Challenges, New Roles, New Capabilities.* San Francisco, CA: Berrett-Koehler.

Lepak, D.P. and Snell, S.A. (1998) Virtual HR: strategic human resource management in the 21st century. *Hum. Resour. Manage. R.* 8, 215–34.

Lieberman, M.B. and Asaba, S. (2006) Why do firms imitate each other? *Acad. Manage. Rev.* 31, 366–85.

Martin, G. (2005) *Technology and People Management: the Opportunity and Challenges.* London: Chartered Institute of Personnel and Development.

Martin, G. and Beaumont, P.B. (2001) Transforming multinational enterprises: towards a process model strategic HRM change in MNEs. *Int. J. Hum. Resour. Manage.* 12, 34–55.

Martin, G. and Hetrick, S. (2006) *Corporate Reputations, Branding and Managing People: a Strategic Approach to HR.* Oxford: Butterworth Heinemann.

Martin, G., Alexander, H., Reddington, M., and Pate, J.M. (2006) Using technology to transform the future of HR: an illustrated model of e-HR. Paper presented to the Academy of Management Annual Conference, Atlanta, USA, 12–16 August 2006.

McKinsey Quarterly. How businesses are using Web 2.0: a McKinsey global survey. July, 2007. Available online at: www.mckinsey quarterly.com (last accessed 11 September, 2007).

Miles, R.E. and Snow, C.C. (2003) *Organization Strategy, Structure and Process: a Standard Business Classic.* Stanford: Stanford University Press.

Morris, S., Snell, S.A., and Lepak, D. (2005) An architectural approach towards managing knowledge stocks and flows: implications for re-inventing the HR function. In *Reinventing*

Human Resources (R. Burke and C. Cooper, eds.). London: Routledge.

Paauwe, J. (2004) *HRM and Performance: Achieving Long-Term Viability.* Oxford: Oxford University Press.

Pfeffer, J. and Sutton, R.I. (2006) *Hard Facts, Dangerous Half-Truths and Total Nonsense: Profiting from Evidence-Based Management.* Boston: Harvard Business School Press.

Rayport, J.F. and Sviokla, J.J. (1995) Exploiting the virtual value chain. *Harvard Bus. Rev.* Nov–Dec, 75–85.

Reddington, M. and Martin, G. (2006) Theorising the links between e-HR and strategic HRM. Paper presented to the First International workshop on e-HRM, Twente University, the Netherlands, 25–26 October.

Reddington, M., Williamson, M., and Withers, M. (2005) *Transforming HR: Creating Value Through People.* Oxford: Butterworth Heinemann.

Reilly, P. and Tamkin, P. (2006) *The Changing HR Function: the Key Questions.* London: Chartered Institute of Personnel and Development.

Ruël, H., Bondarouk, T., and Looise, J.K. (2004) *e-HRM: Innovation or Irritation.* Utrecht: Lemma.

Shrivastava, S. and Shaw, J.B. (2004) Liberating HR through technology. *Hum. Resource Manage.* 42, 201–22.

Snell, S.A., Steuber, D., and Lepak, D.P. (2001). Virtual HR departments: getting out of the middle. In *Human Resource Management in Virtual Organizations* (R.L. Heneman and D.B. Greenberger, eds.) pp. 81–102. Charlotte, NC: Information Age Publishing.

Sparrow, P. and Cooper, G. (2003) The Employment relationship: Key Challenges for HR. Butterworth Heinmann: Oxford.

Sparrow, P.R., Brewster, C., and Harris, H. (2004) *Globalizing Human Resource Management.* London: Routledge.

Swart, J. and Kinnie, N. (2003) Knowledge-intensive firms: the influence of the client on HR systems. *Hum. Resour. Manage. J.* 10, 5–17.

Taylor, W.C. and LaBarre, P. (2006) *Mavericks at Work: Why the Most Original Minds in Business Win.* New York: William Morrow.

Theaker, M. and Vernon, P. (2006) Removing the barriers to success in HR transformation. Mercer Consulting. 31 July, 2006. Available online at: www.mercerhr.com/knowledgecenter/reportsummary.jhtml/dynamic/idContent/1235040 (last accessed 11 September 2007).

Ulrich, D. and Brockbank, W. (2005) *The HR Value Proposition.* Boston, MA: Harvard Business School Press.

Walker, A.J. (ed.) (2001) *The Technologies and Trends that are Transforming HR: Web-Based Human Resources.* New York: McGraw Hill/Towers Perrin.

Whitley, R. (1999) *Divergent Capitalisms: The Social Structuring and Change of Business Systems.* Oxford: Oxford University Press.

Whittington, R.E. (2000) *What is Strategy and Does it Matter?* London: Thomson.

Wright, P.M., Gardiner, T.M., and Moynihan, L.M. (2003) The impact of HR practices on the performance of business units. *Hum. Resour. Manage. J.* 13, 21–36.

Zahra, S.A. and George, G. (2002) Absorptive capacity: a review, reconceptualization and extension. *Acad. Manage. Rev.* 27, 185–203.

PART I

Outsourcing and Shared Services

CHAPTER 2

Lessons on Outsourcing from a Supply Chain Management Perspective

Douglas Macbeth

Outsourcing is but the latest example of the process of managing external resources which has its origins in the buying process. However the strategic imperatives of focusing on core business and enabling cost reduction and value enhancement require that consideration is given to whether the human resources (HR) activity or function is included in the core or if it should be considered for a version of outsourcing. If the outsourcing option in considered this can include the provider of the resource (in this case, part, or all of the HR provision) being either bought in as a package from an outside service provider (OSP) or internal capability is transferred to an outside organization or that some hybrid solution is implemented.

To some extent other resource groupings, for example, information technology (IT), manufacturing, logistics, facilities management, and procurement have already been through some of these developments and lessons can be transferred about good and bad practice (see Kakabadse and Kakabadse, 2000, for an extensive review). There are always managerial options of how a longer-term provision might best be constructed but these are dependent on the different business contexts in which the decisions are located. It is also very important to make a decision based not on short-term financial expediency but on the basis of strategic intent and future-oriented organizational architecture. Such architectures should consider the external provider market and how to interact with it to mutual advantage. In all of this, the evolving global business environment permits new options fueled by convergence in information and communications technology which provides instantaneous response and potentially continuous operation by having strategically placed and collaborative teams of people. The emergence of providers located in low labor cost geographies has also facilitated this and their rapid rise up the experience curve in a number of business sectors has often provided a cost effective and reliable set of choices. However, global businesses are still constrained by the need to be compliant with national and international agreements and standards whose effect is often to retain liability at the client end even when activities actually take place on the other side of the world. Command and control processes are less effective with those organizations that you do not own, so the whole business-to-business relationship becomes based more on influencing and identification of mutual benefits than on the 'customer is always right'.

These features of global supply chains have been studied and developed over many years in the manufacturing environment most notably in connection with the Toyota rise to challenge for the title of the world's biggest car company (e.g. see Womack et al., 1990). Although, it is fair to say that Toyota only exhibits one of the possible architectures we will discuss later. The challenge now is to see how these lessons can be applied to the HR function.

Outsourcing is a word that has come to represent a complete range of activities but we can trace the base concept back to a decision to place outside an organization's boundaries a set of activities that were once contained inside the ownership structure of the organization. However, the term is also used to describe situations where resources from outside an organization are employed in support of the core organization's customer support when they were never inside the organization's boundaries. See, for example, the Microsoft Xbox development and market launch success in which the core company (Microsoft) had the product vision and the marketing spend ability but no other capability to design, manufacture, and distribute the product against a time-critical market launch window (O'Brien, 2001).

This relates to a much older debate going back to early discussions to define the boundaries of the firm (Marshall, 1923; Coase, 1937; Williamson, 1975; 1985; 1986). In academic discussions this was about what conditions made it sensible to own capabilities in order to produce a good or service and when does the market mechanism (the exchange transaction) make more sense. In practitioner terms this is called the 'make/do or buy' decision. In effect, organizations have to decide what is so important to their future success that they need to retain close control and ownership of the capability and its development trajectory (the make/do option) and those that are required to provide a full customer service but which they do not need to own. Even without ownership, however, they must be able to reliably engage with these external resources to ensure a full customer service (the buy option). Harland et al. (2005) provide an extensive review of the literature in this area and for that reason we will leave such discussions at this point.

Experience from other functions' involvement in outsourcing in its various guises suggests that too often insufficient analysis of the strategic options available and their relative merits (in both the short and medium term) takes place and that change is initiated without sufficient thought as to where it might lead and whether the road to be traveled can be used to return to base, if such is required in light of changing market situations in the future.

What many regard as outsourcing is captured in the announcement by DuPont of a major outsourcing deal in 2005.

> 'Convergys will provide comprehensive Human Resources (HR) transactional services to DuPont's 60 000 employees and 102 000 retirees in 70 countries and 30 languages around the world. Convergys expects this contract to generate revenues in excess of $1.1 billion over its 13-year

duration. DuPont expects to realize a 20 per cent productivity improvement as services transition to Convergys, increasing to 30 per cent after 5 years.

Convergys will provide DuPont with a comprehensive suite of HR transactional services such as Organization & Employee Development, Workforce Planning & Deployment, Compensation Management, Benefits Administration, Payroll, Integrated Health Services, Recruiting, Employee & Labor Relations, HR Process Support Administration, Work Environment Support, Performance Management, Employee Data Management, Vendor Management, and HR consultative services. Deloitte Consulting, LLP will support the implementation.

Convergys will implement, host, and maintain a state-of-the-art HR information system.

Jim Borel, DuPont senior vice president, global Human Resources said 'Convergys brings best-in-class global services to its clients, and DuPont will benefit from increased business performance through improved efficiency, reduced administrative costs, and better utilization of strategic workforce information. DuPont will be able to utilize world-class employee and manager self-service tools as well as state-of-the-art service centers located around the globe. Convergys is the right partner to enable the transformation of our HR transactional services by standardizing, simplifying, leveraging, and automating a number of our HR processes.'

Convergys news release 2 November, 2005.

In the above example we can see some of the perceived benefits being outlined but there are concerns from the client's perspective as well as that of the OSPs as shown in Figure 2.1.

From a client perspective, OSPs provide the opportunity to gain expertise from their focus on what the client has decided is non-core business for them. The OSP has this activity as its focus and will be expected to invest to maintain its competitive capability. By providing services other than to the focal client the OSP also gains other experiences which can be used by the focal client in the future. It is also likely that the OSP can justify dedicated computer and communications systems to support

Opportunities for client	Threats to client
OSP provides focus	Loss of control
Investment in focal activity	Opportunistic pricing model
Technology support updated	Limited benefit share
Benefits of scale and scope	Loss of focus to other client's business
Dedicated skills and management	Reduced emphasis on performance and support over time
Overhead reduction	Rigid spec. rigidly adhered to
Provide operational data	Increasing coordination costs with increased complexity
	Reduced compliance data visibility
Opportunities for OSP	**Threats to OSP**
Business growth and extension	Underestimating client complexity and under-pricing
Leverage	Staff transferred are not/cannot be helped to be competent
High efficiency utilization	
Lock in of client, barriers to entry to competitors	Service expectation creep
Sell capability to other clients	Contract re-tendered or repatriated
Capture undervalued skills from client	
Release creativity and motivation in staff	

Figure 2.1

Client and outsourced service providers' opportunities and threats.
Note: OSP, Outside services provider.

their own activities, the expense of which would not be justified inside the client company. The focus on the activity is also expected to provide management data where previously this may have been lacking. This might be important for reasons of compliance with reporting requirements in different countries and in corporate ethics considerations in terms of employment conditions in the outsourced supply chain, perhaps in different world regions.

On the other side of the balance there is usually a perception of loss of control from the client perspective and certainly there is dependence on the OSP for performance and support, but there can be other threats. The fact that the OSP will have other customers might present issues in terms of how the focal client is positioned in the consideration queue when resources are constrained. It can also be the case that since the client did not have a focus on these activities they did not truly understand what the real costs of operating them were. In such circumstance, an opportunistic OSP can drive an aggressive pricing bargain to the client's disadvantage and, subject to contractual terms, this may be difficult to reverse. Another impact of the internal lack of understanding might be in the specifications for the service provision which, if badly framed and implemented, might create opportunities for misunderstanding or manipulation by the OSP. In a changing world, service specifications that are too rigidly defined are unlikely to remain the real requirement so there is a need for a more flexible approach and an evolutionary relationship but who in the focal company's organization understands and can negotiate such matters?

Once the agreement is in operation new business might make the initial focal client's activities relatively less attractive to the OSP and so the client loses visibility of data and emerging trends. If this possibility is realized, mechanisms to span the new boundary between client and OSP need to be agreed not least of which might be how a failing relationship can be cancelled and another OSP introduced but without a major meltdown in performance during the transition. That is, along with the need for 'voice' to discuss the problems they might need to be resolved by 'exit' (Hirschman, 1970), perhaps formulated in the intercompany equivalent of a prenuptial agreement.

The opportunities from the OSP view are to build scale through the acquisition of an important client. The staff transferred are then allowed to focus on the (for them) newly important core business. The transfer of skills and the dependence of the client provide a 'lock-in' of the client and therefore a barrier to entry for the OSP's competitors. It also means that the marketing effort of the OSP can be directed elsewhere.

The major threat to the OSP is that the information provided from the client on which the bid was constructed does not relate to the reality of providing the service and that the contract does not allow this to be re-negotiated. Thus, the projected value of the contract is diminished and with it perhaps the incentive to provide high service to the client (this is a threat to them). There can also be a threat that any staff transferred are actually not capable of performing in the new environment but it might be difficult (through the legalities of the transfer arrangement) to dismiss them or change their employment conditions.

The final threat to the OSP is that the client might choose to reverse their outsourcing decision and repatriate their staff and activities. Of course this possibility is unlikely to have been included in the original outsourcing arrangements and had it been it might have caused the OSP to doubt their commitment from the beginning. However, all contracts will have cancellation clauses so the potential is always there for the OSP to lose the business. In such a circumstance, one has to ask if the OSP will be as motivated given the potential loss of hard won business. The threat of a re-tender and possible replacement of an OSP by another provider must also be factored in if the relationship is not seen as being built for the long term.

There can be little doubt that HR outsourcing is on many organization's agendas. In fact a survey by the Conference Board in 2004 indicated that 76% of the 120 North American and European companies having annual revenues of at least $1 billion have outsourced one or more of the HR functions (called activities in this chapter). In that survey the most popular activities outsourced included 401(k) retirement programs, pensions/benefits, stock options, health benefits, training and development, and payroll (Conference Board, 2004).

What should be outsourced?

The usual answer to this is non-core business and typically 'back office' support activities are seen as less risky but we need to think carefully about the choice (see Conklin, 2005 for some discussions of factors as found in other literatures while Adler, 2003 also discusses these issues). Outsourcing offers the chance to do a number of things including: cost reductions on normal activities; provide increased control information; build capability and possibly capacity with some new investment; enhance current contribution and value added capability and create new business opportunities. Each of these requires different structures and governance processes alongside key performance indicators.

It can also be planned in a sequential manner to sort a problem, develop new capability, and then to bring the activity or function back inside to deliver a better and more controllable service. Alternatively there might be an option to float off the new unit as a separate business entity with new clients and new focus on business growth. These possibilities already demonstrate the need to think more long term so that short-term decisions and processes do not restrict strategic moves later.

Of course the journey also depends on where you start from. It is likely that an HR function that has already coordinated activities across multiple sites perhaps into a shared services organization is more ready to meet the challenges of outsourcing. Alternatively, such a structure might be so embedded that taking it outside the organizational boundaries would present a serious organizational challenge.

Without a complete understanding of the current state of expertise and potential reach it will be very difficult for an external provider to know what they are being asked to take on and it will be extremely difficult for the internal decision makers to evaluate any external bid. The HR function therefore requires a level of process maturity and robustness to be in a position to consider outsourcing.

Outsourcing might be seen as a solution to a failing service which must be sorted at all costs. Such an open-ended commitment is not to be encouraged since the costs can escalate very dramatically. Without detailed internal understanding, any external service provider (SP) will need to consider a considerable consultancy effort to create the baseline performance level on which to build a bid for the contract. The base level description will allow the creation and evaluation of improvement agendas for support to the bid and to support the OSP's decision process that such business can be delivered profitably. Such a consultancy intervention might be even be worth the investment by the client to allow them to become an intelligent customer in evaluating the OSP's bid and might actually re-open the possibility of the in-house options we will discuss shortly.

Scope and scale decisions are also important. It is possible to outsource parts of activities (that is 'cherry pick' from the equivalent of the DuPont list above), complete activities or business processes (e.g. recruitment) or the whole of the HR functional business scope. This again might be a staged process to build experience and confidence without the risks of a complete functional outsourcing from which it may be difficult to retrace the steps.

The range of options or variations on the outsourcing theme which can be available are listed and discussed below (Hermann and Macbeth, 2006).

Soft-in/insourcing

- Features
  - A SP takes over the activities previously provided by the company's own resources.
  - The SP invoices for their services.
- Benefits
  - Cost is visible due to the direct costing.
  - Fixed cost of HR changed to variable cost.
- Dangers
  - All services and cost are defined by a service contract.
  - Loss of competence and evaluation capability.
  - Dependence on chosen SP.
  - Exit or replacement costs unclear.

Hard-out/resource outsourcing

- Features
  - SP takes over the HR functions and processes as well as the staff and other assets.
  - Payment plan for asset transfer.
  - Staff transfer governed by legal conditions.
  - SP invoices the client for their services.

- Benefits
  - Reduced capital cost for the client and increased utilization of assets through SP networks.
  - Cost is visible due to the direct costing.
  - Fixed cost of HR changed to variable cost.
  - All services and cost are defined by a service contract.
- Dangers
  - Loss of competence and evaluation capability.
  - Dependence on chosen SP.
  - Exit or replacement costs unclear.

Total-invest-out/enhanced service outsourcing

- Features
  - Same as hard-out plus a contractual requirement that SP will invest in resources and systems to improve service performance by agreed increments over time.
- Benefits
  - Same as hard-out but with increasing and pre-defined service levels.
- Dangers
  - Loss of competence and evaluation capability.
  - Dependence on chosen SP.
  - Enforcing the improvements.
  - Exit or replacement costs unclear.

Share-in/internal joint venture (JV)

- Features
  - Focal firm and a SP form an HR services JV.
  - SP responsible for operational management of JV and service to their client.
  - The shareholding and voting rights in such a JV may vary.

- JV also acts as an external SP to other clients, but client's competence and know-how is not lost.
- Payment plan for transfers of corporate assets.
- Staff transfer governed by legal provisions.

■ Benefits
- Reduced capital cost for the client and increased utilization of assets through SP networks.
- Cost is visible due to the direct costing.
- Fixed cost of HR changed to variable cost.
- All services and cost are defined by a service contract.
- Strategic option to repatriate expertise is possible.

■ Dangers
- Divergent interests over time between client and SP.

Share-out/trading services entity

■ Features
- Same as share-in except no SP, client invests in new business entity to create new capability and looks to sell services to others.

■ Benefits
- Cost is visible due to the direct costing.
- Fixed cost of HR changed to variable cost.
- HR still core competence but now entrepreneurial as well.
- All services and cost are defined by a service contract with users in client's business but can have different pricing models.
- Sales of services to external parties might reduce core client's internal cost of service.

■ Dangers
- Risks involved in recruiting and managing new staff and solving any existing internal problems.
- External service clients are increasingly seen as more important than internal ones and service levels decline.

How to manage the change

The main dimensions can be captured in the three categories of: type of activity, degree of permanence, and governance arrangements.

Back office operations are often the least problematical and almost commodity-like in that the only differentiating factor is that outsourcing can usually produce lower operational costs to provide the service. Examples might include activities like database recording and maintenance. The term transactional activities is sometimes used to describe these commodity-like activities as well but as there becomes more social interactions these require a more active interface and the development of this might enhance the value of the service experienced by the users. An example might be career development planning and support. The final category in this section is transformational. Here the essence of the activity changes to provide much more added value and service support. This literally transforms the activity to something approaching best in class and capable of competing against other providers in the market place.

Degrees of permanence tend to follow the types.

The commodity type will tend to be permanent in that the activity is unlikely to the repatriated at any time although the provider (in the way that markets work) may have a limited tenure before the contract is put out to competitive tender again.

The interaction type will have an extended timescale, at least in theory and, if it is delivering as intended, may continue indefinitely or until some major industry change causes the whole process to be re-examined. This can include merger and acquisition deals which change priorities for one or more of the parties involved or a new technology or process improvement which removes or reduces the need for the activity.

Permanence is a difficult concept in the transformational case since by definition the after-transformation stage raises new opportunities and potential threats to the existing situation so that, once achieved, the transformed entity might no longer be the appropriate solution for the original client's needs.

Governance possibilities are also related to the types of activity. Commodity services can be managed as one would manage commodities of any other product or service in that it is a market approach and since we bought on price we can manage the outsourcers with an arms-length contract built around the service specification or service level agreement. Since we are aiming for low cost we do not want to incur large management charges to monitor performance.

In the more relational interaction mode, as it develops and more services are designed and implemented, we need to consider a more active involved style which has elsewhere been described as a partnering type of approach.

Interactional types of processes with an OSP require more client involvement since there are more emergent issues to deal with as the requirement is refined over time and as options are identified. This might indicate the need for a partnering type of governance approach. Veludo and Macbeth (2000), in their partnering conceptual framework, made an attempt to define the dimensions and characteristics of partnering. The dimensions are: trust, win–win outcomes where the benefits from waste reductions and market success are shared between the parties, long-term orientation, coordination, problem solving, and flexibility. The characteristics are: an inherent trust, sharing of risks and rewards, increase in joint competitiveness, expectation of continuity, continuous improvement focus, supplier development, joint strategy setting, joint planning, joint research and development (R&D), two-way communication, willingness to help one another, conflict resolution, flexibility in delivery, and flexibility in agreements.

They further assert that partnering is a relationship type which has to be defined and targeted, by the parties involved, at the start of a learning process leading to previously agreed objectives. This up front agreement must be between parties who see economic advantage in working together and wish to commit formally and emotionally to making the relationship one in which there will be benefits to both but for which both parties are required to work diligently. Partnering in this definition is not an easy option and so needs to be evaluated carefully but it has the capability to keep both parties involved and challenged to perform as the relationship matures. Learning in such situations is not one sided. So a client who outsources but partners with the OSP is not abrogating control and knowledge, rather they have the chance to learn from the OSP's complementary skills. A partnering approach might allow the process of outsourcing to be reversed but of course this might destroy the relationship which built the client's capability. The future need for the OSP would need to be seen as minimal to justify such a 'burning bridges' decision. An arms-length relationship will not offer the same learning opportunities and would deny the reversal path as a future option.

The transformational type offers two scenarios depending on whether there is an OSP involved or not. Doing an internal transformation involves bringing the HR activity into clear focus and building capability to perform as required by the parent as client. This can be as a separate group or function or business unit but if there is any prospect of delivering services to external clients in the future it might be as well to create the support infrastructure from the beginning and effective 'trade' with other parts of the client organization. In this way processes and procedures and crucially employee attitudes and support to the future prospects can be developed so that the transition to an external client will not be so disruptive. This requires serious vision, investment, and planning to give it a chance and given that the start point was some weakness in capability (which triggered the need to change) this becomes a major change program and subject to the same concerns as with another other such project which tend not have high success rates.

Once there is an OSP involved the likelihood is that it will need to be governed by a legally constituted JV as it will be constructed as a stand alone company with its shareholders and its own business plan. The original client's interests and rights need to be considered carefully from the outset since, once it is in operation, change will be much more complicated to effect.

Managing the process: in–out balance

Outsourcing an activity or even a function does not mean that responsibility for the results of that activity are transferred. In reality this means that much of the rhetoric of risk transfer much used in for example public–private partnerships (much in vogue for hospital building and operation for example) is at the extreme, nonsense. Of course if a SP fails to deliver the promised service there may be financial penalties and consequences of other kinds but the reality is that if the outsourcing client's customers are adversely affected they do not complain to the OSP (of whom they may have no knowledge), they complain to and feel aggrieved at being let down by the client organization. Thus, in any outsourcing situation there can be headcount reduction (or people transfer) in the immediate area of the transferred activity but the rest of the client organization who interface with that activity still have to function alongside the new arrangements. In fact, the new 'remoteness' of the activity is often found to need more coordinating managerial effort so that these staff numbers and activity levels are found to increase to cope. This raises a real competence issue in the medium terms for the managers in the client organization whose experience and understanding of the OSP's business diminishes in time unless there is a clear and ongoing commitment to share such developments with the client managers so that they can truly evaluate what they are being told by the OSP. They also have to change from managing the activity directly to overseeing the OSP's management performance. They therefore moved from being business activity managers to being business relationship managers, which requires some retraining and changes in measurement and reward systems which increase internal costs. The Conference Board survey referred to earlier also indicated that 60% of respondents are in the process of creating a core competency for managing outsourcing providers within human resources (Conference Board, 2004). The question is, were these costs anticipated when the outsourcing cost–benefit calculations were being made?

Strategy and future proofing

The issues of core competence (Prahalad and Hamel, 1990) that drove the outsourcing decision are fraught with difficulty. How can we be sure that what is regarded as not core competence now remains in that category in 5 years' time? What risks would the client run if the new critical capability was no longer under direct control but now provides a potential new source of bargaining power from an OSP who reverts to adversarial behavior to take advantage of the client dependence created through the outsourcing.

Thus, although the initial client strategy might have been to outsource the activity to an OSP who would sort the problems in the functional area only for the client to cancel the contract and return the activity back in-house, it is not always as easy in practice to follow such a path reversal. For example, the scale effects which the OSP used to permit a lower operational cost would still not be there in-house. Similarly the personnel who had been transferred and had come to see their activity as core to the OSP's business model would yet again be in a more minor supporting role inside the client's organization. Allied to these factors, bringing the activity back in-house will probably require modifications to organizational structures and processes which also need to be managed. Conversely, forming a JV initially to retain options on the future can still allow the sale of a client's interests to the OSP if the decision really is that the activities are never going to be core and that managerial effort needs to be redirected to core business. Thus, a JV or a partnering approach might migrate through time to an arms-length market approach.

This suggests that complete outsourcing of the commodity type needs very careful evaluation at the beginning and regular re-evaluation in case the world changes. All other types require active management and involvement. The need to understand how to work with and get the best support from an external party (even within a JV) will become one of the key skills of HR managers moving in this direction. Perhaps it would be prudent to develop some of those skills before the first outsourcing situation emerges?

Key questions

(1)   Does your organization truly understand what can be involved in HR outsourcing?

(2)   Is everyone clear about the organization's mission and how HR contributes?

(3)   Is it clear what level of experience and maturity is currently available in-house?

(4)   Are there internal people capable of defining the requirements which might be outsourced and of evaluating the service offers from potential OSPs? If not, are you capable of evaluating any support offers from consultants or the OSPs themselves?

(5)   Can required performance objectives and associated measures be created for the activities and for the business relationship with all relevant parties, internal and external? Do the lists of stakeholders include regulators of various kinds in each of the countries in which the organization operates?

(6)   What time horizon is being planned for and what contract duration is being discussed with OSPs?

(7)   What new relationship and project management skills will be needed and how will they be provided? item[(8)] Can you truly specify and cost a program to develop the in-house capability to meet the needs of the internal client users? How long will it take? Can you afford to make and sustain the required investment in people, training, and performance monitoring to get and keep the HR activity up to best practice levels in-house?

Summary

Outsourcing is much hyped and can be highly political as jobs migrate round the globe but there is little likelihood that the option to work this way will diminish. Already some of the major OSPs in a variety of service areas are global players and are moving into their clients' market places and providing yet further value-adding propositions. HR strategists need to have thought about and be prepared to produce the business case for or against it as a support to their organization's future plans. If allying in some way to a truly best in class supplier is the way to produce a more competitive service offering to the client's customers then the business case will drive the behaviors of the senior strategic managers and the HR group better be ready to make the best of the situation.

References

Adler, P.S. (2003) Making the HR outsourcing decision. *Sloan Manage. Rev.* 45, 53–60.

Coase, R. (1937) The nature of the firm. *Economica* 4, 386–405.

Conference Board (2004) *HR Outsourcing: Benefits, Challenges and Trends,* Brussels: Conference Board.

Conklin, D.W. (2005) Risks and rewards in HR business process outsourcing. *Long Range Plann.* 38, 579–98.

Harland, C., Knight, L., Lamming, R., and Walker, H. (2005) Outsourcing: assessing the risks and benefits for organisations, sectors and nations. *Int. J. Oper. Prod. Man.* 25, 831–50.

Hermann, U. and Macbeth, D.K. (2006) Outsourcing of logistics in the German "Mittelstand". European Operations Management Association (EurOMA) Conference 2006 – Moving Up the Value Chain. University of Strathclyde, Glasgow, UK. pp. 1131–40.

Hirschman A. (1970) *Exit, Voice and Loyalty: Responses to Decline in Firms Organisations and States.* Cambridge, MA: Harvard University Press.

Kakabadse, N. and Kakabadse, A. (2000) Critical review – outsourcing: a paradigm shift. *J Manage. Dev.,* 19, 670–728.

O'Brien, J.M. (2001) The making of the Xbox. *Wired* November 9.11.

Prahalad, C.K. and Hamel, G. (1990) The core competence of the corporation. *Harvard Bus. Rev.* 68, 79–93.

Marshall, A. (1923) *Industry and Trade.* London: Macmillan.

Veludo, M.L. and Macbeth, D.K. (2000) Partnering relationships in the automotive industry – empirical evidence from Portugal. In *Proceedings of the 9th International Annual IPSERA Conference,* May 2002. London, ON, Canada.

Williamson, O.E. (1975) *Markets and Hierarchies.* New York: Free Press.

Williamson, O.E. (1985) *The Economic Institutions of Capitalism,* Free Press, NY.

Williamson, O.E. (1986) *Economic Organisation.* Brighton, UK: Wheatsheaf Books.

Womack, J.P., Jones, D.T., and Roos, D. (1990) *The Machine that Changed the World.* London: Macmillan.

CHAPTER 3

HR Outsourcing in Italy

Anna Comacchio, Fabrizio Gerli, Annachiara Scapolan, and Sara Bonesso

Introduction

Various studies have been carried out by providers and consultants on the human resource outsourcing (HRO) process. However, these studies principally concentrate on multinational firms with a divisional structure operating in an Anglo-Saxon environment (USA and UK) and there is still little research on smaller firms situated in continental Europe, arguable with different systems of human resource management (HRM) from the Anglo-Saxon model (Brewster et al., 2007). In Italy, HRO is a developing feature of HRM, though it has not reached US levels (Silvestri and Pilati, 2005). The fact that 66% of Italian businesses have outsourced at least one HRM process and 34% are considering broadening their range of outsourced processes bears witness to this. This chapter aims to shed light on the forms of outsourcing of HRM processes in Italy, and, in so doing, provide some much needed theory and evidence into the outsourcing debate.

The outsourcing phenomenon: antecedents and forms of governance

There is a confluence in the HRO literature (Greer et al., 1999; Adler, 2003) in identifying two principal drivers of the process of unbundling HRM: the operational driver and the strategic driver. The operational driver is linked to cost savings achieved by exploiting provider's economies of scales and standardizing processes. The strategic driver is achieved by freeing up time to concentrate on the internal processes that create added value for the firm and also by improving the quality of service delivery and by acquiring new knowledge which complements the know-how already present in-house.

Analysis of the antecedents aids the understanding of those reasons that drive businesses to outsource an increasing number of HRM processes and the prediction of which processes will be outsourced. Unfortunately, this type of analysis risks limiting our understanding of the HRO process to a decision of whether or not to 'make or buy'. However, as the phenomenon of HRO becomes more widespread and its impact on the number of processes outsourced by each firm increases, a growing and important subject area for human resources (HR) managers is represented by the different forms of outsourcing governance.

This research problem has been dealt with over recent years from two perspectives: transaction cost theory (TCT; Klaas, 2003) and the resource-based view (RBV) of strategy (Baron and Kreps, 1999; Laursen and Mahnke, 2001; Wright et al., 2001; Espino-Rodríguez and Padrón-Robaina, 2006). According to the first perspective (TCT) the decision to outsource is guided not only by the reduction in the production costs of the HR service, but also by the assessment of the transaction costs with the provider. To minimize transaction costs the processes outsourced are those characterized by low specificity and low uncertainty in the determination of performance. These conditions enable the choice of a short-term formal contract, as a governance mechanism, integrated with a detailed service level agreement. The second perspective (RBV) (Baron and Kreps, 1999; Espino-Rodríguez and Padrón-Robaina, 2006) criticizes the efficiency vision of TCT and explains the decision to outsource in terms of core resources. The authors adopting the RBV perspective, at times integrated with that of TCT, argue that activities kept in-house are those that are rare, specific, inimitable, and that generate value for the business. However, in these studies, companies also use HRO to access those processes and resources of the provider that are complementary to key internal abilities and therefore prove strategic for the delivery of the HRM service.

The contribution of this theoretical perspective to the analysis of 'how' to govern the interorganizational relationship between the firm and providers is more limited (Espino-Rodríguez and Padrón-Robaina, 2006), which leads to a third line of research. This perspective focuses on the manner of governance of interorganizational outsourcing relationships and examines the different roles contracts can have on the governance of the relationship, including formal contracts that are settled through application to a third party (i.e. a court), and relational contracts, based on informal agreements, trust, and the longevity of the relationship (Baker et al., 2002). Research is aimed at understanding the antecedents leading to recourse to the two types of contract and inquires whether the two types of contract are substitutes or complements; furthermore it investigates the impact of the choice of one form over another on performance (Poppo and Zenger, 2002; Woolthuis et al., 2005; Carson et al., 2006).

A contribution that enables the specific problem of HRO governance to be analyzed, consistently with this third line of research, is that recently supplied by Sako and Tierney (2005). According to these authors different forms of HRO processes can be described along a continuum bounded by a strategy of *transactional* management of the relationship (only one outsourced process according to a market and short-term logic) and a *transformational* form of management, as in the case of BP-Exult. In contrast to the simplicity of the transactional form, the transformational HRO anticipates more than one outsourced process, high interdependence between the firm and the provider, and a tendency towards the long term aimed at reorganizing the service. The authors maintain that the HRO to which large firms, with a divisional structure and international presence, are moving towards today is that of a transformational kind. This process, which is explained by the authors also on the basis of an analysis of the reorganization of the providers' market, is interpreted as a general tendency to cross the market and hierarchy, in the governance of the relationship between the firm and HR provider, by means of the transition from formal contracts to relational contracts (Sako and Tierney, 2005).

These same authors outline three reasons that drive firms to adopt relational contracts in HRO. First, the complexity of the contracts tends to increase as the breadth of the service rendered by the provider increases, or that of the number of HRM processes outsourced and the geographical spread of the service. This fact makes it more difficult to provide for all the terms of the agreement beforehand. Second, it is not the demand for standard services, which the firm knows the terms of in detail, that increases, but the reorganization processes of the HRM function. Divisional-form organizations interested in redefining HRM policies at corporate level adopt a 'black box developmental contract' (Sako and Tierney, 2005), the terms of which are difficult to define entirely *a priori*. Third, both parties are interested in increasing the duration of the contract to take advantage of a greater payback period. Due to the high costs to start up the relationship, it is estimated that an HRO agreement takes approximately 18 months before it starts to generate a return for the vendor (Sako and Tierney, 2005).

The above propositions explain multidivisional, multinational firms, but to what extent can we apply to smaller, less complicated firms? Italy represents an interesting setting for this question, since firms are smaller, typically without a global international presence, and adopt a functional organizational structure and HRM profiles rather different from those considered by Sako and Tierney (2005); personnel management in Italy still has limited experience in complex and long-term outsourcing (Leiblein and Miller, 2003). Nevertheless, Italy has many firms that are beginning the HR outsourcing process journey, unencumbered by a previous history, so we have a better chance of establishing the key antecedents, untainted by history, and whether one can assume a transition from transactional forms to relational contracts.

The research

Research methods

The research was carried out in two separate steps. First, three case studies were carried out for exploratory purposes (Eisenhardt, 1989; Yin, 1991), to understand the forms of governance of the outsourcing phenomenon in HR processes in Italy and to help refine the structure of the survey questionnaire. Subsequently, in 2005, a questionnaire was prepared and made available on-line, aimed at collecting information concerning the phenomenon under investigation on a wider scale. The questionnaire was divided into three sections: the first part focused on the firm's details; the second part asked questions on HRM departmental structure, size, activities, resources employed, and processes undertaken; the third part was specifically focused on the firm's outsourcing processes. The processes of HRM were identified through an analysis of the literature on outsourcing and on HRM: administrative activities, trade-union relations, recruitment, selection, career management, training, assessment, compensation, organizational development, special projects, and internal communication.

The sample

We sampled 33 firms and considered the individual HRM processes outsourced by the firms themselves as units of analysis. This amounted to 57 in total. All 57 outsourced HRM processes were included in the research. For each process the characteristics, level of outsourcing, operational methods of management, reasons for outsourcing, forms of governance of the relationship, and future prospects in terms of problems or management opportunities were analyzed.

The sample was predominantly made up of medium-to-large firms from the north of Italy, with an average turnover of €179 million and an average number of employees of 843. Firms with fewer than 250 employees made up 30% of the sample, the smallest was 45 employees. The firms show a managerial structure, on average there are 22 managers, 74 middle managers, 322 clerical workers, and 253 workers. Use of flexible forms of contract such as temporary employment or project collaborations was limited. The sectors represented were: mechanical engineering, electronics, agriculture and food, transport, clothing/footwear, credit/insurance, ceramics, paper, chemicals, large-scale retail, tourism/performing arts, and publishing. Analysis of the level of sophistication attained by the HRM department indicates that HR in these firms has a relatively sophisticated level of development, using 'leading-edge' HR practices. For example, the majority of firms in the sample used techniques such as skills analysis, assessment of performance and results, pay surveys, process mapping, and job description. A smaller subsector used more sophisticated techniques such as job posting, assessment centre, e-learning, individual/collective incentive plans, climate analysis, and replacement tables. The staffing ratio of the HRM was 1.63, with a minimum of 0.30 and a maximum of 5.26. The average number of levels of management in the HR departments was 2.6, while the maximum was 5.0.

Research results

The outsourced HR processes: extent of the phenomenon and characteristics of the activities

First, the analysis has enabled us to understand the extent to which particular HR processes are outsourced (Table 3.1). Our data show that training processes are those for which resorting to external providers is most frequent, followed by the personnel administration and selection/recruitment processes. Significant, though less frequent, is the use of external support in the management of special projects, for example, the implementation of performance management or talent management processes or incentive plans. The abovementioned processes constitute those which are most affected by the phenomenon, not only because they are those most frequently outsourced but also because they are planned to be outsourced in the short term.

Table 3.1

Type of processes outsourced (percentage frequency).

HR processes	At least partly outsourced	Not outsourced yet but on the point of being so	Carried out entirely in-house
Administrative activity	55.2	3.4	41.4
Trade-union relations	3.8	0	96.2
Recruitment	24.1	13.8	62.1
Selection	48.3	13.8	37.9
Career management	0	0	100.0
Training	72.4	6.9	20.7
Performance management	7.4	3.7	88.9
Compensation	0	3.7	96.3
Organizational development	22.2	7.4	70.4
Special projects	38.1	4.8	57.1
Internal communication	15.4	0	84.6

With reference to the duration of the outsourcing experience (Table 3.2) we found that outsourcing can be considered as a relatively recent phenomenon, since, in the majority of cases, the decision to outsource was taken only at least 3 or 4 years previously, namely in 2002 or 2001. Only administration processes do not confirm this trend, typically having been outsourced more recently, 1–2 years previously (in 2003 or 2004) or less than one year previously (in 2005) while for special projects temporal proximity is a structural characteristic deriving from their discontinuity.

The duration of the outsourcing experience does not find any parallel with the same duration of the relationship with the

Table 3.2

Percentage distribution of the outsourced processes based on the time period in which the decision to outsource was made.

	< 1 year	1–2 years	3–4 years	≥ 5 years
Administration	20.0	33.3	6.7	40.0
Recruitment	0	0	60.0	40.0
Selection	0	0	18.2	81.8
Training	0	13.3	26.7	60.0
Special projects	25.0	25.0	0	50.0

providers. The fact that the decision to outsource originated approximately 3 to 4 years previously, namely in 2001 or 2002, was not necessarily accompanied by the tendency to build, with the same provider, partnership relations of the same duration.

Degree of outsourcing: internal control to monitor the provider

Few studies have examined the degree of outsourcing of individual HRM processes. In this research the adoption of the level-of-process analysis allows us to consider those aspects of the outsourcing process that may be useful for a more in-depth understanding of HRO characteristics and the relationship with the provider. The results of the research enabled us to conclude that, in the majority of the processes analyzed, outsourcing occurs partially. HR departments seemed to be interested in maintaining a more or less extensive internal control over all such processes. The extent of this control is shown in Table 3.3; one can observe how there are relatively few processes that show a high or total degree of outsourcing, while the majority are located in a middle band, namely a percentage of less than 50% of the process is outsourced. In particular, among the processes with the highest degree of outsourcing are the personnel administration and recruitment processes, while the processes that are most subject to internal control are selection, training and special projects.

Table 3.3

Percentage distribution of the outsourced processes based on the degree of outsourcing.

	0–25%	26–50%	51–75%	76–100%
Administration	6.7	53.3	26.7	13.3
Recruitment	40.0	0	60.0	0
Selection	54.5	27.3	9.1	9.1
Training	20.0	60.0	20.0	0.0
Special projects	50.0	25.0	0	25.0

The presence of internal control of a part of the outsourced processes appears justified by the necessity to continue to fuel internal know-how, thus enabling firms to assess the provider or select new ones. In other words, for firms this meant increasing their absorptive capacity (see Chapter 1: Technology, Outsourcing, and HR Transformation: an Introduction; Cohen and Levinthal, 1990) to make more rational choices of outsourcing and to manage the integration process between the provider's services and their own bundle of internal HRM processes.

Boxes 3.1 and 3.2 illustrate two cases of partial outsourcing, which may help readers understand the details underlying these statistics.

Box 3.1   Gruppo X*: partial outsourcing of personnel administration

Gruppo X is an Italian company which, since the beginning of the 1980s, has operated in the casual clothing sector. Its main office and all of its four factories are localized in the province of Treviso, in northeast Italy.

Its principal brand is famous worldwide so much so that 30% of the turnover is realized in Italy while 70% comes from abroad. There are 200 single-brand sale outlets while there are 130 corners.

In 2005, the Group's turnover exceeded €330 million and the number of employees was 1061.

Ten people work in HR, including the manager. The HRM uses, in addition to the more traditional personnel management instruments, more innovative instruments such as pay surveys, job analysis, corporate climate analysis, and internal marketing. These instruments are employed not only for the managers but also for the middle managers and employees.

Gruppo X's HRM departments turns to the market for HR services, first of all, for the activities of recruitment and selection when these concern particular professional skills that are hard to find on the labor market and whose search requires a specific competence. For these professional figures the company applies, depending on the type, to a few national headhunting and selection companies or local employment agencies.

Since January 2004, the company has decided to outsource part of the personnel administration activities: payroll and the performance of fiscal requirements concerning pay.

Recourse to outside of the company for administration activities is part of a policy aimed at developing HR activities with a higher strategic content and reducing the operational costs of the processes.

The choice of supplier fell on an organizational service provider in Milan chosen based on its skills, specialization, and experience in IT and HRM outsourcing, as well as the cost of the service.

The contract stipulated with the provider is non-exclusive with a duration of 3 years (with a renewal option) and a fixed cost for each pay packet processed. The agreement also provides that the client firm, Gruppo X, uses a special software supplied by the provider to transmit the data necessary for the payroll services.

The HR director defines this process as *basic outsourcing*, since it has outsourced the administration process while keeping the control functions over the operations inside the company.

After payroll services were outsourced, the employee previously in charge of these services took on the role of liaison officer, monitoring and coordinating operations with the external provider. At the beginning of the outsourcing relationship the liaising activity was very intense. Periodic meetings, which were later substituted with telephone calls and e-mails, were necessary to establish this relationship. Gruppo X assesses the provider according to the reliability of the service provided, with regards to the contractual specifications, and on rapidity of response time.

*The company asked to remain anonymous.

Notes: HRM, human resource management; IT, information technology.

Box 3.2   The case of Alcan Packaging Italia: partial outsourcing of the recruitment, selection, and training activities

Alcan Packaging Italia and HRM

Alcan Packaging Italia is part of the Alcan multinational group, world leader in the production of aluminum. The Italian factories deal with the manufacture of packaging for food, pharmaceutical, and cosmetic products. The main plant is in Vicenza, in northeast Italy. The other manufacturing plants, all located in the North of Italy, are situated in Lainate and Arenzano.

In 2005, Alcan Packaging Italia had a turnover of €193 million; there were 821 employees divided into: 18 managers, 251 clerical workers, and 552 workers.

The HR Italia manager, in addition to being in charge of the personnel policies inside Alcan Packaging Italia, is also personnel manager in the plant in Vicenza. In the other manufacturing plants there is a HR manager who answers, hierarchically, to the plant manager and, functionally, to the HR Italia manager. The various manufacturing plants deal, completely autonomously, with the selection and training of their personnel and they work with the HR Italia management with regards to organizational problems, organizational development, and trade-union relations.

The HR area of Alcan Packaging Italia has nine people, including the HR manager. Even though it is a young area, which has existed for a relatively short time, it shows a good level of sophistication, measured by the quantity and type of management instruments used. In addition to the traditional HR instruments (replacement tables, pay surveys), Alcan HR Italia management utilizes more innovative practices (job analysis, assessment center, corporate climate analysis) and it does so for many of the current categories of personnel. This is certainly due to the fact that Alcan Packaging Italia is part of a multinational group equipped with the most cutting-edge instruments in the HR sector. Particularly worthy of note is, for example, the e-HRM system aimed at the managerial figures (management and middle management) and at young talent with high potential: the IPCM assessment system and the internal recruitment channel, Jobs Online, are included this investment.

The outsourced HRM processes

Other than personnel administration, for which the choice is not unequivocal (it depends on the plant), among the HRM processes in Alcan Packaging Italia, the processes of recruitment and selection and training are more concerned with outsourcing. Indeed, for these processes, Alcan Packaging Italia decided to opt for a management which is a cross between market and hierarchy.

For both recruitment and selection, as well as training, it is a partial type of outsourcing, in that it concerns either only several phases in the process or, when it concerns the whole process, only several categories of personnel.

In particular, in the event that blue collar or white collar workers with a maximum of 3–4 years' experience are sought recruitment occurs by consulting the internal CV database and turning to suppliers specialized in the search for these professional figures. In the event that the company turns to external suppliers, the headhunting companies are entrusted not only with recruitment but also the first phases of selection.

However, for the more important middle managers and managers both the recruitment and the first stages of selection are carried out exclusively by the external headhunting and selection companies consulted by Alcan Italia.

For training, Alcan turns to the market for:

–   the purchase of standard training packages (catalogue training);
–   the supply of internally planned training courses;
–   the planning and supply of complex courses, to be realized on the base of training requirements detected internally. These requirements are identified by the line and communicated to the HR manager, who manages relations with the market.

It must be stated that, alongside recourse to the market, for the high-potential professional profiles there are training courses that are specially designed, managed, and supplied by the group's head office.

The principal reasons that drove Alcan Packaging to outsource, for both recruitment and selection as well as training, are ascribed, first, to the necessity of improving processes' effectiveness, by relying on the specialization and experience of the providers. The second reason is linked to efficiency and it concerns the reduction of times and costs.

Another reason is formed by the necessity of focusing on those HRM activities which are core.

Conversely, among those reasons for keeping part of the outsourced processes and other HRM activities in-house, the HR manager indicated the importance of possessing distinctive abilities, sources of competitive advantage, and the consequent risk of spill over, the interdependence with other activities and, lastly, though decidedly a less important reason, the costs, which are less internally compared to the market due to economies of scale.

Alcan Packaging Italia uses three to five providers of recruitment and selection services. These are the largest employment agencies, local headhunting and selection companies and, for the middle managers and managers, headhunting companies.

Alcan Italia has regular relationships with approximately 15 providers of training services – consultants and/or training companies – whose selection took the firm approximately 1 year.

Non-exclusive contracts are made for recruitment; for selection, however, exclusive contracts are made with the supplier.

Those contracts between Alcan and the suppliers of services concerning personnel training are also non-exclusive.

Notes: HR, human resources; HRM, human resource management; IPCM, Individual Performance and Career Management.

The antecedents: the importance of service improvement

Analysis of the antecedents indicates the extent to which firms in the sample used outsourcing to access resources and skills not available internally in order to obtain a higher level of service (Table 3.4). External providers are therefore recognized as suppliers of a specialist service that the HRM department is unable to perform with the same efficiency and effectiveness. Conversely, economic factors, such as the reduction of operating costs or the resort to economies of scale, appear less important in the outsourcing decision. Similarly, less importance is given to aspects of a technological or imitative nature.

Table 3.4

Internal/external factors which have led to a partial or complete outsourcing of HR processes.

Cause	Frequency (%)
Possibility of accessing resources available on the market	23.7
Lack of internal resources or skills	18.5
Increase in quality/professional skills of the service	17.8
Focusing on one/few HR activities to excel in	6.7
Reduction of operating costs	6.7
Increase in reliability/standardization of service	6.7
Impossibility of accessing economies of scale	3.7
Impossibility of realizing activity due to growing volumes	3.7
Re-engineering HR activity	3.0
Simplicity of activity	3.0
Possibility of introducing ICT-based HR platform	2.2
Repeating positive experience of other firms	2.2
Possibility of assessing service rendered without difficulty	1.5
Possibility of accessing technological innovations	0.7

Note: HR, human resources; ICT, information and communication technology.

Therefore, from the analysis it appears, consistent with RBV, that recourse to outsourcing is motivated by considerations of improving the effectiveness of the bundle of HRM processes. This trend is confirmed by the extent to which firms rely on different degrees of outsourcing. The degree of outsourcing of HR processes is greater, the lesser the contribution of the process itself to corporate competitive advantage: in other words, the perceived strategic nature of the process by and large leads to a greater internal control of the same by the firm.

This trend leads to a different approach to outsourcing. Those processes with a higher degree of outsourcing are worth considering, namely those related to personnel administration and recruitment; for these the most important driver is that of reducing HR costs and hours in order to invest in more value-added internal services. Such processes are characterized by a high degree of standardization and are also those processes that absorb considerable working hours.

Box 3.3 is a case illustration of a company that has outsourced the whole personnel administration service, providing an illustration of some of the above points.

Box 3.3   Lowara: the complete outsourcing of personnel administration processes

Lowara is an Italian firm localized in Vicenza; it operates in the sector of development and manufacture of pump systems in the field of water technology and in the sectors of residential and collective construction, irrigation, and industry. In 2004, it had a turnover of €137 million. The firm has two manufacturing plants. In 2004, there were 720 employees plus another 50 temporary workers. The firm, established in 1968, was bought by Goulds Pumps in 1985 and in 1997 became part of the ITT industries group, the main manufacturer worldwide of pumps and pump systems for water and industrial liquids. Since 2003, Lowara has held the role of headquarters of the WTG EMEA.

Lowara's personnel office deals with the management activities of HR and the firm's trade-union relations. The person in charge of the secretarial activities and the person in charge of the 'personnel services' area report to the manager of the personnel office. In total, the number of people employed in the personnel management is five.

The principal activities of Lowara's personnel management include managerial activities such as personnel selection and training programs, performance assessment and compensation, career identification and development, as well as more innovative and highly strategic activities such as the development of organizational competences, communication (in collaboration with other corporate sectors), and the implementation of ITT corporate policies.

Outsourcing of HRM

In 2001, Lowara completely reorganized its personnel management by outsourcing the personnel administration activity, more specifically: attendance and absence, pay and contributions, documentation regarding social security and public bodies due to initiation/termination of employment contracts, training contracts, statistical surveys (e.g. annual disabled declaration).

Lowara outsourced personnel administration activity to reduce the excessive commitment of resources (human and time) in the most routine and least added-value activities, to focus on more strategic activities, such as the involvement in a BPR project at corporate level.

Dissatisfaction with the IT supplier who had developed the software package for the in-house management of the payroll and the performance of fiscal requirements also played a part in the decision. Due to outsourcing the number of people employed in the personnel office passed from eight to five. Through outsourcing the personnel management states it has realized an improvement in the levels of effectiveness and efficiency of the service.

The provider of HRM services chosen by Lowara is 'HRO', a Milanese company, which is part of the larger OSP 'Gruppo Byte'.

Selection was carried out based on the following criteria: reputation, price of service, and supply of accessory services. Accessory services related to pay and contributions fall under these criteria.

The supplier's willingness to absorb the excess staff was also instrumental in the choice: indeed HRO employed two of the three people who, due to the decision to outsource, had to leave the personnel office in Lowara. The third worker was transferred to the firm's administration office.

The first contract had a duration of 3 years, provided for the lease of premises in Lowara's open space and a consideration of a fixed price, within definite tolerance bands.

The services offered by HRO are supplied by means of a virtual platform through which the two firms – the client and the supplier – exchange data from their own information systems. This mechanism does not require the physical presence of the supplier, however, at the beginning of the relationship with HRO, Lowara asked the provider to be present in the firm, giving it a part of the open space, also in order to supply several accessory services considered very important for Lowara's employees (help desk, legislation advice).

In order to monitor the relationship with the provider, the contract also lists the performance indicators and performance levels expected by Lowara. The presence of these elements makes the contract between Lowara and HRO a service level agreement.

According to Lowara, outsourcing has entailed costs that were not entirely anticipated during the decision phase linked to the management of the exceptions encountered until the system was made operative after the first year.

Notes: HRM, human resource management; HRO, human resource outsourcing; WTG EMEA, Water Technology Group Europe Middle East and Africa.

Analysis of the factors that lead firms to choose specific providers supports the importance of the quality of services to the business line. The first factor in these choices is the competence and specialization in the service (27.6%), followed by experience in the sector (21.4%), and by reliability over the long run (10.3%). The quality/price ratio of the service (6.9%) is only at fourth place, and at eleventh place is the lowest cost compared to other providers (2.8%).

If one takes the opposite factors into consideration, namely those that drive the firm to retain their provision in-house (Table 3.5) to keep control over it, one also finds reasons connected to the effective management of value-added and firm-specific HRM services to the line being prominent. Moreover, the principal causes of internal management of a process (or part of a process) are also consistent with TCT perspective, namely process specificity and frequency.

Also, in this case no significant differences based on the type of HR process under consideration was found, with the exception of the selection process, for which the economic valuation takes on greater importance compared to other processes, though subordinate to strategic valuations. It emerged that the cost of the provider for the selection service may be such as to drive the HRM not to outsource at all.

Lastly, confirmation of the reasons that drive firms to outsource also comes from the data related to the assessment criteria used to judge the service supplied by the provider. The principal parameter adopted was the quality of the service (31.4%), in second place was the reliability of the service

Table 3.5

Internal/external factors which have led to the decision not to completely outsource HR processes.

Cause	Frequency (%)
Maintaining control of strategic activity in-house	26.4
High corporate specificity of activities	20.0
High frequency of activities' realization	11.2
Internal management costs lower than market prices	10.4
High complexity of activities	10.4
Lack of satisfactory supply on the market	8.0
Difficulty assessing the service provided by supplier	8.0
Prices of services available on the market too high	4.0
Necessity of saturating resources employed in such activity	1.6

(22.9%), in third place the ability to support changes in the client's needs, and cost was only placed fourth (15.7%). In fifth place was the ability of the provider to propose innovative solutions (10.7%) in processes such as training, selection, organizational planning, and special projects.

The relationship with the provider

Analysis of the relationship with the provider is aimed at understanding whether in Italy, given the still limited diffusion of the phenomenon and the strategic and organizational characteristics of firms, a transactional type of outsourcing approach was typically adopted, namely an approach in which one or few activities were outsourced to different providers underpinned by a short-term logic (Sako and Tierney, 2005).

To elucidate this, we can look at our data on the number of outsourced processes. As we have seen previously, in most cases it is only one activity that was outsourced; the highest portion of firms investigated (47% of cases) state that they outsource only one HR process, while only 29% outsource two and 19% three or more.

Furthermore, firms outsource to more than one provider. Data collected for each process indicated that on average for the management of personnel administration processes 1.4 providers were involved, for the management of recruitment and selection processes there were on average 2.5 providers involved, and 3.6 in training processes. Typically, different HR processes were outsourced to specialist providers, including HR consultancies or IT firms specialized in payroll management. For recruitment and selection, however, mainly employment agencies or headhunters were involved, while for training the choice falls on business schools, universities, trade associations, training bodies, and consultancy firms, the latter are also used for the management of special projects.

Importantly, Italian firms tended to consider one provider as an easy substitute for another. In 61.7% of cases the provider is considered by firms as immediately substitutable with others with minimal cost; in 31.9% of cases the supplier is substitutable but only by sustaining significant costs. Only in 6.4% of outsourced processes is the provider substitutable with difficulty and at a high costs. Consequently, in the majority of cases the high substitutability of the supplier indicates recourse to outsourcing on the basis of a market as opposed to partnership logic.

However, it was also found that substitutability differed according to the HR process under question. As shown in Table 3.6, a high degree of substitutability was found in the processes of selection and recruitment, while for the process of personnel administration, very likely due to the higher installation costs, the degree of substitutability was lower.

In outsourcing HR activities, firms' temporal reference point is still short term. The contracts made with the providers, in the majority of cases investigated, were typically less than 1 year and, moreover, were not automatically renewable in 63% of cases. Only for the process of managing personnel administration was a longer duration and a more significant percentage of contracts with a duration of greater than 5 years (26.7%) found, due to the higher costs of installation and, consequently, change.

These data seem to confirm the hypothesis that a transactional relationship was the norm; outsourcing of an integrated

Table 3.6

Percentage distribution of processes outsourced based on the degree of substitutability of the provider.

	Provider is immediately substitutable with minimal costs (%)	Provider is substitutable but by sustaining significant costs (%)	Provider is substitutable with difficulty and only by sustaining significant costs (%)
Administration	33.3	53.3	13.3
Recruitment	100.0	0	0
Selection	88.9	11.1	0
Training	58.3	33.3	8.3
Special projects	66.7	33.3	0

bundle of HR services to a single provider over the long term was still a long way from being typical in the Italian context. The transactional type of approach is accompanied by the use of formal contracts. In the majority of cases (41.7%) it concerns framework agreements, followed by non-exclusive contracts (31.7%) and by highly prescribed contracts with service level agreement clauses (10.0%). In the management of the relationship shared operating systems or shared or connected roles (respectively 6.7% and 1.7%) are rare, likewise for the sharing of property rights (1.7%) or IT platforms (3.3%).

The supply of the service occurred in the majority of cases by combining on-line and off-line modes (56.3%), while in the remaining cases it occurred only through off-line modes (39.6%) and a small part by only relying on on-line modes (4.2%). These last data were noticeable exclusively in the field of outsourcing the personnel administration process.

Although the services outsourced to a highest degree are, for the most part, standard, some problems in the relationship with the provider also surfaced. These tended to focus on the problems experienced by some client firms of an inadequate level of service for the processes of recruitment and administration. The coordination difficulties were seen as the main problem facing the outsourcing of processes, especially those that required a greater degree of personalization such as selection and training of qualified employees. However, it must be said that in nearly half of the cases no problems were found.

In short, our data indicate the presence of the conditions that Sako and Tierney (2005) proposed as characterizing the employment of transactional relations in the relationship with the provider. As we have seen the extent of outsourcing is typically limited to one process; moreover, the relationship lasts on average no more than 2 years. Finally, it is clear that it is the standard, less strategically critical HR processes that are outsourced to a greater extent, with a much greater degree of internal control being exercised over less standardized processes.

Firm size and the outsourcing process

The sample contained small- and medium-sized firms as well as large firms. This leads us to question whether the different size of the firms in the Italian situation shapes the nature of outsourcing governance.

The type of processes outsourced most is not significantly affected by the size of the firm: unbundling the sample based on the number of employees, one observes a similar outsourcing of processes both by small-to-medium enterprises (SMEs) with less than 250 employees as well as large firms. The only partially dissonant element is constituted by the selection process, which is outsourced more by large firms (55%) compared to others (33%).

Large firms' propensity to outsource diverges from that of medium firms and is greater especially as regards personnel administration, 67% of big companies intend to outsource more of this process, while no medium-sized firms expressed a similar intention. A further difference found between the SMEs and the large firms concerned the parameters for provider assessment: as the size of the firm increased the number of assessment criteria adopted increased, particularly the percentage of firms that relied on the ability to provide innovative solutions and support changes to client needs in addition to the standard cost and quality criteria.

Conclusions

The data collected confirm the importance of outsourcing in the management of HR in Italian firms. However, outsourcing is still somewhat limited in scope and complexity, typically focusing on only one HR process. When firms do decide to outsource more than one process, the principal logic is that of focusing on resources and abilities that are not available internally to obtain a higher level of service. Economic justifications are less widespread among firms, which are also illustrated by the cases; when firms outsource they do so with the objective of reorienting scarce resources towards activities with greater added value. A significant result from the research and analysis at process level concerns the degree of outsourcing of the individual HR activities. Firms are interested in maintaining internal control that guarantees the expertise necessary to monitor the provider and integrate his services within the firm.

Administration and recruitment processes are most susceptible to outsourcing, the drivers of which are the greater degree of standardization and absorption of HR time by the two processes. This finding confirms the tendency of firms to maintain firm-specific and higher value added processes inside the organization, which can benefit from greater resources precisely thanks to outsourcing of the more standard activities or portions of activities. However, when a specialised service is required in order to complement the internal bundle of processes, external consultants can be approached.

With reference to the form of governance, our analysis reveals the reliance of Italian firms' on formal contracts in HRO. Analysis of the number, type of processes, and their degree of standardization confirms the lack of those conditions of complexity and uncertainty of the transaction that, according to Sako and Tierney (2005), drive firms to adopt relational contracts. Moreover, governance of the relationship with one or more providers appears to be designed according to short-term criteria. Furthermore, it is based on framework agreements which, for the most part, are non-renewable automatically and therefore renegotiable. In 80% of cases the service is designed based on the specifications defined by HR managers. The parameters for the assessment of the service are defined by the firm, and in several cases agreed with the provider. Recourse is not made by using coordination mechanisms such as shared operating systems or lateral mechanisms such as shared or connecting roles.

To conclude, further light on these data can be shed by examining the work of Carson et al. (2006), who studied the effects of uncertainty on the recourse to formal or relational contracts by empirically testing the hypotheses on 125 processes of research and development (R&D) outsourcing.

These authors distinguish between two types of uncertainty: volatility and ambiguity (Figure 3.1). *Volatility* concerns the variability of the environment and therefore the uncertainty about the future, while *ambiguity* is an uncertainty which is not determined by change, but which derives from the lack of information, from not knowing the cause and effect relations

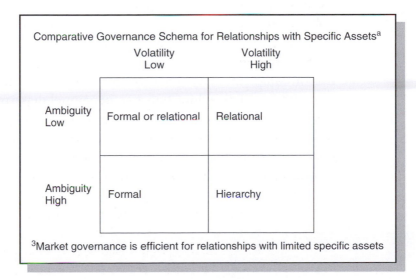

Figure 3.1
Comparative schema for the type of contracts used in interorganizational relationships.
Source: Carson et al. (2006).

or alternative actions. According to these authors, in the presence of specific assets, the different level of the two forms of uncertainty determine the choice of interorganizational relationships based on formal rather than relational contracts, whereas when both are high firms resort to hierarchy.

In the case of our sample firms, we propose that there are conditions of asset specificity, revealed by the request for the service to be personalized, though to differing degrees, from the personnel management. Moreover, the uncertainty of the transaction seems to be characterized by some level of ambiguity. *Volatility* is not present due to the short duration of the relationship and the relative stability of the outsourced processes. One can also speculate on the existence of *ambiguity*, based on the fact that the firms look externally for processes or phases of processes that cannot be realized in-house and therefore do not have all the information and skills necessary for their realization and thus evaluate all the aspects. The internal control of one part of the processes outsourced guarantees, on the other hand, the minimum expertise necessary to define *ex-ante* the required specifications for the services to insert in the contract. Consequently, the firms analyzed resort to formal contracts rather than relational contracts.

In short, this research proposes a new perspective for the study of HRO in Italy, hitherto analyzed in light of TCT and RBV, with their respective limitations. Analysis of the alternative or complementary recourse to relational and formal contracts in the relationships between personnel departments and providers appears to be rich with potential, both for understanding the evolution of outsourcing in Italy and the managerial implications that may stem from it.

Implications for managers

Some important managerial implications can be drawn from the results.

First, in deciding what to outsource and what to keep inside, firm's executives in cooperation with its HR department should identify those activities that are no longer value-added and at the same time are highly time consuming. This represents the first step toward freeing internal HR resources, burdened by tactics tasks, in order to dedicate them to more strategic activities. Our findings show that HR administration process and recruitment and selection of low-skilled personnel are externalized, since these two processes do not affect the firm's competitiveness. This internal analysis, besides detecting the activities for which outsourcing could lead to time-operating savings, might evaluate the services that the HR departments are not able to deliver in-house effectively and efficiently. Effectiveness means satisfaction of internal clients, top management, line managers, and employees. As our research points out, especially in SMEs, where the role of HR function is mainly administrative, the lack of expertise in value-added processes like training, selection of professional skills that are hard to find on the labor market or implementation of special projects (talent management, compensation plans) leads to externalization. A thorough evaluation of the internal capabilities held by the HR staff and the contribution of the HR processes to the firm's core business represents a critical step in order to understand outsourcing decisions. Finally, externalization can also be a source of cost savings. In this case it should be chosen by firms every time it is recognized that a service can be realized more efficiently on the market, for example because the HR provider can benefit from economies of scale that are impossible for the single firm, specially in the context of SMEs. In our research, pay-roll activities and recruitment are externalized because making them in-house would have been more expensive.

A second implication regards the type of HR outsourcing and the degree of externalization. Our research demonstrates that Italian firms are yet far from a transformational outsourcing since they externalize only some HR activities to a variety of specialized suppliers. Moreover, the firms in the sample still maintain an extensive internal control over the majority of externalized processes, especially those of critical nature. This could be ascribed to a lack of trust or to a cultural factor widespread in the SMEs context, that is the high degree centralization. As a consequence, the high level of control can mitigate the advantages expected from the outsourcing decisions, such as gains of productivity and focusing on strategic activities. Also the transfer of best practices, new ideas, and suggestions from the providers to the firm might be compromised. Furthermore, the research highlights that firms have several providers, and each one is specialized in a particular HR process (training, recruiting, administration). However, managing different specialized HR providers increases transactional costs and limits advantages, such as economies of scale, faster and more reliable IT systems for data transfer and elaboration, cross-process synergies, which can be achieved managing a full-service HRO supplier.

In contrast, it is worth noting that HR outsourcing is relatively recent in Italy. In our sample, the majority of firms started to externalize HR services in 2003–2004 and the earliest experiences occurred around 2001. The HR BPO market is emerging in Italy and it is still little known by Italian firms, especially by SMEs which, as we have seen, externalize particularly to traditional HR providers. Moreover, in Italian firms, HR departments are traditionally 'administrative experts' (Ulrich, 1997). They have to perform administrative tasks and to supply efficient and effective procedures and practices for the HR policies (from recruitment to evaluation, from training to compensation). This is also true for the SMEs in our sample, whose personnel offices, though larger, still have limited experience in outsourcing, but are willing to be involved in less operative HR activities, and to introduce more sophisticated techniques and tools, and to start relying on external service providers. Outsourcing is, on the one hand, a way to free up the department of labour intensive processes and on the other, a way to complement internal value added services with external ones. In this context, the transactional approach to externalization of HR activities adopted by Italian firms could be conceived as a way of approaching the new phenomenon of HR outsourcing on a piecemeal basis, by exploring the market of HR BPO, experimenting benefits and problems of externalization, and building up the relationship with providers. An internal control of a part of the outsourced processes appears justified by the need for the client firm to keep fuelling internal know-how enabling the firms to competently assess the provider or select new ones. In other words, for firms this means nurturing the absorptive capacity (Cohen and Levinthal, 1990), which facilitates the choices of outsourcing and the integration process between the provider's services and their own bundle of internal HRM processes. This piecemeal approach can be useful also for HR providers, especially those that are not traditional partners for SMEs. Indeed, HR providers can exploit transactional relationships to gain better knowledge the real needs of SMEs and enter new market segments.

A final implication concerns the evaluation of HR providers and their services. Services are defined based on the specifications defined by HR managers as well as the evaluation parameters that consider traditional metrics such as time, cost, and quality. However, often the level of service (made in-house or externalized) is not formally measured, thus the risk is to continue producing in-house services that would be better externalized, or to rely on suppliers who do not guarantee a competitive service. Firms, especially SMEs, require a new set of managerial skills that support them toward profitable forms of outsourcing. The transactional approach that characterizes Italian SMEs represents a means of nurturing these skills, since firms and providers start to know each other and to understand the mutual benefits stemming from a collaborative relationship. Consequently, a necessary step is to acquire trust, to develop collaboration, to create an appropriate metric system, and, eventually, to evolve towards a different form of outsourcing where both parties – firm and provider – share some risks and rewards in a partnership focused on a shared set of goals for the business.

References

Adler, P.S. (2003) Making the HR outsourcing decision. *Sloan Manage. Rev.* Fall, 53–60.

Baker, G., Gibbons, R., and Murphy, K.J. (2002) Relational contracts and the theory of the firm. *Q. J. Econ.* February, 39–84.

Baron, J.N. and Kreps, D.M. (1999) *Strategic Human Resources.* New York: John Wiley & Sons.

Brewster C., Sparrow P., and Vernon G. (2007) *International Human Resource Management* 2nd edition. Berkshire (UK): McGraw Hill Education.

Carson, S.J., Madhok, A., and Wu, T. (2006) Uncertainty, opportunism, and governance: the effects of volatility and ambiguity on formal and relational contracting. *Acad. Manage. J.* 49, 1058–77.

Cohen, W.M. and Levinthal, D.A. (1990) Absorptive capacity: a new perspective on learning and innovation. *Admin. Sci. Quart.* 35, 128–52.

Eisenhardt, K.M. (1989) Building theories form case study research. *Acad. Manage. Rev.* 14, 532–50.

Espino-Rodríguez, T.F. and Padrón-Robaina, V. (2006) A review of outsourcing from the resource-based view of the firm. *Int. J. Manage. Rev.* 8, 49–70.

Greer, C.R., Youngblood, S.A., and Gray, D.A. (1999) Human resource management outsourcing: the make or buy decision. *Acad. Manage. Exec.* 13, 85–96.

Klaas, B. (2003) Professional employer organizations and their role in small and medium enterprises: the impact of HR outsourcing. *Entrepren. Theor. Pract.* Fall.

Laursen, K. and Mahnke, V. (2001) Knowledge strategies, firm types, and complementarity in human resource practices. *J. Manage. Gov.* 5, 1–27.

Leiblein, M.J. and Miller, D.J. (2003) An empirical examination of transaction and firm-level influences on the vertical boundaries of the firm. *Strategic Manage. J.* 24, 839–59.

Poppo, L. and Zenger, T.R. (2002) Do formal contracts and *relational* governance function as substitutes or complements? *Strategic Manage. J.* 23, 707.

Sako, M. and Tierney, A. (2005) Sustainability of business service outsourcing: the case of human resource outsourcing (HRO). *AIM Research Working Papers*, June. Available from http://www.sbs.ox.ac.uk/NR/rdonlyres/FC74DDA9-8480-4EE1-A324-2176269F1753/1431/HROworkingpapersakoandTierney2009.pdf

Silvestri, G. and Pilati, M. (2005) La gestione strategica delle risorse umane: un nuovo patto tra direzione del personale e management. *Econ. Manage.* 1, 97–113.

Ulrich D. (1997) Human Resource Champion. Cambridge, MA: Harvard Business School Press.

Woolthuis, R.K., Hillerbrand, B., and Nooteboom, B. (2005) Trust, contract and relationship development. *Organ. Stud.* 26, 813–40.

Wright, P.M., Dunford, S.A., and Snell, S.A. 2001. Human resources and the resource based view of the firm. *J. Manage.* 1, 27, 701–21.

Yin, R.K. (1991) *Case Study Research. Design and Methods.* London: Sage Publications.

Further reading

Barney, J. (1991) Firm resources and sustained competitive advantage. *J Manage* 17, 99–120.

Chartered Institute of Personnel and Development. (2006) *HR Outsourcing.* September 2006. Available online at: www.cipd.co.uk (last accessed 23 September 2007).

Lepak, D. and Snell, S. 1998. Virtual HR: strategic human resource management in the 21st century. *Hum. Resource Manage. Rev.* 8, 215–35.

Towers Perrin (2005) *HR Outsourcing: New Realities, New Expectations.*

CHAPTER 4

Outsourcing HR in France: Theory and Practice

Veronique Guilloux and Michel Kalika

Introduction

Hypercompetition, globalization, and information and communication technology (ICT) generalization go together with new organizational forms, networked organizations, and desegregation of the traditional enterprise (Pichault and Rorive, 2003). An increasing focus on core business has led to the outsourcing of non-core activities, though we should be careful about overstating the case as Chapter 1: Technology, Outsourcing, and HR Transformation: an Introduction has indicated. Nevertheless, from 1980 businesses began to abandon obviously peripheral activities such as cleaning and catering. And, over time, more complex activities such as computing and logistics were outsourced and now complete processes are being externalized (known as business process outsourcing; BPO).

There has been a great deal written on the theme of ICT externalization (Lacity and Willcocks, 2001; Fimbel, 2003; Barthélemy, 2004; Meissonier, 2006). Other articles have been concerned with function or operational process externalization (Quélin and Duhamel, 2003), including customer relationship management (CRM) and call centers (Ueltschy et al., 2006), financial services (Jennings, 1996), and human resources (Beaman, 2004; Lawler et al., 2004).

This chapter will deal with the theme of the externalization of human resources (HR). Many authors have worked on the evolution of an HR function 'under pressure'. The HR function, it is constantly argued, must demonstrate its value: indeed, some commentators have signaled the death of the HR function if it does not (Kanter, 2003), though others are more sanguine about its future (Schmidt et al., 2004).

Two factors are supposed to liberate the function: information technology and the externalization of administrative activities into service centers (Spencer, 1995, Kalika, 2002; 2003; 2006). The development of mega-externalization contracts (recent examples include arrangements between Proctor & Gamble and IBM) gave birth to e-HR and the interface between information systems (IS) and human resource management (HRM). This chapter will present a definition of externalization, different forms of HR outsourcing and the strategic role of the HR function. The following questions will also be analyzed: Is BPO a solution for those considering transformation of the HR function and does ICT significantly contribute to BPO?

Definition and different forms of HR outsourcing

Externalization and ICT

The term 'externalization' can be used as an alternative to 'outsourcing', where the needs of the firm are met by an external structure ('out' sourcing) rather than by an internal structure ('in' sourcing). In contrast to 'subcontracting', which has more of a short-term perspective, externalization entails a strong link between the firm and its provider, thus creating a strategic alliance. The French Economic and Social Council's report

(Conseil Economique et Social, 2005, p. II20) proposed the following characteristics of a definition:

■ Externalization could be defined as the resort to an external provider, for an activity so far realized inside the firm;

■ It often goes with material and/or HR transfers;

■ It requires a contractual framework defining remits, deliveries, mutual obligations in a larger way than subcontracting;

■ Outsourcing is consistent with long-term commitment between the enterprise and its service provider.

More specifically, practitioners categorize HR externalization in different ways, as described in Box 4.1 below.

Box 4.1   Different forms of HR externalization

1   An *ASP* delivers an online service to its customers (e.g. the services provided by Cegid/CCMX). A business does not need to purchase, maintain, or operate HR systems but instead pays the service provider for the use of their systems. This may be payable at a transaction level, by numbers of users, or taxed by an estimated income. This kind of HR service is primarily used by small-to-medium-sized businesses.

2   *Application hosting* involves the *external hosting of an HR application.* Here the firm's application is 'taken' and is hosted by the service provider. This is likely to involve *third party application management,* which provides for the maintenance of a software application, and is subject to specific service level agreements. Application outsourcing is the management and the operation of computing resources (materials and networks) which can be localized on the provider's premises. For a firm, externalizing HR processing services consists of entrusting an HR process to the provider (e.g. legal monitoring, social reporting, functional assistance, computation, etc.). The vendor's resources are shared among several clients. The vendor commits himself to achieve contractually agreed results.

3   *BPO* takes this a step further and entrusts the whole business process to the provider (e.g. externalization of the

administrative aspects of the HR function to providers such as IBM, Accenture, ADP GSI). The firm retains its managerial and strategic decisions. The emphasis on rationalization of key business leads some US firms to go further using 'co-employment' by PEOs to externalize employer responsibilities such as contracts, recruitment, and remuneration. It is primarily small firms that use PEOs, which are currently only operating in the USA (Klaas et al., 2005).

Notes: ASP, application service provider; BPO, business process outsourcing; HR, human resources; PEO, professional employer organizations.

HR outsourcing in France

An updated overview of HR outsourcing was developed by Markess International in 2006 (Figure 4.1). It identified different types of vendors. These include:

- Service companies (e.g. Accenture, IBM) are global HR service partners offering outsourcing solutions and technology integration services to the world's largest employers;
- HR services operators (such as ADP GSI, Cegedim SRH) provide the management of certain HR domains and support them with their own software solution;
- Software suppliers may provide HR-specific applications (e.g. Horoquartz) or include HR capability as part of a wider enterprise resource planning (ERP) system (e.g. SAP, Oracle). They can also propose a hosting solution based on their software (e.g. CEGID);
- Application service providers (ASPs) develop HR 'best of breed' applications that they provide through Internet access, e.g. for payroll (e-paye) or recruitment (Monster). Examples of such consulting firms are Hewitt Associates and PricewaterhouseCoopers.

Concerning the outsourcing of HR, different contractual forms appear to exist. In a study of 194 companies in France, the

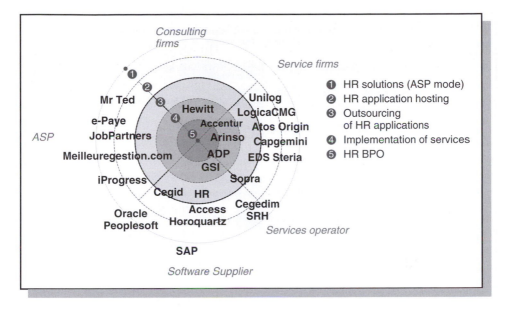

Figure 4.1
Human resources outsourcing vendor marketplace.
Source: Markess International (2006).
Notes: ASP, application service provider; HR, human resources.

most common form of outsourcing of HR was HR processing services (42%); the use of an ASP to manage HR applications was chosen by a further 34% of organizations, while HR application hosting was the choice of a further 29% of respondent organizations (Figure 4.2).

For outsourced applications (Figure 4.3), payroll processing has been the first domain to be addressed. This trend is forecast to continue in the near future. The second domain is the externalization of the training process. The French legal environment with its training rights for employees (DIF, *Droit individuel à la formation*) has boosted the number of firms resorting to outsourcing of training and development. The administration of employees has also been well developed, especially as businesses want to entrust legal compliance to the outsourcer.

Do these general statistics, however, suggest that HR outsourcing strategy leads the firm towards a new HR Model. And does BPO fit with the new HRM model ?

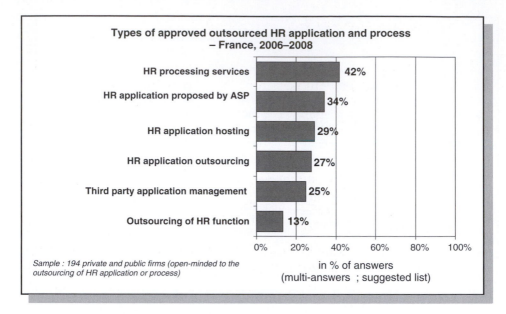

Figure 4.2
Contractual forms.
Source: Markess International (2006).
Notes: BPO, business process outsourcing ; HR, human resources.

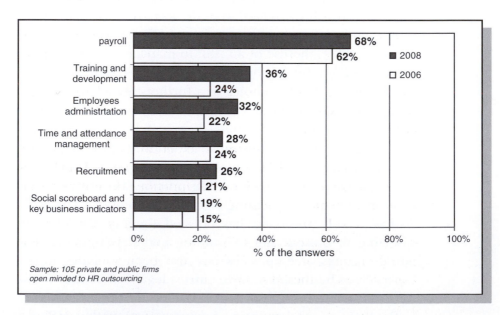

Figure 4.3
Applications concerned by outsourcing.
Source: Markess International (2006).

Towards a new HR model?

In his original work on this subject, Ulrich (1996) described four management roles for the HR function: strategic partner, administrative expert, employee champion, and change agent. The author positioned them on a matrix with two axes: process versus people; strategic focus versus day-to-day operational focus. In each mission, he argued, HR role must reinforce the creation of value for the employees, investors, and customers of the firm. These four profiles also help evaluate the performance of HR.

- The *strategic partner* helps the firm to target its strategic aims and to align HRM practices to the firm's strategic orientations. Becker et al. (2001) encourage the use of an 'HR scorecard' to position the HR function as a business partner;
- The *administrative expert* orientates their action towards operational tasks, managing working contracts, pay-roll, and administrative processes. Different types of software support this work;
- The *employee champion* answers the employees' needs, improving levels of commitment and competence;
- The *change agent* is a catalyst encouraging innovation and contributing to transformation of the organization.

The LENTIC Research Centre (Laboratoire d'Etudes des Nouvelles Technologies de l'Information, de la Communication et des Industries Culturelles, University of Liège, Belgium) associates both the administrative expert and employee champion to a type of HRM they label as *mechanical HRM*. This reflects activities that modern HR functions do not necessarily want to assume, usually focusing on transactional actions such as payroll. In contrast, the change agent and the strategic partner participate in an *organic HRM* model. The argument is that developing and institutionalizing the strategic role of the HR will permit the HR function to become a stakeholder in the firm's creation of value (Becker et al., 1997). Beysseyre des Horts (2005) indicates that the academic literature often shows the introduction of ICT as a means of creating value for all the stakeholders by releasing HR professionals to focus on strategic issues; however, there has been little empirical research to shed light on whether this has occurred. We have carried out some exploratory interviews in 2006 to understand if HR externalization could help the function in its new strategic role, which we touch on in the next few sections.

Can BPO solve the tensions between traditional administrative role of HR function and its new strategic role?

Nowadays in France, HR externalization is more concerned with the HR process than the HR function per se. Our interviewees quote the DIF legislation (2004) as a stimulus to externalization. The 'industrialization' of DIF makes human resource information systems (HRIS) more complex and requires additional resources, often leading firms to outsource the process as a result. Figure 4.4 gives an example of the decomposition of HR externalization.

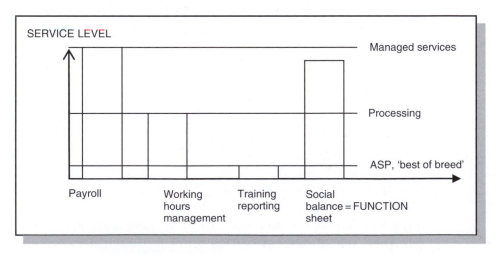

Figure 4.4
Fictitious example of externalized tasks portfolio.
Note: ASP, application service provider.

Recent evidence suggests that genuine BPO is still not used frequently in France compared with Anglo-Saxon countries, although it has received a degree of impetus from foreign-owned multinational enterprises searching for harmonization and coordination of their HR policies and systems.

Box 4.2 summarizes the HR BPO contract between IBM and Proctor & Gamble (noting that it follows a separate agreement of $3 billion with HP for outsourcing its IS infrastructure):

Box 4.2   Procter & Gamble chose IBM Business Consulting Services for Employee Services Business Transformation Outsourcing (BTO)

Procter & Gamble selected IBM Business Consulting Services when they decided to externalize several business processes. The aim of this strategy was reducing costs and improving employee services. This major business transformation could enable it to compete more effectively in the fickle business to consumer market. This transformation rests on outsourcing of some critical, but non-core business processes to improve flexibility and focus on core competencies. One major area that the company sought to outsource was its employee services, or human resources (HR), functions. It needed a strong outsourcing partner with experience and a international presence to support its nearly 98 000 employees worldwide, spread out in 80 countries. The company decided to work with IBM Business Consulting Services for Employee Services Business Transformation Outsourcing (BTO). It will outsource its payroll, benefits, travel etc . . .   IBM will provide process transformation and technology integration in managing these HR functions for its employees. Procter & Gamble will receive employee services in a more jus-in-time, flexible way. The solution should improve decision making by providing management real-time access to employee reporting information that is consistent, accurate and standardized.

Notes: BTO, business transformation outsourcing; HR, human resources.

Some key firms such as IBM and Accenture link BPO to the idea of shared service centers (SSC). Historically, these centers remained internal to the firm. Such operations centralize the various support functions in various geographical establishments. Instead of having independent 'back-offices' at each operational entity (e.g. subsidiaries, plants, factories), support resources are gathered together into a SSC. Unlike administrative centralization, these centers are responsible for cost management and the quality level of the services provided. The SSC has a proper budget and defines its service on a contractual basis with its internal clients, which in turn sets the performance standards in terms of cost, time, and quality. SCCs regularly compare their various costs to external benchmarks from the best firms in the sector. SCCs also constitutes a center of excellence and may be a profit center in the organization.

An SSC which was formerly run inside the firm can nowadays be externalized (involving transfer of personnel) or can be treated by a new service provider (transfer of competence) (Horan and Vernon, 2003). IBM owns several big international centers: in Asia Pacific (Philippine 300 persons; China 100 persons), one in Europe (Budapest 500 persons), and in the USA (Costa Rica 500 persons; Hortolândia, Brasil 300 persons). These number of persons are dedicated to HR, since other teams could be focused on CRM or finance. This reinforces the mutualisation phenomenon (multiclients or multilevel BPO contracts) for the holders of offshore platforms. SSCs are also often 'offshored', i.e. relocated to another part of the world. Geographical areas are selected according to the attractiveness both of the country concerned (infrastructure, political, monetary, financial, fiscal, legal environments, etc.) and of the resources available (salary costs, real estates costs, quality, competence, spoken languages, employment situation, etc.). More specifically transferring personal information outside France requires a CNIL specific procedure (see the French data protection authority see www.cnil.fr/).

In the case of *personnel transfer*, the provider undertakes to take over some or all of the employees of the firm. Thus, in the scope of the global externalization of the administrative HR of Proctor & Gamble, IBM has employed approximately 800 people from Proctor & Gamble as well as three of its multinational SSCs. New forms of organization, particularly externalization, impact heavily on the application of employment law (Morin, 2005). Externalization of functional domains goes with the professionalization of the legal and fiscal frameworks surrounding these operations.

In France, the *L122-12 article* of labor legislation (equivalent legislation to L122-12 across Europe can be found in 'Business transfers across Europe' http://employment-news. lovells.de/download/Business_Transfer_across_Europe.pdf) means that staff transfer is automatic, providing that the transfer relies on a self-governing economic entity. The theme of social responsibility is obviously inherent in these kinds of restructuring (Morin, 2005; Rorive, 2005). Joint ventures (JVs) between the contractors and the providers may be created in order to smooth the transition to outsourcing The purpose of these structures is not to endure: they accommodate employees with L22-12 status when the arrangement notes employees' transfer and houses employees in *'temporary assignment status'*, when the provider wants in fact to reorganize and redeploy them in the firm. The interviews show that the first reluctance is the social risk (e.g. strikes, protest movement). The provider use the JV approach to manage the transition on a longer duration.

In the case of *competence transfer*, the provider does not employ some principal employees.

It is legitimate to question the risks to and the limits of the enterprise which is externalizing its services. Could the increasing cuts in human resources mean the regression of the HR function?

Exploratory interviews within HT service providers show that they defend a strategic vision of HR and do not simply support an economic logic with cost reductions. They maintain that BPO could help to transform the HR function in the firm by resolving the tensions between its administrative traditional role and its new strategic role.

Figure 4.5 can be interpreted as follows: BPO helps liberate the HR function so that it can be more focused on its strategic mission. Providers take into account the SSC (*general HR* in interface with each country) and place an HR Internet portal at the employees' disposal (the Technology block in the diagram). The HR partners work with the business units. In the development stage, priority is given on recruitment, motivation development, etc. In the stabilization level, the role is to fit HR and the competences with the business firm. Finally in the recession stage, crisis management is involved. Corporate HR

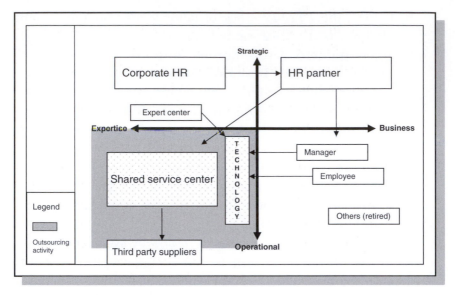

Figure 4.5
Links between BPO and HR.
Note: HR, human resources (adapted from Ulrich's concept).

elaborates the institutional strategy. It is in interface with the expert center (HR process *specialist*).

The different squares of the diagram are interdependent and resemble Ulrich's model. According to Ulrich's terms, several questions can be asked: 'Does this BPO framework support the next HR agenda for adding value and delivering results?' and 'How does IT affect BPO?'

How ICT could positively affect BPO?

Few studies exist on the relationship between BPO and value creation in HRM. Examples where firms have brought outsourced IT operations back in-house ('*back-sourcing*') may surprise some practitioners. In 2002, JP Morgan externalized its IS infrastructure with IBM with a contract of $5 billon over 7 years. But, after merging with Bank One in 2004, JP Morgan reneged on its contract with IBM and decided to re-internalize its IS function. Even if a reversibility clause is now included in BPO contracts, re-internalization of activities is not without cost for the firm. There is little empirical evidence to justify HR externalization and, when it does exist, it can throw up tensions and contradictions. For example, Shis et al. (2005) collected data in 153 large Taiwanese companies, discovering that the HR function's involvement in the company's strategic process was found to negatively influence the relationship between HR outsourcing and perceived effectiveness. Analyzing the Flemish PASO (Panel Survey of Organizations) database, Delmotte and Sels (2005) show that HR outsourcing is not only an instrument of cost reduction, but is also part of a more strategic vision of HR. They observe that internalization (delegation of power to hierarchic lines) and externalization are strongly correlated, and do not necessarily lead to reductions in HR staff. These surveys suggest that combining internalization and externalization allows the HR function to move towards a role of strategic business partner.

Qualitative research through cases helps complement these statistical studies. Cook's (2205) work reminds us that Ulrich did not really discuss the process of interaction by which the distribution of work between in-house HR professionals and outsourced HR staff is determined. When they have outsourcing decisions, firms need to look beyond the resource-based view that helps them to identify their competitive advantage, more specially on the complex institutional context (decision makers' norms and values, corporate history, organizational culture and politics, public and regulatory pressures, and industry-wide norms). Our interviews confirm this point of view. The recent French government elections and current social trends do not suggest that large outsourcing contracts are on the horizon. BPO is considered as strategic, and consequently it is usually more decided by a firm's chief executive than by its HR departments.

Shen (2005) reminds us that good management of the externalization relationship is a vital condition for the success of the collaboration, and also to develop organizational learning. In that way, Schlosser et al. (2006) suggest that managers can possibly influence the relationship between outsourcing and social capital through marketing tactics and enriched psychological contracts.

Even though we possess limited knowledge about the effectiveness of outsourcing and HR duties, we can understand how ICT could affect BPO. Advanced Internet technology furthers a seamless relationship between external vendors and client companies, which is why investment and innovations in an integrated HR information technology are often a selling point of the HR-specialized service providers. This could enhance 'cross-fertilization' between the two firms and perhaps bypass the resistance to change existing in-house. Companies may learn the latest techniques and benefit from benchmarking; they may capitalize on one another's expertise and contribute to organizational memory with ICT. When BPO is well driven, our interviews underline the implementation of HR scorecard, better HR reporting and development of e-HR.

Conclusion

In this chapter, HR outsourcing is not presented only as an instrument of cost reduction but also as a transformational outsourcing and as a process of the organizational and strategic change. As BPO and SSC redefine the shape of the firm, the effective management of human resource outsourcing relies on creating and sustaining a good relationship with the providers. Personal transfer or competence transfer has not the same impact on social risk, which is the greatest barrier to French BPO.

No real empirical evidence sustains BPO's claims of cost reduction, better services, and the creation of value (Conklin, 2005; Belcourt, 2006). Human resource outsourcing leads to significant change in the firm and needs to be well managed. This chapter tries to analyze how IT could go with BPO and what kind of assets IT supplies. As there is an important theoretical literature demonstrating that IT mechanisms provide great insight into a successful management interorganizational coordination in a global supply chain (Kosnik, Wong-MingJi &

Hoover 2006), future research on IT/HR outsourcing and inter/intra supply chain dynamics could help to manage the best of 'BPO spirit'.

References

Barthélemy, J. (2004) *Stratégies d'Externalisation*. Paris: Dunod.

Beaman, K. (2004) *Out of Site: an Inside Look at HR Outsourcing*. Austin, TX: IHRIM Press.

Becker, B., Michel Kalika, Huselid, A., and Ulrich, D. (2001) *The HR Scorecard. Linking People, Strategy, and Performance*. Boston: Boston Harvard Business School Press.

Becker, B.E., Huselid, M.A., Pickus, P.S., and Spratt, M.F. (1997) HR as a source of shareholder value. *Hum. Resource Manage. J.* 31, 1–6.

Belcourt, M. (2006) Outsourcing: the benefits and the risks. *Hum. Resource Manage. Rev.* 16, 269–79.

Bertrand Quélin and François Duhamel (2003) Bringing Together Strategic Outsourcing and Corporate Strategy: Outsourcing Morives and Risks *Eur. Manage. J.* 21, 5, pp. 467–661.

Beysseyre des Horts, C.H. (2005) Création de valeur et TIC: le Cas de l'e-RH. In *e-RH: Réalités Manageriales* (M. Kalika, V. Guilloux, F. Laval, and M. Matmati, eds.) pp. 9–22. Paris: Librairie Vuibert.

Budhwar, P., Luthar, H., and Bhatnagar, J. (2006) The dynamics of HRM systems in Indian BPO Firms. *J. Labor Res.* XXVII, 339–60.

Conklin, D. (2005) Risks and rewards in IIR business process outsourcing. *Long Range Plann.* 38, 579–98.

Conseil Economique et Social (2005) *Conséquences sur l'Emploi et le Travail des Stratégies d'Externalisation d'Activités*. Paris: Journaux Officiels.

Cooke, F., Shen, J., and McBride, A. (2005) Outsourcing HR as a competitive strategy? A literature Review and an assessment of implications. *Hum. Resource Manage.* 44, 413–32.

Delmotte, J. and Sels, L. (2005) *L'Outsourcing des RH: Opportunité ou Menace?* Leuven, Brussel: Editions Université Leuven.

Fimbel, E. (2003) Les facteurs décisionnels de l'externalisation des systèmes d'information: référentiels théoriques, éléments empiriques et proposition typologique. *Syst. Inform. Manage.* 8, 4.

French Economic and Social Council (2005) Conséquences sur l'emploi et le travail des stratégies d'externalisation d'activités. *Ed des Journaux officiels.* pII20.

Horan, P. and Vernon, P. (2003) Expanding HR's Global potential: shared service centers in multi-country regions. *Compensat. Benefit. Rev.* September, 45–53.

Jennings, D. (1996) Outsourcing opportunities for financial services. *Long Range Plann.* 29, 393–404.

Kalika, M. (2002) Le défi du e-management. In *Les Défis du Management* (M. Kalika, ed.) pp. 221–36. Paris: Editions Liaisons.

Kalika, M. (2003) TIC et stratégie. In *E-Management, Quelles Transformations pour l'Entreprise?* (M. Kalika, M. Ledru, H. Isaac, C. Beyou, and E. Josserand, eds.) pp. 71–96. Paris: Editions Liaisons.

Kalika, M. (2006) *Management et TIC: 5 Ans de e-Management.* Paris: Editions Liaisons.

Kanter, M. (2003) Foreword. In *Human Resources in the 21st Century* (M. Effron, R. Gandossy, and M. Goldsmith, eds.) p. vii. New Jersey: John Wiley & Sons.

Klaas, B., Gainey, T., McClendon, J., and Yang, H. (2005) Professional employer organizations and their impact on client satisfaction with human resource outcomes: a field study of human resource outsourcing in small and medium enterprises. *J. Manage.* 31, 234–54.

Lacity, M. and Willcocks, L. (2001) *Global Information Technology Outsourcing.* Chichester, UK: Wiley.

Markess International (2006) *Externalisation RH.* Livre Blanc.

Meissonier, R. (2006) *Externaliser le Système d'Information: Décider et Manager.* Paris: Economica.

Morin, A.L. (2005) Labour law and new forms of corporate organization. *Int. Labour Rev.* 144, 5–30.

Pichault, F. and Rorive, B. (2003) *Restructurations et Nouveaux Périmètres Organisationnels: le Rôle de la Fonction RH, Journée d'Etudes 'Les Restructurations: Volonté ou Fatalité?* Paris: IAE de Paris.

Rorive, B. (2005) Restructurations stratégiques et vulnérabilités au travail. *Rev. l'IRES* 47, 117–34.

Schlosser et al. (2006)

Schmidt, G., Guéry, L., Mercier, E., and Mottay, D. (2004) *La Fonction Ressources Humaines, Levier de Création de Valeur? du Volontarisme des Discours au Scepticisme des Acteurs.* Colloque AGRH.

Shen, J. (2005) Human resource outsourcing: 1990–2004. *J. Organ. Transform. Social Change* 2, 275–95.

Shis, S., Chiang, Y.H., and Hsu, C.C. (2005) Exploring HR outsourcing and its perceived effectiveness. *Int. J. Bus. Perform. Manage.* 7, 464–82.

Shrivastava, S. and Shaw, J. (2003) Liberating HR through technology. *Hum. Resource Manage.* Fall, 201–22.

Schlosser, F., Templer, A., and Ghanam, D. (2006) How human resource outsourcing affects organizational learning in the knowledge economy. *J. Labor Res.* 27, 291–304.

Spencer, L.M. (1995) *Reengineering Human Resources.* New York: John Wiley & Sons.

Stroh, L.K. and Treehuboff, D. (2003). Outsourcing HR functions: when-and when not-to go outside. *J. Leadership Organ. Stud.* 10, 19–28.

Ueltschy, L., Ryans, J., and Herremans, I. (2006) Marketing: who's really minding the store globally? *Bus. Horizons* 49, 139–48.

Urich, D. (1996) *Human Resource Champions.* Boston: Harvard Business School Press.

Further reading

ADP (2002) *Ressources Humaines: L'Externalisation en Europe, une Tendance Profonde, une Evolution Accélérée.* Available online at: www.europe.adp.com/files/site/a/d/adpeuropefr.eu.adp.com/ftp/actualites/Outsourcing-FR.pdf (last accessed 23 September 2007).

Barker, P and Yeates, H. (1985) *Introducing Computer Assisted Learning.* New Jersey: Prentice Hall.

Barley, S. (1996) Technicians in the workplace: ethnographic evidence for bringing work into organization studies. *Admin. Sci. Quart.* 41, 404–41.

Barthe, S. (2001) Les technologies du web: une réponse éventuelle aux nouveaux défis de la GRH. *Rev. Gest. Ressour. Hum.* 41, 5–20.

Kakabadse, A. and Kakabadse, N. (2000) Sourcing: new face to economies of scale and the emergence of new organizational forms. *Knowl. Process Manage.* 7, 107–18.

Kalika, M (ed.) (2002) *E-GRH: Révolution ou Évolution?* Paris: Editions Liaisons.

Kalika, M, Guilloux, V., Laval, F, and Matmati, M. (eds.) (2005) *E-RH: Réalités Managériales.* Paris: Librairie Vuibert.

Kerr, S. and Von Glinow, M.A. (1997) The future of HR: plus ça change, plus c'est la même chose. *Hum. Resource Manage.* 36, 115–9.

Kosnik, T., Wong-MingJi, D., Hoover, K. (2006) Outsoucing vs insourcing in the human resource supply chain: a comparison of five generic models. *Personnel Review*, 35(6), 671–684.

Linder, J. (2004) Transformational outsourcing. *Sloan Manage. Rev.* Winter, 52–8.

Losey, M., Meisinger, S., and Ulrich, D. (eds.) (2005) *The Future of Human Resource Management: 64 Thought Leaders Explore the Critical HR Issues of Today and Tomorrow.* San Francisco: Jossey Bass.

Wils, T., Labelle, C., and Guérin, G. (2000) Le repositionnement des rôles des professionnels en ressources humaines: impacts sur les compétences et la mobilization. *Rev. Int. Gest.* 24, 20–33.

CHAPTER 5

Restructuring the HR Function: HR Shared Service Centers in the Netherlands

Elaine Farndale and Jaap Paauwe

The advent of e-human resource management (e-HRM) combined with globalization is having a significant impact on the human resources (HR) function. We are increasingly hearing questions about how HR is delivered and the quality of this service. In particular we are seeing more and more HR shared service centers (SSCs) being established, housing HRM activities under one roof for a selected domain of an organization. In practice, many stories have been told about these changes to HR, but little has been learned from these examples. This chapter looks at these stories and combines this with newly collected evidence to explore the main motives for companies to establish HR SSCs, the expectations these motives create and the actual outcomes realized. The findings based on HR SSC experiences in 15 companies in the Netherlands show that issues such as cost, quality, and standardization are at the forefront of organizational drivers to establish SSCs, yet few organizations are actually satisfied with their process for monitoring the center's performance. More detailed findings and the implications for HR functions in particular are discussed.

Introduction

Paauwe (2004) identified four logics in the field of HRM. There is the strategic logic of linking HRM strategy with corporate strategy, the societal logic of fitting HRM policies with society at large, the professional logic of the level of quality of the services provided by the HR function, and the delivery logic which focuses on the various ways in which HRM practices can be delivered: by the HR function itself, by line management, through employee self-service, SSCs, web-based and/or through outsourcing and offshoring contracts. Much has been written regarding the first two logics, particularly the strategic logic linking HRM and firm performance. However, here we turn our attention to delivery and professional logic, considering how HRM is delivered in organizations today and in particular on the impact of technology on the structure and performance of the HR function.

With this focus in mind, a relatively new form of organization structure for HR is the SSC. This way of organizing provides a single location to house HRM activities for a selected domain of an organization, be it the whole organization, a geographical region, or for a specific business division. The center is designed to make optimal use of web-based and information systems technology to support this new organizational structure. The ethos behind the service concept is that it is the client that decides which services they would like to receive from the center, rather than the HR function within the organization deciding on which services it will deliver. SSCs are thus designed to deliver services of the highest value and at the lowest cost to internal clients. This structure also transfers increasing responsibility away from HR to line managers for the implementation of HRM, as well as the technology enabling line managers and employees to make use of self-service functionality (Reilly, 1999; Reilly and Williams, 2003).

These are just a few of the issues raised by HR SSCs. As can already be seen, the starting point for this exploration of the impact of SSCs on the HR function is similar to that noted regarding the introduction of e-HRM in recent years: the issue is 'not primarily technical; it is first and foremost a change in the mindsets and behaviors of HR personnel, line managers, and employees' (Ruël et al., 2004, p. 102). However, there is a lack of studies exploring the HR SSC phenomenon as it is largely still in its infancy. Taking an organizational perspective, this chapter considers the main motives and expectations of organizations establishing HR SSCs, and the related anticipated performance outcomes. In the following sections, these motives and expectations are discussed in further detail before looking at evidence gathered from the Dutch context.

Shared service centers: the big questions

Centralization or decentralization?

The introduction of SSCs is a response to the decision particularly facing large organizations, as to whether they should centralize or decentralize their support functions, either to maintain control from the center or to increase local responsiveness. Decentralization of the HR function means that organizations are more flexible locally to respond to changes in market and institutional demands, such as the requirement of new employee skills to match product or service development, or the implementation of changing employment legislation. In addition, decentralization transfers ownership of HRM to local units maintaining local autonomy. However, this mode of operation also runs the risk of missing opportunities for synergies across the organization as a whole, and producing variable levels of service quality (Schulman et al., 1999). In contrast, centralization has the advantages of control and efficiency directed from the center, leading to the avoidance of redundancy and duplication of work (Ulrich, 1995). However, ensuring buy-in to the services by local businesses can be more problematic due to the geographical separation of units.

The shared services concept is claimed to be a form of organizing which can produce the benefits of both centralization and decentralization, whilst minimizing the drawbacks of both. It combines centralized decision making with decentralized delivery: whereas the centralization model focuses on strategic HR at headquarters and operational HR at local subsidiary level, the SSC model centralizes the transactional HR activities, creating more space for strategic HR at the local level. SSCs thus enable companies to maintain control of core support functions, avoid duplication, and offer services more efficiently and at lower cost (Quinn et al., 2000). SSCs can thus be seen as a type of internal outsourcing ('in-sourcing') in the way in which the local business units establish the required service levels from the 'external' SSC.

The SSC can be incorporated into the organizational structure in different operating models: the *basic* model which consolidates transactional activities to achieve economies of scale; the *marketplace* model which adds the professional expertise center dimension to the transactional activities; the *advanced marketplace* model, where the center is considered to be a commercial enterprise, possibly providing services to external customers; and the *independent business model* in which the SSC is defined as a separate business entity, a spin-off from the mother company (Quinn et al., 2000). Strikwerda (2004) also identifies possible organizing structures. SSCs can be an internal joint venture between different business units, where resources are pooled to provide a single-location service. The SSC could also be set up as a separate business unit itself, responsible to the board as all other business units. A more centralized solution is for the SSC to be part of the corporate center, housed alongside the headquarters. For an SSC which is only active for a specific business unit, it may be embedded in that business unit. External models include joint ventures between the organization and an external party, or the SSC being completely independently run by an external party, selling its services to the organization (such as the partnership between Procter & Gamble with IBM running its HR SSCs).

Supporting corporate strategy?

Ultimately, the decision to create a SSC is largely a factor of corporate strategy. Corporate strategy encourages appropriate interdependencies, and hence there are choices to be made between integration and differentiation for the structure of internal operations.

Particularly for a multinational organization, the decision to bring together HRM administrative tasks in a single location to provide services across business divisions or locations indicates a certain desire on behalf of the organization to consolidate its field of operation. For example, SSCs are more likely to be implemented by organizations with a transnational or global internationalization strategy (see: Bartlett and Ghoshal, 1989), whereby the company does not see itself in terms of a collection of host countries supporting the home-country headquarters, but more as an integrated whole, spanning national boundaries. If a company strategy is more polycentric, in which subsidiaries are given full autonomy over HRM practices, then an international SSC would not be an appropriate structure for HR services.

Integration will not always be seen as advantageous by all areas of the organization. For example, as highlighted with the e-HRM phenomenon: 'when implementing e-HRM on a global scale, it is not easy to make it appear advantageous on a local scale' (Ruël et al., 2004, p. 103). However, the integration of activities across business and geographical boundaries within the SSC increases the potential for organizational learning from which all parties can benefit. It can also mean that the HR function is more flexible to change as it is able to respond from one central source to meet the demands of, for example, external changes in employment legislation, or internal changes in corporate HRM strategy (Reilly, 1999).

In addition to intentional corporate strategy, there may also be a certain degree of mimetic institutional isomorphism taking place (Paauwe and Boselie, 2003): there is a trend underway of companies setting up SSCs, with much publicity regarding potential cost savings, and hence other companies may be being seduced into following the same trend to maintain their legitimacy and chances of survival in the marketplace. This could mean that there is a danger that SSCs become a passing fad unless they are genuinely found to add value to the organization and the HR function itself.

Reaping the benefits of technology?

SSCs are almost synonymously linked with e-HRM or web-based HRM technologies. Advanced technological developments have facilitated the ability of widespread communication across organizational and national boundaries, providing real-time information to privileged recipients regardless of their geographical location. Based on the e-HRM model developed by Ruël and colleagues (2004), there is a range of goals which e-HRM is designed to achieve: cost reduction (such as printing, telephone calls, and paper), wider dispersion of information and communication, improving the service quality and productivity of the HR function creating room for increased strategic input, bringing clients closer to HR services through increased empowerment, and time savings for the HR function and for employees. SSCs are arguably the natural progression of these web-based technologies. As ICT has become more sophisticated, this has enabled the consolidation of corporate activities into fewer locations whilst spreading information to a broader audience. In HR terms, the advent of e-HRM thus appears to be culminating in an increasing number of HR SSCs appearing within company structures.

If we look at the extant HR SSC literature, it becomes immediately apparent that the e-HRM goals overlap considerably with those of SSCs, such as a desire to enhance the strategic contribution of the HR function (Reilly and Williams, 2003); to provide a single point of contact for clients and consistency of advice and information (Reilly, 1999); to reduce costs through economies of scale (Forst, 1997); and to make more efficient and transparent use of resources through standardization (Reilly, 1999; Reilly and Williams, 2003). There have also, however, been further potential benefits identified, which go beyond the application of e-HRM technologies and consider the advantages of housing HRM administrative activities in a single location. These include the opportunity to create a focus on service delivery quality and client satisfaction, creating a clear linkage between customer expectations and service delivery; to develop an integrated approach to problem solving and hence enhance organizational learning; and to create a clear division between transactional and transformational HRM activities and hence clarify roles within the HR department.

Delivering cost-effectiveness and quality improvement?

Linked with technology, cost-effectiveness has also been highlighted by many organizations as a reason for wanting to establish a SSC. Economies of scale are largely at play here, as well as considering 'make or buy' decisions. Adams (1991) uses both agency and transaction cost economics in order to highlight various degrees of internalization (make) or externalization (buy). Transaction cost economics suggests that the choice between allocating practices to the external market or to the internal organization is a matter of cost minimization. The focus of agency theory is to determine the most effective contract to control the relationship between the principal and the agent: agency costs must be considered low for externalization of services to be worthwhile. In the SSC structure, transaction costs are thus reduced, processes are more efficient, and ways to cooperate become more flexible.

Bringing together the administrative tasks of the HR function in one location, and the application of advanced e-HRM technologies, not only results in potential cost-efficiencies for the organization, but also in a potential increase in the level of service quality. As noted earlier, SSCs are consumer rather than producer driven and as a result, the attention of the unit is focused on customer service quality, which can represent a source of added-value of the HR function to firm performance. It is common practice also for organizations to put service level agreements (SLAs) in place to define the relationship between the new HR structure and its clients (Strikwerda, 2004).

With the help of advanced e-HRM and HRIS tools, the quality of the HR data itself can also be improved both in terms of its availability and accessibility. The standardization of HRM practices and policies across a whole organization or region to ensure these practices can be managed from a single center also increases the quality of these practices in terms of the consistency of their application and their transparency (Ulrich, 1995).

Many challenges, however, face organizations before such benefits can be realized. These include, for example: senior management support and a clear linkage with corporate strategy and culture for the new organization design; clear boundary management, defining which roles and activities belong where; acceptance of the SSC facility by the clients, to avoid the creation of a shadow HR function within the business unit; the alignment of HRM practices, systems, and policies across the whole organization to ensure both horizontal fit between the practices themselves and with the organization; the management of relationships and communication given the reduced extent of direct interaction between HR and employees or line managers; appropriate career management and skill development for HR professionals within the new structure; and the provision of appropriate access to e-HRM facilities across the organization for all staff (Cooke, 2006; Forst, 2002; Reilly, 1999; Reilly and Williams, 2003; Ulrich, 1995). Cooke (2006) suggests that in reality, SSCs result in higher than expected costs and a fall in client satisfaction with HR services, primarily due to inaccurate planning and setting false expectations.

Restructuring the HR function?

The anticipated outcomes of e-HRM for the HR department are summarized by Ruël and colleagues (2004) along two dimensions: short term/long term and operational/strategic. Short-term operational outcomes can be achieved through the establishment of SSCs which focus on routine administration and transactional HRM practices. Long-term operational outcomes focus more on added value, and often take the form of centers of HR expertise. The latter are often global or regional teams which specialize in a particular HRM discipline, for example compensation and benefits. Today, as e-HRM and SSCs have advanced, a typical organization structure of a large organization which has opted for the HR SSC route can thus be summarized as follows (Reilly, 1999):

- corporate HR function based at the headquarters;
- centers of expertise in HRM disciplines at national, regional, or global levels;
- SSC(s) either for the whole organization or divisions thereof;
- HR business partners at the local business unit level.

There is, however, emergent evidence of a fifth layer in this organizational structure. Between the centers of expertise and the SSCs an intermediary level of governance is being introduced which has the role of monitoring the SLAs in force between the business units and the HR service providers. This is more of a brokerage role, ensuring the management of important relationships.

The SSC concept not only affects the structure of the HR department, but also the roles carried out by the HR professionals. The HR function itself has consistently suffered from role ambiguity within the organizational context. The SSC structure can perhaps provide clarity to the function, by emphasizing the distinction between transactional HR practices, traditional HRM processes, and transformational HR activities (Wright and Dyer, 2000; see Table 5.1). SSCs will typically start with the consolidation of transactional activities such as payroll, benefits management, pensions, and employee records. The longer-term goals can then be to establish centers of expertise around the more traditional and transformational HRM activities. These experts build corporate transparency and consistency through sharing a common base of knowledge. This distinction between transactional and transformational activities in turn reflects the different roles performed by HR managers, particularly the functional expert versus the strategic

Table 5.1

Dimensions of HRM practices, processes, and activities.

Transactional	Traditional	Transformational
Payroll	Recruitment and selection	Strategic HRM
Benefits	Training and development	Organization development
Pensions	Performance management	Knowledge management
Absence	Employee relations	Change management
Employee records	Health and safety	Culture management

Source: Adapted from Wright and Dyer (2000).
Note: HRM, human resource management.

partner roles (Ulrich and Brockbank, 2005). Whilst organizations are always demanding excellence from the administrative, transactional tasks, the HR function itself is demanding greater opportunities for transformational, strategic involvement.

In particular, in the SSC structure, Reilly and Williams (2003) suggest three tiers of job roles for HR staff: HR front-office employees or call-agents (first tier); HR advisors (second tier); and HR experts (third tier). First tier employees have direct contact with clients, and are the first point of contact. Second tier advisors provide more detailed help in a particular functional discipline, whilst third tier experts are called upon to interpret more complex policy issues. Second and third tier staff can either work in the front-office with direct contact with clients, or in a back-office where their expertise is pooled internally to then channel back through the front-office to clients.

In summary, SSCs bring together corporate decisions regarding the centralization or decentralization of HR activities, creating an appropriate degree of interdependency and integration across an organization. In turn, this can impact on organizational learning as well as the organization's ability to survive in the marketplace. Second, the impact of technology means making the best use of available advanced ICT, particularly to deliver cost-effective and high-quality business solutions. Finally, SSCs are about restructuring the HR function itself, with the related impact on roles for HR professionals and for line managers and employees.

Based on this analysis of the literature, three primary levels of drivers are emerging for the establishment of HR SSCs. At the strategic level (1) there are competitive forces at play; at the organizational level (2) it is about the standardization and coordination of structures, systems, and processes; and at the HR department level (3) the key issues are the professionalism of HR and the delivery of HRM. In order to explore the relative weight and impact of these drivers in organizations today, as well as their related organizational outcomes, the following sections describe a study of HR SSCs in the Netherlands.

Case studies and survey

To explore HR SSCs in practice, two rounds of data collection were undertaken. First, case studies of two Dutch multinationals were prepared; one in the financial sector (Bankco) and one in the fast-moving consumer goods sector (Foodco). In Foodco, as part of a larger study of HR roles, there were five interviews held with HR and line management from different business units and the SSC itself. A separate study was undertaken at Bankco, where interviews were held with 13 employees; all but one, a senior manager, were members of the HR function involved with the establishment of a new HR SSC. The interviewees came from a range of business units and corporate HR from different regions and countries across the globe. The interviews gathered information regarding aspects of the external and internal context driving the need for an SSC, and the anticipated benefits and challenges of the new structure for HR.

The second round of data collection was a questionnaire, designed and administered by Berenschot Group in Utrecht, the Netherlands (De Reus et al., 2006). The data collected includes the motives for initiating a SSC, the organizational format adopted, the staffing of the SSC, the kind of HRM activities and HR roles performed, and performance metrics in terms of cost-effectiveness and client-satisfaction. The respondents are all managers responsible for their organization's SSC in large organizations in the Netherlands. In total, 30 questionnaires were mailed from which 14 responses were received (see Table 5.2).

Table 5.2

Questionnaire respondents.

Organization	Turnover 2004 (€ billion)	Industry sector	Coverage of the HR SSC
Universityco	0.6	Education	Complete national
Postco	3.9	Postal services	Partial national
Electronico	14.3	Electronics	Complete national
Insuranceco	1.5	Insurance services	Complete national
Ministryco	0.1	Government	Partial national
Metalco	2.2	Metal manufacturing	Partial national
Drinkco	5.1	Food manufacturing	Partial national
Financeco	55.0	Financial services	Complete national
Oilco	18.2	Oil and petrochemicals	Partial global
Bankco	19.7	Financial services	Complete global
Teleco	11.7	Telecommunications	Complete national
Serviceco	7.6	Insurance services	Complete national
Tempco	5.8	Employment agency	Complete national
Powerco	4.9	Power utilities	Complete national

Notes: HR, human resources; SCC, shared service center.

Survey findings

The findings based on the survey among 14 organizations in the Netherlands which have all recently initiated a SSC are presented here. Table 5.3 gives an overview of the main characteristics of these organizations. Most of these companies are large and operate in various sectors of the Dutch economy.

Table 5.3
The size of the HR SSCs.

Organization	Number of FTE employees in the HR SSC	Number of employees covered by the HR SSC	Ratio of SSC employees to employees covered	Total HR SSC budget/costs (€ million)	Number of transactions (per year)
Postco	196.0	50 000	1:255	8.9	15 020
Financeco	263.7	32 650	1:124	26.1	n/a
Bankco	219.0	27 000	1:123	30.6	60 000
Teleco	86.2	17 800	1:206	12.0	19 500
Tempco	40.3	12 260	1:304	3.9	103 000
Serviceco	258.0	10 600	1:41	30.5	n/a
Metalco	86.3	9900	1:115	10.6	10 000
Powerco	37.5	9441	1:252	n/a	n/a
Oilco	70.0	7800	1:111	10.0	n/a
Electronico	10.4	6850	1:659	2.0	n/a
Universityco	7.2	6000	1:833	0.4	n/a
Drinkco	42.3	4850	1:115	3.4	n/a
Ministryco	91.0	2950	1:32	5.9	28 000
Insuranceco	7.6	650	1:85	0.1	n/a

Notes: FTE, full-time equivalent; HR, human resources; n/a, not available; SCC, shared service center.

Motives for establishing a shared service center

Respondents were asked to indicate the three most important motives for initiating an SSC (see Figure 5.1).

It is not surprising that the most obvious goals relate to cost reduction and quality improvement. What is also interesting is how high the standardization of HR processes appears on organization's agendas. The SSC concept is being used as an enabler or even an enforcer to put in place desired process of standardization of HRM across companies.

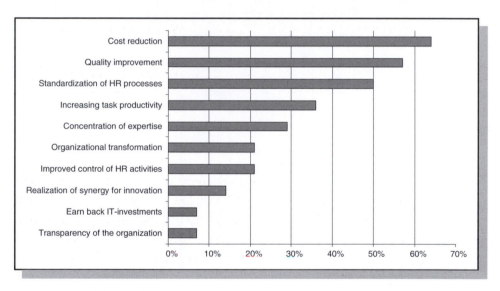

Figure 5.1
The main goals and perceived benefits of HR SSCs.
Notes: HR, human resources; IT, information technology.

We also asked respondents to state the three primary success factors that had contributed most to the actual successful implementation and operation of the SSCs (see Figure 5.2). The most popular factors have a very clear linkage to corporate strategy: a clear vision during implementation, an appropriate focus on service delivery, and high involvement of management in the implementation process to ensure support and buy-in to the service. Interestingly technology was considered a key success factor by few organizations.

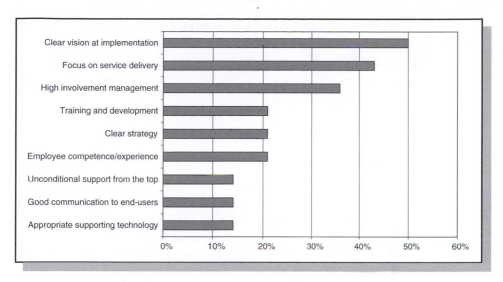

Figure 5.2
The perceived critical success factors for achieving the main goals.

Organizational design

Based on the various options for either an in-house organizational design or an outsourcing model, the companies applied different organizational structures for operating their SSC. Six organizations established SSCs as separate business units, five incorporated the SSC into the corporate center, two established the SSC embedded in existing business units (Drinkco and Bankco), and one (Universityco) opted for an internal joint venture (a separate business unit, managed by other business units).

Related to this issue is whether the SSCs are managed as profit or cost centers. Cost centers aim at cost and expense recovery, whereas profit centers include an element of margin on top of cost to meet internal profit or rate of return targets. In our sample, the majority of companies (nine) work with a budgetary price strategy, indicating that the SSC finances its activities with a predetermined budget and aims to provide necessary services at minimal cost. Two organizations (Oilco and Drinkco) use an activity-based pricing formula, delivering services to the business units using transfer prices determined within the company. The SSC at Powerco charges the actual costs incurred for a service to the relevant business unit.

Most organizations (nine out of the 14) also make use of SLAs, which specify the criteria (such as frequency, quality level, and cost) for the services to be delivered. Four of these organizations have a single SLA in place for all units, whilst the others have different SLAs in place for different organization units.

Resources

The data show that costs related to staffing are by far the largest when compared to other expenses such as housing, ICT, and technical services. Figure 5.3 presents the different cost categories per HR SSC full time equivalent employee. As technology plays such an important role in the operation of SSCs, it is remarkable that automation and ICT costs are only indicated as on average 13% of total costs.

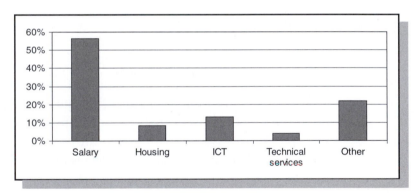

Figure 5.3
Average percentage of total costs per HR SSC FTE.

Referring back to Table 5.1, it is possible to see an overview of the number of full-time equivalent (FTE) employees working for the SSC per company. Figure 5.4 also gives an insight into the number of employees being serviced by one HR SSC employee. As can be seen, the overall size of the organization does not necessarily coincide with the ratio of employees serviced.

The optimum has apparently been achieved by companies employing between 5000 and 10 000 employees in total. However, we need to be careful because the data have not been corrected for the number of HR services provided by the SSC.

It might be that larger organizations simply deliver more services. We consider this issue in the overview of performance indicators below.

Distinguishing between the unrolling, survival and growth phase of the SSC, we can see that as SSCs become more mature, they appear to achieve a higher degree of efficiency (see Figure 5.5).

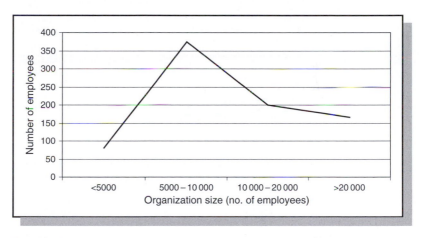

Figure 5.4
The total number of employees serviced by one HR SSC FTE (by organization size).

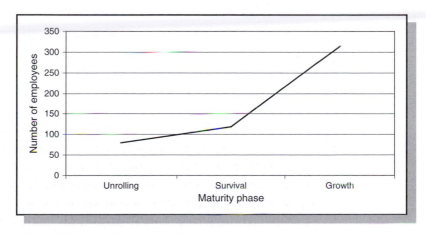

Figure 5.5
The total number of employees serviced by one HR SSC FTE (by maturity phase).

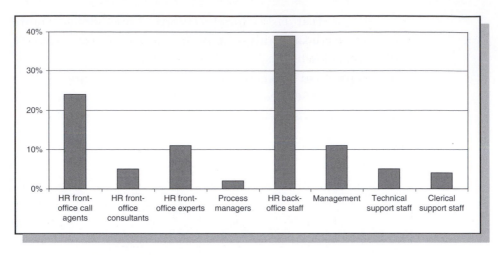

Figure 5.6
Job roles in HR SSCs.
Note: HR, human resources.

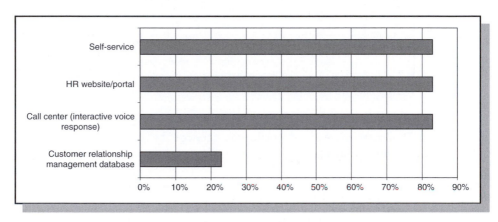

Figure 5.7
The use of technologies by HR SSCs.
Note: HR, human resources.

To give an indication of the actual activities of HR people within the SSC, Figure 5.6 indicates the proportion of HR SSC staff undertaking the different job roles within the center in the different companies. The roles are based on those identified by Reilly and Williams (2003) mentioned earlier. It is interesting to note that in the companies surveyed, the majority of staff is actually found in back-office rather than customer-facing roles.

With respect to technology, the different tools and the degree to which they are being used in SSCs are represented in

Figure 5.7. We can see that customer relationship management databases are being used only on an occasional basis, whereas self-service, web-based, and call center technologies are all in more widespread use.

Self-service HRM

The range of HRM practices covered by the SSCs in the survey is represented in Figure 5.8. Companies were asked to indicate which web-based self-service applications they had available either to line management only, or to employees only, or to both. They were also asked which of these applications they planned to introduce in the future. Self-service systems for the management of expenses and sick leave are most widely in current use, whilst least use is being made of salary information systems. This latter observation may be a result of many companies having outsourced their payroll systems previously, therefore there is little requirement for further in-house salary information provision.

Performance indicators

A range of indicators can be used by organizations to consider the financial impact of SSCs, such as the costs per FTE employee within the center, the number of employees serviced per single SSC FTE, and related cost-efficiency ratios. Due to the variety of ways in which each company made these calculations it is difficult to present an overview of comparative performance indicators here. However, companies were asked in a more general sense what issues they were coming up against in attempting to achieve their performance targets. Figure 5.9 shows that the most common problem faced is actually gathering performance information. Companies do not know whether the centers are producing the desired outcomes. The technological systems themselves are also identified as the second largest problem they have faced in implementing the SSC.

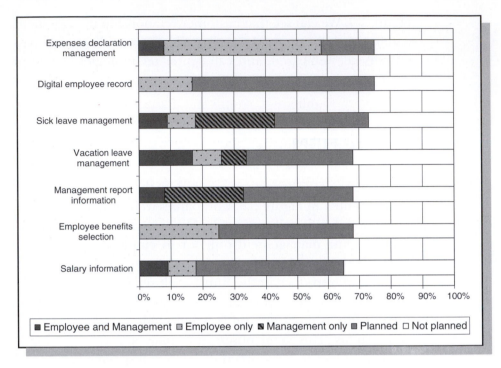

Figure 5.8
The use of self-service applications in HR SSCs.

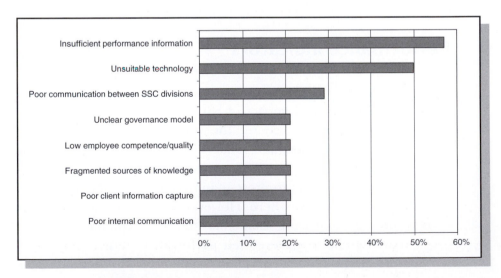

Figure 5.9
The main problems facing HR SSCs.

Motives, expectations, and outcomes

Earlier, we highlighted a number of strategic drivers for the establishment of HR SSCs. In turn, these lead to expectations at the organizational level about service delivery and costs. The HR SSC concept itself was also described as leading to certain outcomes in terms of the shape and scope of the structure of the HR function and the roles of HR employees. This framework is presented in Figure 5.10. In this section, we look in more detail at the extent to which these motives, expectations, and outcomes described in the literature coincide with the experiences of the companies surveyed and interviewed in this study.

The primary motives of SSCs show many overlaps between extant literature and the experience of organizations themselves. The SSC concept is claimed at the strategic level as being

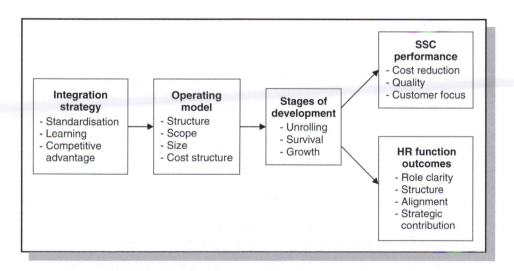

Figure 5.10
SSC goals and outcomes.
Notes: HR, human resources; SSC, shared service center.

designed to create a centralized unit but which remains responsive to local business needs. The more detailed aspect of the SSC being designed to support a corporate strategy of integration and to increase opportunities for organizational learning was not so widely cited amongst companies. However, there was evidence of the importance of these dimensions in the interview data (presented in summary in Boxes 5.1 and 5.2). The introduction of an HR SSC appears to be primarily centered at the organizational level on cost savings and quality improvements.

Box 5.1   Foodco HR SSC

This SSC, which carries out all transactional HRM activities across the Netherlands for Foodco, was established to realize the following goals:

- To centralize administrative tasks;
- To create expertise teams and improve HRM innovation;
- To make HRM more transparent, simple, and clear;
- To act as an employee relations interface;
- To increase employee responsibility, e.g. for personal development;
- To create a channel for knowledge transfer across the company;
- To allow HR to take on more of a business partner role in the business units.

The center is run as a business. HR managers have daily contact, and although the transactional activities are considered a hygiene factor, they still need to be running perfectly. Because of the structure, any errors at operating level are clearly visible and can be addressed more readily. If issues are not addressed, there is always the danger that if local sites do not feel they are receiving the level of service they require, they are more likely to recruit someone locally to take on the tasks, creating a shadow HR function in the business unit.

Notes: HR, human resources; HRM, human resource management; SSC, shared service center.

Box 5.2   Bankco HR SSC

At the point directly before implementation of the HR SSC at Bankco, the following drivers for the establishment of the center were identified:

External drivers:
- Competitive market forces to improve flexibility and responsiveness, to cut costs and improve efficiencies, and to leverage the company's global network to become more geocentric;
- To take advantage of new technology enabling the implementation of the shared service concept and particularly self-service to transfer responsibilities to the line/employees;
- To make employment conditions more flexible, transparent, and clear, cutting across national cultures and institutions.

Internal drivers:
- To reduce internal fragmentation and encourage a more holistic approach to HRM, providing a central point with accountability and responsibility for global employee data;
- To improve the image and consistency of the HR function and allow performance monitoring, and providing employees with a clear, single point of contact to discuss HRM issues;
- To release time for HR to take on more value-adding activities as business partners.

The challenges Bankco anticipated include:
- The quality of the technology implemented: its ability to deliver quality products and solutions that meet the business needs and demands;
- The change management process for introducing the new structure;
- The capabilities of the individuals in the SSC to manage the cultural differences of all the different countries it serves.

The goals Bankco anticipate include:
- Higher quality HR across the company;
- Cross-border collaboration and knowledge sharing;

- Lower costs: less duplication and lower headcount;
- HR being able to make more of a strategic contribution as business partners.

Notes: HR, human resources; HRM, human resource management; SSC, shared service center.

The availability of advanced technologies was not always seen as a primary driver for setting up the SSC, and indeed having appropriate technology was not considered by many as a success factor for achieving the goals of the center. This is also supported by the fact that by far the largest cost of running an HR SSC lies in salary costs and not in technology or technological service costs. However, one of the main obstacles for companies was indeed finding suitable information technology (IT) systems for their HRM processes.

Specific to the HR function, half of the companies surveyed saw the standardization of HR processes as an important goal of the SSC. Achieving clarity between transactional and transformational HR roles is also an important goal for the HR function, particularly to achieve an improved strategic contribution. Although not covered by the survey data, this point was highlighted particularly in the interviews were carried out in Bankco and Foodco (see Boxes 5.1 and 5.2). Equally, the standardization, consistency, and transparency of HRM practices and better quality HR data highlighted in the literature were in evidence in the interviews.

The actual outcomes for organizations in terms of the HR SSC structure and scope have also been explored here. Different forms of organizing have been suggested in the literature, and two forms in particular are being used by organizations today: most organizations opt either to set up the SSC as a separate business unit, or to incorporate it into part of the corporate headquarters, operating the center with its own budget and SLAs. It appears that although the size of the organization may not determine the most effective ratio of SSC employees to total company employees, the stage of development of the center is more consequential. The survey data shows that as centers mature, the ratio becomes more efficient.

With regard to the different job roles being operated within SSCs, a predominance of advisory and expert back-office rather than customer-facing call agent roles in the companies surveyed implies the important role that SSCs play in establishing centers of expertise in addition to the delivery of more transactional activities via front-line call center staff. Again, this may mean that organizations are indeed focusing on the development of centers of excellence in HRM practices by pooling knowledge and experience in a single location (e.g. see Bankco in Box 5.2).

Despite the many advantages and positive outcomes of HR SSCs, there are of course problems incurred in the process of implementation and operation. The companies surveyed stated problems such as not having performance information on how well the center is operating and technology not being suited to the HRM processes required. More general issues of communication, cooperation, boundary management, acceptance of the new structure, and the horizontal alignment of HRM practices have also been highlighted.

Seven HR shared service center lessons

What can we learn from these company experiences? The following points highlight key lessons when adopting an HR SSC structure.

1   The implementation of SSCs appears to be less driven by a strategic vision of integration and transformation than by organizational level goals of cost reduction and quality improvement. Organizations must however ensure that the SSC is not seen as a 'must have fad' but is actually designed to *support corporate strategy* in terms of integration, flexibility, knowledge sharing, and learning. It is crucial that the creation of an SSC has clear *top level leadership* and a strong vision to guide implementation.

2   SSCs can create opportunities to reap the *benefits of both centralization and decentralization* if planned appropriately by creating a geographically centralized unit but which is locally client-driven. The SSC itself is most frequently an independent business unit or a subunit of corporate HQ: the choice being related to the coverage of the unit and its strategic goals. Likewise a budget structure is most common, but a corporate goal may be to develop the unit as an external profit center over time. The key point is to ensure that at all stages of development the roles and responsibilities of HR, line management, and employees remain clearly articulated and communicated. Ultimately, organizations also need to be careful to get the staffing of the SSC right as this is the single major source of cost of running the unit.

3   Organizations can take the opportunity to *benefit from available technology* to facilitate the creation of an SSC, but they need to ensure the technological systems are capable of supporting corporate processes rather than technology dictating practice. Although not perceived from the outset as a potential inhibitor, technology is recognized by many in later stages of development as hindering the desired progress of the introduction of new HR systems.

4   It has been shown that there are considerable *cost-savings* to be achieved through the introduction of SSCs; however, it is important to remember that it may only be in the later stages of operation that these are actually realized.

5   What appears to be highly important in the early stages of implementation is improving the *standardization of HR practices*, enhancing corporate transparency and consistency. These 'quick wins' are an essential part of encouraging buy-in and satisfaction with the service. In particular, an important pre-implementation activity is to establish the desired standardization activities to ensure the SSC can deliver these outcomes.

6   *Quality improvements* are also high on the list of SSC desired outcomes and are often reinforced with the

introduction of SLAs with clients. However, most organizations admit that once their SSC is up and running,
it often falls short of expectations, largely because realistic expectations were not set at the start. Companies
are finding that it is very difficult to monitor performance and to track changes in quality and/or cost. It
is therefore advisable to have *clear performance measurement systems* identified in advance of implementation
to ensure this monitoring capability.

7   Finally, the whole process of introducing an SSC is
most likely best undertaken as a *gradual restructuring* of
the HR function, moving from the inclusion of basic
administration activities to more advanced expert support. This allows the gradual transfer of roles and
responsibilities and gives the opportunity to carry out
quality checks as new processes and systems are added
to the new structure. Overall, the SSC creates the
opportunity to provide more space for HR to take on a
more strategic role at both corporate and local levels.

Conclusion

Focusing on two of the logics of HRM, the delivery and professional logics (cf. Paauwe, 2004), this chapter has considered
the HR SSC concept in terms of motives and expectations
compared with actual outcomes. We have seen how SSCs
restructure the delivery of HR through a client-driven model of
organization. We have also highlighted that SSCs are not primarily technology-driven phenomena, but are actually about
restructuring how employees and line managers interact with
and experience HR.

There are a multitude of consequences for organizations
arising from the HR SSC concept. At the strategic level, issues of
technology are not seen as primary drivers of the HR SSC concept, yet they are seen as one of the main problems companies
face in terms of being able to find the right solutions to deliver
the HRM services and processes the company requires. At the

organizational level, issues of cost and quality are at the forefront of the organization's mind when it comes to establishing these new organizational forms, however postimplementation, performance monitoring is highlighted as the main challenge facing the company. At the HR department level, the SSC concept is forcing attention on the division between activities which can be delivered with a transactional focus, and those that are more transformational in nature. The division of responsibility between line management and HR is also coming further to the fore. In the long term, companies are hoping that this will deliver results for the organization by increasing service quality, reducing costs, and creating time for a more strategic contribution from the HR department to firm performance.

Acknowlegments

The authors would like to thank Berenschot Group (Utrecht, The Netherlands) for their permission to use the quantitative data in this study.

References

Adams, K. (1991) Externalisation vs. specialisation: what is happening to personnel? *Hum. Resource Manage. J.* 4, 40-54.

Bartlett, C.A. and Ghoshal, S. (1989) *Managing Across Borders: the Transnational Solution.* Boston: Harvard Business School Press.

Cooke, F.L. (2006) Modeling an HR shared services center: experience of an MNC in the United Kingdom. *Hum. Resource Manage.* 45, 211-27.

De Reus, H.J., Westerhof, N.J., and Hoeksema, L.H. (2006) A case of trust: summary of Berenschot HR Shared Service Research 2005. *Oracle User Conference*, Diegem, 14 March 2006.

Forst, L.I. (1997) Fulfilling the strategic promise of shared services. *Strat. Leader.* 25, 30-4.

Forst, L.I. (2002) Measure internal customer satisfaction. Industrial Manage. 44, 12–17.

Paauwe, J. (2004) *HRM and Performance: Unique Approaches for Achieving Long-Term Viability*. Oxford: Oxford University Press.

Paauwe, J. and Boselie, P. (2003) Challenging 'strategic HRM' and the relevance of the institutional settings. *Hum. Resource Manage. J.* 13, 56-70.

Quinn, B., Cooke, R., and Kris, A. (2000) *Shared Services: Mining for Corporate Gold*. Harlow: Pearson Education Limited.

Reilly, P. (1999) *HR Shared Services and the Realignment of HR*. Brighton: Institute for Employment Studies, report 368.

Reilly, P. and Williams, T. (2003) *How to get the Best Value from HR: the Shared Service Option*. Aldershot, UK: Gower.

Ruël, H.J.M., Bondarouk, T., and Looise, J.C. (2004) *E-HRM: Innovation or Irritation? An Exploration of Web-Based Human Resource Management in Large Companies*. Utrecht: Lemma Publishers.

Schulman, D.S., Lusk, J.S., Dunleavy, J.R., and Harmer, M.J. (1999) *Shared Services: Adding Value to the Business Units*. New York: John Wiley & Sons.

Strikwerda, J. (2004) *Shared Service Center: Van Kosten Besparing Naar Waardecreatie*. Assen: Koninklijke Van Gorcum.

Ulrich, D. (1995) Shared services: from vogue to value. *Human Resource Plann.* 18, 12-33.

Ulrich, D. and Brockbank, W. (2005) Role call. *People Manage.* 11, 24-28.

Wright, P.M. and Dyer, L. (2000) *People in the E-Business: New Challenges, New Solutions*. Working paper 00-11, Cornell University, USA: Center for Advanced Human Resource Studies.

PART 2

The Theory and Practice of e-HR in Different Countries

The Impact of e-HR on Line Managers and Employees in the UK: Benefits, Problems, and Prospects

Martin Reddington and Claire Hyde

Introduction

Recent literature that has reviewed the relationship between technology and people management, focussing on the e-enablement of HR (e-HR), has shown that although the literature on technology, organisations and people is vast, dating back to the 1960s and earlier, there is surprisingly little independent, academic work on information and communications technology (ICT) and the Human Resources (HR) function, especially in the UK or wider European context. A lot of claims have been generated by consultants and some academics, supported by a limited number of headline cases, concerning the potential for the e-HR, with significant claims having been made for cost reductions and even the virtualization of HR itself. However, it is also clear that organizations do not all look at e-HR in quite the same way. Although enabled by it, e-HR is defined by much more than the technology used.

For example, Kettley and Reilly (2003, p. 13) assert:

'E-HR practices vary considerably in the extent to which they include the redesign of e-HR processes and service delivery methods. Consequently, the level of ambition has fundamental implications for the future configuration and design of HR roles, for the capability of HR staff and for the management of change.'

As discussed in Chapter 1: Technology, Outsourcing, and HR Transformation: an Introduction and in some of our previous work (Reddington and Martin 2006), it is possible to see e-HR outcomes as both intended and unintended, and positive and negative (depending on where one stands). Some examples of these are shown in Table 6.1.

This view begins to surface the potential difficulties associated with the wider transformation of HR, as more activities are devolved to line managers and employees, supposedly liberating HR to perform more strategic, value-adding work. This is based on the assumptions that the HR function has the capability in place to support these higher value-adding roles and indeed the motivation, two assumptions not borne out by evidence on how HR uses it time over the last decade, which seems to have changed little (Boudreau and Ramstad, 2007).

The nature and extent of the inter-related implications, both for HR and line managers are now examined in more detail and we found it helpful to adapt and reorganize the impacts of e-HR shown in Table 6.1 into three main categories, as featured in the report by Parry et al. (2007):

- The impact on HR activities and processes;
- The impact on employee communication and engagement;
- The impact on the changing roles and skills of HR and line managers.

Table 6.1

Classifying e-HR impacts.

Intended positive	Intended negative
Transactional	**Transactional**
1) Reduced costs of HR transactions and HR headcount reduction	1) HR headcount reduction
2) Greater responsiveness to needs of managers and employees' needs for (real-time) information and tailored HR solutions on demand	**Transformational**
3) Increased self-efficacy among managers and employees	1) Lack of face-to-face contact and remoteness of HR staff from 'clients'
	2) Intellectual property and data ownership transferred to outsourcing partner
Transformational	
1) Greater accountability of managers for people management	
2) Greater access to individual learning	
3) More time for HR to focus on expert/strategic issues	
Unintended positive	**Unintended negative**
Transactional	**Transactional**
1) Spill over of information from HR into other areas of business	1) Displacement of existing HR staff and loss of organizational knowledge
Transformational	2) Lack of job satisfaction among HR staff working in shared service centers
1) Greater sense of organizational innovativeness/progress Modelled through adoption of sophisticated e-HR	3) Manager/employee frustration over ease of use and value of information

Source: Adapted from Reddington and Martin (2006).
Note: HR, human resources.

For each category, we begin by reviewing the relevant literature but also enhance this with illustrations from our own recent research in a large UK mobile telephone company.

The impact of e-HR on the efficiency of HR activities and processes

Though the use of information technology (IT) in human resource information system (HRIS) has been quite widespread since the 1980s, this has to be distinguished from e-HR for two key reasons. First, HRIS is focused on automating the systems used by the HR function itself; thus its main 'customer' has been HR staff rather than managers or employees. Second, the use of HRIS does not enable the creation of the new HR business model discussed in the introduction. So, for example, HRIS has concerned itself with automating systems such as payroll and personal information, usually with little or no attempt to make such data interactive or available to staff outside of HR. In contrast to HRIS, e-HR is concerned with the application of Internet and web-based systems, and increasingly, mobile communications technologies to change the nature of interactions among HR staff, line managers, and employees from a pure face-to-face relationship to one that is increasingly mediated by such technologies (Ruël et al., 2004). In doing so, it replaces or complements face-to-face relationships and HRIS with a 'smart self-service relationship', customized content, and greater individualization of services.

Much of the existing literature has focused on the benefits of e-HR adoption (see Box 6.1) but it is becoming increasingly recognized that there are potentially negative consequences from e-HR adoption for HR staff and their internal clients, especially if the issues connected with change management and technology acceptance are not handled effectively (see Chapter 16: Strategic Amplification of HR: New Forms of Organization Or Social Disintegration?).

Box 6.1   Headline findings on the impact of e-HR on the efficiency of HR activities and processes

Two key reports (CIPD 2004; Martin 2005) reveal that around 60% of the survey population, on average, rated 'improving productivity' and 'reducing operational cost' to be 'as expected'.

The results were less convincing in respect of 'reducing the headcount', with an average of 42% of respondents reporting this to be 'as expected'.

In all cases, however, no actual value or relative percentage, measured against a baseline value, was provided. Also, the population sample consisted of only HR managers.

US evidence from 2002 studies pointed to reductions of 33–50% in HR staff following the implementation of self-service technology, with forecasts of spending on e-HR set to increase (Gueutal and Falbe, 2005). Other consultancy-based surveys reported dramatic reductions of 43% in average transaction costs, 62% in the length of time taken to deal with queries, 50% reductions in enquiries directly to HR and service centers, and 37% average reductions in headcount associated with HR administration (Towers Perrin, 2002; Watson Wyatt, 2002).

Other work reported increases up to 50% in employee satisfaction with HR and impressive returns on investment, showing payback times of less than 2 years (Cedar, 2002; Singapore Ministry of Manpower, 2003).

Interestingly, payback times have increased in line with the sophistication provided by suppliers in line with organizational demands, with average payback period increasing from 12 months in 2001 to 22 months in 2003 (Cedar, 2002, quoted in Gueutal and Falbe, 2005).

Parry et al. (2007) cited savings of £120 000 ($241 000) through HR headcount reductions at Norwich Union and anticipated savings of around £100 000 when on-line payslips are introduced. The same report also identified a reduction in absence rates of 50% over 6 months at East Thames Buses (London), through the intelligent use of performance information.

For example, the temptation to promote the cost-saving aspects of e-HR may disguise a plethora of tensions concerning the wider organizational and relational impacts. Reddington et al. (2005) draw attention to the need to manage the inherent tensions between cost savings and human interaction – a key aspect of the service delivery challenge:

'The potential danger of over-stretching on the cost-saving aspects, to the detriment of the 'human side' of HR must be borne in mind. Customer intimacy, a key driver of the perception of service quality, can be compromised if a transactional mentality, driven by cost reduction targets, dominates the service delivery philosophy.' Reddington et al. (2005, p. 68)

The vital observation here is that e-HR should not be viewed simply as a discrete, technological solution to automate HR processes and improve access to data. Rather, it is an enabler of transformation within HR and the wider business.

The impact on improving employee communication and engagement

Technology can play an important part in ensuring effective communication. The use of electronic methods for communication and people management may have an impact on relationships within an organization and the engagement of individuals both with each other and with the company as a whole. The basic assumption behind much of the drive to e-enable HR has been to improve employee access to HR information and processes; in doing so it represents a cultural shift away from the traditional, centralized, and hierarchical structure to sharing information and encourages the perception of a more personalized HR service (Cedar, 2006).

Giving employees 'round-the-clock' access to critical personal information, as well as the responsibility for ensuring that the information in that system is accurate and complete, may empower the workforce and allow employees to develop some ownership of this data, by making them self-sufficient. This in turn helps to build and improve employee communication and engagement through a process in which employees have greater control over relevant information, a greater voice in the organization, a sense of corporate identity, and a deeper and more timely understanding of the needs of the business (e.g. through web-based portals, employee input, HR surveys, and employee communications reports). In turn, the hoped for outcomes are higher levels of organizational identification and engagement (Martin and Hetrick, 2006, Parry et al., 2007).

However, there are a number of cautionary observations and findings that question this central premise. As Kettley and Reilly (2003) assert:

'The jury is still out on whether there is cause or effect between e-HR and employee motivation and performance. HR remains rightly cautious, despite the persuasive logic of the consultants and vendors of how much can really be achieved with technology.' (Kettley and Reilly, 2003, p. 38)

Even consultants and practitioners, perhaps more naturally inclined to see the positive side of technology, have also been skeptical of the promised benefits and impact on employees. For example, Watson Wyatt (2002) and O'Farrell and Furnham (2002) draw our attention to this point and the need for e-HR services to be sufficiently attractive, from a user perspective, to stimulate take-up. John Meelow, a senior HR practitioner at BP makes a similar observation, in discussing BP's e-HR implementation:

'This has not been a challenge putting e-HR on the web, but more to do with getting people to use it. Our IT and HR departments led this project but we needed to start with the business wanting to do it in the first place! We forgot about the people and the processes and didn't get buy-in from line managers.' (People Management, 2002)

We suggest the focus on employee communication and engagement is partial because it does not explicitly make reference to the role and problems faced by line managers. Our preliminary research shows this aspect to be one of the most important forms of resistance to e-HR implementation.

The impact on the changing roles and skills for HR and line managers

This focuses on the claim and evidence that e-HR frees up scarce time for HR practitioners to allow them to focus on more strategic, valued-added activities. This challenge implies a greater potential for HR professionals to become business partners, strategic partners, and leaders (Ulrich and Brockbank, 2005). However, a note of caution about the impact of e-HR on the levels of competence among HR function practitioners needs to be sounded:

'On paper, taking the administrative work out of HR sounds right, but I sometimes question whether the remaining people have the ability to be more strategic. HR directors must look at what skills they would need in their departments after automating the admin functions.' (Foster, 2002, p. 7)

This situation seemingly highlights a paradox that the HR function must solve. Institutionalized devaluation of the HR function is connected with the perception of HR being stuck in a primarily administrative role and lacking the capabilities to occupy the higher value, business-partnering role. And yet,

'If the basic HR processes such as administrative activities are not in good order, especially on sensitive issues such as executive pay, no strategic contribution is likely to be considered of value until the administrative problem has been fixed.' (Holbeche, 2001, pp. 17–8).

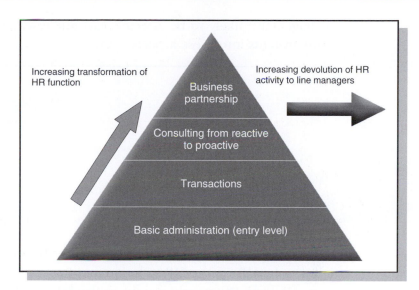

Figure 6.1
HR value pyramid.
Source: Adapted from Reddington et al. (2005).

Perversely, HR teams which concentrate on administration and policing policy:

'have been seen as expensive: a necessary evil consuming resources disproportionate to the value they add to the company.' (Lawler and Mohrman, 2003, p. 6)

This paradox, also highlighted by Reddington et al. (2005), is illustrated in the 'HR Value Pyramid' featured in Figure 6.1 above. As the HR function moves up the so-called value pyramid, through the adoption of e-HR, it results in more displacement or devolution of traditional HR activities into the line-manager communities, often through web-based, self-service tools.

These considerations extend well beyond cost reductions and process efficiency and lead us to ask key questions: Just how does e-HR impact the delivery of HR services and more particularly, how are those impacts perceived by managers, both in HR and the line? In unpacking these questions, it is helpful to look at how the roles of HR professionals and line managers are likely to be affected and our research provides some insights into these aspects.

A case study on implementing e-HR systems in a large UK mobile telephone company – what are the impacts?

Remarkably little data exists that explicitly seeks to explore the impact of e-HR on the HR function and line-manager populations. These findings add weight to the relevance and nature of our research, which seeks to establish the impact of e-HR on the HR/line-manager relationship and deliberately embraces data from both HR and line-manager populations. The host organization is the UK-based part of one of the largest mobile companies in the world, which serves over 86 million mobile customers worldwide. The strategic drivers of the investment in e-HR, which commenced in 2001, were primarily concerned with improving service quality and freeing up time for HR staff to address more strategic issues rather than basic administration. This led to the development of a common HR portal, through which all on-line services could be accessed. The intention of this portal was also to help HR to create a greater sense of corporate identity among employees in the extended enterprise using an internal employer branding strategy (Martin and Hetrick, 2006). The real benefit being sought was an improvement in HR service quality, providing more accurate and reliable data, and enabling more informed management decisions.

Recently, the company embarked on a major project to upgrade the enterprise resource planning (ERP) software package, as the previous version had reached the end of its commercial life and eventually would not be supported by the supplier. The organization agreed to support this research in order to achieve a meaningful assessment of the impact of e-HR on both the HR and line-manager population, with a view to improving the service offering, where practicable, in the future.

Research approach

Our research into the impact of the e-HR initiative was carried out during 2006 and 2007 and comprised two stages of data collection. The first tranche of data were collected using a web-based survey of HR and line managers. The total number surveyed was 94, representing about 10% of the overall manager population. Seventy managers responded, yielding a response rate of approximately 75%. Within that total, 65 responses were from line managers and five from HR managers, which was broadly representative of the ratio across the wider organization.

The survey was designed to elicit information on three aspects of the e-HR implementation, including line-managers' views on usage and benefits of the e-HR tools; data quality and maintenance; and the effectiveness of communications, support, and training connected with the e-HR system (see Appendix 1 for a list of illustrative survey statements). These aspects were designed to enable key impacts of the investment in e-HR to be investigated, leading to clear indicators in respect of where improvements could best be targeted.

The survey was followed up by three focus groups, involving a total of 15 line managers, to probe some of the findings of the survey. A qualitative method was used in the form of a case study approach to create an in-depth, rich account (Yin, 2003) of how one organization has implemented an e-HR system and what line managers think about the organization's efforts.

Respondents were selected using purposive sampling; participants were purposely chosen because of their relevance to the research. Each respondent had completed the web-based survey and confirmed his or her willingness to be chosen for subsequent follow up research aimed at obtaining more detailed insights into their views of the e-HR system.

Focus-group respondents were provided with a list of topics for discussion beforehand and permission was granted to tape-record the sessions for analysis purposes; confidentiality throughout the process was assured. The transcript of each session was sent back to participants for validation. Summary reports of the main findings were sent to the host HR function as a basis for discussion and the identification of follow up actions. At the time of writing, these discussions were at a preliminary stage and therefore no official response from the HR team can be reported.

Results of web-based survey

Table 6.2 provides a summary of the results of the questionnaire based on a simple aggregation of percentage of favorable responses to each of the questions corresponding to the three dimensions. The favorable percentages combine the favorable/agree and very favorable/strongly agree scores; the middle percentage represents neutral scores, while the unfavorable percentages combine the unfavorable/disagree and highly unfavorable/strongly disagree scores.

A cursory examination of the headline data shows that HR managers recorded higher favorable percentages on all aspects of the e-HR implementation. This topography of sentiment revealed in the web-based material serves to highlight the importance of obtaining results from both HR and line-manager communities. The dangers of omitting line managers from research work aimed at assessing the future direction of change initiatives, were also articulated in a Chartered Institute

Table 6.2
Results of web-based survey among HR and line managers on e-HR.

Dimension	Aggregate (%)			Line manager (%)			HR manager (%)		
	F	N	U	F	N	U	F	N	U
Use and benefit	54	24	22	53	24	23	69	24	7
Data accuracy and maintenance	73	13	14	71	14	15	90	8	2
Communications, support and training	45	28	27	44	27	29	60	37	3

F = Favourable; N = Neutral; U = Unfavourable.

of Personnel and Development (CIPD) Report (2002), which refers to the:

'Weakness of research that asks a senior HR manager to complete a questionnaire about HR in his or her firm and then relies on those responses for analysis.' (CIPD, 2002, note 13)

It is clearly apparent from the headline results in Table 6.2 that perceptions of data quality and maintenance dominate the favorable results, whilst perceptions of communications support and training are least favorable.

Closer inspection of the survey statement responses (for more details contact Martin Reddington) shows that within the line-manager community only 34% reported an appreciation of the benefits of e-HR, from the perspective of return on investment. There were similar reservations about the impact of e-HR on HR services; only 30% reported that e-HR had increased the effectiveness of human resource management (HRM) in their organization.

These results, amongst others, were probed during the focus group sessions and the main findings have been adapted to fit the three categories of impact defined earlier: the impact on HR activities and processes; the impact on employee communication and engagement; and the impact on the changing roles and skills of HR and line managers.

The impact of e-HR on the efficiency of HR activities and processes

It is understood that the introduction of new technologies, such as e-HR, to deliver HR advice and services to line managers, as well as generating significant organizational benefits, can also cause potentially negative consequences if the implementation process is not managed effectively (see Table 6.1). For example, Whittaker and Marchington (2003) conducted research finding that there were concerns among the line-manager community that the HR function lacked visibility and that it had become remote with increasing usage of electronic data systems and self-service HR.

They commented:

> '… having the chance to talk with someone from the HR function was regarded as essential, if only to seek clarification face-to-face about how to deal with specific problems.' (Whittaker and Marchington, 2003, p. 258)

This lack of emphasis on 'the human side' of HR was reflected in our research, which highlighted the need for HR professionals to remember that they are dealing with individuals and they are providing a service; their work is about people, not processes. Line managers made the following observations:

> 'It would be helpful if they [HR] came and talked to you like a human being…'
>
> '[I] actually speak to HR and say, 'this is the situation, am I right in this or am I wrong in that?' Usually, that's the best way and it also keeps up the human contact, which is important.'
>
> 'I think they've [HR] got to be consultative, they've got to be visible and they've got to be accessible to managers at a particular level but also, I think, from an employee perspective.'

The organizational benefits of e-HR implementation should not, however, be forgotten. At the host organization some of the tools were quite heavily used, providing significant support to both line managers and employees. This is revealed in comments such as:

> 'There's a lot of good material in there, there's a lot of good material on the website …'

More specifically, line managers praised the HR e-mail service as illustrated in the following remarks:

'I find they're really responsive [the HR e-mail] … they connect right away and give you the information and if you go back to them [with further queries,] they'll come back to you.'

'… more staff are now starting to use the e-mail system because they know they get a response quite quickly.'

One important factor in the e-HR transformation process, which is often neglected by both academics and practitioners, is that e-HR needs to be considered in the wider context of HR service delivery. If change occurs in organizations it does not do so in isolation, it affects all other elements of the service delivery model. This is reinforced by Reddington et al.:

'The adoption of e-HR … triggers a chain reaction of other consequences that have a profound bearing on the way organisations do HR …' (Reddington et al., 2005, p. 32)

In our research, participants observed that the implementation of a new e-HR system signaled the need for a cultural shift within HR in order to ensure that the function was not just paying 'lip service' to line-managers' expectations and aspirations. As one line manager remarked:

'… I think there needs to be some shift where you get like a 'wow' factor; if you contact HR for any reason through any channel you should feel, 'wow that was great!' That's how we should feel ……… I think at the moment that wow factor isn't there, it's here and there, now and then, but it's not consistent.'

From this it is apparent that overall perceptions are very mixed towards e-HR, in terms of its impact on the efficiency of HR activities and processes.

The impact on improving employee communication and engagement

Our research demonstrates the importance of effective communication in ensuring that both line managers and employees 'buy in' to e-HR. This is illustrated in the comments below:

'New systems ... should be communicated well and users need to understand why these things are happening. This would lead to less resistance.'

'... the message that comes across is mixed and it's not a constructive message. I think they've [HR] got to develop how to execute that message and once they get that right then I think things will come through ... we're having to find [things] out for ourselves and it leads to people using different methods and certain tools in certain ways and it becomes a kind of a mixed bag.'

Participants also highlighted the importance of intuitive systems and comprehensive training in order to secure line manager and employee engagement.

'The tools should be intuitive and designed around us, the internal customer, so that tasks that are done very often, like approving leave and expenses, should be the easiest but often they seem really difficult. ... Maybe it's a criticism of [the system] that we have to adapt to it rather than it adapting to us ... Why don't we have something that is more suited to us?'

'When we implement new systems ... every department should send someone along to be trained up to use it.'

'HR could ... get floor walkers, for example, on the day it goes live. You could have one experienced user per floor to show people how the new system works ...'

'I think the super user concept wouldn't be a bad thing ... if people are confused, then the super user is best placed to learn the nuances of it (new tool).'

Linked to this, we found that there was often line manager and employee frustration regarding the usability of the system. The solution, as advocated by the users, was to create a more personalized and tailored HR solution. For example, whilst participants praised the e-mail service provided by the HR team both in terms of the speed and quality of responses it provided, they acknowledged this service was only helpful in answering simple, self-contained problems and line managers experienced difficulty when they required more detailed advice from HR.

> '[The e-mail service] is really good because all you do is send an e-mail, ask the question and they [HR] tell you what to do.'
>   '[The e-mail service] can be great for certain things. An example would be if I had a direct report with a sick child, but no holiday entitlement left. I can [send an] e-mail ... and I know that I will have the answer. So that sort of very simple, self-contained problem can be easily answered. However, as soon as it's something less specific or more open ended, it's very difficult to know how to get that information out of HR.'

Reddington et al. (2005) highlight it is essential that line managers are involved in the implementation process in order to ensure that the new HR delivery model is client-centered. This can be achieved in a variety of ways: through early consultation with all managers; active, hands-on senior level involvement in the e-HR project team, and a customer references panel that engages with the proposals throughout. As one line manager explained:

> '[A] good parallel is when we think about launching things to customers. The way it should work is ... figuring out how they want to do business with us and then we adapt to them because that's how you'll be a successful company. The same philosophy should apply to our internal offering – the HR tools and services. The tools should be intuitive and designed around us, the internal customer.'

In spite of these criticisms regarding the impact of e-HR on improving employee communication and engagement, it is clear that line managers at the host organization were making a significant effort to engage their teams, encouraging them to discuss areas that could be improved.

> '… what we do try and do is to get the engagement of the team. We ask the team, 'you tell us what we can do differently to get this working; what can we do?' I think the team as a whole can see that you try to take action on their issues and this creates an improved employee engagement score.'

From the evidence presented, it is clear that the perceived impact of e-HR on improving employee engagement and communication is disappointing. Despite this, the line managers presented a range of constructive suggestions to alleviate the issues identified.

The impact on the changing roles and skills for HR and line managers

In a transformed state, the HR function is unlikely to place a premium on administrative skills and the HR positions available will be strategic in focus requiring a higher capability of candidates. This is supported in research conducted by Bell et al. they found that:

> 'Information Technology has allowed the HR function to focus less attention on routine, administrative tasks and dedicate more energy to delivering services that add value to the business.' (Bell et al., 2006, p. 303)

Thus, it is clear that e-HR can leave more time for HR to focus on expert or strategic issues and is therefore one way of facilitating the transition from operational to strategic HRM.

Indeed, many line managers emphasized the important contributions made by the HR team and praised their ability to carry out job roles effectively.

'I think there are brilliant staff [in HR]; I know who to go to and I've been really impressed by their customer focus. I think they're right on … giving advice and I would definitely give them accolades.'

'I find the learning and development team fantastic … If I've got an issue to discuss (with Learning and Development), I'll go and talk to [someone] and [they] will then sit down with me for an hour and talk me through the courses and tell me specifically what courses might be suitable for my people.'

'I find the [people] in recruitment are fantastic; I deal with two of them on a regular basis.'

However, as one line manager commented:

'If you're not careful HR is viewed with a degree of cynicism or scepticism it probably doesn't deserve …'

This is illustrated in our research by the following negative perceptions of the HR function:

'Everyone knows that the HR function is an overhead (cost to the business)… Very rarely, it seems, you get someone who says something good about HR; more often than not it's seen as the part of the organisation which stops you doing things.'

'I really don't know what HR does. I only think of them as people who pay us or tell us we've got the sack …'

This selection of comments illustrates that the views of line managers towards the HR function are quite patchy and that if, as Ulrich (1998, p. 125) states, 'HR should be defined not by what it does but by what it delivers', the quality of HR service delivery needs to be high to ensure that the perceptions of line managers are largely positive. The HR function is required to improve and market convincingly its value contribution to the business in order to diffuse the type of negative sentiment revealed here by the line-manager community. Indeed, as Reddington et al. emphasize:

'The challenge for each HR function is to define for itself a way of making a value-adding contribution that is right for its organisation.' (Reddington et al., 2005, p. 130)

Thus, in order to manage this challenge effectively, HR needs to be clear about how it can add value in a way that is appropriate to its organization's unique context. If HR fails to achieve this, the threat is that the business will turn elsewhere for that contribution and the in-house HR function will become insignificant and impotent (ibid).

The line-manager community surveyed in this research argued that the creation of service level agreements (SLAs) could provide one way of measuring HR performance and therefore help to define its value contribution.

'My perspective as far as service delivery is concerned is that HR needs to have a strategy backed up by SLA's (service level agreements)... If they don't operate like that, how do you measure the performance of the department? ... HR needs to be accountable.'

In addition, line managers felt that performance assessment criteria should make their *own* people management responsibilities more explicit.

'There isn't a very clear way for [line managers] to understand their responsibilities; no-one really knows what their responsibilities are.'

'The aim of the [performance management] guidance is
that we should have five objectives [but] there's not a lot of
suggestion as to what those objectives should comprise ...'

'If you manage people then you're the first line of HR in
any business and I think we could save ourselves a lot of
time and trouble or even money if we got that little bit
right.'

Linked to the issue of establishing clear accountabilities for
both HR and line managers, participants emphasized that partnership needs to be built between HR and the line to ensure
the effective delivery of HR services. As one respondent commented:

'It's a matter of having to try and advise each other as to
how we can reduce each other's burden by making sure
that once we understand what the issue is, whose
responsible for dealing with it, then we get on with it ...'

These findings illustrate that the impact of e-HR on the
changing roles and skills for HR and line managers is a complex
picture and encompasses a broad range of aspects that must
be appreciated and successfully addressed, if positive outcomes
are to be achieved.

Conclusions

The review of the literature and our research exposes a range
of tensions and dilemmas concerning the benefits, problems
and prospects for e-HR, a position that is summed up well by
Towers Perrin (2002, p. 2):

'This gap (between what has been promised by e-HR and
what has been delivered) underscores an important fact
about technology that more and more employers are now
coming to understand: Implementation is only the beginning
of the process. The web is just the means to an end, and

> that end – widespread acceptance of self-service as the 'way' to manage HR, for both employers and managers – takes planning, time and dedication. It represents a significant internal change for most organisations, and has to be supported with education, communication, the right tools and processes, and frequent and consistent reinforcement.'

There is certainly evidence available that points towards e-HR having a positive impact on the efficiency of HR activities and processes, as neatly described by Parry et al. (2007):

> 'The use of technology can make HR processes faster and more efficient, more accurate, more consistent and transparent and cheaper. Some processes would not be possible without an e-application.' (Parry et al., 2007 p. 28)

However, it is also recognized that these effects may be problematic to evaluate and our research highlights a very mixed picture indeed when viewed from the perspective of line managers. In terms of the impact on improving employee communication and engagement it is apparent that technology can facilitate employee engagement, through the greater ease of communication and the increased availability of information. However, our research shows that unless the e-HR tools are intuitive to use and attractive in terms of relevance and personalization, then problems concerning alienation of the user can result. This is also confirmed by Martin (2005, pp. 35–6) when he comments that:

> '... while virtual meetings and education can remove the problems of time and space from social interactions, some employees feel alienated from their essential human nature and from the product or service they are producing.'

These concerns also reflect a wider issue – the one of 'customization' of e-HR versus the adoption of easily configurable 'out of the box' solutions (sometimes called 'vanilla solutions') from the ERP software vendors. The internal pressures created by the 'pull' of personalized solutions from line managers and employees, which require customization of the standard software offering, often conflicts with the need to limit and control implementation costs. Customization can result in significant additional initial and ongoing costs and presents a dilemma for the HR function, which has to balance the cost and quality of the eventual solution. Perhaps the real challenge here is directed towards the software vendors, who will face increasing demands to provide more flexible, intuitive functionality in their vanilla product.

From the perspective of the impact on the changing roles and skills for HR and line managers, our contention is that e-HR not only requires changes in technology but involves changes in the whole structure of work and relationships. Indeed authors such as McDonagh (2001, cited in Shrivastava and Shaw, 2004), suggest that success in implementing e-HR systems relies on the ability of managers to manage change. When embarking on an e-HR transformation journey, organizations need to consider the future configuration and design of HR roles and establish what HR capability needs to be in place to secure their vision of a changed HR function.

We believe that our research has underlined an important point: line managers want and value high-quality HR services and would be prepared to work collaboratively with HR to improve overall service delivery. HR should therefore seek to use the intrinsic goodwill that can exist among the line-manager community to guide future HR activities. If HR service delivery can become more client-centered, then this unleashes the possibility of the significant reputational enhancement of the HR function that has been talked about for many years but has not yet been fully realized.

References

Bell, B.S., Lee, S., and Yeung, S.K. (2006) The impact of e-HR on professional competence in HRM: implications for the development of HR professionals. *Hum. Resource Manage.* 45, 295–308.

Boudreau, J.W. and Ramstad, P.M. (2007) *Beyond HR: a New Science of Human Capital.* Boston: Harvard Business School Press.

Cedar (2002) Cedar 2002 human resources self-service/portal HR survey. Available online at: http://www.cedarcrestone.com/ whitepapers.php.

Cedar (2006) *Workforce Technologies and Service Delivery Approaches Survey.* Available online at www.cedarcrestone.com (last accessed 23 September 2007).

CIPD (2002) *Sustaining Success in Difficult Times: Research Summary.* London: Chartered Institute of Personnel and Development.

CIPD (2004) *People and technology: Is HR getting the best out of IT?* Survey Report. London: Chartered Institute of Personnel and Development.

Foster, S. (2002) e into HR could save you millions. *Human Resources e-HR Portfolio* 2002, p. 7 Haymarket.

Gueutal, H.G. and Falbe, C. (2005) eHR: Trends in delivery methods. In H.G. Gueutal and D.L. Stone (Eds.) (2005) *The Brave New World of eHR: Human Resources in the Digital Age,* San Francisco: Josey Bass, pps. 190–225.

Gueutal, H.G. and Stone, D.L (eds.) (2005) *The Brave New World of eHR: Human Resources in the Digital Age.* San Francisco: Jossey Bass.

Holbeche, L. (2001) *Aligning Human Resources and Business Strategy.* Oxford: Butterworth Heinemann.

Kettley, P. and Reilly, P. (2003) *eHR: An Introduction.* IES Report 398, Brighton, UK: Institute of Employment Studies.

Lawler, E.E. and Mohrman, S.A. (2003). *Creating a Strategic Human Resources Organization.* Stanford: Stanford University Press.

Martin, G. (2005) *Technology and People Management: the opportunity and the challenge.* Research Report. London: Chartered Institute of Personnel and Development.

Martin, G. (2005a) *HR Outsourcing: the Key Decisions.* London: Chartered Institute of Personnel and Development.

Martin, G. (2005b) *People Management and Technology: Progress and Potential.* Survey Report. London: Chartered Institute of Personnel and Development.

Martin, G. and Hetrick, S. (2006) *Corporate Reputations, Branding and People Management: a Strategic Approach to HR.* Oxford: Butterworth Heinemann.

O'Farrell, B. and Furnham, A. (2003) *European e-HR Survey.* University of London and IHRIM Europe, October 2002.

Parry, E., Tyson, S., Selbie, D., and Leighton, R. (2007) *HR and Technology: Impact and Advantages.* London: Chartered Institute of Personnel and Development.

People Management (2002) BP learns outsourcing lessons. *People Manage.* 7, 22 November.

Reddington, M., Williamson, M., and Withers, M. (2005) *Transforming HR: Creating Value Through People.* Oxford: Elsevier: Butterworth-Heinemann.

Reddington, M. and Martin, G. (2006) *Theorizing the Links between e-HR and Strategic e-HRM: A Framework, Case Illustration and Some Reflections.* Paper presented First European Academic Conference on e-HR: Twente University, the Netherlands, 25–26 October 2006.

Ruël, H., Bondarouk, T., and Looise, J.K. (2004) *e-HRM: Innovation or Irritation.* Utrecht: Lemma.

Shrivastava, S. and Shaw, J.B. (2004) Liberating HR through technology. *Hum. Resource Manage.* 42, 201–22.

Singapore Ministry of Manpower commissioned report (2003). *E-HR: Leveraging Technology.* March 2003. Available online at: www.outsmart.com/art-MOM.htm.

Towers Perrin (2002) *HR on the Web: New realities in service delivery.* For online access contact: http://www.towersperrin.com/hrservices.

Ulrich, D. (1998) A new mandate for human resources. *Harvard Bus. Rev.* 76, 124–34.

Ulrich, D. and Brockbank, W. (2005) *The HR Value Proposition.* Boston: Harvard Business School Press.

Watson Wyatt (2002) *B2E/e-HR: Survey Results 2002.* Last accessed on 16 November 2007 online at: http://www.watsonwyatt.com/research/resrender.asp?id=2000861&page=1.

Whittaker, S. and Marchington, M. (2003) Devolving HR responsibility to the line: Threat, opportunity or partnership? *Employ. Relat.* 25, 245–61.

Yin, R.K. (2003) *Case Study Research: Design and Methods* (3rd edn.), London: Sage Publications.

CHAPTER 7

Exploring the Relationship between e-HRM and HRM Effectiveness: Lessons Learned from Three International Companies

Huub J.M. Ruël and Tanya Bondarouk

The basic expectations when implementing e-human resource management (e-HRM) are that its use will decrease costs, improve the human resources (HR) service level, and give the HR department space to become a real strategic partner. Or, in other words, HRM will become more effective through the application of e-HRM. This basic expectation is emphasized by software companies and e-HR consultancies, but it has not been subjected to extensive academic research. In this chapter, we present the outcomes of a comprehensive qualitative study on the link between e-HRM and HRM effectiveness. This study was conducted in three large international companies from contrasting sectors. It shows that, overall, the content and the structure of e-HRM applications can have a positive effect on technical and strategic HRM effectiveness. In terms of the link between e-HRM and the commitment of employees, it seems that through using e-HRM applications, respondents sense that they are receiving more attention in terms of receiving information and development opportunities, which may make them more committed to the organization.

Introduction

e-HRM, the use of web-based technologies for human resource management practices and policies, is maturing within organizational life. Much is claimed and expressed about the advantages of e-HRM, but proof of these advantages is scarce. There is no clear evidence that answers the question as to whether e-HRM contributes to HRM effectiveness. Consultancy firms, rather than academics, have made the initial attempts to investigate whether the efforts put into e-HRM lead to the expected outcomes, but these attempts tend to be somewhat subjective. The involvement of academia in this topic is more recent and has not yet led to rigorous answers.

In this chapter, we present the results of a predominantly qualitative study on the question as to whether e-HRM contributes to HRM effectiveness. The chapter is structured as follows: first, we summarize developments in research on e-HRM and on HRM effectiveness; second, we focus on our specific line of reasoning, present the research model used, and describe our research methods; third, we present our extensive qualitative results; and, finally, we end with some conclusions and a discussion of what they mean for academics and practitioners.

Developments in research on e-HRM

We define e-HRM as a way of implementing HRM strategies, policies, and practices in organizations through the conscious and directed support of, and/or with the full use of, channels based on web technology. The word 'implementing' in this context has a broad meaning, such as making something work, putting something into practice, or having something realized. e-HRM, therefore, is a concept – a way of 'doing' HRM (Ruël et al., 2002; 2004). Note, that this does not ignore the fact that e-HRM can transform the nature of HRM strategies, policies, and practices, as is indeed suggested by the model of Ruël et al. (2002; 2004). However, this is seen as a consequence that emerges over time and which is difficult to manage. This makes it a very interesting topic for research – but it is beyond the scope of this chapter to consider how e-HRM is conceptualized.

The literature on e-HRM suggests that, in general terms, the three goals of e-HRM are cost reduction, improving HR services, and improving strategic orientation (Brockbank, 1997; Lepak and Snell, 1998; Stanton and Coovert, 2004; see also Chapter 1: Technology, Outsourcing, and HR Transformation: an Introduction). Some empirical findings have added to these goals with globalization seen as a driving e-HRM force in international large organizations. However, empirical findings also show that these goals are not clearly defined in practice and that e-HRM is mostly directed at cost reduction and increasing the efficiency in HR services, rather than at improving the strategic orientation of HRM (Gardner et al., 2003; Ruël et al., 2004; Ruta, 2005). A recent study has found that in nearly half of the companies investigated with a completely integrated human resource information system, HR was not seen as a strategic partner (Lawler and Mohrman, 2003).

Ruël et al. (2002) noted an aspect that is fairly well covered by the above summary but which is, nevertheless, interesting to highlight, namely the changing nature of the employment relationship in many business systems. With a supply shortage in many labor markets (during the economic upturn of the 1990s), the individualization of society and the increased educational level of citizens (and thus of employees), the power balance in the employment relationship shifted in the direction of employees: and they wanted to set their own career paths. In our view (Ruël et al.,

2002), a move towards the greater use of e-HRM can provide tools to support this development. This aspect adds to the earlier-mentioned drivers, and can be seen as improving the service towards internal clients, albeit with an external societal drive.

We have also shown (Ruël et al., 2004) that although, in practice, the e-HRM types adopted are mixed, establishing a good basis for e-HRM at the operational level seems to be an essential prerequisite for relational and transformational e-HRM; and that this requires changes in the tasks of HR professionals (less paper-based administration and more e-communications with employees, and requires the acquisition of the skills needed to operate IT). Further, it was also shown that there is a 'gap' between e-HRM in a technical sense (the available functionality) and its use and adoption by employees and line managers. Actual usage/adoption can lag 3 years behind what is available.

Other available research evidence suggests that, in many organizations, e-HRM has led to a radical redistribution of the work that HR managers used to do. Many of the reporting activities, previously performed by HR professionals, can now be performed on-line by managers and employees (Ruël et al., 2004; Ruta, 2005). On their own desktops, line managers now have to perform appraisals, evaluate employee costs, generate HR reports (turnover, absenteeism), process training requests, and oversee competence management. Further, employees have access to everything they need in order to change and manage their personal files, plan their development, process financial documents, and apply for new internal jobs (Roehling et al., 2005).

The literature suggests that the various e-HRM goals, and the different types of e-HRM, are expected to deliver outcomes including a greater efficiency in HRM processes, a higher level of service delivery, and a better strategic contribution. The expected outcomes can, however, be 'encapsulated' in a single concept: HRM effectiveness. e-HRM is expected to contribute to the effectiveness of HRM, which in turn should contribute towards achieving an organization's goals.

HRM effectiveness

HRM effectiveness is addressed in a great number of studies that strive to demonstrate the value of what HR professionals do for the rest of the organization, and how HRM practices are linked to desired organizational outcomes (Huselid, 1995; Boxall, 1996; Baron and Kreps, 1999, Wright et al., 2001). Following Wright et al. (2001), we note that attempts to demonstrate HRM effectiveness have focused on just a few areas.

HRM – firm performance

HRM effectiveness is often mentioned as HRM's contribution to firm performance (e.g. see Kane et al., 1999; Ostroff and Bowen, 2000; Wright et al., 2001). Especially during the past decade, the HRM literature has attempted to show that progressive HR practices result in higher firm performance (Hope Hailey, 2005; Wright et al., 2005). Huselid's (1995) pioneering study has shown that a set of HR practices labeled high performance work systems were related to turnover, accounting profits, and firm market value. Since then, a growing number of studies have attempted to empirically test the relationships between HR practices and firm performance (see the elaborated overviews by Delery and Doty, 1996; Ostroff and Bowen, 2000; Boselie et al., 2001; Tsui and Wang, 2002; Wright et al., 2005). For example, MacDuffie (1995) found that certain bundles of HR practices were related to productivity and quality in his sample of car assembly plants. Delery and Doty (1996) found significant relationships between HR practices and accounting profits among a sample of banks. Youndt et al. (1996) found that certain combinations of HR practices in their sample of manufacturing firms were related to operational performance indicators. More recently, the study by Batt (2002) that examined the relationship between HR practices, employee resignation rates, and organizational performance in the service sector revealed that resignation rates were lower and sales growth higher in call centers that emphasized high skills, employee participation, and human resource incentives such as good employment security.

The international arena for recent studies into HRM and firm performance is quite broad. A quantitative research study in 62 manufacturing Chinese-Western joint ventures has shown a positive relationship between firm performance and the extent to which firms use a 'high-performance' HRM system as well as the degree to which they integrate HRM into the firm strategy (Bjorkman and Xiucheng, 2002). Another study, conducted among 52 Japanese subsidiaries of multinational corporations (Park et al., 2003), revealed that the relationships between HR systems and firm outcomes were mediated by employees skills, attitudes, and behaviors. A survey of 102 Israeli organizations found positive associations between HRM practices stressing the promotion of women and organizational effectiveness (Harel et al., 2003). A further study of 45 software companies in India by Paul and Anantharaman (2003) has shown that every HRM practice found in the sample had an indirect influence on operational and financial organizational performance. Findings from another study conducted among 132 publicly traded manufacturing companies in the USA, indicate that the impact of high-performance work systems on productivity is influenced by industry capital intensity, growth, and differentiation (Datta et al., 2005).

Technical and strategic effectiveness of HRM

Huselid et al. (1997) introduced the concept of the technical and strategic effectiveness of HRM, guided by the idea that HRM seeks approval for its activities in 'socially constructed environments' (p. 172). Meeting the expectations of stakeholders means, for HRM, gaining legitimacy and acceptance in the organization. The expectations of 'traditional' HRM activities in the research by Tsui (1990), and of HR services (Wright et al., 2001), tend to be similar for all firms. These traditional HRM activities, given the label 'technical' by Huselid et al. (1997), were seen as effective in the eyes of the stakeholders.

In contrast to technical HRM activities, 'strategic' HRM activities are considered to be HRM-based innovations for companies. Huselid et al. (1997) noted that, despite an absence of full agreement on what is meant by strategic HRM, there is a broad consensus that it involves the development and implementation of policies that are aligned with business strategy. They found that strategic effectiveness was significantly associated with firm performance, whereas technical HRM effectiveness was not.

Nowadays, increasingly confronted with electronic HRM, we observe that we are left to wonder to what extent the use of e-HRM makes HRM more effective overall. In other words, if an organization decides to introduce digital HRM, will its HRM processes have the desired impact on employees' skills, behavior, and attitudes? Further, it is unclear what conditions e-HRM has to meet in order to contribute to strategic and technical HRM effectiveness.

The research model

In our study, we attempted to find out whether e-HRM applications contribute to HRM effectiveness. We assumed that it is essentially the use of e-HRM applications, and more specifically the appreciation of the use of e-HRM applications, that affects users' (employees, managers, HRM professionals) perceptions of strategic and technical effectiveness. Recent studies on the implementation of e-HRM have moved towards addressing the dynamic nature of HRIS implementations, and used concepts such as innovation implementation, learning, change management and the technology acceptance model (Keebler and Rhodes, 2002). The inclusion of the technology acceptance model (Davis et al., 1989) in e-HRM studies has resulted in ideas that the use of e-HRM by targeted employees is largely determined by the level of usefulness of the HR information technology and its ease of use (Ruta, 2005; Voermans and Van Veldhoven, 2005). A good recent example is the study into the implementation of an HR employee portal in the Italian subsidiary of Hewlett-Packard (Ruta, 2005).

Inspired by the concepts incorporated in the technology acceptance model, usefulness, and ease of use, we chose to distinguish three aspects of e-HRM appreciation: its job relevance (slightly different to usefulness), its quality, and its ease of use. Of particular note is the fact that we added quality, referring to the content (HRM policies and practices) and the structure of the e-HRM tools.

How these ideas fit together in our model is illustrated in Figure 7.1 below.

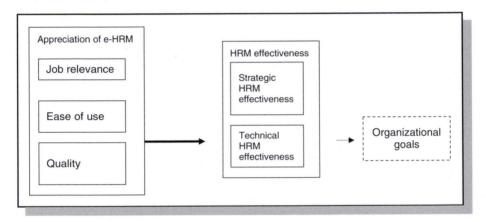

Figure 7.1
Research model: the link between e-HRM and HRM effectiveness (Ruël et al., 2007).
Note: HRM, human resource management.

Research methodology

We later present the results of a qualitative study that set out to investigate the relationship between the appreciation of e-HRM and HRM effectiveness. This study would lay the basis for theoretical generalization (see Yin, 1994). The study's goal was to draw conclusions on the use of e-HRM and the way in which HRM goals are achieved (i.e. HRM effectiveness), and therefore we considered it important to include a range of companies. Furthermore, we selected large companies (> 10 000 employees) as research by Ball (2001) has shown that large companies tend to implement large comprehensive HRM software packages and, in order to present and explore interesting cases, we selected companies that had a good reputation regarding developments in e-HRM. Based on these criteria, we subsequently collected data from the following three companies: Dow Chemicals, the Ford Motor Company, and IBM. All had commenced implementing e-HRM some years ago and, since then, had been extending e-HRM in a stepwise fashion. In our study, we considered the Benelux site of Dow Chemicals (the largest outside the USA), Ford's German site in Cologne, and IBM's Dutch site. The unit of analysis chosen for this qualitative study was the entire organizational unit or, in other words, each of the three organizational units was considered as a case.

Table 7.1

Definitions of the main concepts.

Aspects	Definition	Topics
Job relevance	The extent to which users believe that using an e-HRM tool is critical in their work situation	Increase in efficiency, increase in productivity
Ease of use	The extent to which a user of an e-HRM application finds the application straightforward in its operation and related interactions	Input efforts, simplicity
Quality	The extent to which a user finds the application well designed and well set up in its HR content	Content, structure
Technical HRM effectiveness	How well the operational HR activities are performed	Work conditions, communications
Strategic HRM effectiveness	How well employee behaviors that support organizational needs in the longer term are promoted	Commitment, competence development, change

Note: HRM, human resource management.

For this qualitative study, we chose conversational interviews as our main technique. We included representatives of many relevant parties (employees, project team members, HRM professionals, line managers), resulting in a so-called multiview of e-HRM perceptions in the selected companies. In addition, we also interviewed employees, line managers, and HRM managers using structured interviews, carried out an evaluation of e-HRM applications (job relevance/usefulness, quality of the applications, and ease of use) and technical and strategic HRM effectiveness. Table 7.1 provides the definitions of the main variables used in the research model.

Results

Case 1: e-HRM at Dow Chemicals Benelux

Dow's web-based people success system (PSS) was launched in 1997. Within 15 weeks, all Dow employees worldwide had received one day of training on the system. By navigating the site, employees could find plenty of information about Dow's HR philosophy, which was in itself important since this was completely new and different from Dow's earlier HR approach. Thus, initially, the PSS was mainly an information provider. However, from that first moment, new tools have been regularly implemented and in 2007 Dow Chemicals claims to be one of the largest investors in information and communication technology (ICT) over recent years. With the implementation of these additional tools, the PSS has become more increasingly interactive in providing HR instruments for use by employees and line management.

Job relevance

When we looked in greater depth, we could see that various groups 'incorporated' the PSS differently. Within the chemical company, the support staff was 'getting along' with the PSS more easily than plant employees. Overall, many people did not go that *deeply* into the system. A lack of time was one of the explanations that people gave for this. It was found, in some cases, that non-involvement was an excuse for not accepting responsibility for one's own development.

Elderly workers were initially reluctant to work with the system because of their lack of computer skills and because most of the information was in English. However, much of the information was later translated to remove this barrier. Tools, such as those used for feedback and learning, were used by some employees, but others found these tools too vague and difficult (a common complaint among plant operators).

Quality of the e-HR application

Although everybody had received considerable information on the system, a general opinion was that there were simply too many screens and steps to go through. It was argued that operators, in particular, needed more precise interfaces.

A significant number of employees chose not to use the 360° feedback tool because they were afraid that their managers would view a negative outcome as evidence of poor performance. There was apparently no guarantee of anonymity in using the system.

A widely expressed opinion was that the PSS content, especially in the recruitment area, emphasized social issues (training, conflict management, language, and social skills) rather than the development of professional and technical skills. As one person close to this area said:

'We simply rely on their (new employees) education; presuming that they have the technical and professional skills. In my view, many mistakes were made in recruiting new employees because of the issues in the system: too much attention is given to social aspects and not to the normal professional skills.'

Further, performance rating had been a major issue among the employees. From a team leader perspective, the PSS lacked a real performance evaluation tool. It provided extensive explanations about the subject, but did not include a tool to evaluate technical professional skills.

Ease of use

The PSS did, however, stress learning and development. A half-day course every 2 months was perceived to be an appropriate amount of time for employees to be able to get what they wanted out of the system. Usage varied by application and by department. For example, employees working in the plants were unlikely to access a computer when they had dirty hands. In 2001, a people strategy was implemented, and part of this strategy was that, by the end of 2004, all employees would have a personal development plan. This meant that they would all have to use the PSS tools. People were then 'forced' to schedule time (in advance) to work with the system, in order to learn how to work at Dow, or for personal development purposes. However, there were departments where this was not taking place. A general impression existed that, in general, it took employees (both line managers and plant employees) 3 years to get used to the PSS. Those who did use it knew what to do, or they knew whom to ask. Others were taking longer to get started. Generally, departments seemed to have two or three employees who were interested in searching for information using the Internet and these were open to the idea of using the PSS. In particular, young people were the more enthusiastic users.

Technical HRM effectiveness (performance of operational HRM activities and communications)

In terms of the technical HRM effectiveness at Dow Chemicals, communications within the company and between the HRM function and employees became quicker and easier, and many considered it had become simpler to communicate. In the plant, however, there were still employees who never checked their e-mails. Overall, as a result of introducing the system, it was observed that direct contact with HRM staff has been dramatically reduced.

In the plants, there were views expressed that employees had to go through too much information in the PSS, that there were not enough computers, that there was too little time to work with the PSS, and that some employees had difficulties with the English (although the main materials had been translated).

At Dow, people had become more aware of what the company wanted from them. Employees had become more interested in trying to enhance their own knowledge and skills. All the information on how to develop was on-line, so there was no longer a need to physically go to the HR department.

Since, through the e-HR system, performance evaluation criteria and processes were now clear, and information about this could be found on the Internet, supervisors could no longer do whatever they wanted because employees were better informed over the correct approach. This, therefore, increased accountability.

Strategic HRM effectiveness (commitment and competence development)

A new system does not in itself change the commitment of employees. Commitment may improve, but this is always difficult to test and measure, and it may not necessarily be a *direct* result of the e-HR system. However, we did find an *indirect* connection: the transparency at Dow increased and its policies became more open – the same information was available to both the management and the employees. The most impressive example was the openness of the compensation component of the PSS. The salaries of all positions were visible to all, anyone could see how much their bosses were paid, and what people earned in the various countries where Dow was active.

Although no direct or linear relationship between e-HRM at Dow Chemicals and commitment has been established – and it is uncertain whether the relationship was strengthened by the PSS – our respondents seemed certain that the system had not destroyed their commitment.

Overall, it can be said that the competencies of people at Dow had increased: 60–70% of the employees had enhanced their competencies through using the PSS. There were amusing anecdotes in the company about how some employees had been forced to learn how to operate a computer because of the PSS implementation, and now some of the older employees were proudly telling their grandchildren that they had learned to work with a computer.

Since the implementation of the PSS, employees could see how to change and develop, and this was very new to them. Some argued that the concept of career self-management was not yet fully working: employees needed more time, and this had to be granted by their team leader. However, there was a commonly held view that there were many individuals who had successfully developed themselves at Dow through using the PSS. With about 2000 operators, it would be unrealistic to expect all of them to develop careers at Dow, but it seems that many had taken the opportunity. The job announcement system (JAS) was seen as having contributed greatly to personal development. Being a user-friendly and well-designed tool, it provided an opportunity to plan a career within Dow and some of the respondents considered the JAS to be the best part of the PSS.

People generally learnt the English terminology used in the PSS very quickly, and did not need to wait until the information was translated, and people's computer skills also improved. Further, the extent of communication with non-Benelux managers, often viewed as 'outsiders', had increased.

The learning component was also experienced as very new. Now, if you wanted to learn, you could. An impression gained was that the general opinion was that the e-learning tool was being used in a different manner than had been intended. This could be due to the American style of the courses that sometimes seemed to teach obvious things. The e-learning tool in itself was felt to be a good idea, and people enjoyed using it, but the content was not always seen as relevant to a person's position and needs.

Overall, at Dow, the PSS resulted in significant cost savings, around $45 million in 2001 through the use of the e-learning facility. In 2002, more than 42 000 individual courses were completed at a much lower cost than with the previous approach. The JAS resulted in improved functioning of the internal labor market. A substantial number of employees used on-line development tools. Overall, through adopting e-HR, HRM became

Table 7.2

Summary of e-HRM appreciation and HRM effectiveness at Dow Chemicals (Benelux).

e-HRM appreciation	Job relevance	Quality of application	Ease of use
Qualification	Moderate	Low	Moderate
HRM effectiveness	**Technical HRM effectiveness**		**Strategic HRM effectiveness**
Qualification	Increased		Increased

Note: HRM, human resource management.

more cost efficient at Dow, supported internal labor mobility, and encouraged employees to accept responsibility for developing their own competencies. Superiors also needed to act more responsibly since employees knew more about their objectives, targets, and rewards (Table 7.2).

Case 2: e-HRM at Fords (Cologne, Germany)

At the Ford Motor Company, an HR intranet site – *HR online*, had been available since 1998 in the USA and 1999 worldwide. Since 1998, Ford's global HR strategy has been to transform HR from an essentially administrative unit to a strategic supportive unit. This transformation could not be achieved, in the view of Ford's management, without centralizing HR administration activities. It was also felt necessary to provide employees with self-service facilities, not only to reduce the administrative work of the HR department, but also to increase the employee satisfaction with HR services.

The core qualities of *HR online*, as communicated within the organization, were that it should be: comfortable, safe, fast, exhaustive, easy, and immediate. With *HR online*, employees and line managers would be able to look upall kinds of

HR-related information, complete transactions, and inspect and change their own personal data.

Job relevance

Using the training-planning tool, employees could see what types of competences were necessary in general, or would need to be developed for the future. Employees could develop a plan for their self-development with the help of this tool, and then go to their manager to discuss it. In this way, the tool would support employees in telling their line manager what they wanted, and the line manager could then start appropriate coaching. This was the 'official HR guideline', as rolled out, but styles differed among line managers and therefore also the application of this guideline.

Line managers stated that the number of times they contacted their HR consultant for day-to-day information had decreased significantly with their increased use of *HR online*. Line managers used *HR online* to check regulations, for example when employees asked whether they could have a day off because a family member was sick. The on-line lease-car program was also frequently used by managers. The system included an online payroll system, and an online training management system.

In general, *HR online* was not used daily, but it was used regularly. Line managers used the 'Managers Toolbox', looked up information, and used the 360° feedback tool to report on their own performance to their managers. The general opinion was that *HR online* provided nearly all the information that line managers needed on an operational level. For more advanced or specialized information, or for advice, line managers could still contact an HR professional through the intranet or by telephone.

Quality of the e-HRM application

HR online was perceived as very well structured and very comprehensive. Among employees who had access, *HR online* was experienced as an appropriate and handy tool. Overall, *HR online* was perceived as a well-functioning information tool with self-service elements covering all the basic arrangements.

To quote a training management assistant:

'As an employee, I can develop a training plan and discuss it with my manager. This can be done through the web, I can register for courses through the web, and I can see whether my boss agrees with this…'

Ease of use

Three years on from the introduction of *HR online*, employees were frequently using it for all kinds of purposes, such as seeking out internal job opportunities and applying for them online, and using the salary function with its option to look back over time. With this, they could assess their salary progression in a very clear way, and this opportunity was seen as very useful and was frequently used by employees.

The impression obtained was that employees were typically using *HR online* around three times a week, frequently to double-check holidays or to see if they were entitled to additional overtime pay. The tool used the most often during our research was the pension calculator! However, despite all the positive elements, it was recognized that some people might miss the personal touch now that all HR-related forms were available online at the company.

Technical HRM effectiveness (performance of operational HRM activities and communications)

HR online was introduced in December 1999 at the Ford Motor Company. Since then, certain outcomes in terms of commitment, competence, congruence, and cost effectiveness have become apparent. In terms of cost effectiveness (based on comments by an expert source), a real return on the *HR online* investment will take at least 5–7 years to achieve, and will only occur if real process innovations are made such as automating the back office (using *HR online* to handle inputs made by employees and management). In practice, there were only very limited workflows behind the tools and although it was

Ford's aim to improve this situation this would need significant investment and, at a time of economic slowdown, the management was cautious about new investment. In fact, the company had only achieved its current advanced stage of operational/relational e-HRM through the direct support of one of the Board members in the 1990s. The general opinion of the system was clear: *HR online* provided a one-stop shop for all HR information, at least on an operational level, and it was easy to use.

In terms of communications affecting the employee–management relationship, one line manager was very clear: employees are better informed and they do not approach their line manager with questions so often. Instead, they now come with their vacation plan to the line manager and say '*Please sign this!*'. Employees have all the information they need in advance. Naturally, there were some people who still preferred to ask their line manager rather than looking on *HR online*, but they were viewed as 'Internet innocents' or 'cyber-dinosaurs', and regarded as about to become extinct!

HR online has made communication between management and non-management much easier. According to a professional from the HR department, there are two sides to this: delivering information to employees from HR, and receiving information as an employee. Previously, it had been very difficult for Fords, as a large company, to 'push' information onto employees: half of them were not interested, and the other half overloaded with too many e-mails. With *HR online* it became much easier for employees to access only the information they wanted – on demand, at any time, and without needing to ask HR staff.

Strategic HRM effectiveness (commitment and competence development)

In terms of *HR online*'s effect on the competences of employees, there were few outcomes to note. Within Ford's Cologne plant there had not been any measurements carried out related to this topic, and there was also the question as to whether this would even be relevant at this stage. *HR online* was very much a form of operational e-HRM, albeit with some relational e-HRM components. Competence development tools (i.e. online training and development, online career planning) were not included, or only available to employees in management positions (i.e. the 360° feedback tool). As is generally the situation, at this Ford plant the e-HRM system is under continuous development and so the situation is changing.

We judge *HR online* at Fords to be the operational/relational type of e-HRM described earlier. Since *HR online* has been in use for a number of years, employee commitment towards the organization could have been influenced by their use of its online tools. Overall, at the Ford Motor Company, 70% of employees had access to the system, although in Germany it was only around 50%. The employees who did have access were very well informed about HR policies and practices, and found *HR online* very useful. *HR online* was the most visited site on Ford's intranet and, for about 80% of the people who had access, it was their basic source of information. *HR online*'s satisfaction rating was recorded as 98%. In 2002, the most used tool was the pension calculator, and among the most accessed information were holiday regulations and salary information.

None of these are directly related to employee commitment, but in an indirect way they did lead to employees expressing positive signals towards the organization (Table 7.3). One employee said that when she compared the online HR tools at Fords with other companies, where some of her friends worked, she felt very positive about Fords.

Table 7.3

The link between appreciation of e-HRM and HRM effectiveness at Fords (Cologne, Germany).

e-HRM appreciation	Job relevance	Quality of application	Ease of use
Qualification	High	High	High
HRM effectiveness	**Technical HRM effectiveness**		**Strategic HRM effectiveness**
Qualification	Increased		Increased

Note: HRM, human resource management.

Case 3: e-HRM at IBM (Amsterdam, the Netherlands)

Since 1998, the policy, framework, contents, and structure of e-HRM at IBM have been renewed and redeveloped. From that year on, a new HR intranet has been launched around the globe. The content of the new HR intranet has been extended in a stepwise fashion with the quantity of information, tools, and functionality gradually increasing.

At IBM, the online HR site is mainly concerned with efficiency and providing a self-service facility for employees and management in order to foster HR's strategic role and to reduce costs. Further, the HR intranet stemmed from IBM's HR strategy, which was revised in 2002, with five focus areas: talent, leadership, climate, performance, and HR capability. All communications with employees through the intranet should be related to one of these five areas, and within each area there were various sources of information and tools.

Job relevance

The available tools were perceived of as very useful but, as with any new application, awareness had to be stimulated and employees needed to be guided and supported. According to the personal development managers (PDMs), the tools' usefulness and necessity had to be stressed and explained. Some people asked why they should put their efforts and skills into understanding a new tool when they had already done this three times with earlier systems at IBM.

In those departments where employees were stimulated to use the new system, the use of the available tools was good. Some tools, such as those for personal development, had to be used by employees because there was no alternative option and without them the appraisal process could not be finalized. One manager said that he was quite often asked to explain the usefulness and necessity of the tools. Conversely, when he had asked employees who had made use of the goal-setting tool, the skills scan tool, and other features whether they thought the picture they obtained from the tools about themselves was a picture that fitted their personal view, their answers were generally positive.

One line manager commented:

'I am also sometimes surprised by certain applications. For example, there are the so-called business conduct guidelines. Employees are expected to have knowledge of these guidelines, to show that they have read them and that they are committed to them. As a manager, you can monitor the progress of the employees in reading the guidelines through the technology.'

When the individual development tool was introduced, it was observed that people started to use it spontaneously. Some were already familiar with a tool for the goal-setting process and then suddenly reading that there was a new individual development planning tool was apparently enough to provoke action. With the individual development tool, employees could establish their own development plan and use the tools that were available to accomplish it. Managers could follow their employees' use of the system through the workflow processes behind the tools. In this way, it can be seen that these tools did became part of the manager–employee relationship. They were coupled in a chain and this enabled managers to monitor where an employee 'stood' in terms of their own development.

Quality of the e-HR applications

The tools were generally experienced as good. The process adopted was that HR would inform employees and management about new tools using e-mail, and at the same time provide links to the new tools. Some line managers would follow this up immediately, while others would not. IBM employees are used to experiencing an enormous amount of information on the HR web, and sometimes too much. The content itself was judged as good but the problem could be to find what you wanted. The information was perceived as very open and transparent, but it was difficult to say whether this actually helped the employees.

Line managers, as the employees themselves, frequently used the HR web. The availability of information and also of services provided had increased. Employees were positive about the fact that more information, especially person-specific information, was available. A good example was the pension planner which was seen as very useful and was the most frequently used tool during our investigation period.

Ease of use

Even before the 'web-based era', there was a lot of HR-related information available within IBM, but the introduction of web technology and a web-based interface made it easier to use. It was also seen as more attractive and accessible. However, employees continued to experience the relational e-HR tools that were available in distinct ways. Some said that it took too much time to work with them, and some said that they were too complex.

Technical HRM effectiveness

In general, at IBM, the opinion was that what was currently available through the HR intranet could never have been achieved through paperwork: it would have been too complex and extensive. In terms of the specific topics we have discussed, the following can be concluded in terms of cost-effectiveness and information accessibility.

It was confidently expected that the use of e-HR at IBM would be cost effective. Figures from HR sources suggested that cost reductions of 57% had been achieved (including the costs of setting up the shared service center *Ask HR*). The fact that one PDM was coaching 47 employees, which would have been impossible without online HR development tools, is further evidence that e-HRM at IBM Netherlands has had a positive effect on reducing costs.

HR information had become much more accessible, which greatly helped employees to become better informed. The

HR department sent important links to employees to ensure that they could find the most relevant information and tools. The HR department played a key role in communicating about the HR intranet. In general, managers were informed first, and then employees. In this way, the managers could prepare for the questions that were likely to arise from the employees.

This availability of information could also have a 'downside' with respect to the employee–manager relationship. If employees can privately access information, there is the danger that they will read into it what they want to read. This could result in problems concerning differences in interpretation between employee and line manager. Furthermore, the fact that most HR information distribution and communications now involve the use of technology has led to the fear that HR communication will become 'colder' and less personal. However, overall, client satisfaction with HR has clearly improved with this new system.

Strategic HRM effectiveness

The online HR tools, as such, did not increase the commitment of people to the organization, although the quality of the information did have a positive influence, as did the accessibility of the information and the speed of access. Although e-HRM at IBM was well developed, it still needed to grow. To stimulate this through the use of e-HR tools, as we have already discussed, employees were supported in their personal development by the appointment of a PDM who could coach them in using the available online development tools.

The competence of employees also improved through the use of the online HR tools, although this was largely reliant on an individual's initiative and desire to develop. Overall, at IBM Netherlands, the competence level of employees was influenced positively through using the development-oriented tools. It is not that there were no thoughts of employee development before the introduction of e-HR, but rather that since the introduction of e-HRM it has become a more structured process. The fact that tools were available online contributed to this (Table 7.4).

Table 7.4
The link between appreciation of e-HRM and HRM effectiveness at IBM.

e-HRM appreciation	Job relevance	Quality of application	Ease of use
Qualification	High	High	High
HRM effectiveness	**Technical HRM effectiveness**		**Strategic HRM effectiveness**
Qualification	Increased		Increased

Note: HRM, human resource management.

Discussion and conclusions

In this chapter, the central question considered was whether e-HRM contributes to HRM effectiveness. In order to assess this, we considered the results of three qualitative studies on this topic. In this way, richer and broader evidence could be presented.

We investigated three international companies that had introduced e-HRM some years earlier, and we observed a clear picture: a greater appreciation of an e-HRM application translates into an increase in both technical and strategic HRM effectiveness. Further, from the cases we learn that, in general, the link and even the influence of e-HRM on technical and strategic HRM effectiveness is perceived as direct. Only when it comes to the link between e-HRM and the commitment of employees (an aspect of strategic HRM effectiveness) does it seem that e-HRM influences respondents' commitment in a more indirect way: we have suggested that respondents experience that they are receiving more attention in terms of receiving information and through being offered development instruments, and this may make them more committed to the organization.

Here, we will consider each of the five areas used in measuring e-HRM in turn, compare the three companies and look at the implications of these findings.

Job relevance

Here, there were clear differences in the three companies. At Dow, there was some resistance from older employees and those people working in the plant, and overall experience was shallow and superficial. At Fords, usage of tools depended on the attitudes and the styles of an individual's manager but, overall, there was less need to resort to HR staff as a result of the e-HRM instruments. The greatest appreciation, by far, of the job relevance of e-HRM was at IBM. There was nevertheless also some reluctance to adopt the latest system as there had been many system changes in the past and (as at Fords) the managers played an important role. However, IBM also effectively made individual e-HRM adoption mandatory by making it a necessary step in completing HR procedures including appraisals. So, overall, it seems that the job relevance of e-HRM is easier to grasp in technology-oriented companies that emphasize services rather than manufacturing, widely depends on sympathetic and well-informed managers, and may be adopted more quickly when integrated into existing frequently used HR procedures.

Quality of the e-HR application

Perceptions of the quality of e-HRM offerings also varied. At Dow (probably the least developed of the three companies in terms of e-HRM usage), there were complaints that there were too many screens and steps to follow. Some e-HRM subfields were not used and others were missing. The 360° tool was not widely used, the recruiting tool did not question applicants about their professional and technical skills, and there was no performance evaluation facility. Fords had a better structured, convenient, and well-functioning e-HRM system in which staff could become empowered in using HR applications for their personal needs. IBM employees, used to an online HR system and gaining informing in this way, liked the content of their system but sometimes found it hard to locate specific tools.

However, once they found them, they considered them – such as the pension planner – to be of high quality and useful. Thus, it would seem that e-HRM provisions have to be well communicated and clearly presented in order for their quality to be appreciated and utilized. Piecemeal attempts at e-HRM are liable to be criticized as being of poor quality.

Ease of use

Related to job relevance and quality, ease of use is another crucial component in e-HRM usage and therefore in its effectiveness. It was initially thought that with half a day every 2 months given over to the system that Dow employees would easily learn to use the system, but it would still take 3 years to achieve widespread adoption. Plant workers had the worst experiences of the system in terms of ease of use, young people were the most positive. The introduction of compulsory personal development plans based on the e-HRM system was gradually bringing more people into the fold, and they generally began to find it easier. Employees at Fords had similarly taken 3 years to get used to their system, but then they used it 3 times a week on average. Over time, they were gradually finding it easier and easier to use, but they still missed the personal touch of the old HR system. IBM employees were so used to web-enabled tools that ease of usage was rarely a problem. They did, however, experience some issues in using the more relational-based tools. Thus, ease of usage depends on time and practice, and is encouraged by the integration of the new into the old. Operational e-HRM systems were the quickest in terms of becoming seen as easy to use.

Technical HRM effectiveness (performance of operational HRM activities and communications)

In terms of the availability of basic HR information, guidelines, and forms, all three companies experienced dramatic improvements. Acquiring information became faster and simpler, and reduced the need for face-to-face contacts with HR staff. However, particularly at Dow, there was a need to encourage regular e-HRM usage, by providing sufficient computers and building in time for the process in people's daily routines. The cost of automating operational HR activities and communications was a barrier for Fords, and this factor limited the complete, holistic development of e-HRM at the company, but all respondents agreed that accessing basic HR information had become much easier. IBM employees felt that operational HR on the scale that had been adopted would be impossible manually, and they were already keenly measuring the cost-effectiveness of operational e-HRM with positive results. However, both Dow and IBM respondents made the point that this new form of empowerment raised new issues. They were increasingly questioning the role and performance of their managers (now that they knew their pay and responsibilities in detail), and they also challenged the interpretation of some of the e-HRM tools. These issues had not emerged earlier when paper-based and face-to-face practices dominated HR activities.

Strategic HRM effectiveness (commitment and competence development)

e-HRM applications in this more advanced area were much less widespread in our sample companies than in their operational HR activities. However, Dow – despite its problems with e-HRM usage, especially by older employees and plant workers – recorded notable successes in the take-up of its e-learning offerings. Seeking out new internal jobs on-line was also popular. Employees appreciated the greater transparency, and the majority used the competency-developing opportunities – if only to improve their computer skills! Fords, in contrast, focused on operational e-HRM, and had not yet attempted to measure competency-development through e-HRM applications. The greater transparency and widespread use of e-HRM tools seemed to have given people more confidence and pride in their company, but this has not been quantified. At IBM, employees, although were used to e-HRM tools for competence development, still needed coaching, and any success in building skills was as much due to individual initiative as to the provision and availability of e-HRM tools.

Limitations and areas for further research

First of all, we would note that the three companies had different cultures and there will have been a range of factors impacting on their individual e-HRM adoptions that we have not considered. Some corporate cultures, especially those that are transparent and people-oriented, favor advanced HR (even in its traditional, non-electronic form), whilst others do not. Reflecting this, the money put into HRM can be seen either as an investment or as a cost.

The question can be raised as to whether e-HRM could be used to change an organization's HR focus completely: from limited, narrow, and secretive to widely used and transparent. Could an organization with a very limited HR function suddenly become advanced in HR terms through a 'leap-frog' approach in which it did not progress through traditional paper-based and face-to-face HR but moved directly to e-HRM implementation?

Another limitation with our overall study is that we did not include contextual variables including the various characteristics of the implementation project, such as user training, communication methods, and support from colleagues and managers, in our research model. Respondents mentioned such aspects but we did not include them in our analysis. It seems reasonable to assume that such variables do have an impact on the relationship between e-HRM and HRM effectiveness and, therefore, future studies should consider expanding the research model. Barriers to e-HRM implementation could be analyzed and recommendations provided for overcoming these.

References

Ball, K.S. (2001) The use of human resource information systems: a survey. *Pers. Rev.* 30, 677–93.

Baron, J.N., and Kreps, D.M. (1999) *Strategic Human Resources.* New York: John Wiley & Sons.

Batt, R. (2002). Managing customer services: Human Resource practices, quit rates, and sales growth. *Acad. Manage. J.* 45, 587—97.

Björkman, I., and Xiucheng, F. (2002). Human resource management and the performance of Western firms in China. *Inter. J. Hum. Resource Manage.* 13, 853–64.

Boselie, P., Paauwe, J., and Jansen, P.G.W. (2001) Human resource management and performance: lessons from the Netherlands. *Int. J. Hum. Resource Manage.* 12, 1107–25.

Boxall, P. (1996) The strategic HRM debate and the resource-based view of the firm. *Hum. Resource Manage. J.* 6, 59–75.

Brockbank, W. (1997) HR's future on the way to a presence. *Hum. Resource Manage.* 36, 65–70.

Datta, D.K., Guthrie, J.P., and Wright, P.M. (2005). Human resource management and labor productivity: does industry matter? *Acad. Manage. J.* 48, 135–45.

Davis, F.D., Bagozzi, R.P., and Warshaw, P.R. (1989) User acceptance of computer technology: a comparison of two theoretical models. *Manage. Sci.* 35, 982–1004.

Delery, J.E., and Doty, D.H. (1996) Modes of theorizing in strategic human resource management: tests of universalistic, contingency, and configurational performance predictions. *Acad. Manage. J.* 39, 802–835.

Gardner, S.D., Lepak, D., and Bartol, K.M. (2003) Virtual HR: the impact of information technology on the human resource professional. *J. Vocation. Behav.* 63, 159–79.

Harel, G.H., Tzafrir, S.S., and Baruch, Y. (2003). Achieving organizational effectiveness through promotion of women into managerial positions: HRM practice focus. *Inter. J. Hum. Resource Manage.* 14, 247–63.

Hope Hailey, V., Farndale, E., and Truss, C. (2005) The HR department's role in organizational performance. *Hum. Resource Manage. J.* 15, 49–66.

Huselid, M. (1995) The impact of human resource management practices on turnover, productivity, and corporate financial performance. *Acad. Manage. J.* 38, 635–72.

Huselid, M., Jackson, S., and Schuler, R. (1997) Technical and strategic human resource management effectiveness as determinants of HRM performance. *Acad. Manage. J.* 40, 171–88.

Kane, B., Crawford, J., and Grant, D. (1999) Barriers to effective HRM. *Int. J. Manpower* 20, 494–515.

Keebler, T.J., and Rhodes, D.W. (2002) E-HR: becoming the 'path of least resistance'. *Employment Relat. Today* Summer, 57–66.

Lawler, E.E., and Mohrman, S.A. (2003). HR as a strategic partner: What does it take to make it happen? *Hum. Resource Planning*, 26, 15–29.

Lepak, D.P., and Snell, S.A. (1998) Virtual HR: strategic human resource management in the 21st century. *Hum. Resource Manage. Rev.* 8, 215–34.

MacDuffie, J.P. (1995). Human resource bundles and manufacturing performance: Organizational logic and flexible production systems in the world auto industry. *Indust. Labor Relations Rev.* 48, 197–221.

Ostroff, C., and Bowen, D.E. (2000) Moving HR to a higher level. HR practices and organisational effectiveness. In *Multilevel Theory, Research, and Methods in Organisations* (K.J. Klein and S.W.J. Kozlowski, eds.) pp. 211–66. San-Francisco: Jossey-Bass.

Park, H.J., Mitsuhashi, H., Fey, C.F., and Björkman, I. (2003). The effect of human resource management practices on Japanese MNS subsidiary performance: a partial mediating model. *Int. J. Hum. Resource Manage.* 14, 1391–1406.

Paul, A.K., and Anantharaman, R.N. (2003). Impact of people management practices on organizational performance: analysis of a causal model. *Int. Hum. Resource Manage.* 14, 1246–66.

Roehling, M.V., Boswell, W.R., Caligiuri, P., Feldman, D., Graham, M.E., Guthrie, J.P., Morishima, M., and Tansky, J.W. (2005) The future of HR management: research needs and directions. *Hum. Resource Manage.* 44, 207–12.

Ruël, H.J.M., Looise, J.C., and Bondarouk, T. (2002) e-HRM: een verschijnsel nader in kaart gebracht. De ontwikkeling van een model voor praktijk en onderzoek. [e-HRM: a phenomenon observed more closely: developing a model for practice and research] *Tijdschr. HRM* Winter.

Ruël, H.J.M., Bondarouk, T.V., and Looise, J.C. (2004) *e-HRM: Innovation or Irritation. An Exploration of Web-Based Human Resource Management in Large Companies.* Utrecht: Lemma Publishers.

Ruël, H.J.M., Bondarouk, T.V., and Van der Velde, M. (2007). The contribution of e-HRM to HRM effectiveness: results of a quantitative study in a Dutch Ministry. *Employee Relations.* 29, 280–91.

Ruta, C.D. (2005) The application of change management theory to the HR portal implementation in subsidiaries of multinational corporations. *Hum. Resource Manage.* 44, 35–53.

Stanton, J.M., and Coovert, M.D. (2004) Turbulent waters: the intersection of information technology and human resources. *Hum. Resource Manage.* 43, 121–26.

Tsui, A.S. (1990). A multilevel-constituency model of effectiveness: an empirical examination at the Human Resource Subunit level. *Administrative Science Quarterly,* 35, 458–83.

Tsui, A., and Wang, D. (2002). Employment relationships from the employer's perspective: current research and future directions, *Int. Rev. of Indust. and Organ. Psychology.* 17, 77–114.

Voerman, M., and Van Veldhoven, M. (2005) De attitude van werknemers ten aanzien van e-HRM verklaard. Een empirische studie bij Philips. [Employee attitudes towards e-HRM explained. An empirical study at Philips] *Tijdschr. HRM* Winter.

Wright, P.M., McMaham, G.C., Snell, S.A., and Gerhart, B. (2001) Comparing line and HR executives' perceptions of HR effectiveness: services, roles, and contributions. *Hum. Resource Manage.* 40, 111–23.

Wright, P., Gardner, T.M., Moynihan, L.M., and Allen, M. (2005) The relationship between HR practices and firm performance: examining causal order. *Pers. Psychol.* 58, 409–46.

Yin, R.K. (1994) Applications of Case Study Research. Thousand Oaks: Sage Publications.

Youndt, M.A., Snell, S.A., Dean, J.W., and Lepak, D.P. (1996). Human resource management, manufacturing strategy, and firm performance. *Acad. Manage. J.* 39, 836–66.

Further reading

Boxall, P., and Purcell, J. (2003) *Strategy and Human Resource Management.* New York: Palgrave Macmillan.

Wright, P.M., and Dyer, L. (2000) People in e-business: new challenges, new solutions. Working paper 00–11, Center for Advanced Human Resource Studies, Cornell University.

CHAPTER 8

The Potential for Privacy Violations in Electronic Human Resource Practices

T. Nichole Phillips, Linda C. Isenhour, and Dianna Stone

Introduction

In recent years there has been a growing concern about information privacy in organizations. One reason for this is that organizations are increasingly using electronic human resource management systems (e-HR) to collect, store, and disseminate data about job applicants and employees. e-HR systems focus on the use of technology to collect, store, and disseminate data about job applicants and employees (Gueutal and Stone, 2005). These data are used to enhance HR decisions, maintain employee records, and streamline HR processes, including recruitment, selection, training, performance management, and compensation (Gueutal and Stone, 2005). For example, most large organizations now use web-based systems to post job openings, collect job applications, and conduct initial screenings of job applicants (Stone et al., 2005). As a result, organizations now have access to a wide array of data about individuals (e.g., background, training, work experience, address, and telephone number) that can easily be disseminated to third parties (e.g., credit agencies, potential employers, and the US government). For instance, recent reports revealed that organizations often sell online recruitment data to third parties, including the US government, without the applicant's knowledge or permission (cf. Stone et al., 2005. As a result, these systems may readily violate individuals' expectations of privacy (Stone et al., 2005).

Thus, an important concern with the use of e-HR systems is the extent to which they have the potential to invade the privacy of individuals (i.e. job incumbents and applicants; Stone et al., 2003; Stone-Romero, 2005). Not surprisingly, e-HR systems are often used to collect and store vast amounts of personal data about individuals, including social security numbers (SSNs), credit reports, personality data, performance data, addresses, telephone numbers, and benefits or medical data (e.g., domestic partners, health insurance, and prescription data) As a result, individuals are justifiably concerned about the extent to which these data can be revealed to others inside (e.g., supervisors) and outside the organization (e.g., employee records sent to governmental agencies; Crutsinger, 2006). As a result, there has been a growing public outcry about the importance of privacy rights; and surveys show that 62% of individuals in the USA believe that legislation is needed to protect their personal privacy (Fox et al., 2000). To date the USA has no private-sector legislation protecting the privacy of employees, but the EU passed privacy legislation in 1998 (EU Countries Implement the Directive, 1998).

Furthermore, given the rise in use of web-based information systems, many individuals are concerned about the theft of their identity. Some estimates indicate that over 80 000 individuals are victimized each year when others use their SSN or credit data to take on the person's identity and purchase products or apply for jobs under an assumed identity (Dixon, 2003). With the increase in Internet-based transactions and information sharing, this number is expected to increase (Dixon, 2003). As a result, many individuals are leery of engaging in activities and information sharing via e-HR systems that could make them susceptible to identity theft. For instance, some research shows that applicants are often reluctant to submit their job applications online because they worry that their personal information will fall into the wrong hands (Harris et al., 2003). Thus, surveys show that 76% of people in the USA are concerned with the use and dissemination of personal information through computerized networks, such as e-HR systems (Fox et al., 2000).

Purpose of chapter

Given the increasing use of e-HR systems and the growing concerns about information privacy, the current chapter will consider the extent to which e-HR systems have the potential to invade the privacy of employees and job applicants. In order to understand these issues the chapter will use the seminal model of organizational privacy developed by Stone and Stone (1990) as a basis for understanding the relation between privacy and e-HR systems. More specifically, the chapter will consider privacy and e-HR systems in terms of several key elements in the Stone and Stone (1990) privacy model, including (1) information factors (e.g., types of information collected, purpose of the data collection, accuracy of information collected), (2) individual factors (e.g., sociocultural, age, ethnicity), and (3) procedural factors. In addition, the chapter will provide directions for future research on privacy and e-HR systems. Finally, we will also provide suggested guidelines for practitioners on the strategies that can be used to protect the privacy of individuals in organizations.

Privacy defined

There are numerous definitions of the privacy construct in various fields such as law, political science, and sociology (Stone and Stone (1990). Most often privacy has been described as the regulation of interactions with others (Altman, 1976; Derlega and Chaikin, 1977; Sundstrom et al., 1980; Sundstrom, 1986), freedom of control by others (Kelvin, 1973), and the control of information about the self (Westin, 1967; Derlega and Chaikin, 1977; Stone and Stone, 1990). Following Stone and Stone's (1990) model of organizational privacy, the current chapter will define privacy as a:

'state or condition in which the individual has the capacity to…control the release and possible subsequent dissemination of information about him or herself.'
(Stone and Stone, 1990, p. 358)

According to the 'privacy as information control' perspective, individuals have privacy when they are able to:

'manage or control information about them and the subsequent impressions that others form about them.'
(Stone and Stone, 1990, p. 385)

This management is accomplished through the individual controlling outflows of information communicated in verbal and non-verbal ways and the subsequent disclosure or dissemination of such information. Through limiting self-disclosure, individuals prevent others from obtaining complete information about the person's past, present, or future intentions (cf. Goffman, 1959; 1963; Jourard, 1966; Derlega and Chaikin, 1977; Stone and Stone, 1990).

The concept of privacy serves to keep others in the world from knowing a person's private thoughts. Individuals would undoubtedly experience embarrassment or social disapproval if others were made aware of all their thoughts, words, or deeds (Wasserstrom, 1984). Societal pressures often lead people to believe that they should be ashamed or embarrassed by personal thoughts or actions that are not consistent with societal norms. Thus, privacy allows individuals to think or say things that are unpopular (Fried, 1968) and enables them to protect their personal dignity and emotional wellbeing (Klopfer and Rubenstein, 1977).

For organizational researchers, a better understanding of privacy and e-HR systems is important because it may enable organizations to identify successful strategies for collecting and using data about individuals while still maintaining their personal privacy. It merits noting that this is a non-trivial task, but is needed if organizations are to use e-HR systems to manage and store employee data. Failure to obtain a solution to the violation of privacy issue can place organizations in a situation where they are faced with legal challenges from employees and job applicants, potentially placing the company in financial jeopardy. In addition, job incumbents or applicants who perceive that their privacy has been invaded may feel that they have been treated unfairly and forego initial job offers or leave the organization (Stone and Kotch, 1989; Stone-Romero et al., 2003). Thus, organizations are increasingly concerned about balancing their needs for information against employees' actual or perceived rights to privacy.

Privacy and e-HRM

The potential of e-HR systems to violate individual privacy expectations is a topic that has been considered by a number of researchers (Linowes, 1996; Harris et al., 2003; Stone et al., 2003; Stone-Romero, 2005). As noted above, the current chapter will utilize the Stone and Stone (1990) model of organizational privacy as a framework for examining the factors affecting privacy and e-HR systems. Although all e-HR functions could be considered, we consider only three HR functions (i.e., e-recruiting, e-selection, and e-performance management) in the interest of brevity. Definitions, examples, and a brief review of relevant research for these three e-HR systems are provided below before proceeding to examine selected privacy model factors (Stone and Stone, 1990). Specifically, we consider (1) information factors (e.g., types of information collected, purpose of the data collection, accuracy of information collected), (2) individual factors (e.g., sociocultural, age, ethnicity), and (3) procedural factors and how each might be related to the extent to which e-HR systems invade, or are perceived to invade, personal privacy. In addition, we offer suggestions for future research, as well as suggested guidelines for HR practitioners on privacy and e-HR systems.

e-Recruiting

In order to facilitate the recruitment process, organizations are increasingly using web-based job sites, portals, and kiosks to attract job applicants (Stone et al., 2003). Some of the most commonly used practices for e-recruiting include adding recruitment pages to existing websites, developing interactive tools for processing applications (e.g., online applications), using specialized recruitment websites (e.g., online job boards), and using online screening techniques (e.g., keyword systems; Galanaki, 2002). The use of these and similar techniques is currently widespread, and some estimates indicate that 95% of large firms use them (Cappelli, 2001; Cedar, 2003; CedarCrestone, 2006). In some cases organizations have resorted to an all-online format where they require that all applicants apply for jobs through the Internet (Cascio, 1998).

There are many uses for e-recruiting. In addition to attracting new employees, some companies use their e-recruiting websites and/or portals as a means of identifying internal job candidates for new positions or promotions (e.g., SAP, People-Soft). Organizations also use their websites to establish 'brand identities' to help distinguish themselves from their competitors (Ulrich, 2001; Stone et al., 2003) and to increase employee retention, surveying competitors' salary rates to ensure that employees' salaries are consistent with the labor market, making it less attractive to search for alternative employment (Cedar, 2003). Thus, e-recruiting systems have become an important aid to organizations by helping to establish a brand identity, attract talented workers, and retain valuable employees (Stone et al., 2005). e-Recruiting strategies increase the effectiveness of the recruiting process by reaching large numbers of applicants, reducing recruitment costs, and allowing organizations to evaluate the success of their recruitment strategies (Cappelli, 2001; Stone et al., 2003).

e-Selection

Organizations are now using e-selection systems to assess and select job applicants, manage applicant flow, and evaluate the effectiveness of selection decisions (Kehoe et al., 2005). These systems are beneficial to both applicants and organizations. Applicants are able to review job descriptions and complete tests, personality inventories, and interviews online. In addition, they often receive immediate feedback about their suitability for the job. Organizations also benefit from e-selection systems because they can streamline and simplify their selection screening processes. For instance, many organizations use sophisticated resume scanning systems to electronically scan applicants' resumes for key words associated with job requirements (Stone et al., 2003; 2005), as well as conducting assessment and background checks online. The data provided from these systems can easily be used to determine the extent to which applicant's knowledge, skills, and abilities meet job requirements. These systems can also help generate applicant strengths and weaknesses, which can be used to tailor specific interview questions for managers (Ulrich, 2001; Kehoe et al., 2005). Finally, these systems can be used to combine assessment data and help managers make final hiring decisions.

e-Performance management

Technology has increasingly been used by organizations as a means of managing employee performance (Cardy and Miller, 2005). Electronic performance management (EPM) technology is the use of electronic instruments, such as audio, video, and computer systems, to collect, store, analyze, and report individual or group performance data (Nebeker and Tatum, 1993). In some cases, these systems record the number of work units employees complete in a given time period; and these data are used to provide timely feedback to employees (Cardy and Miller, 2005). Estimates indicate that 27 million workers are monitored utilizing EPM (DeTienne and Abbot, 1993; Staunton and Barnes-Farrell, 1996). This tool is believed to be beneficial to organizations because it helps streamline the performance management process and enhances productivity in organizations.

Technology also facilitates performance management through computer monitoring (e.g., recording the amount of time spent on each call in a call center) and as a means of assisting managers with writing reviews and providing performance feedback (Cardy and Miller, 2005). In fact, some software packages provide managers with prewritten text, which allows them to focus on the content rather than just the format of the feedback (Cardy and Miller, 2005). In some cases e-performance management system use may increase the frequency and timeliness of feedback in organizations (Adams, 1995; Cardy and Miller, 2005). Finally, technology can afford organizations the opportunity to monitor absenteeism, grievance rates, safety records, and turnover levels over time (Stone et al., 2003).

Privacy and e-HR systems

Not surprisingly, these new e-HR systems make it easier for organizations to collect, store, and use employee data for HR decision-making. However, these same systems have greater potential to violate individuals' privacy. Therefore, in the following sections we consider selected factors that may be related to the extent to which individuals' perceive e-HR systems as invasive of privacy. Specifically, we discuss, in turn, (1) information factors, (2) individual factors, and (3) procedural factors thought to influence perceptions of invasion of privacy below (Stone and Stone, 1990).

Information factors

According to the model of privacy presented by Stone and Stone (1990), there are a number of information factors that may affect individuals' perceptions of privacy. For instance, the type of information collected, the purpose of the information, and the accuracy of the information are all factors that may affect individuals' perceptions of privacy. Each of these factors will be discussed in relation to e-recruiting, e-selection, and e-performance management.

Type of information collected. The type of information collected and stored in an e-HR system is important because it influences the types of inferences that can be made about individuals and the positive or negative outcomes individuals will experience in organizations (Stone and Stone, 1990). Not surprisingly, previous research has shown that individuals are likely to perceive that some types of data are more invasive of privacy than others (Rosenbaum, 1973). For instance, individuals typically perceive the collection of medical data, financial data, and personal history data as more invasive of privacy than the collection of other types of data (Rosenbaum, 1973). Thus, the types of data collected and stored in various e-HR systems may affect individuals' perceptions of privacy.

Type of information collected and e-recruiting. In terms of e-recruiting, organizations typically require applicants to submit their resumes or complete online application forms (Stone et al., 2005). These applications often ask for information about the individuals' education, training, previous work experience, address, telephone number, e-mail address, citizenship, skills, and interests. Given the wide array of information collected in the online application process, applicants may be concerned about their ability to control the collection, storage, use, and dissemination of these data. For instance, some research shows that organizations often sell the information collected via e-recruiting systems to marketing firms and other types of organizations (Stone et al., 2005). Given that individuals typically expect that their personal data will not be disseminated without their permission, we believe that individuals may be more likely to perceive that e-recruiting systems are more invasive of privacy than traditional recruiting systems. To our knowledge, no research exists on this issue; therefore, we propose the following proposition to guide future research on privacy and e-HR systems:

- ■ Proposition 1: Individuals will view online applications as more invasive of privacy than traditional paper applications.

In some cases, organizations also gather data on the person's race or ethnicity, age, gender, and disability status for governmental reporting purposes (e.g., Equal Employment Opportunity requirements). In manual application systems, these data are collected via separate forms. However, when e-HR systems are used, these data are collected as part of the same online application process. Thus, individuals may be more likely to perceive that sensitive data about their ethnicity, age, or disability status will be used to make hiring decisions about them when e-recruiting, rather than traditional paper, systems are used. Thus, they may be more likely to perceive that e-recruiting systems will stigmatize them and violate their privacy, when compared to other recruiting sources. We know of no research on this specific issue; therefore, we propose the following proposition:

- ■ Proposition 2: Individuals will view online collection of ethnicity, age, or disability status as more invasive of privacy than traditional paper collection of such data.

In an effort to ameliorate individuals' concerns about invasion of privacy, we suggest that organizations develop a set of fair information policies regarding e-recruiting and communicate these policies to all job applicants. For instance, organizations might assure applicants that all data provided for the application process will not be released without applicants' permission or used for purposes other than the application process. Likewise, organizations might specify a privacy policy on their websites indicating that data for EEO reporting purposes will be kept separate from the application and will not be used to make hiring decisions. Given the absence of research on these strategies for protecting privacy, we offer the following propositions to guide research on the topic:

- ■ Proposition 3a: Individuals will view online applications as less invasive of privacy when organizations specify policies limiting the use and dissemination of such data than when they do not.
- ■ Proposition 3b: Individuals will view online collection of EEO reporting data as less invasive of privacy when

organizations specify policies that preclude the use of such information for hiring decisions than when they do not.

Type of information and e-selection. As noted above, e-selection systems are often used to collect a vast amount of information about an applicant's knowledge, skills, abilities, and other job requirements (KSAOs). For instance, these systems are used to collect data about cognitive ability and personality through online testing systems. As a result, applicants may be concerned that one failure on an online test may permanently stigmatize them because online data can easily be networked or disseminated to others. Interestingly, some reports indicate that organizations in the USA are developing centralized databases and networking data about job applicants (Stone and Stone-Romero, 1998). Thus, applicants may perceive that online selection systems have a greater capacity to invade their privacy because one youthful transgression or poor performance rating early in one's career may preclude an individual's being hired for jobs (Stone and Stone-Romero, 1998).

In addition, individuals may feel that the compilation and storage of such sensitive information in a potential employer's e-HR system could subject them to harmful privacy violations either through unauthorized access by individuals within the firm or unauthorized disclosure to third parties. Therefore, we maintain that individuals may react more negatively to e-selection than traditional selection systems because online systems may be perceived as more invasive of privacy. We know of no specific research on this topic and, thus, propose the following proposition to guide future research:

■ Proposition 4: Individuals will view e-selection processes as more invasive of privacy than traditional paper selection processes.

Apart from online testing, e-selection systems are also used to conduct background checks and may gather data about individuals' work experience, education, SSN, driving record, financial resources, and criminal history (Gueutal and Stone, 2005). For example, banking firms may specifically request permission to access an applicant's financial records to assess whether debt is a problem that might lead to theft. In the USA, these systems require applicants to reveal their SSNs as part of the hiring process. However, when organizations access other databases to check an applicant's background, there is always the risk that the data in these databases will be inaccurate. As a result, the applicant will be denied a job based on incorrect data. For instance, one of the authors had a student named 'Michael Kelly', a 51-year-old truck driver with a clean driving and criminal record. However, when the person applied for a job, the organization gathered incorrect data from a database about a person named 'Michael Kelley' who was 25 years old, with numerous driving and criminal offenses. As a result, Michael Kelly was repeatedly denied jobs until he identified the problem and corrected the data about him in online databases. It follows that applicants may be more concerned about the accuracy of online selection systems than traditional selection systems. Thus, we offer the following proposition to guide future research on the topic:

- ■ Proposition 5: Individuals will perceive that data collected via online background checks are more inaccurate than data collected via traditional background checks.

Type of information and e-performance management systems. As noted above, e-performance management systems are used to collect and store information about individuals' work performance (e.g., productivity and quality), promotion potential, and compensation history (Gueutal and Stone, 2005). For example, management support systems (MSS) are used by many firms to reduce the involvement of HR professionals in the performance appraisal process by allowing line mangers to enter and maintain both performance and compensation data. Thus, any manager in an organization may be able to view an individual's performance ratings or salary data. As a result, individuals may be concerned that others in the organization (e.g., secretaries, technical specialists) might have access to, or misuse, such data. Specifically, individuals may feel that there is a greater likelihood that they will be denied promotions or transfers when all performance data are permanently stored in such systems. Moreover, as noted above, when online performance management systems are used, individuals may perceive that one transgression or mistake can permanently stigmatize them and negatively affect their long-term outcomes in organizations. Furthermore, some researchers (Stone et al., 2006) argue that computerized monitoring systems are likely to be viewed by individuals as highly invasive of privacy. One reason for this is that these systems often count the quantity of work produced, but do not consider the quality of the work. As a result, these systems often focus on extremely deficient criteria and fail to assess all the behaviors necessary for individual or organizational success adequately (Casio and Aguinis, 2004). Thus, they may not provide an accurate picture of the employee's performance. Likewise, these systems severely limit the freedom of individuals and may evoke reactance or resistance (Stone et al., 2006). For example, individuals may perceive that computerized monitoring systems are invasive of privacy because they gather data associated with a person's bathroom or rest breaks. Not surprisingly, some research shows that individuals whose performance was monitored by computerized systems have lower satisfaction and higher anxiety rates than those who are monitored by supervisors (Ambrose et al., 1998).

In view of the arguments noted above, we believe that individuals may be more likely to perceive that e-performance systems are more invasive of privacy than traditional performance management systems. To our knowledge, there is no specific research on the issue. Therefore, we offer the following proposition:

■ Proposition 6: Individuals will be more likely to view e-performance management systems as more invasive of privacy than traditional paper performance management systems.

Purpose of data collection. Another factor thought to affect individuals' perceptions of privacy is the purpose for which the data are collected (Stone and Stone, 1990). Organizations collect information for a variety of decision-making purposes (e.g., selection, promotion, compensation). Previous research shows that individuals are less likely to perceive that their privacy has been violated if they perceive that the information is being used for specific, job-relevant purposes (Simmons, 1968; Stone and Stone, 1990). However, an individual's vulnerability increases in any data collection context that diminishes the individual's ability to make an informed decision regarding whether or not he or she wants to provide the information that is being sought (Schein, 1977; Stone and Stone, 1990). Therefore, individuals who are knowledgeable of all potential uses of the information they provide and how that information impacts job-related decisions may be less likely to believe that their privacy will be violated (Stone, 1978; London and Bray, 1980; Stone and Stone, 1990; Stone-Romero and Stone, 1998).

Purpose of data collection and e-recruiting. In using e-recruiting systems, individuals may be more likely to believe that their privacy has been invaded if the data are collected for the job application process and then used for other purposes (e.g., marketing, sold to job board). In addition, individuals should be more likely to perceive that their privacy has been invaded if e-recruiting systems gather data that are not perceived to be directly related to job requirements (e.g., data about marital status or family planning) than if they collect only job-relevant data (e.g., years of job-related experience). The collection of information unrelated to the capacity or willingness of applicants to work in a specific job may be a key determinant of individuals' perceptions of invasion of privacy (Stone and Stone, 1990; Stone et al., 1994). It follows from these arguments that organizations may be able to reduce the extent to which applicants perceive their privacy has been invaded by ensuring that only job-relevant data are collected in the application process. The research available in this area is limited. Therefore, we propose the following proposition to help guide future research on this topic:

- ■ Proposition 7: Individuals will be less likely to view online e-recruiting systems as invasive of privacy when all data collected are perceived as job-relevant than when data are perceived as unrelated to the job.

Purpose of data collection and e-selection. Similarly, e-selection systems that require applicants to take online tests to ascertain whether they possess the skills required for a particular job may affect individuals' perceptions of invasion of privacy. For example, individuals applying for an administrative assistant position may take one of several online job sample tests available commercially that assess abilities to use Microsoft Word, Excel, and Access programs. Such tests would be consistent with job description duties and would be unlikely to be perceived as a violation of the applicant's privacy. However, requests to complete other types of assessment tests (e.g., personality inventories), for which no perceived link between the assessment and job performance might exist, may lead individuals to believe their privacy has been invaded. Indeed, results of research reveal that selection procedures

> 'believed to probe the minds of applicants...result in an uneasy feeling by applicants and are perceived as invading the individual's privacy.' (Stone-Romero et al., 2003, p. 352)

Given these arguments, we suggest that one way to reduce applicants' perceptions of privacy invasion is to implement e-selection practices that ensure that all assessment methods are perceived as directly related to successful job performance. If these methods do not have obvious face validity, then the organization could explain the relevance to the job in the application process. We know of no research on this issue; therefore, we propose the following proposition:

- Proposition 8: Individuals will be less likely to view e-selection systems as invasive of privacy when data collected are clearly job-related than when data are not clearly job-related.

Purpose of data collection and e-performance management systems. As noted above, e-performance management systems that collect data via computerized monitoring systems may also be viewed as invasive of privacy. One reason for this is that, regardless of organizations' claims that they are collecting data to manage performance, individuals may perceive that the data are being collected for other purposes (e.g., reduce their autonomy, restrict their freedom, basis for layoffs). For instance, individuals may view the use of computerized monitoring systems to measure e-mail access and usage, timing of restroom breaks, or time spent on tasks as overly restrictive of their freedom and, therefore, believe their privacy has been invaded. To our knowledge, no research has directly assessed the extent to which data collected for e-performance management systems are viewed as irrelevant to their purpose. Therefore, we propose the following:

■ Proposition 9: Individuals will be more likely to view e-performance management systems as invasive of privacy when data are collected for purposes other than performance management than when they are collected solely for performance management purposes.

Accuracy of information. Another important factor that influences perceptions of violations of privacy expectations is the accuracy of the data collected and stored in e-HR systems. Individuals generally expect that organizations will make decisions based on data that are unbiased and error free (Stone and Stone, 1990; Bies, 1993). Stone and Stone (1990) suggest that individuals may believe that their privacy has been violated when the information used to make important decisions (e.g., promotion, compensation) about them may be inaccurate. Moreover, individuals may be especially concerned when data is collected from third parties (e.g., medical suppliers, credit agencies, police agencies) because such data may be unreliable and invalid (Stone, 1978; Stone and Stone, 1990). Individuals may be unaware of such information and, therefore, unable to control it. Finally, individuals may feel that their privacy has been violated when they are unable to access or correct their collected and stored data. In particular, individuals may be concerned that information collected and maintained in e-HR systems is more likely to be inaccurate than information collected through more traditional means.

Accuracy of data and e-recruiting. Individuals who provide information through e-recruiting systems generally enter their information directly by typing data in the format specified by the website. Alternatively, they use a combination approach of attaching a resume, typing in some data, and using 'cut and paste' technique to enter the resume. Such systems generally do not provide spell checking or other means of checking the accuracy of the data. Thus, individuals who are not proficient typists may misspell or enter inaccurate data in the system. This can be especially harmful when the resume is typed directly and errors occur, because key word software that prescreens the resume for job-related, specific phrases (e.g., engineer) may be unable to recognize misspellings (e.g., ingeneer). As a consequence of these errors, applicants may be rejected inappropriately. Indeed, resume word scanning systems used to prescreen job applicants may do a better job of assessing which applicants were savvy enough to include the terms listed in the job announcement or posting in their resume, as opposed to identifying applicants who are actually qualified for the jobs (Stone et al., 2005).

Other researchers argue that resume scanning systems may not be reliable or valid because key words are not based on job analysis (Mohamed et al., 2002). As a result, the keywords in the system may not be accurate or job-related. Finally, additional information collected during the prescreening effort is entered by organization members. Thus, applicants may be unaware of the data entry or unable to confirm the accuracy of the data entered by others. As a consequence applicants may view e-recruiting systems as invasive of privacy because they fear that data in these systems are inaccurate, and they have no means of verifying that the data are correct. Given these arguments we offer the following proposition:

■ Proposition 10: Individuals will be more likely to view e-recruiting systems as invasive of privacy when they cannot access and confirm the accuracy of data collected than when they can access and confirm the accuracy of data.

Accuracy of data and e-selection. Similarly, e-selection systems also may be a source of inaccurate information that leads individuals to perceive their privacy has been invaded. For example, organizations that conduct background checks, including reviewing credit reports or driving records of job applicants and incumbents, may be basing selection decisions on inaccurate data. Recent estimates indicate that 79% of the reports held by the three largest credit reporting agencies (i.e. Trans Union, Experian, and Equifax) contain errors (Cassidy and Mierswinski, 2004). The fact that data in these credit reports and other databases are flawed may lead applicants to perceive that decisions about them will be based on invalid data. Thus, they are likely to view e-selection systems as unfair (Bies, 1993) and invasive of privacy. We believe that organizations should interpret the data from online background checks and other databases with caution and develop strategies for ensuring applicant data are accurate before using them to make selection decisions. For example, employers may want to give applicants the opportunity to review and correct the errors in all data collected for selection purposes. To our knowledge, no research has assessed this strategy. Therefore, we make the following prediction to guide research:

■ Proposition 11: Individuals will be less likely to view e-selection systems as invasive of privacy when given an opportunity to access and correct erroneous data than when they are given no opportunity to access and correct erroneous data.

Although some researchers suggest that online assessment is less biased than traditional selection systems (e.g., inability to discern race, ethnicity, gender), others believe that online ability tests and personality assessments are less reliable and valid than traditional methods (Mohamed et al., 2002; Jones and Dages, 2003; Stone et al., 2003). The primary reason for this is that online tests are often conducted without monitors, and applicants may have the opportunity to research the answers or gain assistance from others. Thus, online selection systems may be based on less accurate assessments than traditional selection systems (Chapman and Webster, 2003; Stone et al., 2005). Organizations have devised techniques such as computer-adaptive testing to reduce this uncertainty (Jones and Dages, 2003). Research, however, is needed to examine the reliability and validity of online assessment methods.

Accuracy of data and e-performance management systems. Individuals' beliefs about the accuracy of data in e-performance management systems are also likely to affect their perceptions that their privacy has been invaded. The primary reason for this is that performance data are often used as the basis for promotions, pay raises, and other positive outcomes in organizations. As a result, when performance appraisals are based on inaccurate data, individuals are less likely to receive the outcomes they deserve. Furthermore, research on feedback and performance management suggests that individuals are unlikely to change their behaviors if they do not believe that performance feedback is accurate (Ilgen et al., 1979; Stone and Stone, 1984; 1985). Thus, managers who wish to improve performance in organizations are less likely to be successful if they base their ratings or feedback on inaccurate data.

As noted above, e-performance management systems have the potential to produce inaccurate data in a number of ways. In particular, computerized monitoring systems may not adequately assess all important elements of performance. For instance, when e-monitoring systems are used to count the numbers of calls completed in a call center, an increase in the number of calls taken may serve to decrease the quality of service provided to customers (Stone et al., 2006). Furthermore, a person who provides outstanding service to customers may be viewed as a poor performer on this system if he/she does not complete a large number of calls. As a result, the use of e-performance systems may provide an inaccurate depiction of the true performance of individuals. To our knowledge, research has not focused on this issue. Therefore, we make the following prediction:

■ Proposition 12: Individuals will be more likely to view e-performance management systems as invasive of privacy when performance data are perceived to be inaccurate than when data are perceived to be accurate.

Individual factors

The model of privacy developed by Stone and Stone (1990) also suggested that individual factors affect perceptions of privacy. Therefore, we believe that there may be individual differences in reactions to the use of e-HR systems. Although a number of individual factors may influence reactions to e-HR systems, we limit the discussion below to sociocultural, age, and ethnicity factors.

Sociocultural factors and reactions to e-HR systems. A number of researchers have argued that cultural norms and values influence individual's expectations of privacy and perceived rights to privacy (Kelvin, 1973; Stone and Stone, 1990). In particular, social norms and mores regulate the amounts and types of information individuals will exchange with each other and the degree to which intrusions into privacy will be viewed as acceptable (Schwartz, 1968; Kelvin, 1973; Derlega and Chaikin, 1977; Laufer and Wolfe, 1977). Norms regarding privacy seem to be a reflection of the norms in various nations or societies. For instance, European norms about privacy protection seem to be stricter than those in the USA. As a result, the EU passed legislation in 1998 that imposes restriction on the transmission and disclosure of employment data.

Interestingly, although there are no formal constitutional rights to privacy in the USA, most Americans still perceive that they have a right to personal privacy (Stone and Stone-Romero, 1998). US cultural norms dictate that information used to make employment decisions about individuals be job-related and accurate (Stone and Stone-Romero, 1998). Similarly, individuals in the USA believe that they should have control over their personal data and have a right to participate in all decisions about the disclosure of data (Stone and Stone-Romero, 1998). As a result of these norms, there are several state and federal laws concerned with privacy in the USA (i.e. Privacy Act of 1974; Smith, 1992).

Given that cultures vary regarding individuals' needs and expectations of privacy, it should be the case that there are cultural differences in reactions to e-recruiting and e-selection systems. For instance, some researchers have argued that individuals from diffuse-oriented cultures (e.g., China, Venezuela), which value privacy highly, may be less likely than those from specific-oriented cultures (e.g., UK, USA) to use e-recruitment and e-selection systems (Trompenaars and Hampden-Turner, 1998; Stone-Romero, 2005). Similarly, others have argued that individuals from particularistic and highly ascriptive cultures may react negatively to e-HR systems (e.g., e-recruiting, e-selection, e-performance management systems) because the former cultures emphasize personal relationships more than the latter (Stone et al., 2004). Furthermore, e-HR systems create very standardized, impersonal recruitment processes (Stone et al., 2004), which is incongruent with the relationship-oriented values of particularistic and ascriptive cultures. Despite these arguments, we know of no specific research on the issue (cf. Stone et al., 2004, and Stone-Romero, 2005, for specific hypotheses regarding individual differences in cultural values and privacy). Therefore, we suggest the following proposition to guide future research:

- Proposition 13: Individuals with differing cultural values will differ in their view of the invasion of privacy associated with e-recruiting and e-selection systems.

As noted above, cultures also vary in terms of their beliefs about individual rights and freedoms. For instance, those in individualistic cultures and low power distance cultures often believe that they have 'rights that even kings must respect' (Stone-Romero and Stone, 1998). However, those in high power distance cultures are much less likely to believe they have individual rights. Thus, we believe that there may be cultural differences in reactions to e-performance appraisal systems. The primary reason for this is that e-performance management systems often decrease individual autonomy and place restrictions on individuals' freedom (cf. Stone et al., 2004, and Stone-Romero, 2005, for specific hypotheses regarding privacy and individuals' cultural values). Therefore, we suggest the following proposition to guide future research:

- Proposition 14: Individuals with differing cultural values will differ in their view of the invasion of privacy associated with e-performance management systems.

Age and e-HR systems. We also believe there may be age differences in the extent to which individuals view e-HR systems as invasive of privacy. More specifically, we believe that older individuals should react more negatively to e-recruiting and e-selection systems than those who are younger (Galanaki, 2002; McManus and Ferguson, 2003). The primary reason for this is that older individuals may have a greater desire to control personal information because they are more likely to be aware of how data can stigmatize people in organizations.

Older individuals have been found to be less likely to use e-recruiting and e-selection systems, preferring traditional methods such as newspaper advertising over the more advanced web-based methods (McManus and Ferguson, 2003). Accordingly, organizations that use only e-recruiting and e-selection formats risk missing out on a large percentage of the workforce, limiting the organization's ability to attract and hire the most qualified applicant.

Similarly, older employees may be less willing to accept or use e-performance management systems. In addition to concerns that their private information will be easily available to others in the organization in a less formal way, older employees may expect and prefer traditional one-on-one interaction with managers. e-Performance management systems may be viewed as leading to less personal contact between managers and subordinates. Having experienced and relied on such relationships over time, older employees may believe that their privacy will be violated if performance information is not limited to such a relationship. Thus, older employees may be reluctant to utilize electronic resources to complete tasks and share information due to the risk that the information will be intercepted by a third party. Thus, we propose the following:

■ Proposition 15: Older individuals will be more likely than younger individuals to view e-HR systems as invasive of privacy.

Ethnicity and e-HR systems. Little research has evaluated the role that ethnicity plays in the privacy perceptions and reactions of individuals (cf. Gandy, 1993, for an exception). However, we believe that there may be ethnic differences in the development of expectations of privacy and individuals' reactions to e-HR systems. One reason for this is that members of some ethnic minority groups may be more concerned with privacy protection and rights than members of more dominant groups

in a society. For example, research has shown that African
Americans in the USA are more concerned about privacy pro-
tections than white people, Anglo Americans with 64% indicating they are very concerned about privacy issues as compared
to 43% of white people (Westin, 1990). African Americans
are also more likely than white people Anglo Americans
to believe that organizations should be limited in the types
of information that they collect about potential employees
(Westin, 1990). This strong commitment to personal privacy
values and expectations may be based in the historical experiences of ethnic minority groups. Historically, ethnic minorities
have been relegated to a lower power status in both society
and organizations, being subjected to numerous instances of
discrimination and unfair or unequal treatment. In addition,
ethnic minorities have often been prevented from accessing
and maintaining the information that is held and used to make
decisions about them. Studies show that groups deprived of
certain rights and opportunities in the past and, thus, required
to sacrifice much in the fight for equal opportunity, have a
strong commitment to those rights and privileges and are very
defensive of attempts to challenge them (Brehm, 1966).

Previous research reports that members of ethnic minority
groups are less likely to use e-HR systems such as e-recruiting
and e-selection (McManus and Ferguson, 2003). e-Recruiting
and e-selection systems require individuals to disclose substantial amounts of personal information to organizations in applying for jobs. Thus, some ethnic minorities may be less willing
to use e-HR systems to provide personal information because
they feel powerless to control its use or dissemination and have
little confidence that organizations will respect their privacy
rights. Similarly, ethnic minorities may be less willing to use
or accept e-performance management systems because they do
not believe that information in such systems will be kept private, leading to stigmatization and negative employment outcomes. Moreover, e-performance management systems reflect
an organization's desire to control behavior. Due to individual differences in experiences, members of ethnic minority
groups may be less likely to willingly participate in a system
that is designed to control their behavior. Such experiences
are likely to increase concerns of privacy violations associated

with e-HR systems. We know of no research that has assessed the role of race/ethnicity in the development of privacy expectations. Therefore, we present the following proposition to guide future research in this area:

- Proposition 16: Racial/ethnic minorities will be more likely than majority group members to view eHR systems as invasive of privacy.

Procedural factors

According to the model of privacy presented by Stone and Stone (1990), procedural factors also affect individuals' perceptions of privacy. Consistent with these arguments the Privacy Protection Study Commission (1977) presented a set of recommended procedures that would protect individuals' actual or perceived rights to privacy in organizations. These recommendations suggest that private sector employers in the USA voluntarily develop fair information management policies and procedures designed to protect individual privacy. To date however, not all organizations have taken steps to develop these policies or practices. Thus, we believe that one procedure that may be used to protect individuals' privacy is to develop a set of fair information policies. Policies such as these serve two purposes and benefit both organizations and employees. First, they clearly state the organization's position on privacy issues and enable individuals to assess the match between their privacy expectations and an organization's privacy protection strategies. Second, these policies act as a contract between employer and employee such that an organization's failure to adhere to the specific guidelines can result in the organization facing legal ramifications due to breach of contract (Denis, 1986).

Another procedure that can be used to protect individual privacy with respect to e-HR systems is the use of participation. In the USA, cultural norms dictate that individuals should have a voice in the design and use of any control system that may affect them (Trice and Beyer, 1993). As a result, individuals often expect to be included in most, if not all, decisions regarding the uses of information about them. For example, if organizations disseminate personal information about employees without their permission, individuals are likely to perceive that their privacy has been invaded (Fusilier and Hoyer, 1980; Tolchinsky et al., 1981; Stone and Stone-Romero, 1998). However, when employees provide authorization for the disclosure of their personal information, they are less likely to perceive that their privacy has been invaded (Fusilier and Hoyer, 1980). The opportunity to give permission for disclosure of personal information collected by organizations should provide employees with a greater sense of control over their information. In support of these arguments, results of research by Tolchinsky et al. (1981) and Fusilier and Hoyer (1980) revealed that when employees authorized the release of information they were less likely to perceive their privacy had been invaded. Similarly, research (Lukaszewski et al., in press) shows that the ability to choose the type of HR system influences perceptions of invasion of privacy.

We believe, as do others, that organizations have a responsibility to safeguard the information they collect and store about their employees (Fox and Ostling, 1979). As a result, company policies and procedures related to an organization's commitment to privacy protection should clearly state the organization's position on matters such as the collection, storage, dissemination, and uses of information about job applicants and employees (Stone and Stone, 1990). In addition, organizations should take special measures to ensure that employees and applicants are aware of the organization's privacy policies and understand its terms and their rights contained therein.

In view of these arguments, we believe that organizations should develop privacy protection policies when using e-recruiting, e-selection, and e-performance management systems. In particular, we believe these policies should (1) be clearly communicated to applicants and employees on all company websites and (2) require applicants and employees to signify their understanding or agreement with these policies prior to completing online applications or assessments. In addition, we also contend that individuals should be allowed to participate in all decisions about the release or dissemination of their personal data both inside and outside the organization. We know of no research that assesses the extent to which privacy protection policies or participation affect individuals' perceptions of privacy. Therefore, we offer the following proposition to guide research:

■ Proposition 17a: Individuals will be less likely to view e-HR systems as invasive of privacy when organizations establish and communicate individuals' rights to control dissemination of their data than when they do not establish and communicate such policies.
■ Proposition 17b: Individuals will be less likely to view e-HR systems as invasive of privacy when organizations publish and require acceptance of their policies at company websites than when they do not publish and require acceptance of such policies.

Based on the above, researchers have many future opportunities to expand understanding of individuals' perceptions of privacy violations and e-HR. However, human resource professionals are faced today with the potential conflict between the use of e-HR systems to support achievement of strategic goals and the protection of the privacy of applicants and incumbent employees. Accordingly, we discuss guiding principles in the next section to assist them in required day-to-day decisions.

Guiding principles for HR professionals

Consistent with the recommendations presented above, we offer general guiding principles for organizations regarding policies and procedures that may be effective in reducing the violation, or perceived violation, of privacy expectations of applicants and employees. Note, however, that we caution HR professionals that these guiding principles are not based on empirical research, as outlined above. Moreover, we reiterate that research is needed to test the propositions suggested above before these guiding principles are implemented in organizations.

In light of the potential for violation for privacy violations associated with types of information collected, we suggest that human resource professionals consider the following:

- Guiding principle 1: When seeking data from job applicants and incumbent employees through e-HR systems, collect only information that is required for the current decision being made (i.e. selection). Determination of the information that is deemed relevant should be based upon a thorough job analysis, identifying job knowledge, skills, and abilities that are required to successfully perform that job.
- Guiding principle 2: Safeguard the information that is included in electronic databases by establishing specific record retention policies regarding the length of time each type of information should be maintained electronically. Utilizing processes such as layered system access and data encryption lessen the likelihood that stored data will be deciphered and used by unauthorized individuals inside or outside the organization.

In light of the potential privacy violations associated with the purpose of data collection in e-HR systems, human resource professionals may wish to consider the following:

- Guiding principle 3: Provide applicants and employees with explanations regarding why information is being collected and the specific decisions for which it will be employed.
- Guiding principle 4: Electronically monitor only those behaviors that are associated with performance in a position. Inform individuals that they are being monitored and for what reason the data are being collected.
- Guiding principle 5: Establish database error rate goals and conduct monthly audits to identify and correct data errors. Establish error rate performance goals for company employees responsible for data entry.
- Guiding principle 6: In order to increase the reliability and validity of decisions, utilize e-HR systems in conjunction with traditional systems (e.g., online assessments

and face-to-face test administration; resume scanning systems and visual review).

In light of the potential privacy violations associated with procedural factors, human resource professionals may wish to consider the following:

- Guiding principle 7: Provide policies and procedures for employees to access their information contained in organizational databases. Additionally, ensure that there is a detailed mechanism by which employees are able to change or correct erroneous entries.
- Guiding principle 8: At the time they apply for jobs, inform applicants that a background check will be performed and information collected from third parties. Advise applicants of any negative information that was discovered from the reports and permit them to either confirm or deny the information, especially if the presence of the data results in negative outcomes (i.e. rejection of job) for the applicant.

In light of the potential for e-HR systems to violate privacy expectations based on individuals' sociocultural beliefs and experiences, HR professionals may wish to consider the following:

- Guiding principle 9: Develop privacy policies related to e-HR methods and enforce and follow them. In addition, be sure that these policies are publicized to the employees, either through websites, intranets, e-mail, or newsletters.
- Guiding principle 10: Recognize that individuals with different sociocultural backgrounds may differ in their acceptance of e-HR systems, requiring alternative approaches to recruitment, selection, and performance management, including collection of performance data (e.g., drug testing, electronic monitoring). Whenever possible allow job applicants and employees to choose the type of human resource information system they will use (e.g., traditional HR versus electronic HR system).

In light of the potential for violation of privacy expectations associated with an individual's age and ethnicity, HR professionals may wish to consider the following:

- Guiding principle 11: Employ HR specialists who are knowledgeable regarding the e-HR systems and the information contained therein so they can assist employees with access or use of these systems. These specialists should also be able to handle exceptions and special circumstances as they arise.
- Guiding principle 12: Ensure that the e-HR systems employed are accessible and attractive to all potential and current employees, regardless of age or ethnicity, in order to reduce the likelihood of adverse impact. The design should be such that the systems can be utilized by all employees without extensive training, including those having minimal computer skills, experience, and education.

Conclusion

Electronic human resource management systems provide organizations with numerous benefits. However, there are also some dysfunctional consequences associated with their use, including their potential to violate individuals' expectations of privacy. Organizations have a need to gather, store, and disseminate information about their applicants and employees. Individuals have an expectation that they will maintain the rights to the information that is collected and disseminated about them. This presents a conflict between individuals and organizations, as both parties have valid and justifiable reasons for the handling of information. However, it is our position that individual rights take precedence over those of organizations, unless there is a bona fide reason for the opposite to occur. For example, organizations conduct criminal background checks for individuals employed in the school system to protect children, other employees, and the general public. To insure that individuals' privacy expectations are not violated, organizations must understand that information collected and maintained (i.e. type of information, purpose for collecting information, and accuracy of information), procedures associated with collecting and dissemination such information, and individual factors (i.e. sociocultural, age, and ethnicity) are likely to be related to whether an individual perceives or experiences violations of privacy expectations. To preclude potential violations, organizations can establish, communicate, and enforce privacy policies and procedures associated with collecting, maintaining, and disseminating individuals' private data.

Although extensive research has examined privacy expectations, less attention has been focused on privacy and electronic human resource management systems. However, research is important to organizations facing more and more pressure to implement such systems in an increasingly competitive global environment. The propositions that are presented above can be useful in directing future research in this area. A summary of the propositions is presented in Box 8.1. Guiding principles identified above can also be useful in directing future research, as well as providing guidance for practitioners. A compilation of those guidelines is presented in Box 8.2. It is our hope that organizations can utilize this information to reduce the likelihood that their e-HR processes will violate the privacy expectations of applicants and employees and, thus, reduce the negative outcomes for both organizations and individuals that can be associated with such violations.

Box 8.1   Summary of propositions

- Proposition 1: Individuals will view online applications as more invasive of privacy than traditional paper applications.
- Proposition 2: Individuals will view online collection of ethnicity, age, or disability status as more invasive of privacy than traditional paper collection of such data.
- Proposition 3a: Individuals will view online applications as less invasive of privacy when organizations specify policies limiting the use and dissemination of such data than when they do not.
- Proposition 3b: Individuals will view online collection of EEO reporting data as less invasive of privacy when organizations specify

policies that preclude the use of such information for hiring decisions than when they do not.

- Proposition 4: Individuals will view e-selection processes as more invasive of privacy than traditional paper selection processes.
- Proposition 5: Individuals will perceive that data collected via online background checks are more inaccurate than data collected via traditional background checks.
- Proposition 6: Individuals will be more likely to view e-performance management systems as more invasive of privacy than traditional paper performance management systems.
- Proposition 7: Individuals will be less likely to view online e-recruiting systems as invasive of privacy when all data collected are perceived as job-relevant than when data are perceived as unrelated to the job.
- Proposition 8: Individuals will be less likely to view e-selection systems as invasive of privacy when data collected are clearly job-related than when data are not clearly job-related.
- Proposition 9: Individuals will be more likely to view e-performance management systems as invasive of privacy when data are collected for purposes other than performance management than when they are collected solely for performance management purposes.
- Proposition 10: Individuals will be more likely to view e-recruiting systems as invasive of privacy when they cannot access and confirm the accuracy of data collected than when they can access and confirm the accuracy of data.
- Proposition 11: Individuals will be less likely to view e-selection systems as invasive of privacy when given an opportunity to access and correct erroneous data than when they are given no opportunity to access and correct erroneous data.
- Proposition 12: Individuals will be more likely to view e-performance management systems as invasive of privacy when performance data are perceived to be inaccurate than when data are perceived to be accurate.
- Proposition 13: Individuals with differing cultural values will differ in their view of the invasion of privacy associated with e-recruiting and e-selection systems.
- Proposition 14: Individuals with differing cultural values will differ in their view of the invasion of privacy associated with e-performance management systems.

■ Proposition 15: Older individuals will be more likely than younger individuals to view e-HR systems as invasive of privacy.

■ Proposition 16: Racial minorities will be more likely than the indigenous population to view e-HR systems as invasive of privacy.

■ Proposition 17a: Individuals will be less likely to view e-HR systems as invasive of privacy when organizations establish and communicate individuals' rights to control dissemination of their data than when they do not establish and communicate such policies.

■ Proposition 17b: Individuals will be less likely to view e-HR systems as invasive of privacy when organizations publish and require acceptance of their policies at company websites than when they do not publish and require acceptance of such policies.

Box 8.2   Summary of guiding principles

■ Guiding principle 1: When seeking data from job applicants and incumbent employees through e-HR systems, collect only information that is required for the current decision being made (i.e. selection). Determination of the information that is deemed relevant should be based upon a thorough job analysis, identifying job knowledge, skills, and abilities that are required to successfully perform that job.

■ Guiding principle 2: Safeguard the information that is included in electronic databases by establishing specific record retention policies regarding the length of time each type of information should be maintained electronically. Utilizing processes such as layered system access and data encryption lessen the likelihood that stored data will be deciphered and used by unauthorized individuals inside or outside the organization.

■ Guiding principle 3: Provide applicants and employees with explanations regarding why information is being collected and the specific decisions for which it will be employed.

■ Guiding principle 4: Electronically monitor only those behaviors that are associated with performance in a position. Inform individuals that they are being monitored and for what reason the data are being collected.

■ Guiding principle 5: Establish database error rate goals and conduct monthly audits to identify and correct data errors. Establish error rate performance goals for company employees responsible for data entry.

- Guiding principle 6: In order to increase the reliability and validity of decisions, utilize e-HR systems in conjunction with traditional systems (e.g., online assessments and face-to-face test administration; resume scanning systems and visual review).
- Guiding principle 7: Provide policies and procedures for employees to access their information contained in organizational databases. Additionally, ensure that there is a detailed mechanism by which employees are able to change or correct erroneous entries.
- Guiding principle 8: At the time they apply for jobs, inform applicants that a background check will be performed and information collected from third parties. Advise applicants of any negative information that was discovered from the reports and permit them to either confirm or deny the information, especially if the presence of the data results in negative outcomes (i.e. rejection of job) for the applicant.
- Guiding principle 9: Develop privacy policies related to e-HR methods and enforce and follow them. In addition, be sure that these policies are publicized to the employees, either through websites, intranets, e-mail, or newsletters.
- Guiding principle 10: Recognize that individuals with different sociocultural backgrounds may differ in their acceptance of e-HR systems, requiring alternative approaches to recruitment, selection, and performance management, including collection of performance data (e.g., drug testing, electronic monitoring). Whenever possible allow job applicants and employees to choose the type of human resource information system they will use (e.g., traditional HR versus electronic HR system).
- Guiding principle 11: Employ HR specialists who are knowledgeable regarding the e-HR systems and the information contained therein so they can assist employees with access or use of these systems. These specialists should also be able to handle exceptions and special circumstances as they arise.
- Guiding principle 12: Ensure that the e-HR systems employed are accessible and attractive to all potential and current employees, regardless of age or ethnicity, in order to reduce the likelihood of adverse impact. The design should be such that the systems can be utilized by all employees without extensive training, including those having minimal computer skills, experience, and education.

References

Adams, J. (1995) Four performance packages add ease and speed to evaluations. *HR Mag.* 40, 151–5.

Altman, I. (1976) Privacy: a conceptual analysis. *Environ. Behav.* 8, 7–29.

Ambrose, M., Adler, G., and Noel, T. (1998) Electronic performance monitoring: a consideration of rights. In *Moral Management of People and Processes* (M. Schminke, ed.) Mahwah, NJ: Lawrence Erlbaum.

Bies, R. (1993) Privacy and procedural justice in organizations. *Soc. Justice Res.* 6, 69–86.

Brehm, J. (1966) *Psychological Reactance to Threats on Behavior Freedom.* Oxford: Academic Press.

Cappelli, P. (2001) Making the most of on-line recruiting. *Harvard Bus. Rev.* 79, 139–46.

Cardy, R., and Miller, J. (2005) eHR and performance management: a consideration of positive potential and the dark side. In *The Brave New World of EHR* (H. Gueutal and D. Stone, eds.) pp. 138–65. San Francisco: Jossey-Bass.

Cascio, W. (1998) *Managing Human Resources: Productivity, Quality of Work Life, and Profits* (5th ed.). New York: Irwin, McGraw-Hill.

Cascio, W. and Aguinis, H. (2004) *Applied Psychology in Human Resource Management.* Upper Saddle River, NJ: Prentice-Hall.

Cassidy, A. and Mierswinski, E. (2004) *Mistakes do Happen: a Look at Errors in Consumer Credit Reports.* US Public Interest Research Group.

Cedar (2003). Cedar 2003 Workforce Technologies Survey. Available online at http://www.cedarcrestone.com/whitepapers/Cedar_2003_Workforce_Technologies_Survey.pdf (last accessed 21 November 2007).

CedarCrestone. (2006) *2006 HCM Survey White Paper.* Available online at: www.cedarcrestone.com/whitepapers.php (last accessed 23 September 2007).

Chapman, D. and Webster, J. (2003) The use of technologies in the recruiting, screening, and selection processes for job candidates. *Int. J. Select. Assess.* 11, 113–20.

Crutsinger, M. (2006) U.S. Bank-Record Snooping Called 'Government at its Best'. *Chicago Sun-Times* 24 June 2006. Available online at: www.findarticles.com/p/articles/mi_qn4155/is_2006 0624/ai_n16506850 (last accessed 23 September 2007).

Denis, M. (1986) Privacy rights and drug testing: is there a conflict? *Employ. Relat. Today* 15, 253–68.

Derlega, V. and Chaikin, A. (1977) Privacy and self-disclosure in social relationships. *J. Soc. Issues* 33, 102–15.

DeTienne, K. and Abbot, N. (1993) Developing an employee-centered electronic monitoring system. *J. Syst. Manage.* 44, 12–5.

Dixon, P. (2003) *2003 Job Search Privacy Study - Job Searching in the Networked Environment: Consumer Privacy Benchmarks.* 11 November 2003. Available online at: http://www.worldprivacyforum.org/wpfjobstudy.pdf (last accessed 21 November 2007).

EU countries implement the Directive in various ways. (1998) *Privacy Laws and Business International Newsletter,* 45, 3. Available online at: http://www.privacylaws.com/templates/publicationpage.aspx?id=973 (last accessed 21 November 2007).

Fox, J. and Ostling, P. (1979) Employee and government access to personnel files: Rights and requirements. *Employee Relat. Law J.* 5, 70.

Fox, S., Rainie, L., Horrigan, J., Lenhart, A., Spooner, T., and Carter, C. (2000) *Trust and Privacy Online: Why Americans Want to Rewrite the Rules.* Available online at: www.pewinternet.org/pdfs/PIP_Trust_Privacy_Report.pdf (last accessed 23 September 2007).

Fried, C. (1968) Privacy: a moral analysis. *Yale Law J.* 77, 475–93.

Fusilier, M. and Hoyer, W. (1980) Variables affecting perceptions of invasion of privacy in a personnel selection situation. *J. Appl. Psychol.* 65, 623–26.

Galanaki, E. (2002) The decision to recruit online: a descriptive study. *Career Dev. Int.* 7, 243–51.

Gandy, O. (1993) African Americans and privacy: understanding the black perspective in the emerging policy debate. *J. Black Stud.* 24, 178–95.

Goffman, E. (1959) *The Presentation of Self in Everyday Life.* Garden City, NY: Doubleday.

Goffman, E. (1963) *Stigma: Notes on the Management of Spoiled Identity.* Englewood Cliffs, NJ: Prentice-Hall.

Gueutal, H. and Stone, D. (eds.) (2005) *The Brave New World of EHR.* San Francisco: Jossey-Bass.

Harris, M., Van Hoye, G., and Lievens, F. (2003) Privacy and attitudes towards Internet-based selection systems: a cross-cultural comparison. *Int. J. Select. Assess.* 11, 230–6.

Ilgen, D., Fisher, C., and Taylor, S. (1979) Consequences of individual feedback on behavior in organizations. *J. Appl. Psychol.* 64, 349–71.

Jones, J. and Dages, K. (2003) Technology trends in staffing and assessment: a practice note. *Int. J. Select. Assess.* 11, 247–52.

Jourard, S. (1966) Some psychological aspects of privacy. *Law Contemp. Prob.* 31, 307–18.

Kehoe, J., Dickter, D., Russell, D., and Sacco, J. (2005) E-Selection. In *The Brave New World of EHR* (H. Gueutal and D. Stone, eds.) pp. 54–103). San Francisco: Jossey-Bass.

Kelvin, P. (1973) A social-psychological examination of privacy. *Br. J. Social Clin. Psychol.* 12, 248–261.

Klopfer, P. and Rubenstein, D. (1977) The concept of privacy and its biological basis. *J. Soc. Issues* 33, 52–65.

Laufer, R. and Wolfe, M. (1977) Privacy as a consent and a social issue: A multidimensional developmental theory. *J. Soc. Issues* 33, 22–41.

Linowes, D. (1996, April 22) *Many Companies Fail to Protect Confidential Information.* Available online at: www.epic.org/privacy/workplace/linowesPR.html (last accessed 23 September 2007).

London, M. and Bray, D. (1980) Ethical issues in testing and evaluation for personnel decisions. *Am. Psychol.* 35, 890–901.

Lukaszewski, K., Stone, D., and Stone-Romero, E. (in press) The effects of the ability to choose the type of human resource system and type of information disclosed on perceptions of invasion of privacy and system satisfaction. *J. Bus. Psychol.*

McManus, M. and Ferguson, M. (2003) Biodata, personality, and demographic differences of recruits from three sources. *Int. J. Select. Assess.* 11, 175–83.

Mohamed, A., Orife, J., and Wibowo, K. (2002) The legality of key word search as a personnel selection tool. *Employee Relat.* 24, 516–22.

Nebeker, D. and Tatum, C. (1993) The effects of computer monitoring, standards, and rewards on work performance, job satisfaction, and stress. *J. Appl. Soc. Psychol.* 23, 508–36.

Privacy Protection Study Commission. (1977) *Personal Privacy in an Information Society.* Washington, DC: US Government Printing Office.

Rosenbaum, B. (1973) Attitude toward invasion of privacy in the personnel selection process and job applicant demographic and personality correlates. *J. Appl. Psychol.* 58, 333–8.

Schein, V. (1977) Individual privacy and personnel psychology: the need for a broader perspective. *J. Soc. Issues* 33, 154–67.

Schwartz, B. (1968) The social psychology of privacy. *Am. J. Sociol.* 73, 741–52.

Simmons, D. (1968) Invasion of privacy and judged benefit of personality test inquiry. *J. Gen. Psychol.* 79, 177–81.

Smith, R. (1992) *Compilation of State and Federal Privacy Laws.* Washington, DC: Privacy Journal.

Staunton, J. and Barnes-Farrell, J. (1996) Effects of electronic performance monitoring on personal control, task satisfaction, and task performance. *J. Appl. Psychol.* 81, 738–45.

Stone, D. and Kotch, D. (1989) Individuals' attitudes toward organizational drug testing policies and practices. *J. Appl. Psychol.* 3, 518–21.

Stone, D. and Stone, E. (1985) The effects of feedback consistency and feedback favorability on self-perceived task competence and perceived feedback accuracy. *Organ. Beh. Hum. Dec.* 36, 167–85.

Stone, D. and Stone-Romero, E. (1998) A multiple stakeholder model of privacy in organizations. In *Moral Management of People and Processes* (M. Schminke, ed.) pp. 35–60. Mahwah, NJ: Lawrence Erlbaum.

Stone, D., Lukaszewski, K., and Isenhour, L. (2005) Online strategies for attracting talent. In *The Brave New World of EHR* (H. Gueutal and D. Stone, eds.) pp. 22–53). San Francisco: Jossey-Bass.

Stone, D., Stone-Romero, E., and Hyatt, D. (1994) *Some potential determinants of individuals' reactions to personnel selection procedures.* Paper presented at the meeting of Society for Industrial and Organizational Psychologists, Nashville, TN.

Stone, D., Stone-Romero, E., and Isenhour, L. (2004) Die zunkunft von eHR: Pontenzielle vortielle, nachteile und kulturelle einflusse auf ihre akzeptanze und effektiviatat. In *Human Resource Management in Inter- und Intranet* (G. Hertel and U. Konradt, eds.) pp. 326–46. Gottingen, Germany: Hogrefe.

Stone, D., Stone-Romero, E., and Lukaszewski, K. (2003) The functional and dysfunctional consequences of human resources information technology for organizations and their employees. In *Advances in Human Performance and Cognitive Engineering Research* (D. Stone, ed.) pp. 37–68). San Francisco: Jossey-Bass.

Stone, D., Stone-Romero, E., and Lukaszewski, K. (2006) Factors affecting the acceptance and effectiveness of electronic human resource systems. *Hum. Resource Manage. Rev.* 16, 229–44.

Stone, E. (1978) *Research Methods in Organizational Behavior.* Glenview, IL: Scott-Foresman.

Stone, E. and Stone, D. (1984) The effects of multiple sources of performance feedback and feedback favorability on self-perceived task competence and perceived feedback accuracy. *J. Manage.* 10, 371–78.

Stone, E. and Stone, D. (1990) Privacy in organizations: Theoretical issues, research findings, and protection strategies. In *Research in Personnel and Human Resources Management* (G. Ferris and K. Rowland, eds.) Vol. 8, pp. 349–411. Greenwich, CT: JAI.

Stone-Romero, E. (2005) The effects of eHR system characteristics and culture on system acceptance and effectiveness. In *The Brave New World of EHR* (H. Gueutal and D. Stone, eds.), pp. 226–54. San Francisco: Jossey-Bass.

Stone-Romero, E. and Stone, D. (1998) Religious and moral influences on work-related values and work quality. In *Advances in the Management of Organizational Quality* (D. Fedor and S. Ghosh, eds.) pp. 185–285. San Francisco: Elsevier/JAI Press.

Stone-Romero, E., Stone, D., and Hyatt, D. (2003) Personnel selections procedures and invasion of privacy. *J. Soc. Issues* 59, 343–68.

Sundstrom, E. (1986) *Work Places: The Psychology of the Physical Environment in Offices and Factories.* Cambridge: Cambridge University Press.

Sundstrom, E., Burt, R., and Kamp, D. (1980) Privacy at work: architectural correlates of job satisfaction and job performance. *Acad. Manage. J.* 23, 101–17.

Tolchinsky, P., McCuddy, M., Adams, J., Ganster, D., Woodman, R., and Fromkin, H. (1981) Employee perceptions of invasion of privacy: a field simulation experiment. *J. Appl. Psychol.* 66, 308–13.

Trice, H. and Beyer, J. (1993) *The Culture of Work Organizations.* Englewood Cliffs, NJ: Prentice-Hall.

Trompenaars, F. and Hampden-Turner, C. (1998) *Riding the Waves of Culture: Understanding Cultural Diversity in Global Business.* New York: McGraw-Hill.

Ulrich, D. (2001) From e-business to eHR. *Hum. Resource. Inform. Manage. J.* 5, 90–7.

Wasserstrom, R. (1984) Privacy: some arguments and assumptions. In *Philosophical Dimensions of Privacy: an Anthology* (F. Schoeman, ed.) pp. 317–332. New York: Cambridge University Press.

Westin, A. (1967) *Privacy and Freedom.* New York: Atheneum.

Westin, A. (1990) *Harris-Equifax Consumer Privacy Survey 1990.* Atlanta, GA: Equifax, Inc.

CHAPTER 9

Diffusion of HR-ICTs, an Innovations Perspective

Miguel R. Olivas-Luján and Gary W. Florkowski

Introduction

'Innovation' has become an increasingly fashionable term in the business lexicon over the last few decades. Consultants, academics, journalists – even governments – tout it as a crucial organizational capability to remain competitive in today's global economy, or perhaps merely survive. Innovation events are being staged around the world to showcase the latest products and evolve new models for innovation management (e.g. Welsh Assembly Government, 2006; Cambridge-MIT Institute, 2006; Financial Times Innovate 2006 Summit). Business magazines and famed consultants produce yearly lists of 'the most innovative companies', innovation guides, etc. (e.g. FastCompany, 2006; InformationWeek, 2006; McGregor, 2006; etc.). Academic programs designed to study and foster the generation and dispersal of innovative concepts are appearing in some of the most prestigious institutions around the world. Even Finnish prime minister Matti Vanhanen, whose country holds the EU presidency, proposed innovation as the first theme of the bloc's October 2006 Summit (Finland's European Presidency Website, 2006). It can be safely said that we live in a society that seeks, celebrates, and rewards innovation, perhaps to the point of losing sight of what the very word truly stands for!

Indeed, innovation means different things to different people. For some, any kind of novelty, improvement, or advancement is indicative of innovation, even if it is marginal in nature. Others have argued that the change must be significant in a meaningful way, even momentous. Similarly, there are those who only recognize changes which are material or tangible in form as true innovations (e.g. a new product), while others would include altered production processes, business models or organizational structures in the mix.

Not surprisingly, scholars around the world have dedicated vast efforts to make sense of these apparently diverging perspectives. A robust body of interdisciplinary literature known as diffusion of innovations (DOI; Rogers, 1962; Daft, 1978; Tornatzky and Klein, 1982; Damanpour and Evan, 1984; Kwon and Zmud, 1987; Rogers, 2003) has been evolving since the mid-1900s, offering an array of definitions, paradigms, and inferential analytical models to help our understanding of:

- What constitutes an innovation?
- How to describe it?
- Who is more likely to adopt an innovation?
- What characterizes the process of adoption, and perhaps most interestingly?
- How to foster the development of an organization's innovativeness?

Martin (2006) noted that this is a most promising, but little used, perspective in the study of electronic human resource management (e-HRM); a deficiency we seek to redress in three ways. First, the chapter highlights how human resource information and communication technologies (HR-ICTs) can be described and classified in the mindset of DOI investigators. Table 9.1 summarizes the DOI elements reviewed, key questions that they raise, and their practical significance. Second, early results are profiled from an ongoing research program of HR-ICT innovation in several English-speaking countries. Finally, we advance suggestions that should be helpful to managers who are intent in increasing their organization's

Table 9.1

DOI theory elements applied to HR-ICTs.

DOI elements	Key questions	Practical significance
For the HR-ICT innovation		
Type of innovation	Is the HR-ICT a product, a procedure, a process, or a model?	Products and simple procedures may be easier to understand and justify; processes and models may be more abstract and involve more organizational stakeholders
Locus of impact: departmental, organizational, or interorganizational	Does the innovation affect only the HR function, several organizational units, or several organizations?	More potential allies – or contrarians – will be involved in the different stages of adoption
Compatibility	Are the targeted users ready to use the HR-ICT?	Introducing radical departures from the status quo may invite rejection of the technology
Relative advantage	Is the HR-ICT a clear improvement over the way things were done before?	Larger improvements to the status quo are easier to justify
Trialability	Are HR-ICT demos available?	Demos help demystify the innovation for its targeted users
Complexity	Is the HR-ICT easy to use? Or, do users have to 'jump through hoops' and go through long training before they can utilize it?	The more complex an innovation, the less likely it will be adopted rapidly and by all intended users
Observability (of benefits)	Are the positive consequences of using the HR-ICTs easily observable?	Resistance to change will decrease to the extent that users can see its benefits
Categories of adopters or HR-ICT users		
Innovators	Who are the key users that might adopt the innovation early?	By focusing your energy on members of this group, you will struggle less to get support for the HR-ICT overall; this group is a 'natural choice' for pilot implementations
Early adopters	Who are the users that might soon follow the innovators?	Your unit should be able to provide easy and more robust access to those that immediately follow the innovator group

(continued)

Table 9.1

(Continued)

DOI elements	Key questions	Practical significance
Early majority	What users are likely to adopt the HR-ICT before the 'average adopter'?	The ability to serve well this group early might determine the eventual, final level of acceptance for the HR-ICT; without a visible group of adopters, the HR-ICT may rapidly fall in disuse
Late majority	Which users will adopt the technology after the 'average adopter'?	By the time this group is reached, the innovation should be completely tested and capacity issues must have been resolved
Laggards	What HR customers are more likely to wait until they have no choice but to use the technology?	This group of users will need back up systems, pre-adoption style, for a longer time than the rest of the adopters
Non-adopters	How large is the proportion of employees that might never use the innovation?	Rarely will an innovation reach 100% of its targeted users; your personnel department must be ready to face this fact and keep offering a small proportion of its services 'the old way'
For the adopting organization		
Top management support	Is top management indifferent, supportive, or hesitant about using HR-ICTs in the firm?	Studies on the acceptance of innovations in information systems, in HR, and in HR-ICTs show this is a strong predictor of adoption
Innovation climate in the HR department	Are HR employees encouraged to innovate, try new things? Is there tolerance for unintentional error?	HR departments with a climate that does not contain curiosity in its employees, that will not punish occasional trials for new ways tend to use more HR-ICTs better
System of eventual adopters	Who are the 'peer organizations' adopting the HR-ICT in question?	Industry pressures and/or imitation of 'leaders' can be a very significant motivation to acquire and use the HR-ICT

Notes: DOI, diffusion of innovations; HR, human resources; HR-ICT, human resources information and communication technologies.

potential for innovativeness in the human resource (HR) function. Indeed, the very use of the terminology used in this article should aid HR managers better identify, explain, and even 'sell' and manage the adoption of technological innovations within their organization.

What constitutes an innovation? What are the key descriptors?

The innovations we will consider in this chapter are HR-ICTs. They may be web-based (e.g. intra- and extranets), telephony-based (e.g. interactive voice response (IVR) systems), or computer-based technologies (e.g. database application tracking applicants' demographic information for equal employment opportunity (EEO) compliance purposes that does not require a web-interface). Within the DOI literature, an innovation is any concept (i.e. product, procedure, process, model, etc.) that was previously unknown to a potential group or system of adopters. While the 'concept' clearly may be a new product (e.g. computerized kiosk for HR transactions, software application for testing or record keeping), it also encompasses a new procedure (e.g. self-service infrastructure enabling employees, managers, or executives to find HR information online instead of having to interact with an HR staff person), process (e.g. workflow for job postings, online updating of records, etc.), and even model (e.g. supporting the company's strategy by aligning HR-ICT investments in such a way that the most fitting candidates are hired, most adequate work behaviors rewarded, etc.).

The emphasis is not on how long the innovation has been in existence per se, but on the fact that the idea is novel to a cohort of potential adopters. DOI studies have focused attention on the innovation itself, on the potential adopter, and on the processes of adoption, acceptance, and diffusion within a system of adopters. (Related topics have drawn interest, such as change agent characteristics and how communication networks help innovations diffuse, but they are outside the scope of this chapter.)

A useful, separate distinction is whether the innovation fundamentally affects the HR department, company-at-large, or adopting organization *and* its external stakeholders (i.e. the *locus of impact* of the innovation, Prescott and Conger, 1995). For example, an electronic application system designed to speed up tracking of applicants' competencies, demographic information, etc. is likely to impact *directly* the HR department only; of course, other departments might notice that HR is now able to send them résumés more rapidly and accurately, but they are not the information and communication technology (ICT)'s target users. Compare this with a self-service system that enables employees to modify their personal records so they can claim benefits such as insurance, tax exemptions, etc. Such a system impacts both the HR department *and* the rest of the organization; its locus of impact is *organizational*. Lastly, consider an extranet system facilitating seamless service-delivery between a client firm's employees and the outside vendor handling pension-plan administration on an outsourced basis. There, the locus of impact is *interorganizational*. Identifying the locus of impact for the ICT is helpful to build the business case and prepare for better adoption of the innovation. For example, if the personnel department is the only one that will be affected by the adoption of a new tracking system, in most companies there will be fewer executives to convince, fewer potential users to train, and so on, than if the locus of impact for the innovation is organizational or (even worse!) interorganizational.

HR-ICTs also may be gainfully described by five key DOI attributes: compatibility, relative advantage, trialability, complexity, and observability of benefits (Rogers, 2003; Teng et al., 2002). (Teng et al. (2002) include five additional characteristics found in the literature that will not be discussed here: cost, communicability, divisibility, profitability, and social approval. Several of these characteristics are so strongly linked with the ones in this chapter that we decided to focus our attention on these five.) *Compatibility* refers to an innovation's perceived congruence with the existing needs, past experiences, and current priorities of potential adopters. In companies where telephony and computer systems are not used extensively, HR-ICTs have a lower probability of being adopted. DeSanctis (1986) found that most HR subfunctions in the USA were ill-prepared to use information systems for human resource information system (HRIS), except for compensation and payroll management. At the time of her study, many HRIS were run in mainframes or minicomputers and point-and-click graphical user interfaces (GUIs) were not prevalent. A global survey conducted soon thereafter identified two major impediments to the full realization of HRIS' potential in the near future: insufficient budgets/executive commitment, and a lack of HRM understanding among systems designers (Towers Perrin/IBM, 1992, pp. 96–7). The former constraint was most likely to be cited in the Americas, the latter in Asia Pacific countries. Furthermore, only one-third of the overall sample expressed the view that HR staffers were computer literate. Foreshadowing what was to come, however, approximately 80% predicted that computer literacy would become a critical requirement for the profession by the end of the 2010 (p. 38). A majority also felt that executives and line managers would enjoy a great deal of access to HRIS (p. 52). We have certainly come a long way! Today, most people are quite familiar with Windows and Macintosh GUIs upon which many HRIS run. In addition, personal computers have become powerful enough to run or interact with system hosts via client-server architecture. HR operatives, professionals, and executive are more and more likely to be equipped with information technology (IT)-competencies. Ninety-four per cent of the respondents in one survey identified software and Internet skills as extremely or somewhat important competencies for HR hires in their organization (Society for Human Resource Management, 2005). Still, a smart HR innovations manager must assess the extent to which the targeted users may sense that the innovation does not match their preferences, the company culture, or is in any way ill-suited to local conditions, and work diligently to help users overcome any incompatibilities – themes we will return to later in the chapter.

Relative advantage is defined as the extent to which potential adopters perceive an innovation is capable of delivering results that are superior to what was experienced beforehand. Until the late 1990s, there was little reason to believe that tangible benefits would redound automatically from HR-ICTs adoption. Computers, software, and other technologies used for HR purposes tended to be very expensive, limited in their functionality, and inefficiently managed. DeSanctis, for example, reported the HRIS under study tended to be disconnected from other management information systems, and that personnel who could adequately manage the HRIS and information requirements of internal customers were being neglected. Things changed dramatically in the 20 years that followed. For example, Microsoft extracted more than $1 million per annum in savings from its American operations by opting for a totally electronic payroll function (Greengard, 2000). Approximately 80% of the savings were achieved by eliminating the printing, distribution, and mailing costs for employees' earnings statements, 17% by fully automating time-card reporting for exempt and non-exempt personnel, and 3% by universally instituting electronic W-4 (tax retention) forms and direct deposits. Humana, Inc., an American managed healthcare firm, reduced its average advertising cost-per-qualified resume from $128.00 to $0.06 through web-based recruiting and the use of smart-agent software to manage applicant flows (Greengard, 1998). One multinational reportedly saved $22 million by leveraging these two technologies across multiple labor markets (Anderson Consulting, 1999). IBM's global rollout of a comprehensive e-HRM system not only saved the firm $350 million on an annual basis, but also increased employee satisfaction with HR services from 30% to 90% (Personnel Today, 2002). Nowadays, expectations that HR-ICT implementation will decrease administrative costs increase customer satisfaction, and free up HR staff to engage in more transformational work as strategic partners for their organizations are commonplace (e.g. Watson Wyatt, 2002a; 2002b; Olivas-Luján, 2003; Gueutal and Stone, 2005; Society for Human Resource Management, 2005; Strohmeier, 2007). (Geographically diverse, practitioner surveys signal noticeable progress on these fronts with much upside potential remaining (e.g. Towers Perrin 2001; Watson Wyatt Worldwide 2002a; Cedar 2004; CIPD, 2004; Cedar, 2005; 2006; SHRM, 2005). Reallocating time to strategic initiatives has been the slowest of the three objectives to materialize. Gardner et al.'s (2003) inability to confirm a hypothesized link between level-of-IT-infusion in HR and relative-time-spent on transformational activities by HR professionals is consistent with this observation. Thus, the envisioned shift in task demands requires more than IT-investment alone.)

Trialability has also increased for HR-ICTs since the mid-1990s. This characteristic makes it possible for users to experience how the innovation works before adoption takes place. Before GUIs became prevalent, HR decision makers would only be able to see the benefits of HR-ICTs indirectly, perhaps by interacting with colleagues or attending vendors' demonstrations. In our time, most HR-ICT providers will have a demonstration website, CD, or at least a video available (in addition to multiple other promotional materials) for any potential customer who wants to see how the technology is used. To illustrate, SAP's website enables potential adopters to preview how employees and managers can create and approve leave requests using ESS/MSS features of the human capital management suite within mySAP ERP. Arinso International, a global HRO and consulting firm, provides an e-HR solutions demo CD to interested persons who register online. An emerging class of vendors goes even further, facilitating cross-vendor, product comparisons by congregating links to HR-software demos and trial versions on a single webpage (e.g. HR-Software.net, 2020software.com). Needless to say, taking full advantage of demos and free trials can make a great difference when the business case is presented to the executives that have to authorize the acquisition, or when presenting prototypes to current users to increase the chances of their acceptance.

In contrast, the more complicated or difficult to understand and use an innovation is perceived to be, the less likely it will be promptly embraced; a characteristic that has been labeled *complexity*. The proliferation of personal computers and their connectivity via local area networks (LANs) and TCP/IP communication protocols, combined with the expanded functionality of cellular and line telephones, have increased the probability that non-technical users of computers and telephony systems will perceive their needs can be met by applications housed in the firm's larger IT architecture. Testing and training administration, résumé tracking, compliance reporting, performance appraisals, career planning, and many other functional activities in HRM have been automated in user-friendly ways that no longer scare away staff.

The IT-competencies of HR professionals have risen in parallel. Kavanagh (1998) cites survey research documenting marked advancement on this dimension by UK personnel managers during the latter half of the 1990s. Over a 3-year period, the number of persons acknowledging no IT expertise fell from 16% to 0%, while those professing to have excellent knowledge in this area increased from 11% to 52%. Society for Human Resource Management (SHRM)'s 2005 technology survey suggests that their counterparts in the USA followed suit. Seventy per cent of the respondents classified themselves as having some IT technical expertise; another 22% denoting an extremely high level. Identifying technically proficient users at the firm- and subunit levels still will be key, though, to reduce complexity's potential drag on adoption as we explain below.

Lastly, *observability* of the innovation's benefits must be taken into account when trying to explain adoption behaviors. Anecdotal success stories like those at Humana, Inc. and IBM certainly lend credence to HR-ICT initiatives, but they are unlikely to close the deal for most non-users. As the cumulative evidence of their beneficial effects grows, however, more potential adopters should be spurred to act. The number of sources reporting aggregate performance data from hundreds of firms in domestic and international settings has increased substantially since 2000. The outcome measures are very broad at times, such as 'effectiveness in capturing the expected ROI on HR technology investments' (Mercer HR Consulting, 2003, pp. 26–7), 'effectiveness of e-HR systems' (IRS Employment Review, 2002), and 'achievement of B2E/e-HR program goals' (Watson Wyatt Worldwide, 2002a, p. 12). In other instances, discrete criteria are evaluated (e.g. Chartered Institute of Personnel and Development (CIPD), 2004, p. 11; SHRM, 2005, pp. 15–6). (More accurate employee information, decreased cycle time for employee transactions, and a reduction in the HR department's administrative workload were the highest rated HR-ICT successes in both cases.) A series of workforce-technology surveys published by CedarCrestone lists the average gains that users achieved in average-cost per transaction, cycle time, headcount changes, return on investment, and employee satisfaction (CedarCrestone, 2002; 2003; 2004; 2005; 2006). These benefits are easily perceived by the HR department's main constituencies, and their existence should increase the rate of HR-ICT adoption.

Unfortunately, this information is more difficult to come by in emerging markets, where external reporting has been spotty at best. Watson Wyatt Worldwide's (2004) e-HR survey in Greater China is an exception, although the findings are not likely to convert high numbers of potential adopters into actual users. While 51% of the respondents believed that past investments in HR technology had generated benefits, less than one-quarter of these organizations had metrics in place to assess the ROI of their investments formally. Regrettably, efforts to document the presence of HR-ICTs in Latin America (Watson Wyatt Worldwide, 2000; Mercer HR Consulting, 2002) and Central and Eastern Europe (Deloitte, 2005) have not commented on their perceived or actual effects.

Overall, these five innovation characteristics have changed radically since the mid-1980s in ways that encourage the diffusion of HR-ICTs. While others studies have cast HR technology as an innovation (e.g. Shrivastava and Shaw, 2003; Ngai and Wat, 2006), none have examined the cross-firm, and ultimately cross-national, dynamics of their proliferation. In the sections that follow, we describe how DOI theory utilizes time-of-adoption to stratify potential users into distinct subgroups, and how the system-wide diffusion process can be modeled to facilitate the job of an HR innovations manager.

Who is more likely to adopt an innovation?

Identifying what organizations, or within organizations, specific employees that are more likely to use an HR-ICT should be a priority for managers. Adopters (organizations or individuals, but our discussion will focus on HR-ICT users within the firm) may be placed on a distribution that has been inferred to be similar to a normal (the famous symmetrical 'bell') distribution with respect to the time in which they accept the innovation. Adopters' place along the horizontal axis determines whether they should be classified as innovators, early adopters, early majority, late majority, or laggards (Gurbaxani, 1990, p. 66; Rogers, 2003, p. 281). *Innovators* have been conceptualized as the very first adopters (individuals, organizations, etc.) in a system that embraces the innovation. Popular press would say they are the 'leading edge' (or even 'bleeding edge') innovators. Rogers states that the first one in 40 (2.5%) of all eventual adopters would be part of this group which differs significantly from the next four subgroups of adopters. A manager that wants to implement HR-ICTs in a company should try hard to identify the innovators in the organization and request their help for testing and promoting the innovation. They are a natural choice for implementing or 'beta-testing' the HR-ICT before it goes 'live' for a larger audience.

The second group is named *early adopters*, the next 13.5% of ultimate users that take up the innovation early, but after the innovators; again this group is expected to differ from the previous and the following sets of adopters, and should be treated differently. For example, easy but more robust access must be provided to members of this group in comparison with the earlier one. A 'bare-bones' version of the HR-ICT, together with some imperfections may be satisfactory for the innovators, but the early adopters need less imperfections and more capacity due to their larger number and their lower tolerance to technological 'bugs' and 'burps.'

The next group (defined as approximately the following 34% of adopters in the organization) are called the *early majority*, and they would have adopted the innovation within one standard deviation before the average adopter. In other words, they still take on the innovation before the bulk of eventual users, but after the innovators and the early adopters have become familiarized with it. The ability to serve well this group early might determine the eventual, final level of acceptance for the HR-ICT; without a visible collection of adopters, the technology may rapidly fall in disuse. At the time members of this user group become customers, the technology should have been thoroughly tested and debugged, and issues regarding capacity, bottlenecks, and 'weaker links' requiring spare parts or periodical updates anticipated. If the technology is complex enough that it had to be implemented running the old way of doing things in parallel, this is the time to notify users that soon the old way will be dropped.

The following 34% of adopters are the *late majority* (up to one standard deviation after the average adopter), and they are followed by the *laggards* who are the remaining 16% of actual, eventual adopters in the system. By the time the former group is reached, the HR-ICT should be completely tested and capacity issues must have been resolved satisfactorily. Members of the late majority group tend to be more skeptical and conservative than their peers from previous categories. The latter group of users might need back up systems, pre-adoption style, for a longer time than the rest of the customers. Fear of change is not unusual among laggard adopters; therefore expecting that everybody will use the technology is unwise.

Clearly, these five categories are not symmetrically located around the mean. Still, this taxonomy is used across a variety of disciplines as the members within each subgroup are fairly homogeneous in a variety of important ways, and different from the adopters in the other groups. It is also prudent to remember that these entities are *actual* adopters. For any given innovation, there will almost always remain a number of 'potential' adopters that never actually accept it –the *non-adopters*. It is uncommon for any given innovation to reach 100% of its targeted users; your personnel department must be ready to face this fact and prepare to keep offering a small proportion of its services 'the old fashioned way'.

Are there any other important factors for an organization to adopt an HR-ICT?

Based on both literature and the results from our ongoing research program, three factors in particular are strongly related to organizational success in HR-ICT adoption. *Top management support* is a factor that has been found to predict a wide variety of organizational HR outcomes (Kossek, 1989), and the 'intensity' with which an organization will use HR-ICTs is no exception. A recent study of 155 firms in Canada and the USA showed that organizations where support from the executive board for HR-ICTs is present resulted in higher quantity and more advanced levels of HR-ICT usage (Olivas-Luján, 2003). The same study also found that *HR departments with an innovation climate* that does not curb intellectual curiosity in its employees or punish occasional trials for new ways of doing things tend to use more HR-ICTs and/or use them in a more widespread fashion. Lastly, there is strong evidence that the *system of eventual adopters* itself may be a very important influence on HR-ICT uses. Frequently, there is pressure within industries to do what the 'leader' is doing, even when the reasons and the benefits are not fully understood (i.e. mimetic isomorphism). The study summarized below adds evidence to this theory. Larger organizations with relatively high levels of HR transactional work were viewed as the population of potential adopters (see Florkowski and Olivas-Luján, 2006 for more details). We now describe the diffusion research that was used to model, understand, and forecast the adoption of HR-ICTs in the USA, Canada and to a lesser degree in other English-speaking countries.

How do we describe the process of innovation adoption?

Three competing diffusion models have been utilized to explain an innovation's growing acceptance over time, represented by S-shaped curves with different parameters (Teng et al., 2002; Rai et al., 1998): external, internal, and mixed influences models. The *external influence* model assumes that adoption is driven primarily by messages from mass media and other sources outside of the social system of likely adopters (e.g. consultants, vendors, etc.). An exponential equation with parameters m (total number of eventual adopters in the system) and p (coefficient of external influence) was used to capture these forces on technology adoption.

To illustrate external influences, Human Resource Executive® has been fielding its annual HR Technology Conference and Exposition in the USA since 1998, drawing senior HR executives and professionals from at least 12 nations. Besides orchestrating numerous stateside events, the International Quality and Productivity Council (IQPC) has conducted multiday, e-HRM conferences for executives in Singapore, Shanghai, and Brussels since 2002, with two more slated for Sydney and Berlin in 2008. Workshop and presentation themes include:

- Designing and implementing a portal-based HR intranet;
- Successfully marketing the e-HR concept to the company;
- Rolling out e-HR on a global basis with one solution;
- Developing the HR model for e-enabled shared services;
- Integrating people and process to transform e-enabled HR from potential to reality;
- Optimizing the global delivery of HR through your intranet;
- The ABCs of preparing a business case for employee self-service (IQPC website).

Watson Wyatt Worldwide maintains a dedicated website, eHR.com, which affords members a comprehensive information channel and diagnostic resources (e.g. e-HR Journey Tool) to foster the spread of information technologies within HRM. Technology Evaluation Centers (TEC) offers subscribers a decision-support tool to make customized HR-software comparisons, as well as an HR product rating report that incorporates 644 functional, technical, and business criteria. (The report is divided into six modules that rates product functionality for different kinds of HR activities and IT support requirements. Detailed ratings for each vendor's solution are paired with the corresponding values for the lowest- and highest-rated competitors in TEC's knowledge base.) The HR-XML Consortium, an international, non-profit group linking major software vendors, HR-service suppliers, XML technology companies, HR professional associations, and individual employers, continues to spearhead the development and publication of standardized data protocols for interfirm exchanges of HR information. Among its major accomplishments are set protocols for certain aspects of staffing and benefits administration, a software certification program, and a freely available testbed enabling implementers to test their XML versions against consortium specifications.

In contrast, *internal influence* models assume that adoption patterns are driven primarily by 'word-of-mouth' and other imitation effects. Gompertz and Logistic equations are the two most common means of operationalizing internal-influence models, with q depicting the coefficient of internal influence. Social-system members, particularly HR executives and HRMS managers, have numerous modalities available to them to research, debate, and ultimately inform decision-making about HR-ICTs. Leading professional associations in the USA and abroad have worked aggressively to facilitate such communications. To give an idea about these influences, the SHRM administers an HR-technology e-newsletter and online discussion community. A webcast library also can be accessed to complement technology-related articles that regularly appear in its flagship publication, *HR Magazine*. A 'killer apps' webpage encourages individuals to pilot test featured solutions. In addition, the International Association for Human Resource Information Management (IHRIM) maintains several list servers to increase the sharing of ideas and advice online among HR systems professionals, as well as publishing two influential periodicals (*IHRIM.link*, *IHRIM Wire Newsletter*) and an online buyer's guide. Like its American counterparts, the CIPD enables members to participate in online communities with technology-oriented threads. It also organizes an HR Software Show to afford direct access to leading vendors and existing users of HR-ICTs (akin to IHRIM's annual Conference and Technology Exposition). All three organizations sponsor and publish white papers, technical reports, and surveys to increase members' technology awareness and savvy. The Australian Human Resource Institute has instituted a network of HRIS Special Interest Groups with varying levels of activity across individual chapters. More modest, but increasingly relevant support, has been extended by Honk Kong's Institute for Human Resource

Management, where members have access to an e-HR glossary, a guide to products and services, and service-provider profiles that have been compiled by its e-HR Interest Group.

Finally, Bass' forecasting model (1969) included both external and internal influences into the same equation – a *mixed influence* model – facilitating comparisons of their respective effects (Mahajan et al., 2000).

In our study, non-linear regression provided the means of testing which diffusion model best approximated the observed timing of more than 492 distinct HR-ICT purchases over a 34-year period (1970–2003). (Overall, 158 companies participated in the study – 94 based in the USA, 56 in Canada, 11 in the UK, and six in Ireland. Data were collected by means of a web-based survey that was accessed by HR/Personnel executives or their delegates (survey administration details may be found in Olivas-Luján, 2003).) Table 9.2 summarizes the equations which drove our analyses. Their ability to furnish accurate replications was embodied in the R-square values. Parameters m, p, and q, in turn, symbolized the expected number of adopters in the system, the coefficient of external influence (i.e. the strength of factors that are promoting the innovations from outside the social system) and coefficient of internal influence (i.e. extent to which prior adoptions in the system are important in generating more adoptions).

Table 9.2

Equations used to model the number of adoptions considering external, internal, and mixed influences.

Exponential	$N(t) = m\,(1 - \exp(-pt))$
Gompertz	$N(t) = m\,(\exp(-c\,(\exp(-qt))))$
Logistic	$N(t) = 1 / (1/m + c\,(\exp(-qt)))$
Bass	$N(t) = m\dfrac{1 - \exp(-t(p+q))}{1 + (q/p)(\exp(-t(p+q)))}$

Notes: $N(t)$ = number of prospective adopters having acquired the technology in question at time t ($0 < N(t) < N(m)$); m = total number of eventual adopters in the social system; c = constant; p = coefficient of external influence (i.e. factors outside the social system such as the use of media); and q = coefficient of internal influence (i.e. impact of prior adoptions in the system, often via 'word of mouth' and other similar mechanisms).

As stated above, a useful distinction among MIS innovations is based on their locus of impact –the IS unit, intraorganizational, and interorganizational. In a similar fashion, we decided to classify the technologies under investigation into two groups depending on whether they were designed to be used by HR staff or HR's internal customers. The former included HR functional applications, integrated HR suites, and HR extranet applications; the latter IVR systems, HR intranet applications, employee self-service applications, manager self-service applications, and HR portals. (We originally requested information on 'wireless HR services' as well, but found virtually no responses to that subset of questions.)

Our empirical results suggested that HR-ICT diffusion is motivated more importantly by influences *internal* to the system of potential adopters than by external influences, with one exception. Integrated HR suites and HR intranets, which might possibly be diffusing via company-wide efforts to standardize computer systems is the only one of eight HR-ICTs from our study that returned a higher value for p than the corresponding q coefficient. Analyses by primary user group (HR unit versus HR users or company employees) did not yield significantly different results either, thus supporting the idea that this set of HR innovations is adopted by personnel departments by way of somewhat similar stimuli: influences that are internal to the system of adopters, rather than external influences. Lastly, analyzing the subsamples by nationality (i.e. comparing the US with the non-US responses) did not show any meaningful differences in diffusion pattern parameters (p, q, and m) or in explanatory power (R square for the non-linear regressions).

How can we foster the development of an organization's innovativeness?

As Martin (2006) has noted, HR departments with a stronger capacity to identify, assimilate, and utilize innovations (technological or otherwise) are more likely to survive and add value to their firms. The question then becomes, what can personnel managers do to increase this capacity to capitalize from HR-ICT innovations? Clearly, some advice has already been presented in the previous sections of this chapter in the form of useful theories and paradigms that may be used to understand this phenomenon, to describe it and to foster it. Still, we have included in Table 9.3 a summary of suggestions

Table 9.3
Suggestions for practice.

Make sure the consequences of adoption will fit with company strategy
Beware of innovating for innovations' sake
Create a business case with multiple justifications (e.g. do not only mention cycle times but also greater company appeal for stakeholders, less overtime likely, etc.)
As early as it may be prudent, identify and involve key users – not just top managers – in the decision process
Bandwagon arguments (i.e. 'our competition already is using it') might not be very logical or rational, but they tend to be very effective!
For HR-ICTs that target the employees, use socialization programs and events to bring them up to speed
Keep in mind that certain transactions (e.g. terminations, mortality in record-keeping, etc.) cannot be automated without losing required compassion and human touch
A sense of urgency is frequently a pre-requirement to innovation adoption (e.g. ERP implementation in the firm)
The past matters: successful marginal adoptions of HR-ICTs pave the ground for more radical innovations
Consider company seasonality to schedule training programs
Confirm, rather than assume familiarity with the innovation platform (e.g. advanced use of browsers for web-based applications)
Prepare answers in advance of meeting with resistors
Resist the urge to demand or expect 100% acceptance – keep the organizational goals and strategy as your priority
Tolerance of error is critical to foster an innovative organization

Notes: ERP, enterprise resource planning; HR-ICT, human resource information and communication technology.

that HR managers should consider in the adoption of HR-ICTs firmly grounded in the findings described above and our own experience and research.

Probably the most important suggestion is to ensure that the expected outcomes for introducing the HR-ICT will fit corporate strategy (Olivas-Luján et al., in press). For example, cost-savings might not be the most fitting outcome for firms that want to distinguish themselves as giving a personalized service to their customers. Some companies might argue that the service provided to employees does not have to mirror the service the company will give its external customers, but the fact of the matter is that organizational cultures are created through consistency, not by treating employees as second-rate citizens. Remember also that the past matters: successful marginal adoptions of HR-ICTs pave the ground for more radical innovations. Industry (or company) seasonality is also important to schedule training programs for using a new innovation; for example, December would be the worst month for training employees on how to use a new online record-keeping system in a retailer firm!

Similarly, one should not try to adopt HR-ICTs (or any other type of innovations) simply to be able to claim being the first; beware of championing a new idea for the sake of innovating. Still, bandwagon arguments (i.e. 'our competition already is using this ICT!') might not be very 'rational', but they are powerful! Relatedly, a sense of urgency is frequently a pre-requirement to innovation adoption and other types of organizational change. As early as it may be prudent, identify and involve key users – not just top managers – in the decision process, and confirm, rather than assume familiarity with the innovation platform (e.g. advanced knowledge of browsers for web-based applications cannot be guaranteed for most organizations). In the best case scenario, your proposal or your support for an innovation is a well thought-out business case with multiple justifications. Include a description of current and expected cycle times, cost savings in an annualized basis (without neglecting the typically heavy upfront investment that many innovations require), and as many indicators as you see needed to fairly make your case in a way that is congruent with your organizational culture.

Qualitative work on e-HRM by Ruël et al. (2004) suggests that, at least for some firms, the promise that automation of personnel processes will lead to a more strategic approach is less immediate than cost and service cycle time reductions might be. In their study of five large firms in Europe, they found that competencies were hardly improved, but administrative burdens were decreased. For managers, this might suggest keeping a good dose of cautious optimism when making the business case for the acquisition and deployment of an HR-ICT. In particular, for innovations that will be used by the company employees, use socialization programs and events to bring them 'up to speed' while resisting the desire to demand or expect 100% acceptance –have the organizational goals in perspective, not HR's subgoals.

Keep in mind also that certain transactions (e.g. terminations, mortality in employee record-keeping, etc.) cannot be automated without losing required compassion and human touch. Furthermore, the way that the implementation of an e-HRM strategy impacts organizations is an evident priority that must be more closely researched in the near future.

Conclusion

Much remains to be studied in this novel field that is effectively transforming the HR function. Effects of e-HRM on the personnel staff's job attitudes, productivity, and other outcomes should be carefully and systematically studied (e.g. the work of Ajzen and Fishbein, 2005 or Venkatesh et al., 2003 on attitudes' effects on adoption of technologies, or Galang and Ferris, 1997 on HR power may be of great help). Including other countries, particularly those whose native language is not English, should also advance our understanding in a way that is useful for companies with an international presence. Numerous possibilities open as we make progress in what effects might culture, industrial relations systems, and similar national-level variables might have in acceptance of HR-ICTs and ultimately, on productivity for firms in different nations, and for organizations that cross-borders such as multinationals and other growing organizational forms.

DOI theory offers a powerful set of tools to improve our understanding of who, when, and how HR-ICTs will be adopted in organizations. In this chapter, we have summarized some of the most important elements for using this very well-known and useful paradigm. We have shown results from our ongoing research program, interspersing suggestions for practice and concluded with suggestions for future study. It is our hope that this chapter will be of great help for its readers in managing the deployment of HR-ICTs in their organizations.

Acknowledgments

This study was supported by research grants from the International Business Center, U. of Pittsburgh, from the College of Business, Clarion U. of Pennsylvania, CONACyT (Mexico's science foundation), and Tecnológico de Monterrey, main campus.

References

Ajzen, I. and Fishbein, M. (2005) The influence of attitudes on behavior. In *The Handbook of Attitudes* (D. Albarracín, B.T. Johnson, and M.P. Zanna, eds.) pp. 173–221). Mahwah, NJ: Erlbaum.

Anderson Consulting (1999) What is virtual HR? *Change Management* online magazine.

Bass, F.M. (1969) A new product growth model for consumer durables. *Manage. Sci.* 15, 215–27.

Cambridge-MIT Institute (2006) *Centre for Competitiveness and Innovation Events*. Available online at: www.innovation.jbs.cam.ac. uk(last accessed 21 November 2007).

CedarCrestone (2002) *Human Resources Self Service/Portal Survey*. 5th Annual edn. Baltimore, MD: Cedar Group.

CedarCrestone (2003) *Workforce Technologies Survey*. 6th Annual edn. Baltimore, MD: Cedar Group.

CedarCrestone (2004) *Workforce Technologies Survey.* 7th Annual edn. Alpharetta, GA: CedarCrestone.

CedarCrestone (2005) *Workforce Technologies and Service Delivery Approaches Survey.* 8th Annual edn. Alpharetta, GA: CedarCrestone.

CedarCrestone (2006) *Workforce Technologies and Service Delivery Approaches Survey.* 9th Annual edn. Alpharetta, GA: CedarCrestone.

Chartered Institute of Personnel and Development. (2004) *People and Technology: is HR Getting the Best out of IT? Survey Report.* London: CIPD.

Daft, R.L. (1978) A dual-core model of organizational innovation. *Acad. Manage. J.* 21, 193–210.

Damanpour, F. and Evan, W. M. (1984) Organizational innovation and performance: the problem of 'organizational lag.' *Admin. Sci. Quart.* 29, 392–402.

Deloitte (2005) *The State of HR in Central Europe: Do you Measure up?* Prague: Deloitte Czech Republic BV.

DeSanctis, G. (1986) Human resource information systems: a current assessment. *MIS Quart.* 10, 15–27.

FastCompany. (2006) *Innovation and Creativity Guide.* Available online at: www.fastcompany.com/guides/innovation.html (last accessed 21 September 2007).

Financial Times Innovate 2006 Summit (2006) *FT Innovate 2006: Innovation for Growth.* Available online at: www.ftinnovate.com/2006/home.asp (last accessed 21 November 2007).

Finland's European Presidency Website (2006) *Prime Minister Matti Vanhanen's Views Prior to the Lahti Summit: Growth from Innovation.* Available online at: www.eu2006.fi/news_and_documents/other_documents/vko42/en_GB/1161247315865 (last accessed 21 September 2007).

Florkowski, G.W. and Olivas-Luján, M.R. (2006) The diffusion of human-resource information-technology innovations in US and non-US firms. *Pers. Rev.* 35, 684–710.

Galang, M.C. and Ferris, G.R. (1997) Human resource department power and influence through symbolic action. *Hum. Relat.* 50, 1403-26.

Gardner, S.D., Lepak, D.P., and Bartol, K.M. (2003) Virtual HR: the impact of information technology on the human resource professional. *J. Vocation. Behav.* 63, 159–79.

Greengard, S. (1998) Putting online recruiting to work. *Workforce* 77, 73–6.

Greengard, S. (2000) Virtual paper cuts. *Workforce* 79, 16–8.

Gueutal, H.G. and Stone, D.L. (eds.) (2005) *The Brave New World of eHR: Human Resources in the Digital Age*. San Francisco: Jossey-Bass.

Gurbaxani, V. (1990) Diffusion in computing networks: the case of BITNET. *Commun. ACM* 33, 65–75.

InformationWeek. (2006) *Innovation 100: The Customer*. Available online at: www.informationweek.com/816/i100splash.html (last accessed 21 September 2007).

IRS Employment Review (2002) *Still waiting for the e-HR revolution*. Issue 763, 11 November.

Kavanagh, J. (1998) Personnel managers emerge as IT pioneers. *Financial Times FT-IT Review* 7 October 1998, XIII.

Kossek, E.E. (1989) *The Acceptance of Human Resource Innovation: Lessons for Management*. New York: Quorum Books.

Kwon, T.H. and Zmud, R.W. (1987) Unifying the fragmented models of information systems implementation. In *Critical Issues in Information Systems Research* (J.R. Boland and R.A. Hirschheim, eds.) pp. 227–51. New York: John Wiley.

Mahajan, V., Muller, E., and Wind, Y. (2000) *New-Product Diffusion Models*. NY: Springer.

Martin, G. (2006) Reconceptualizing absorptive capacity to explain the e-enablement of the HR function (e-HR) in organizations. *Proceedings of the First European Academic Workshop on e-HRM*. Enschede, the Netherlands: University of Twente.

McGregor, J. (2006) The world's most innovative companies. *BusinessWeek* 24 April 2006; pp. 63–76.

Mercer HR Consulting (2002) *Using the Power of HR to Create New Value: a Study of HR Transformations in Latin American Organizations*. New York: Mercer Human Resource Consulting.

Mercer HR Consulting (2003) *Transforming HR for Business Results: a Study of US Organizations*. New York: Mercer Human Resource Consulting.

Ngai, E.W.T. and Wat, F. K. T. (2006) Human resource information systems: a review and empirical analysis. *Pers. Rev.* 35, 297–314.

Olivas-Luján, M.R. (2003) *Determinants of the assimilation of information and communication technologies in human resource service delivery in Canada and the United States of America*. Doctoral dissertation, Katz Graduate School of Business, U of Pittsburgh, Pittsburgh, PA. Available online at: http://etd.library.pitt.edu:80/ETD/available/etd-07232003-191847/ (last accessed 21 September 2007).

Olivas-Luján, M.R., Ramírez, J., and Zapata Cantú, L. (2007). e-HRM in Mexico: adapting innovations for global competitiveness. *Int. J. Manpower* 28, 418–34.

Personnel Today (2002) HR budget at IBM slashed through e-HR. 4 June, 1, 8.

Prescott, M.B. and Conger, S.A. (1995) Information technology innovations – a classification by IT locus of impact and research approach. *Data base Adv. Inf. Sy.* 26, 20–41.

Rai, A., Ravichandran, T., and Samaddar, S. (1998) How to anticipate the Internet's global diffusion. *Commun. ACM* 41, 97–106.

Rogers, E. (2003) *Diffusion of Innovations*. (5th edn.), New York: Free Press.

Rogers, E.M. (1962) *Diffusion of Innovations*. New York: Free Press of Glencoe.

Ruël, H.J.M., Bondarouk, T.V., and Looise, J.K. (2004) E-HRM: innovation or irritation? An exploration of web-based human resource management in five large companies. *Manage. Rev.* 15, 364–80.

Shrivastava, S. and Shaw, J.B. (2003) Liberating HR through technology. *Hum. Resource Manage.* 42, 201–22.

Society for Human Resource Management (2005) *2005 HR Technology Survey Report*. Alexandria, VA: SHRM Research Department.

Strohmeier, S. (2007) Research in e-HRM. Review and implications. *HRM Rev.* 17, 19–37.

Teng, J.T.C., Grover, V., and Guttler, W. (2002) Information technology innovations: general diffusion patterns and its relationships to innovation characteristics. *IEEE Trans. Engin. Manage.* 49, 13–27.

Towers Perrin (2001) *Web-Based Self-Service: The Current State of the Art. Executive Summary*. New York: Towers Perrin.

Towers Perrin/IBM (1992) *Priorities for Competitive Advantage: A Worldwide Human Resource Study*. New York: Towers Perrin.

Tornatzky, L.G. and Klein, K.J. (1982) Innovation characteristics and innovation adoption-implementation: a meta analysis of findings. *IEEE Trans. Engin. Manage.* 29, 28–45.

Venkatesh, V., Morris, M.G., Davis, G.B., and Davis, F.D. (2003) User acceptance of information technology: toward a unified view. *MIS Quart.* 27, 425–78.

Watson Wyatt Worldwide (2000) *O efeito net: Internet, intranet e eHR, pesquisa conduzida no Brasil em 2000*. Available online at: www.watsonwyatt.com/research/resrender.asp? id=w-421& page=1 (last accessed 21 September 2007).

Watson Wyatt Worldwide (2002a) *B2E/eHR Survey Results 2002. Report Summary.* Available online at: www. watsonwyatt.com/ asia-pacific/research/resrender.asp? id = 2000861 &page =1 (last accessed 21 September 2007).

Watson Wyatt Worldwide (2002b) *eHR™: Getting Results Along the Journey – 2002 Survey Report Summary.* Available online at: www.watsonwyatt.com/asia-pacific/research/resrender.asp? id=W-524&page=1 (last accessed 21 September 2007).

Watson Wyatt Worldwide (2004) *2003/2004 Greater China eHR Survey Report.* Available online at: http://www.watsonwyatt. com/ canada-english/research/resrender.asp?id=E-204&page=1 (last accessed 21 September 2007).

Welsh Assembly Government (2006) *Innovative Companies in Wales.* Available online at: www.wda.co.uk/ index.cfm/ technology_ and _innovation /innovation _works/innovative_welsh_ companies/en8690 (last accessed 21 September 2007).

CHAPTER 10

Designing and Implementing e-HRM — a Structurational Approach to Investigating Technological and Organizational Change

Elke S. Schuessler

Introduction

Electronic human resource management (e-HRM) – the use of information technology (IT) to support HRM processes – is increasingly being applied in human resources (HR) departments to increase their efficiency and effectiveness by standardizing and streamlining HR processes and by relieving HR personnel from administrative burdens (Lengnick-Hall and Moritz, 2003). However, little systematic research has been completed to-date which analyses the processes of technology design and implementation in specific organizational contexts or assesses the impact of e-HRM on the delivery of HR services.

'Despite evidence of increasing use of HR-related technology by individual firms, there has been little theory development in this area.' (Shrivastava and Shaw, 2003, p. 202)

And, as argued by Huselid (2004), there is a need to develop new approaches for doing research and guiding practitioners on the intersection of HRM and IT to fill this gap.

In the related literature on organizational change and information technology, however, there is a good deal of theory which is useful in guiding new research programs and practice, and in making sense of the empirical data gathered within HRM. Robey and Boudreau (1999), for example, outlined the potential of IT to transform organizations, which has been a prominent theme in the management and information systems literatures ever since computers were introduced commercially in the 1950s. Beginning with deterministic approaches in which IT is either considered as an inescapable force imposed on organizations or as an enabler of change used by management to transform organizations, recent approaches have evolved which have argued for a more complex relationship between IT and organizational change.

Particularly promising in this respect is the research drawing on Giddens' (1984) structuration theory (e.g. Barley, 1990; Orlikowski and Robey, 1991; Orlikowski, 1992; 2000). From this perspective, the introduction of technology constitutes an inherently dynamic process in which human agents create and continuously change technology whilst the technology at the same time acts as a mediator of their action; agency and structure are therefore not independent but closely interlinked. Whilst structuration theory emphasizes the importance of the structures that agents refer to in their (inter)actions, it also stresses that these structures are not fixed but are continuously re-negotiated and takes into account the unintended consequences which might emerge from such action. These ideas connect two aspects of information systems research that appear to play a very important role in the e-HRM context, namely the questions of how information systems are developed and physically shaped by the actions of the users and how information systems influence the organizations in which they are implemented (Orlikowski and Robey, 1991).

What follows is an attempt to draw on existing structurational models of IT and organizational change to answer the following core research question: *How do organizational contexts influence the design and implementation processes of e-HRM initiatives and how do the design and implementation of e-HRM initiatives influence organizational contexts in turn?* In answering this question, I will first outline some of the core concepts and arguments put forward by the structurational framework. I will then describe the change processes of four organizations which have implemented e-HRM using the Pettigrew and Whipp (1991) framework of strategic change. Finally, I will discuss these findings in line with the concepts described, assess their contribution to future research, and summarize the implications for practitioners in the field.

Proposing a structurational model of technology in organizations

Structurational models of technology in organizations start from the intellectual divide between objectivist and subjectivist approaches to IT, the former treating IT as an independent variable capable of having a certain desired impact on organizations and the latter denying that information technology systems have any objective characteristics since their meanings are always mediated by the social interpretations offered by users (e.g. Orlikowski and Robey, 1991). Since both approaches neglect important aspects of the other, several authors have proposed a more complex relationship between IT and organizations. Drawing on Giddens' (1976; 1979; 1984) theory of structuration, they have integrated a role for both structure and agency (e.g. Barley, 1990; Orlikowski, 1992; 2000). Before turning to these models in more detail, however, it is necessary for non-specialists to give a brief overview of Giddens' core ideas.

First and most importantly, Giddens' concept of the *duality of structure* holds that the structure of social systems is constituted and physically shaped by human actors but at the same time mediates – *facilitates and constrains* – human action. Structures, analytically divided by Giddens into the dimensions of signification, domination and legitimation, gain relevance as agents explicitly or implicitly draw upon their knowledge of these structures when engaged in purposeful action. In so doing, they either reproduce or modify these structures over time. This process is called *structuration*. The rules agents draw on may be formal ('we have to clock in at 8 a.m.') or informal ('we usually have lunch at 1 p.m.') and, depending on their type as well as on the available resources, will have different implications for the structuration process.

Second, whilst agents in the structuration process are essentially viewed as *knowledgeable and reflexive* about their actions, Giddens also emphasized the *unacknowledged conditions* and *unintended consequences* of action. For example, a company's decision to make mobile telephones widely available to all employees may have the intended consequence of improving the availability of these employees but also the unintended consequence of increasing stress among them as they feel pressured to be available at all times – the 24/7 syndrome.

Third, Giddens analytically distinguishes three *modalities* of structuration which link the structural properties to agency, thus mediating social action. When enacting structural properties, actors draw on a stock of knowledge (*interpretative schemes*), use the allocative or authoritative resources available to them (*facilities*), and are guided by the *norms* applying to their social context (see Figure 10.1). In so doing they reconstitute their organization's institutional structure but are also able to transform it – especially when a social system is faced with an exogenous shock such as the arrival of a new technology (Barley, 1986). In his famous study of the introduction of identical computerized tomography (CT) scanning technology in two hospitals Barley found that, whilst the existing hierarchy between radiologists and technologists was re-affirmed in both cases, new and very different role definitions and behavioral

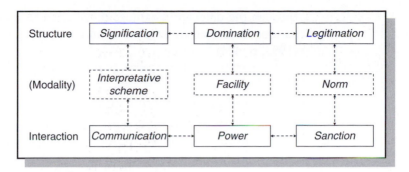

Figure 10.1
Dimensions of the duality of structure.
Source: Adapted from Giddens (1984, p. 29).

patterns emerged as unintended consequences of the technology being accommodated in the social settings. In one case, the technologists increasingly gained more responsibility, whereas in the second case they became more and more insecure and dependent on the radiologists until new radiologists were staffed.

The most important insight to be drawn from Giddens' abstract theorizing for an IT context is the recognition that structures do not exist apart from the human agents who enact and interpret it. Technology should therefore not be conceived of as some kind of static, external structural device, but rather as a set of structuring elements which only gains relevance as people regularly interact with certain properties of the technology in an ongoing process of structuration. Human agents thus shape the set of rules and resources that at the same time serve to shape their interaction with the technology. Put simply, a software package can only become a structure if it is used in some ongoing human action (Orlikowski, 2000).

In her earlier work, Orlikowski (1992) calls this the *duality of technology*:

'Technology is the product of human action, while it also assumes structural properties. That is, technology is physically constructed by actors working in a given social context, and technology is socially constructed by actors

> through the different meanings they attach to it and the various features they emphasize and use.' Orlikowski (1992, p. 406)

In her structurational model of technology she summarizes the four key influences operating continuously and simultaneously in the interaction between technology and organizations: IT is the product of human action as well as its medium; the organization's structures of signification, domination, and legitimation mediate the IT interaction; the IT interaction acts upon these organizational structures, either maintaining or changing them (see Figure 10.2).

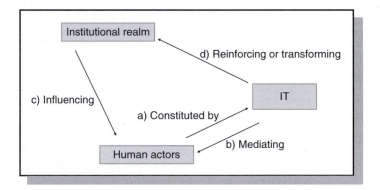

Figure 10.2
A structurational model of information technology.
Source: Adapted from Orlikowski (1992, p. 410) with permission. Copyright 2007, the Institute for Operations Research and the Management Sciences, USA.

According to this model, IT can play a central part in an organization's structuration process and vice versa. By representing social practices, for example, IT can provide a set of interpretative schemes through which users come to understand the world. Furthermore, by formalizing rules, an information system can reinforce the existing institutional order of authority. Finally, by formalizing sanctions, an information system can create an institutionalized moral order which helps to control behavior. At the same time, actors – whilst constrained by existing structures – also have opportunities to modify these structures as they engage in the social processes of software development and use.

It would, therefore, be misleading to view information technology as a separate entity existing outside the duality of structure and agency. The emerging structures of technology use should rather be viewed as part of the institutional realm, as a set of rules and resources (re-)constituted only in recurrent social practice, which was the position Orlikowski took in her later work (Orlikowski, 2000). This view acknowledges that, whilst users might use technologies in the way they were designed, they might also find ways to circumvent them or use them for another purpose. When looking at the development and implementation stages of a new technology as intended in this paper, it nonetheless proves useful to analytically separate the four processes as outlined in the model to be able to analyze how the current institutional realm of an organization influences the creation of a new one and vice versa.

Research methodology

Case selection

The four cases were selected following Yin's (1994) theoretical replication logic. Some form of e-HRM has been implemented in each of the organizations and all the cases are thus theoretically relevant. At the same time, the cases differ along several dimensions – targets, degree of organizational restructuring, or technology. So each case fulfils a different purpose in the analysis and produces contrasting results but for predictable reasons.

An overview of the cases, which are four German companies with an average headcount of 160 000 employees from the automobile, logistics, technology, and transport industries, is set out in Table 10.1.

The cases can be clustered in two groups. In the first group, the focus of the e-HRM initiative was on improving the effectiveness of particular higher-value-added HRM processes, with

Table 10.1

Case overview.

Company	Project description	Main target	Technology
Spring AG	Implementation of ESS/MSS scenarios to support the target agreement/achievement, performance appraisal, salary adjustment, and training processes as part of a larger e-HRM program.	Process effectiveness/ efficiency	Own development/ web
Summer AG	Implementation of an integrated recruitment system with automated pre-selection and fully integrated workflows as part of a larger e-HRM program.	Process effectiveness/ efficiency	Own development/ web
Autumn AG	Restructuring of the HRM department towards an HRM shared service centre. Concentration on the mere adjustment of the existing PeopleSoft modules.	Cost cutting, quality increase	PeopleSoft
Winter AG	Restructuring of the HRM department towards an HRM SSC organization. Implementation of SAP-based workflows for administrative processes. Implementation of an order management system.	Cost cutting	SAP

Notes: ESS, employee self-service; HRM, human resource management; MSS, manager self-service.

the initiative being part of a larger e-HRM project. In the second group, the focus was on cutting HR costs by standardizing administrative tasks and was accompanied by a major organizational restructuring effort, i.e. the building of an HR shared service center (see Chapter 5: Restructuring the HR Function: HR Shared Service Centers in the Netherlands). It is therefore possible to generate some initial theory on such different uses of technology in HRM from these cases and different contexts.

Data collection

This study employed a participant observation methodology, which is particularly useful for studying processes in detail and over a period of time as required by a structuration-based research approach (e.g. Jorgensen, 1989). In three of the cases I was involved as a management consultant working on projects in the companies – Spring AG, Summer AG and Winter AG – for an average period of 8 months each. However, only in the first case was I able to accompany the e-HRM project from the beginning until the roll-out and training phases. To overcome these limitations, I conducted additional semi-structured interviews with a consultant and a client-side member of the project management team in each of the three cases. This has been done to get additional information on outcomes and to be able to reflect my own interpretations critically. In the fourth case, Autumn AG, data were collected from three successive interviews with a member of the project management team over a 6-month period. Finally, I analyzed the project documentation (PowerPoint presentations, strategy/vision documents, cases, etc.), which were made available to me in all of the four cases.

Data analysis

In order to structure this vast amount of information, I defined some a priori categories for coding the data on the basis of Pettigrew and Whipp's (1991) well-known framework of strategic change, which fits in well with the basic assumptions of structuration theory. Pettigrew and Whipp regard strategic change as a continuous and iterative process occurring in and influenced by a given historical, organizational, and economic context. Therefore, not only the *content* of a chosen change initiative is important, but also the *process* of change and the external and internal *context* in which it occurs. Furthermore, as argued by Pettigrew in a later paper on processual analysis (1997), the analysis of processes needs to be linked to the outcomes of the process under investigation. A further category of outcomes was therefore included.

Whilst coding the data, a larger number of subcategories (e.g. HRM vision/mission, project structure, major obstacles, sources of resistance) were developed inductively in the first case which guided the coding of the remaining cases. New categories were added in each new case where necessary and the previous cases were then revisited on the basis of these new categories. After the coding was completed all the categories were compared again across the four cases and revised where necessary and possible ('open coding'; Strauss and Corbin, 1990). Former consulting colleagues who were interviewed in each case were then asked to check the coded information, and the case descriptions below were developed on this basis.

Research results

Case 1: Spring AG

Context

As the Spring AG was part of a global group and had many partner organizations spread all over the world, the central HRM department was faced with the challenge of integrating different country and company cultures, different management personalities, and different HRM guidelines and processes within the framework of the corporate network. The HRM mission, directly derived from the business strategy, was to attract, retain, and develop exceptional people by creating a truly international working climate, to provide instruments for steering the overall HRM processes, to link the partner organizations in all HRM related issues, and to be a strategic partner of management in achieving the corporate targets.

These targets were expected to be achieved through an extensive e-HRM strategy which would allow for an integrated management of all processes on an international level. A number of legacy systems custom-developed by the consulting firm in previous projects were already in place: an organization management system, a recruiting solution, a communication platform connecting the European HRM departments, an HRM portal, and an employee database. Additionally, the SAP payroll module was used.

Content

Due to the particular importance attached to developing and retaining excellent employees, personnel development was selected as the first area in which e-HRM should be implemented. These processes seemed the most promising in bringing benefits to all stakeholders as several problems had been identified, which were expected to be solved by system support. First, the personnel development processes of agreeing targets, appraising performance, adjusting salaries, and defining training measures were not standardized across the different locations. Second, there was no transparency about salaries and bonus payments due to a lack of generally binding guidelines leading to confusion and dissatisfaction amongst the employees. Third, the executives were not very reliable in completing the processes on time for the annual salary round, and HRM had to invest much time in following up on those executives.

In order to tackle these problems, HRM had developed a new compensation and benefits system and had revised the target agreement and performance appraisal forms accordingly. These instruments were to be implemented company-wide with the support of a technical solution building upon the legacy systems in place and providing end-users with an easy-to-use web interface. In this way, transparent guidelines could be communicated, standards could be enforced, and the process status could be monitored easily by all stakeholders.

A project team was set up consisting of three consultants and, on average, eight software developers who also belonged to the consultant firm. A designer was responsible for designing the web interfaces. According to the initial plan, the project was to follow the standard stages of software development: optimizing processes, developing a vision document, writing use cases, developing the technical concept, and then building a prototype. However, as the project was subjected to an immense time pressure – the system had to be ready and running for the next salary round which was 4 months ahead – the phases could not really be followed through systematically as will be shown in the next section.

Process

The project started off smoothly as the project team soon agreed on the new processes and on the functionalities of the system, and the HRM department was very supportive of the project. The developers, however, soon realized that they were not able to develop a stable solution in such a short amount of time. Whilst the project manager on the consultant side signaled this risk very early on, the project manager on the Spring AG side was neither willing, nor able, to make any compromises. The deadline was set by the annual salary round; no additional resources were available, and the scope of the project could not be reduced as the system was presented to high-level executives, whose salaries had to be calculated by the system.

As Spring AG's project manager had no expertise in software development, he did not take the risk of not being able to provide a bug-free system seriously and, instead of working on a solution, he simply increased the pressure on the project team by pressing for more and more features to be included in the system, realizing that his career was at stake if the system would not be accepted by the executives. The chief executive officer (CEO) of the consulting firm, who was a friend of Spring AG's project manager, followed him in this strategy and gave no backing to his employees.

The morale in the project team sank accordingly as it felt incapable of providing a stable solution if new features had to be added all the time whilst at the same time its concerns were ignored and no alternative strategy could be negotiated. However, despite the increasing dissatisfaction and frustration, everyone in the team worked overtime for the entire period as the direct pressure exerted by both the client and the CEO was very high.

As expected, the first pilot version of the system, which was released shortly before the official roll-out, was very unstable and the project manager on the client side was shocked to see what he refused to take notice of before. Only then was it possible to negotiate a new implementation strategy with him, which involved focusing on stabilizing the core feature – the calculation of executive salaries – and leaving out additional features such as the reporting tool and the target agreement process, as new targets did not have to be agreed before the completion of the salary round. In the last days before the roll-out, everyone working on the project, including the project managers, was testing the system day and night and the developers tried their best to stabilize the system.

Parallel to the system development a change and training process took place in which executives and employees separately were informed about the new processes and the new system by the HRM department. Three HRM employees were trained in using the system by the consultants, and these HRM employees then gave first-level support to the employees and executives.

Outcomes

In the end, a system was provided in which there were no more salary related mistakes, but many features that were promised to the executives were not working properly and the expected management buy-in was much lower than expected. As several complicated mistakes emerged when new features were added after the roll-out, these had to be fixed by 'work-around' solutions with the code becoming very complex and difficult to handle. The relationship between the two project managers and between the project managers and the CEO was severely disrupted, and the relationship with the consulting firm only continued because of the initial friendship between the client and the CEO.

To finish the system and to prepare the international roll-out – which was to follow the national roll-out – a new project team was set up with new project managers on both the consultant and the company side. This second project was not under the same time pressure and, as reported by one of the consultants, could be completed without any major disruptions. However, quite a lot of resources had to be invested in simplifying the code in order to make the system more readily applicable in other organizational contexts. This investment could have been avoided had the project not been subjected to the immense pressure outlined above. The effectiveness targets that were set could nonetheless be achieved.

Case 2: Summer AG

Context

The HRM department of Summer AG was faced with the challenge of supporting the company target of securing the successful recruitment of employees, particularly in technical areas where the applicant market was very tight. Additionally, the HR department itself had the vision of setting standards in 'best practice HRM'. This entailed cutting administrative tasks, increasing the availability of HR personnel, increasing transparency, solving communication problems, and improving the service for employees with the help of information technology, as well as extending the counseling function for employees and becoming a strategic business partner of management.

A comprehensive e-HRM strategy was therefore developed to help HR to achieve these targets. The introduction of technology aimed to achieve explicitly a fundamental organizational change and to avoid the danger of simply supporting existing processes with a system.

No wide-ranging legacy systems were in place, except for a self-developed administrative system as well as a self-developed recruitment system, whose development had been stopped a couple of years before the e-HRM project was approved.

Content

The improvement of the existing recruitment solution together with the optimization of the recruitment process was the first step on the way to e-HRM due to the high strategic importance of recruiting for Summer AG. Because there was to be a number of other e-HRM developments, this project assumed a high level of symbolic importance. The project was divided into several subprojects and followed the standard stages of software development: optimizing processes, developing a vision document, writing use cases, developing the technical concept, and then building a prototype. Additionally, a business case was calculated and an international feasibility study was conducted. On average, 20 people worked in the core team of the project at any given time, with a larger number of consultants in the first phases and a higher number of system developers in the later stages. All subprojects were staffed with at least half of HRM-IT department employees and half with external consultants. The consultants, therefore, had a dual function: to simply provide manpower whilst applying their expertise in HRM process optimization and system development.

Several major changes were to be achieved with the project: All applicants would enter their profile online so that an extensive applicant pool could be established, in which the operational departments could actively search for suitable applicants. A highly detailed and comprehensive matching algorithm would pre-select the right applicants for a job posting, and service level agreements between the HR department and the operational departments would increase transparency and provide for more flexibility. As a result, the operational departments would take more responsibility for clarifying their requirements and for actively searching for suitable candidates.

Process

From the beginning, the project had been characterized by a high degree of consultation between the different participants and stakeholders – consultants, HRM-IT employees, central HRM employees and decentralized HRM departments – as attention to all stakeholder interests was deemed to be important in ensuring commitment to the project. For example, regular workshops were held with the recruiters from the decentralized HR departments, which held a vote on the functions to be included in the new system. These coordination costs, together with the technical complexity of the system envisaged, led to delays in the project progression very early on. The project also began with some tensions between the consultants and the HRM-IT employees as no clear role could be attributed to the consultants. They had to act both as an employee, thereby working on the same hierarchical level, and as a consultant. As a consequence, the relationship was somewhat competitive and defined by a lack of trust on both sides.

The roll-out strategy was to present the end-users with a pilot version of the system that comprised all modules but with limited functions in each module, so that the end-users could get a feeling for the entire process. The 'go-live' of this pilot version was delayed by 6 months, but even then the pilot system was not ready to be presented and rather than being a success this roll-out lead to a major crisis. Many of the functions displayed in the pilot led to a system crash and many of the functionalities important to the users were missing. Also, the interface of the system was highly complex and difficult to use, and the end-users, who had only seen and agreed to the new system on the basis of previous paper presentations, were very upset and disappointed by what they saw. This resulted in a fundamental lack of trust in the new system.

The roll-out was accompanied by a comprehensive change program and a special service provider was hired for this purpose. The focus of the change program was on gaining user acceptance, which was done by explaining how the users would get perfect support from a system which was tailor-made to their needs rather than a standard solution. As a consequence, expectations were high and, as argued by one of the consultants, these unrealistic expectations added to the crisis of the first roll-out: rather than preparing the end-users realistically for what they would see in the pilot version and informing them about the hurdles and stages in software development, the users were given promises that could not be fulfilled by technical development. Expectations rose further due to the 6-month delay of the roll-out, and again this was not counteracted by the change managers.

In response to this crisis, the change process was modified and the end-users were involved more closely in the development and testing of the second prototype. Additionally, users were trained and informed about the new processes in several workshops, using multipliers to spread the information throughout the organization. The consultant concluded that, to avoid these problems, small pilots should be developed very early in the process. Only in this way could such unexpected shocks be avoided, and user feedback be taken into account in time.

Resistance to the project mainly came from the executives in the operational departments who were forced to stick to the processes set by the system, and who were made responsible for entering their required skill profiles for applicants themselves in a very structured and detailed way, rather than just calling up the HR department as they had done before. The recruiters and HR employees were generally quite positive about the system, even though they were reluctant to support the matching functionality as they did not feel that a task they had previously completed themselves could now be handled automatically by a system, which implies that their competence was no longer required.

Outcomes

The system went live 1 year later and required about twice as much programming capacity as originally planned. Therefore, the project – at least in the short run – was a huge financial strain. User satisfaction continued to be low after the implementation as the system was still very complex and had performance problems. The initial target of forcing all applicants to use online applications also could not be reached due to the usability and performance problems of the system. In the course of time, however, another consultancy firm was hired to develop a concept for improving the usability of the system, and the system has been improved accordingly. At the time of writing in April 2007, about 80% of all applications are submitted online, and the effectiveness of the process, measured by the improved matching and the improved supply of candidates, has increased.

According to the official information given by the project manager, applicant surveys have been conducted which showed that applicants were generally pleased with the services offered on the new website. In contrast, the consultant reported that several applicants were very dissatisfied with the level of detail required for entering a skill profile. This, however, may not be a problem inherent to the Summer AG solution, but may be related to a more general problem of online applications: applicants have to enter their data anew into very different online application forms for each company they are applying to, rather than being able to send a standard curriculum vitae to several companies at once. As some applicants may not be up to this task, it is questionable whether the company target of recruiting the best candidates can be met by an all-electronic strategy.

Case 3: Autumn AG

Context

In the Autumn AG, several attempts have been made in the past to transform the HR function into a business partner model, the main targets being higher efficiency and effectiveness, better services, and more strategic involvement. As the company consists of several subsidiaries at many locations, more than 30 HR departments are presently in place and about half of the administrative HR tasks are being dealt with at over 150 different locations. Accordingly, processes, products, and role definitions are very inconsistent and the qualification level of HR employees varies widely.

The projects conducted in previous years attempted to achieve this transformational change in incremental steps, such as a change in role definitions in one project and a redefinition of processes in another. However, no lasting effect had been achieved in these projects as the informal structures were kept alive and in many divisions the status quo simply remained under a different label.

Content

The reasons for the concerted change are as follows. In a concerted change, about 200 processes, role definitions, organizational structures, and systems shall now be simultaneously adjusted to achieve the desired transformation of the HRM function. A first subproject has been set up to define the role definitions of the local HR staff and to develop and conduct the according qualification measures and the quality management. In a second subproject processes are harmonized, standardized, and optimized, and the PeopleSoft module in place is expanded in order to automate a larger part of these processes. In a third subproject, seven shared service centers (SSCs) are being established in different regions in which all the administrative HRM tasks would be handled. This will be implemented in three successive steps. The final subproject is responsible for the change management and for communication. A total of 25 full-time equivalents work for this project and, as a result of the failing predecessors, no consultancies are involved.

Project progression

The project is now in the first implementation phase and up until now the most critical issue concerned the establishment of the SSCs and the corresponding organizational changes. Resistance has mainly come from two sources. First, the HR departments have been very reluctant due to a high uncertainty about their future role and tasks. A massive communication campaign has therefore been started, which helped broadening the support for the project.

Second, the works council, whose approval is required for the establishment of the SSCs, has always been very critical concerning the targets of the project and has strongly interfered at several stages. The number of SSCs, for example, would have been lower if it was not for the works council's concern for a reasonable commuting distance for all the employees moving to the SSC. The works council recently threatened to stop the informal negotiations and enter a legal dispute, and thus a new settlement of interests has been negotiated in which the project management team had to make further concessions. Until there is an electronic personnel file, for example, the files cannot be moved to the SSCs so the records will need to be sent by mail or fax between the different locations.

Outcomes

Because of the seven locations, it was relatively easy to staff the SSCs on a voluntary basis and the harmonization and standardization of the first group of less complex processes was unproblematic. Changing the role definitions of the local HR staff, however, proved to be much more difficult. Despite several communication and qualification sessions, HR employees still feel insecure about their future tasks and it can be expected that they will not approve of many of the changes required for the more complex and influential processes which will be defined in the second stage of the project. Since the Head of HR is in charge of the project, however, certain changes could nonetheless be enforced formally if necessary.

Technically only those processes which could be supported by the existing PeopleSoft solution have been implemented so far, so nothing can be said as of now about the technological challenges of establishing a ticketing system and fully automated workflows.

Case 4: Winter AG

Context

In Winter AG, the HR department was faced with rapidly increasing overhead costs and very high workforce variable and fixed costs, and so was forced to develop a strict cost-cutting strategy. The mission therefore was (1) to optimize and automate HRM processes as much as possible, (2) to build a highly standardized 'HRM factory' for administrative tasks and, (3) in the long run, to be a major player in HR outsourcing, offering services to other companies.

The HR department had been in a period of transition for approximately 10 years before the e-HRM project was initiated. In the first change project, HRM staff was trained to develop broad skill profiles, covering a range of administrative as well as higher value-added tasks to offer better services to employees. Then, in line with the general trend of making HR a strategic business partner and reducing administrative tasks, this process was reversed and the personnel function was split into an administrative 'HRM services' function and an 'HRM department' function for higher value-added tasks.

As the company consists of several divisions managed quite independently from each other, each division has its own HRM department. A subsequent project was therefore started to harmonize the different HRM processes between these divisions. Within this context, the HR services function became more centralized (reduced from more than 10 down to six locations) and an SSC was established at the headquarters.

This SSC was equipped with an order management system and became the central entry point for all administrative tasks. The processes, however, were still completed manually. The SSC employees were provided with electronic checklists listing all the necessary steps that had to be completed. As the processes had not yet been standardized, several checklists existed to take account of the differences between the divisions.

Even though an increasing number of employees followed the new processes and contacted the administrative HRM staff via the hotline, a parallel, informal structure remained in place where employees could call up 'their' HRM administrators on their old telephone numbers and where many SSC employees followed the old procedures as they were not forced to follow a standardized procedure. The head of HRM services was still under pressure to cut costs in his department massively.

Content

This was the ground on which the e-HRM project was planned. The main focus was to further optimize and standardize the already harmonized processes and to automate them as much as possible. There was a very clear vision of what 'lean HRM' should look like, and the long-term vision was to become a service provider for administrative HRM tasks for other companies as well.

On a technical level, the aim of the e-HRM project was to harmonize the very heterogeneous software landscape, which consisted of SAP as the standard solution and more than 50 self-developed stand-alone solutions. Due to a lack of standardization, however, the quality of the data held in these systems was very low.

Process

After an evaluation study, a project team was set up to optimize and implement 35 processes which were expected to have the largest savings potential. The project was divided into three subprojects and several consultancies were involved. The first subproject was responsible for defining products and optimizing processes and was staffed with up to eight people. The second subproject was responsible for the technical implementation and was staffed with 10–15 people. The third subproject was responsible for the change management and was staffed with two people. No consultants were involved in this last subproject.

To understand the further developments in this project, it is important to know that the person in charge of the project was the head of HRM services, who was under pressure to cut costs. However, he did not have the authority to actually define the new processes – this authority was held by the different divisions who had to agree to all the changes that were presented by the project team. As the divisions had no real incentive for supporting the standardization of processes but rather had to sacrifice some of their privileges, the project was in a way doomed from the start.

The product and process team (subproject 1) started off with the mission to 'really innovate' the processes, i.e. to design the 'leanest' processes irrespective of what the employees thought would never pass the revision by the divisions. This task was already met with apprehension, particularly from the side of the employees who 'knew' their organization and felt they were wasting their time on something which would not come through afterwards anyway. Whilst the consultants in the team were commissioned to keep up the motivation to innovate, they also felt that it was necessary to involve the rest of the organization early on in the process to avoid a big disappointment afterwards. This was considered especially important as the morale of many HRM employees was already quite low due to the long history of changes, which kept the HRM organization in a constant state of transformation and which gave rise to high levels of insecurity about what would come next.

Additionally, the technical team, which had drafted up the basic architecture of the system, soon required properly defined processes in order to keep on working on the technical specification, which meant that the processes had to go through the revision by the divisions. Several meetings were held in which these major threats to the success of the project were discussed, but due to the architecture of the project outlined above the management team was uncertain about how to involve the rest of the organization in order to get a positive response to the innovations. Finally, a small number of processes with a high benefit for managers to secure a management buy-in was selected and presented in the revision. As expected, the processes were not accepted in the presented form. The processes had to be changed backwards to re-include the divisional specificities, and processes were sometimes discussed down to the level of codes in long and laborious meetings.

Simultaneously, the calculation of a new business case was commissioned, and it became clear that the basis for calculating the savings potential has never been very sound. The data were mainly taken from self-reports or from estimations of HRM employees and could be expected to be very biased. Also, slack times were not included in the calculation and the estimated savings potential was much too high. Therefore, the management team as well as the project members became more and more uncertain about the actual savings potential of the project. The project was therefore put on hold and the focus shifted to the change management tasks severely neglected before.

Outcomes

As described by one of the consultants who has now become an employee of Winter AG, the resistance from the divisions could never really be overcome and the project had to be severely downsized. The processes were clustered into three groups – simple self-service type processes, processes with a simple approval step, and processes with complex approval workflows – and only the 15 simple processes have been implemented for now.

Technically, a platform has been developed on which the other, more complex processes can easily be implemented in the future, but here it is already clear the processes will not be implemented in the very streamlined form originally envisioned. The personnel departments in the divisions refused to give away any of their decision-making power and thus all the processes still have to pass the local divisions. This, however, is still considered as an achievement, as the alternative would have been to still have to consult with the local HR departments before being able to start a workflow electronically, which is something employees and managers are now able to do.

This technical platform, however, is not available as part of the SAP standard solution, so again a self-made system had to be developed, increasing rather than reducing the complexity of the system landscape. Furthermore, some workflows do not run through automatically due to inconsistencies in the database – data have to be stored in a parallel system until fully approved – and the role of an administrator had to be established who is manually taking care of these problems. Again, SAP is being blamed here as the system should be able to deal with these inconsistencies automatically but is not.

The organizational change has been met with some resistance as well, especially from the (powerful) executives and the (less powerful) administrative HR staff. Both sides felt and probably still feel very uneasy with working under factory-like conditions with a cockpit showing work tasks and the status of each process. However, no hard data are available at the present stage of actual system usage and satisfaction with the system.

The works council did not take much interest in the project due to a major trade dispute about the pending agreement on tariffs, but now with a new tariff agreement due in April 2007 a number of change requests have already been made as some of the processes need to be changed accordingly.

Discussion

Regarding the research question of how organizational contexts influence the design and implementation processes of e-HRM initiatives and how the design and implementation of e-HRM initiatives influence organizational contexts in turn, it is clear that in all of the cases the existing institutional structure as enacted by organizational agents heavily influenced the technological and organizational change processes and this in turn either reinforced or changed the existing institutional structures. As structures live through the enactment of human agents, new structures could not simply be imposed on the organization. Rather, each project can be seen as an ongoing process of structuration, with different agents drawing on the existing rules and resources, thereby reproducing or changing them. The three dimensions of structure can hereby only be separated analytically. In reality, they are interlinked (Giddens, 1984).

When looking at the structures of signification, the main influence in case of Spring AG was the project manager's lack of knowledge about the management of technology problems. This heavily influenced the course of the project and was mainly responsible for the initially unsatisfactory outcome. His inability to recognize the potential consequences of the problems voiced by the developers may by related to the resource dimension: since no additional resources were deployed, the system had to be stripped of several important features and became a technically not very elegant solution, which had to be re-programmed after the deadline. Furthermore, the existing norms about how the salary round should be conducted were formalized through the technology and, by providing greater transparency for the HRM department, make it much easier to sanction deviations from this norm as the technology is used.

In Summer AG, one major issue was the norm of a highly democratic company culture. As every stakeholder was included in the development process, many functions and features had to be added, which made the system very complex and caused a delay. This, of course, was only possible because additional resources were made available to the project, probably because of the high symbolic and strategic meaning attached to it. The unrealistic management of expectations in the communication campaign, however, which was probably felt to be necessary to legitimize the changes that were being made to the recruitment processes, resulted in an immediate lack of trust in the system and as a result users were more likely to work around the system wherever possible.

The most salient point in the case of Autumn AG is the power important stakeholders can use to alter significantly the content of a change project to make if fit with existing values and regulations. Without the works council, less then seven SSCs would have been established and many of the processes would have looked differently. A second important aspect is the difficulty to depart from existing structures of signification, as the HR employees cannot envision their new role as a strategic business partner and therefore cling to their existing role definitions.

Similar aspects emerge in the final case, Winter AG. Again, powerful actors – here in form of the divisions who actually had more influence than the project manager – interfered with the project and altered the content of the changes. As the project manager only was instructed to cut costs and was therefore not commissioned to actually establish an SSC and to automate processes, the project as such had a very low level of legitimacy in the organization. Additionally, the project manager tried to change the organization's view of how HR work should be conducted by promoting the vision of an HR factory. This, of course, was met with apprehension as it did not match existing norms and believes.

When comparing the four cases, it is interesting to see that the e-HRM project in each case was initiated with the vision of transforming the HRM function by reducing administrative tasks and by enhancing the role of HRM as a strategic business partner. Interestingly, this target was pursued by two very different strategies. In the cases of Spring AG and Summer AG, the focus was much more on the 'business partner' aspects, where strategically important HRM processes such as personnel development, compensation, and recruiting were optimized with the help of information technology systems. No major restructuring effort was involved. In contrast, Autumn AG and Winter AG focused much more on the 'cutting administrative costs' aspects and attempted to optimize administrative processes by fundamentally altering the structure of the HRM organization, i.e. by establishing an SSC.

Several questions arise from this observation: are these organizations really following the same vision, but by using different means? What might be organizational variables leading to one strategy being chosen over the other? One answer may be given by looking at the signification dimension. According to Storey (1992), the term HRM carries a variety of meanings. To some, it implies taking humans seriously as a powerful resource of strategic importance. To others, it is simply a modern label for personnel management and the traditional assumption of treating employees mainly as a cost factor is retained. Both these views appear to be subsumed in the 'business partner' model and thus, depending on each organization's perspective on how to manage its HRs, such different strategies may be derived from a seemingly equal vision.

Another explanation may be given by drawing on the legitimization as well as on the domination dimensions. As has been argued by Hiltrop (1999), the relationship between HRM and financial performance may not be due to the positive effect of HRM on company performance but to the reverse causality. Such a reverse causality explanation may also be applied to the two patterns observed in the present study: high-performing, resource-rich organizations may be more willing and able to invest in HRM, whereas low-performing organizations need to focus on cutting costs. 'HRM as a business partner' may just be a strategy for good times – and it may be used as a label to legitimize a cost-reduction strategy during others. This argument seems plausible, as the levels of resistance of HRM employees and the works councils were much higher in the last two projects than in the first two, indicating that employees may well have been aware of any 'hidden agendas'.

Table 10.2 shows a summary of the main rules and resources influencing the process of technology design and implementation in each case:

Table 10.2
Dimensions of the duality of structure in the four cases.

	Signification	**Domination**	**Legitimation**
Spring AG	Lack of knowledge about system development	No deployment of further resources	Formalizing norms and providing sanctions regarding the salary round
Summer AG	High symbolic meaning of the project	Availability of additional resources	Democratic culture Poor expectation management
Autumn AG	Dominance of existing role definitions	Power of the works council	Importance of employees' rights
Winter AG	Vision of an HR Factory	Power of the divisions Lack of power of the project manager	Low legitimacy of the project

Conclusion

The cases illustrate how the design and implementation processes of e-HRM initiatives are influenced by the context of each organization, specifically by the predominant structures of meaning, by the existing financial and power resources and by the norms guiding behavior. It shows how an apparently similar vision can be pursued by very different strategies, implying that different meanings might be attached to the 'HRM as a business partner' model or, as an alternative interpretation, suggesting that this label might simply be used to legitimize a cost-cutting strategy. It also shows the importance of existing meaning and power structures when trying to fundamentally alter the organization and the way work is done like in the last two cases. In the first two cases, where only single processes were changed, existing structures mainly influenced the course of the project and the way the project was managed and less the actual content of the change.

To explore the structuration process in more detail, however, more data will have to be collected. Interviewing system users or even observing them at their workplace would have generated very valuable insights, particularly for analyzing the actual use of the technology and for obtaining more information on the impact of the projects in general. It also would have been useful to conduct interviews with the system developers, as they would have been able to provide useful information of how the technology has actually been structured by their own actions – a very important aspect of the structuration process. It is intended to extend the data set accordingly in later stages of this project, as this appears to generate some very promising insights for both theory and practice on the intersection of HR and IT.

Further research should expand on these insights and take a closer look at how these structuration processes actually took place. It should furthermore examine not just the system development processes but also the system use in order to gain more insights on the impact technology actually has on organizational – in this case HRM – structures as it is actively shaped and enacted by the users.

Implications for practitioners

These cases provide a number of lessons for practitioners, which I have provided as a list. Though they may seem obvious to some managers, others may benefit from being reminded of them, since if neglected, they can pose a serious threat to any e-HRM initiative.

- Have a good database. A clean and complete database including role definitions is the basis for any kind of workflow management. Creating such a database should come first in every e-HRM project. Clear-cut organizational structures are required;
- Ensure system flexibility. Organizations are complex, and roles, rules, and regulations change all the time. Make sure your system can accommodate to these changes easily;
- Get the numbers right from the start. Have a sound business case and remember: About 40% of the working time is spent with tasks unrelated to your processes;
- Present a pilot version early. If the rest of the organization is involved in an e-HRM project, they should see a pilot version early on so they know what is going on and can give better feedback;
- Manage expectations realistically. There is no point in promising that everything will improve with the new technology. Users should know about the problems every new system has at the beginning – otherwise their frustration and levels of resistance will increase;
- Leave enough time for testing and bug-fixing. Developers know about this, project managers often do not. A faulty system can damage your reputation and it may even cost your job;
- The more you want to move towards an 'HR Factory', the higher the technical demands. It is never easy to represent organizational complexity in a system. Without the right technology, it becomes impossible;
- Know what you mean by 'business partner'. If you do not know what you really want from your HR

specialists, how should they? If they do not understand their new role, HR specialists are likely to hold onto old ways of working;

■ Do not look down on your administrative HR staff. Let your SSC staff develop into functional HR specialists, so they do not feel like second-class employees. Everybody's job is important;

■ Make sure you have the power to actually change things. Someone will always object to your project, and you need to be fully in charge to be able to overcome this resistance;

■ Do not forget your stakeholders. Line managers and employees will not like your system – unless you make life easier for them. Do not think only about your savings potential, particularly when selecting the first processes.

Acknowledgments

I thank Cornelius Fischer, Graeme Martin, Nadia Pestrak, and Joerg Sydow for their comments on earlier versions of this chapter. I also thank Christian Krohn for his help with the data collection and all my interview partners for their cooperation.

References

Barley, S.R. (1986) Technology as an occasion for structuring: evidence from observations of CT scanners and the social order of radiology departments. *Admin. Sci. Quart.* 31, 78–108.

Barley, S.R. (1990) The alignment of technology and structure trough roles and networks. *Admin. Sci. Quart.* 35, 61–103.

Giddens, A. (1976) *New Rules of Sociological Method.* New York: Basic Books.

Giddens, A. (1979) *Central Problems in Social Theory: Action, Structure and Contradiction in Social Analysis.* Berkeley: University of California Press.

Giddens, A. (1984) *The Constitution of Society. Outline of the Theory of Structuration.* Berkeley: University of California Press.

Hiltrop, J.M. (1999) The quest for the best: human resource practices to attract and retain talent. *Eur. Manage. J.* 17, 422–30.

Huselid, M.A. (2004) Editor's note: special issue on e-HR: the intersection of information technology and human resource management. *Hum. Resource Manage.* 43, 119.

Jorgensen, D.L. (1989) *Participant Observation: a Methodology for Human Studies*. Newbury Park: Sage Publications.

Lengnick-Hall, M.L. and Moritz, S. (2003) The impact of e-HR on the human resource management function. *J. Labor Res.* XXIV, 365–79.

Orlikowski, W.J. (1992) The duality of technology: rethinking the concept of technology in organizations. *Organ. Sci.* 3, 398–427.

Orlikowski, W.J. (2000) Using technology and constituting structures: a practice lens for studying technology in organizations. *Organ. Sci.* 11, 404–28.

Orlikowski, W.J. and Robey, D. (1991) Information technology and the structuring of organizations. *Inform. Sys. Res.* 2, 143–69.

Pettigrew, A. (1997) What is processual analysis? *Scand. J. Manage.* 13, 337–48.

Pettigrew, A. and Whipp, R. (1991) *Managing Change for Competitive Success*. Oxford: Blackwell.

Robey, D. and Boudreau, M.C. (1999) Accounting for the contradictory organizational consequences of information technology: theoretical directions and methodological implications. *Inform. Sys. Res.* 10, 167–85.

Shrivastava, S. and Shaw, J.B. (2003) Liberating HR through technology. *Hum. Resource Manage.* 42, 201–22.

Storey, J. (1992) *Developments in the Management of Human Resources*. Oxford: Blackwell.

Strauss, A. and Corbin, J. (1990) *Basics of Qualitative Research: Grounded Theory, Procedures, and Techniques*. Thousand Oaks, CA: Sage Publications.

Yin, R.K. (1994) *Case Study Research. Design and Methods*. Thousand Oaks, CA: Sage Publications.

Further reading

Orlikowski, W.J. (1993) CASE tools as organizational change: investigating incremental and radical changes in systems development. *Manage. Inform. Sys. Quart.* 17, 309–40.

PART 3

Practitioners Forum

Going Forward with e-HR: What Have We Learned and What Must We Become?

Martyn Sloman

Introduction

Technology and human resources (HR) are not always the most comfortable of bed-fellows. Indeed, when I see how many human resource practitioners react to technology, I am reminded of a comment on my school report in the year before I took the university entrance level examination in physics. It read: 'this boy has a strange attitude to the subject – almost one of resentment that it should exist.' However I gritted my teeth and achieved sufficient mastery to achieve my objective – in this case university entrance.

Does this indicate a way forward for the profession as it wrestles with all these new delivery channels: that we must gain enough awareness to achieve the minimum objectives? We can then concentrate on those areas which interest us and where our skills can best be applied – in developing, managing, and directing interpersonal relationships.

Alas this comforting analogy simply does not work. The brutal truth is that, as HR professionals, we have failed to secure an adequate understanding (let alone mastery) of the HR/technology interface. We cannot allow this to continue, because ultimately it will put the credibility of the HR profession at risk. The way in which technology is applied by people in the business is becoming a critical driver; it is an area where HR specialists need to acquire and demonstrate expertise.

This opening statement may sound unduly gloomy; however there are some positive notes to be struck. Difficulties over the application and implementation of technology are not the sole preserve of human resources. Such problems have arisen across a range of organizations; indeed there have been some high-profile failures. A prominent example of failure in the UK concerned the very public difficulties with 'Choose and Book'. This is described in Box 11.1, which is included at the outset since it highlights some important issues which we will discuss in this chapter.

Box 11.1   Choose and Book

In 2002, The Department of Health committed to 'Ensure that by the end of 2005 every hospital appointment will be booked for the convenience of the patient, making it easier for general practitioners (GPs) to choose the hospital and consultant that best meets their needs' (2002 Public Service Agreement, Objective 1, No.4, Dept. of Health). This target applied to around 9.4 million patients referred for hospital treatment by their GP each year, or around 4% of the total consultations (NAO, 2005, p. 1). Such an ambitious change could only be achieved through a technology interface that would be used to deliver choice to the patient. To quote from a National Audit Office (NAO, 2005) progress report published in January 2005:

'Choice at referral will be delivered most effectively and efficiently through electronic booking (e-booking, also known as Choose and Book), in which the Electronic Booking Service, commissioned by the Department's National Programme for IT (NPfIT), is linked to upgraded or new computer systems in hospitals and GP's surgeries.'

The chosen supplier of IT software delivered a functioning system and the first booking using e-booking was made in July 2004. Departmental projections in July 2004 estimated that by the end of December 2004 there could have been a total of over 205 000 bookings. However, in its January 2005 report 'Patient choice at the point of GP Referral' the NAO commented that:

'...the roll-out of e-booking has been slower that planned and at the end of December 2004 only 63 bookings had been made. Problems have included the reluctance of users to work with an unreliable end-to-end system, limited progress in linking to GP and hospital systems, and the limited numbers of GPs willing to use the system.' (NAO, 2005)

It is not evident, from the report whether the 63 bookings were made by one GP (perhaps an eager and ambitious recently qualified clinician in Hampstead) who used the system 63 times or whether they were made by 63 separate individuals who made one exploratory attempt each!

Investigations were undertaken to discover the views of the GPs on choice and e-booking technology. Accordingly an electronic survey of 1500 GPs was undertaken. Again to quote:

'We commissioned a survey of GPs from Doctors.Net, a research agency specializing in online surveys of medical professionals. The work was carried out between the 13 and 29 October, 2004, following an endorsement of the survey by the Royal College of General Practitioners, which encouraged all its members in its monthly bulletin to complete the survey at Doctors.Net. Of the approximately 25 000 General Practitioners registered with Doctors.Net at that time, all 11 500 members who had used the site in the previous 90 days (some 33% of all GPs), were invited by e-mail to complete our questionnaire which was made available to them electronically from the Doctors.Net web-site. Doctors.Net accepted, on our instructions, the first 1500 responses.' (NAO, 2005, p. 35)

This approach was bound to be biased in favor of the views of the more technologically literate GPs. They would be the ones who would be likely to respond to an electronic survey, so the findings made even more depressing reading.

'Choice cannot be delivered without support from GPs but our survey of GPs found that around half of GPs know very little about it and 61% feel either very negative or a little negative. GPs' concerns include practice capacity, workload, consultation length and fears that existing health inequalities will be exacerbated. The Department has deliberately held back its main effort to inform and engage GPs about choice until it has had a working e-booking system to show GPs, but it intends to mount a campaign to inform and engage GPs during 2005.' (NAO, 2005, p. 2)

Not surprisingly the NAO noted that:

'The Department needs urgently to address the low level of GP support for their plans for implementing choice at referral.' (NAO, 2005, p. 3)

Recognizing that there have been failures elsewhere, however, offers small comfort. As HR professionals, we must develop a more effective forward agenda. First, however, we need to consider the context in which we are operating – the changing role of HR and the emerging importance of technology.

The changing role of human HR

At heart HR is about delivering value to the business: effective people management and development are the critical enablers that allow the organizations to achieve profitability objectives in the private sector and service delivery in the public or voluntary sectors. As we move towards an economy which is increasingly service-led and knowledge-driven, so there is increasing emphasis on the way that human resource management must become a holistic activity. The Chartered Institute of Personnel and Development (CIPD), the UK professional body for HR specialists, has identified and promoted a set of practices called high performance working. To quote from a January 2006 publication '*Smart Work*':

'CIPD research shows that these practices encompass recruitment, training, job appraisal and reward, job design, job quality, flexible working and communication with staff. More specifically, they include ongoing work-based learning, self-managed team working and profit – or performance-related pay systems. Used in the appropriate combination and tailored to the circumstances of each organisation and its workforce, these practices create the conditions for a high level of employee commitment and performance.' (CIPD, 2006a)

The interface between technology and people is central to smart working. Again to quote from '*Smart Work*':

'The challenge to all organisations – not just global players but also commercial and public sector organisations serving purely domestic markets – is to compete on the basis of quality, design, personalised service and efficiency of delivery. This means being responsive to customer demand and innovative in both product and service development to keep ahead of the game. Moreover, increasing competition, continual advances in technology and changing consumer tastes also mean that organisations must be prepared for change and able to constantly adapt and reorganise.

'Quality products and services are typically rich in design specification and brand value, often customised, and delivered in a personalised way. They normally require heavy investment in technology and make particular use of information and communications technology (ICT). But of crucial importance is the contribution of the people who produce or provide them, the knowledge they input and/or the personal touch they bring to delivery.' (CIPD, 2006a)

HR and technology

Given its growing importance the interface between technology and human resources became a major research stream for the CIPD in 2005. In that year we commissioned Professor Graeme Martin to produce a research report '*Technology and People Management*'. He offered a wide definition of technology, but firmly emphasizing its application:

'Broadly speaking, any given technology can be defined in the means by which a desirable goal is achieved, such as that used to develop a new product (e.g. automobiles), or a service (e.g. online delivery of a research report), or a new process (e.g. the e-enablement of HR).' Martin, 2005

He went on to argue that technology has three inter-related components: the physical objects or artifacts; the activities or processes; the knowledge need to develop and apply these physical objects and processes to produce a particular output.

In the following year the CIPD commissioned a 2-year project on HR and technology. The first output was a Change Agenda produced in 2006. The author, Emma Parry of Cranfield School of Management, Cranfield University, Bedford, UK, drew attention to the way that technology was affecting human resources beyond administrative role played by human resource information systems (HRIS). These had been defined by the CIPD as computer-based information systems for managing the administrative and strategic processes related to an organization's employees.

Parry argued that:

'The use of technology in human resource management has grown considerably in recent years. Human resource information systems (HRIS) have developed – from being largely used to administrative and data recording purposes to being used in processes such as recruitment and selection, flexible benefits, development and e-learning. Technology is now being used to support integrated call centres, shared services and self-service environments. As technology improves, organisations can use information systems to manage an increasing number of HR processes in an effective manner to contribute to the availability of information and knowledge. This in turn can lead to improved competitive advantage.' (CIPD, 2006b)

This 2006 Change Agenda was subtitled '*Beyond Delivery*' because it reflected a view that the profession needed to develop its thinking beyond seeing technology as an administrative tool to improve transactions. The survey undertaken for the Human Resource Software Show in 2005 (CIPD, 2005a) was broader in scope than those that had been attempted in previous years. As well as reviewing the progress and prospects in the use of human resource information the survey ventured into two other areas. It examined the use of electronic communication in delivering HR policies and procedures; it also considered the use of technology as a tool in the workplace.

It is the first of these 'new' areas, electronic communication, that has so much potential and as the 'Choose and Book' case illustration shows, can cause so many problems and disappointments. Self-service, where employees make use of information accessed through a portal or gateway on their computer has enormous attractions. As Martin (2005, p. 19) put it in his research report:

'Thus the e-enablement of HR became a 'hot topic' amongst HR professionals in the early part of the new millennium for three main reasons ... The first was the increasing cost of administering human resources during the 1990s with more and more time required by human resource staff to enforce policy and undertake essentially routine, but important, administrative tasks. The second has been the increasing expectations and low levels of reported satisfaction of employees with HR services. So, as employees – as customers – have had increasing access to ICT – enabled services in other area such as personal banking, shopping, and other information, their expectations of what they

---

might receive at work regarding personal information – have also increased … Third it has also been seen as a way of freeing-up scarce time for HR practitioners to allow them to focus on more strategic valued-added activities.'

Parry reiterated the last point in the 2006 Change Agenda. Historically, the HR function has been an administrative function whose role is largely focused on administrative activities such as the maintenance of employee and payroll records. The use of technology in HR, however, may facilitate a change in emphasis to that of HR playing a more strategic role within the organization.

So the e-enablement of HR, if we can get it right, is enormously attractive to the organization, the HR function, and potentially the individual. The increasing sophistication of technology, and the wider availability of computers, allows us to move beyond interactive operation. In her analysis for the CIPD, Parry offered two related definitions with a preference for the latter. She defined an intranet as:

'a system where computers are linked so that they can share information within an organization or within part of an organization,'

---

and a portal as

'a tool or platform by which internal two-way communication including employee or manager self-service can be facilitated.'

She saw the two terms, 'intranet' and 'portal' as generally being used interchangeably by HR. However defined, the potential use of such portals is considerable but we are at an early stage in understanding, let alone realizing, such potential. The CIPD 2005 People Management and Technology Survey showed that almost all (98%) the systems in use offered access to HR information (this raises the question of what they were for if they did not!); the overwhelming majority allowed a facility for down-loading forms (88%), but less than half (48%) allowed a facility for staff feedback. The functional uses of e-HR were shown to be concentrated on recruitment and selection, pay and benefits, and training and performance management.

Not only are there an ever-growing range of potential uses, but some organizations are implementing innovative and effective solutions. Two very different examples, from the Scottish Fire and Rescue Service and Penna Plc are set out as Boxes 11.2 and 11.3.

Box 11.2 Technology enablers: the Scottish Fire and Rescue Service IPDS

Building on a national system of standards and using new channels created by technology, the Scottish Fire and Rescue Service has developed an innovative approach to determining and meeting the needs of the individual learner. It has moved away from a traditional top-down training model, and used a competency framework to encourage Firefighters to take responsibility for their own learning. Requirements and opportunities are made explicit through the need to produce a personal development plan.

This shift in focus has been given impetus by a significant cultural change process that is taking place throughout the UK Fire and Rescue Service. A climate for change was created by a wide-ranging modernization agenda which coincided with a period of industrial action, culminating in a review of pay structures. In England, the Bain Report (2002) proposed that pay should be linked to demonstrated competence. Likewise, in Scotland, the Scottish Executive produced two important reports outlining their modernization objectives. One of these reports, '*The Scottish Fire Service of the Future*' emphasized the importance of firefighters taking responsibility for their own personal performance and development. It wholeheartedly endorsed the new national occupational standards (NOS), which had been produced for the fire service in the UK.

An integrated system
These standards, which were linked to the framework of National Vocational Qualifications and Scottish Vocational Qualifications have

formed the basis of a fire service Integrated Personnel Development System (IPDS). This system is designed to encompass the development needs of all fire service employees from entry level to the most senior positions. The IPDS allows for a more flexible, tailored approach to delivery of development opportunities – supporting a move away from training as courses to developmental learning, based on demonstrating and maintaining competence. This is a far cry from the very traditional 'train me' culture that has been prevalent in the UK fire service for more than 50 years. This new approach has afforded the Scottish Fire and Rescue Service the opportunity to research alternative delivery methods, including the use of electronic media.

Bob Virtue, director of fire service training for Scotland, in his guidance circular, expressed the possibilities in the following terms:

'Records must indicate where and how competence has been achieved, identify role related development needs and describe how these have been or will be satisfied. Recording systems that are non-bureaucratic save management time and encourage people to feel they 'own' their development.'

At the heart of the approach is an electronic browser-based personal development record (the system is called 'PDR*pro*'). Each individual firefighter has a personal record which is embedded in the NOS for the fire service.

At the recruitment stage the firefighter undertakes a selection assessment which involves aspects of these competency standards, other core skills and physical fitness. If successful, he or she then joins and spends 12 weeks on an initial foundation program; in the course of which the new entrant receives a development plan showing the competency standards to be developed. These are recorded electronically using the PDR system. The new firefighter is then assigned to a fire station and, since every station has a different risk profile, the individual development priorities set out in the PDR are amended accordingly.

Progression in the fire-service is based on a movement from 'under development' to 'competent'. Each starter in a new grade (there are seven grades in the structure extending from crew member at the bottom to brigade manager) is considered 'under development'.

An essential part of their move to 'competent' is the recognition and demonstration of relevant skills and this recorded on the PDR system.

There is a strong link between the incident monitoring and recording system and the individual's PDR. Each time a 'watch' at the fire station attends a significant incident they are obliged to conduct a debriefing to review how effectively the incident was handled. As part of this debriefing process the watch manager creates an incident record which is transferred electronically to the individual records of all watch members who were involved. This generates an appropriate list of competencies that would have been deployed in an incident of this nature, and also a list of equipment that may have been used. The firefighter must himself or herself personally tick the boxes indicating the competencies deployed or equipment used. This ensures that the PDR is linked to operational activity and is a live document, rather than a static electronic filing cabinet.

Two other features of electronic enablement are currently under development. The first is what is described as the individual's matrix. This is a color-coded display of the NOS competencies that are relevant to the individual in his or her role: red is 'acquired'; green is 'under-development', and gray is 'non-applicable'. Potentially this technology offers an important operational application: when a 'red acquired' competency has not been used for some time it can 'decay' automatically to green indicating a training or development need.

The second feature is a list of learning modules which are linked to the competencies – some are self-contained e-learning modules, some are guidelines for self-study or instructor intervention. All the competencies are covered in one way or another. These modules taken together are branded as the Scottish Fire Services Virtual College.

All the Fire Chiefs have committed to support the overall approach. At the time of writing, in summer 2006, the main emphasis is on rolling the system out across all of the eight Fire and Rescue Services in Scotland. The first step is to ensure that the records are created for all the 10 000 firefighters in Scotland. So far progress has been good and reactions favorable.

As part of a National Joint Agreement between management and unions published in autumn 2005 much more emphasis will be placed on career assessment in the fire service. Specifically it has been agreed that 'everybody under development must be assessed'. Recorded progression using the PDR will be part of this process; however, additional systems will be needed. The Scottish fire service is therefore creating formal assessment centers for promotion. It is also formulating a performance management system which will include an element of development review and objective setting. The PDR process will, however, remain at the heart of all the enhanced human resource development strategic interventions for the fire service.

Box 11.3   Technology enablers: Penna online

Penna Plc offers outplacement to individuals facing redundancy from organizations across the private, public, and voluntary sectors. The client sponsor is the organization offering outplacement, but the relationship is held with the individual leaving the organization. The individual is known as 'the client', the organization 'the client sponsor'.

Each client is assigned a coach whose role is, through a series of meetings, to support the client in meeting their individual objectives for the future. The timing of these meetings is dependent on the client's program and is agreed between the coach and the client as their relationship progresses.

Penna's outplacement programs reflect a blended learning approach, taking advantage of online learning to supplement their coaching sessions. The programs include the provision of information on job opportunities, assistance with the preparation and marketing of curriculum vitae, the provision of assessment and test tools, and the opportunity to look at various options apart from job search. Penna also employs a team of specialist researchers who provide a 'knowledge coach' service to clients undergoing outplacement when they need tailored research assistance to help them achieve the career outcome they are aiming for.

In 2007, over 12 000 clients will work with Penna across 12 regional centers, or resource centers across the UK.

The Penna Online portal was launched in 2001. All clients can access Penna Online through individually protected usernames and passwords. The portal was developed in-house and a team of researchers and career coaches are responsible for keeping the information up-to-date and relevant to client needs. The portal offers the following facilities:

- A workspace where the client can receive and send e-mail;
- A calendar to track meetings and interviews;
- A facility to create and store information;
- A series of career assessment and planning tools; e.g. self-assessment, writing curriculum vitae, planning for interviews;
- Access to research information, for example, to allow a client to prepare a detailed analysis in a sector, or a company within it, to assist with their job search.

The portal is generic – all clients have access to the same system, but they will use the available functionality on an individual basis, as guided by their career coach. Penna is considering the development of additional functionality for senior directors in the near future.

The portal was introduced for the following reasons:

- Clients were increasingly demanding the opportunity to work remotely and outside normal business hours;
- The numbers that base themselves at the Penna offices had declined and 'we live in a technological age and our clients accept and enjoy it'.
- The portal 'allows the one-to-one coaching session to become more effective by concentrating on the issues that need face-to-face discussion'.

The Penna Online service undergoes continuous development in order to meet the client's needs in an ever-changing market. Penna will be shortly launching its accessibility compliant version to meet the requirements of the Disability Discrimination Act. There will also be increased functionality to improve connectivity with career opportunities and information sources around the globe. Client use of the portal is ever increasing, and Penna's coaches use the portal to enhance the effectiveness of the one-to-one relationship.

When Penna Online was first launched, the initial challenge to it use lay not primarily with the client, but with some of the Penna coaches. They had seen their role as focused on a model of face-to-face coaching and did not see how an electronic tool could enhance that process. Penna provided, and still provides, training on an ongoing basis on the use of the portal through their professional development groups. As awareness grew, it showed coaches that the portal was not replacing them, but by introducing a blended approach, giving them the opportunity to use their skills to better effect in the length of program available. Clients take the information from the portal and then build on that information in their session with their coach. These sessions therefore become true individual coaching sessions and not just teach-ins.

In December 2004, Penna surveyed users of Penna Online. The results showed that over 72% of clients thought that the guidance and assistance received from the career coach was excellent or very good and over 70% worked together with their career coach either reviewing work online remotely or reviewing the outcomes as part of their coaching session.

There are also some clients that do prefer not to use the portal. The two primary reasons for this are:

- Lack of skill and understanding of the technology. Where requested Penna will provide this training that in turn enhances client's employability and life skills;
- Lack of access to technology – resource centers provide this or alternative methods are identified – family, libraries, Internet cafes, etc.

In the end the client is the driver and if they do not want to use Penna Online, Penna provides other media to meet individual client needs.

Penna Online is an important part of the services offered and features prominently in any presentation to clients. Bev White, managing director of Career Transition at Penna, believes that while the portal improves productivity and efficiency, and thereby reduces costs, one-to-one coaching is at the heart of Penna's programs.

Research carried out by Penna in July 2005 exploring the value of outplacement confirms Bev White's view.

Sixty-five per cent of individuals stated that the personal coach was the most valuable part of their program with a further 56% citing curriculum-vitae review with their coach also featuring prominently.

Bev White says,

'A portal could not, and should not, ever replace the one-to-one relationship. Our programmes are about blended learning to best meet the client's needs.'

One of the most sophisticated and thoughtful organizational applications of e-HR I have come across in my work for the CIPD is located in the BBC in the UK. Speaking at the 2006 CIPD-HRSS Conference, Caroline Prendergast, the Head of BBC Training & Development Delivery, and Nick Shackleton-Jones, the BBC online and Informal Learning Manager, outlined the details of 'gateway' an intranet portal at had been developed for the BBC, which was subsequently fleshed out during a further interview (Box 11.4).

Box 11.4 Experience with the BBC gateway

When installing the gateway portal the BBC recognized that ease of use was critical and adequate bandwidth was essential. The corporation was keen to learn and build on the experience of others and took a considered approach rather than seeking to become an early adopter. Gateway in its present form emerged in 1996.

From the outset there was much emphasis for securing a high degree of personalization – individual users needed to 'own' and to be able to configure their own portal. Unlike most intranets, there is also a great deal of variety in terms of page design: only the gateway title-bar remains the same across all pages. Although, to an extent, this could be regarded as diluting the overall brand, local ownership is seen as encouraging creativity, resulting in more innovative activities and ultimately higher use.

In mid-2006, there were some 25 000 people employed in the BBC and over 2 million web pages were available to them through gateway. A study at that time revealed that the top three uses were 'searching for people', 'reviewing pay and expenses', and 'learning'. These three reflect the broad categories of usage planned at the outset – news and information, self-service and learning and informal learning.

Penetration has been high – for example, 87% of current BBC staff have participated in some online learning through gateway.

Given the emphasis on individual ownership rather than pre-scribed use, some unanticipated but welcome developments have been observed. The information on 'searching for people' for example, has not merely taken the form of access to an electronic filing system; the biographies that individuals have provided are wide-ranging and included photographs, skills, and areas of personal interest.

One particular success has been the wide interest shown in the blogs that senior managers (including for example the director of BBC Global News) have made available on the system. Such interest has been spontaneous, but it has been encouraged as a way of communicating to-up-date information on activities and as offering insights to more junior people seeking to develop their careers. Whilst there are only some 180 blogs on the system – as many as one-third of BBC staff regularly read a blog.

These blogs, and indeed the people search facility, are regarded as an important part of learning and development activity within the cor-poration. Caroline Prendergast and Nick Shackleton-Jones emphasize the importance of informal, socially mediated learning and see the future of e-learning in terms of increasing service and solution diver-sity. They do still see considerable value in preparing and distributing specific e-learning material on important topics. One recent example concerns information in the form of a key point guide in Israel and Palestine. This 'reference-ware' approach typically works hand-in-hand with an 'awareness' module which highlights the key issues in a way which is compelling and contextualized. It can be seen that this involves a much wider perspective of e-learning where the boundaries between learning and performance support will disappear.

Caroline Prendergast and Nick Shackleton-Jones provided their top 10 tips or principles for the effective use on an e-HR portal, which are worth reproducing:

- Ensure you have sufficient bandwidth;
- Support video and interactivity;
- Personalize: feature people and stories;
- Foster user-generated, dynamic content;
- Carry the latest information;
- Encourage diversity and local ownership;

- Ensure that the intranet is properly supported;
- Use it to make good learning opportunities available;
- Simplify navigation;
- Make it an indispensable tool, not merely a library;
- Set it as the default homepage in Internet Explorer.

(Reproduced by permission from Caroline Prendergast and Nick Shackleton-Jones, 2006.)

Change management

Although there is plenty of good practice about, as a profession we have some ground to make up in proving our value to our organizational colleagues and gaining credibility. We are embarking on a major change management process. Here it is evident that good practice is about the effective management of change. This is a well-researched area for the HR function. We know what promising practices looks like – the only problem is doing implementing them.

As has been noted, a 2005 CIPD survey considered the use of technology as a tool in the workplace. The survey showed that respondents were generally involved in implementing technology-related change processes: 71% said that they might be involved in managing the change process, 63% in monitoring its effectiveness, and 66% in reviewing the process. A higher percentage, 83%, said that they might be involved in managing the ongoing training. For respondents who are not involved in any of these activities, however, their influence on important business change activities must be correspondingly limited (CIPD, 2005a).

The following extract from the 2005 Survey reports the result of some of the telephone interviews carried out by the researchers at the Work Research Institute at the University of Sheffield, who undertook the survey on the CIPD's behalf.

'Our telephone interviewees were asked why they didn't get involved in decisions when technology was being introduced in the wider organisation. Most answers to this question were variations on the themes of 'it's nothing to do with us,' 'decisions of that sort are taken at departmental level,' and 'I don't have the expertise in the operational area under discussion so I would not have anything positive to contribute.' There was also some indication that HR's non-involvement may be due to operational departments wanting to have complete control over how their own budget is spent.

If they were involved, the telephone interviewees were asked what benefits their involvement provided to the organisation. They saw the benefits for of the human element being factored into the decision-making process right at the start as leading to fewer problems during implementation. They saw their involvement as an 'indication of where HR sits in an organisation. One interviewee thought that HR non-involvement in other organisations may also be an indication of the preferences and interests of those who choose HR as a career.' (CIPD, 2005a)

What have we learned?

Some clear messages emerge from the four case illustrations of Choose and Book, Penna, the Scottish Fire and Rescue Service, and the BBC. What is interesting is that they are clear in retrospect; they follow from an application of some well-established human resource principles. The first point is that new systems depend on active consent and support of those who are about to make use of them. They must be seen to be relevant to the parties concerned. One of the most important of the ongoing CIPD research projects is of relevance here. This is the people and performance model (Purcell et al., 2005), the CIPD's efforts to explain how the link between effective human resource policies and business benefits worked in practice.

This research suggests that the crucial factor linking HR practices to performance is the way that these practices lead to discretionary behavior. This was defined in the following terms:

'Discretionary behaviour means making the sort of choices that often define a job, such as the way the job is done – the speed, care, innovation and style of job delivery. This behaviour is at the heart of the employment relationship, because it is hard for the employer to define and then monitor and control the amount of effort, innovation and productive behaviour required. The most obvious example here is front-line service work dealing with customers either face to face or over the phone. It concerns the sort of everyday behaviour that the employer wants but has to rely on the employee to deliver.' (Purcell et al., 2005)

The second major lesson is that progress is not about 'automating' but about 'support and automate'. There is a crucial judgment to be made about what elements of process can or should be delivered through technology and what parts require human interaction – whether this is delivered by the individual's manager, their peer workers, or the human resource department. Getting this right in practice is a challenging process and we human resource professionals can take comfort that we have been here before.

One of the most evocative pieces of human resource folk memory concerns the early work of the Tavistock School conducted by Trist and Bamforth (1951), which gave rise to the notion of socio-technical systems thinking. Ken Bamforth was a coal miner who returned to the industry as a social researcher to investigate the organization of miners' ways of working. He discovered that, under certain conditions, the miners had developed a composite system of working, which involved commitment to the group task and greater cooperation (or discretionary behavior!). Perhaps the most important implication was recognition that a separate approach to the design of the social and the technical systems of an organization was inappropriate. Effective work design needed to optimize and integrate both technical and social concerns. A full 50 years on this message is fundamental and it is to our shame that we seem to have forgotten it. We need to rediscover the socio-technical approach – whatever we label it in the twenty-first century. Only through effective social-technical design principles will the user or workers consent that we need to secure support to achieve the potential of the new technology.

Finally, we should at all costs avoid being seduced by the technology (or more accurately by the potential of the technology). Even if we succumb our workforces will not necessarily fall under its spell (as illustrated in Chapter 6: The Impact of e-HR on Line Managers and Employees in the UK: Benefits, Problems, and Prospects.

References

Bain Report (2002) The Future of the Fire Service: Reducing Risk, Saving Lives, Office of the Deputy Prime Minister, London.

Chartered Institute of Personnel and Development. (2005a) *People Management and Technology: Progress and Potential.* London: CIPD.

Chartered Institute of Personnel and Development. (2005b) *Training and Development Report: Annual Survey Report 2005.* London: CIPD.

Chartered Institute of Personnel and Development. (2006a) *Smart Work; CIPD Public Policy Perspectives.* London: CIPD.

Chartered Institute of Personnel and Development. (2006b) *HR and Technology: Beyond Delivery, Change Agenda.* London: CIPD.

Martin, G. (2005) *Technology and People Management.* CIPD Research Report.

National Audit Office (2005) *Department of Health: Patient Choice at the Point of GP Referral (Report by the Comptroller and Auditor General).* London: The Stationary Office: HC 180 Session 2004–2005.

Purcell, J., Kinnie, N., and Hutchinson, S. (2005) Open minded. *People Manage.* 9, 30–7.

Purcell, J., Kinnie, N., Hutchinson, S., Rayton, B., and Swart, J. (2003) Understanding the People and Performance Link: Unlocking the Black Box, CIPD Research Report, London: CIPD.

Trist, E.L. and Bamforth, K.W. (1951). Some social and psychological consequences of the longwall method of coal getting. *Hum. Relat.* 4, 1.

CHAPTER 12

The e-Enablement of People Management in BT

Margaret Savage and Heather Alexander

Introduction

In this chapter, we set out an account of business change – its pace, scale, and impact – as the underlying driver for the radical overhaul of the BT Group strategies for people, human resources (HR), and its HR systems. The case illustrates how the four key drivers mentioned in Chapter 1: Technology, Outsourcing, and HR Transformation: an Introduction played a significant part in the emerging e-HR system, with transformational rather than transactional change being the primary reason underlying the developments. It also illustrates the design and implementation problems of e-HR and HR transformations, including the need to re-engineer existing HR processes. We conclude with some lessons learned that may have implications for other organizations seeking to implement an e-HR transformation on a global scale.

The starting point for the case was the aftermath of the 'dot-com' collapse in 2001 and the convergence of information and communications technologies (ICT) occurring at that time, which impacted the telecommunications sector greatly.

From this, BT emerged in 2002 under new executive leadership with an ambitious strategy for transformation. Success would depend on the successful defense of the existing profitable domestic markets which were under competitive attack, allied with the stimulation of revenue growth from 'new wave' technologies and markets. By the end of 2006, the latter were to account for around half of the Group's profits.

The overarching goal was to be recognized as a major 'new breed' services business with a 'telco' inside. Successful execution of this long-term strategy depended on the delivery of a range of demanding objectives. These were as follows:

- Revitalizing the customer/brand promise;
- Realigning this with values established for the company and its people;
- Growing and sustaining profitable revenue streams;
- Retaining cost leadership;
- Investing in a systems-enabled network;
- Developing an innovative portfolio of services, solutions, and products;
- Re-establishing a global footprint with multinational/multisite corporate clients.

As a result of this strategy, the BT Group is recognized today as one of Europe's leading providers of globally networked Information and Communications Technology (ICT) services and solutions. It has a strong domestic market to which it offers a range of products and services: telephony, mobility, broadband, and, most recently, vision. BT's expectations of its people during this period were for high performance and engagement. The workforce was geographically dispersed and richly diverse, comprising highly skilled, customer-centric people; according to our attitude surveys, many of them shared the BT values and the vision of stimulating growth in a global, digitally networked economy. Strong leadership, performance, and people management capabilities were identified as critical success factors for company transformation.

Nowhere, however, would the implications of this change be felt more strongly than in the HR function itself. The question asked of HR was: could it step up to meet the challenges facing

BT, the leadership team, the management team, the workforce, and the re-organization of the HR department?

HR in BT

BT Human Resources (BTHR) had long been recognized as having a key role to play in delivering strategic objectives. Judged by mentions in the UK business press, it had an impressive track record of successfully creating and delivering innovative people solutions at crucial moments in the organization's history. Consequently, it was actively engaged in assessing the people implications of the evolving business strategy. It determined and designed the strategic interventions needed from the HR strategy to trigger changes in behavior, competence, capability, and confidence. Its goal was simply to achieve 'business success through high-performing teams of highly engaged people'.

In addition, delivery of the people and HR strategic plans needed to address four other factors:

- Expansion, including multiple acquisitions, meant that there were a growing number of employees in a growing number of countries around the world;
- Demand was intensifying for faster, direct access to management information on HR, people, and people-related cost data, in order to inform operational decision making and to aid improvements in people management practices and employee engagement;
- Commercial contracts with the HR and payroll outsourcing provider/s were due for renewal;
- BTHR had to deliver a 20% reduction in its own operational cost base – a significant challenge coming after 10 successive years of delivering significant cost and efficiency improvements.

Structurally, HR comprised a small central strategic leadership team, functional specialists in a number of centers of expertise;

a larger, distributed, 'business partner/generalist' HR community; and an outsourced shared services, which administered high-volume people, pensions, and payroll transactions, as well as training at that time. This organization reflected the so-called 'Ulrich' model, discussed in Chapter 1: Technology, Outsourcing, and HR Transformation: an Introduction.

The HR business model was mature with sophisticated tracking of operational/process costs, comprehensive service level agreements, and rigorous performance metrics. There was already an excellent understanding of the drivers behind these and the company's total labor cost base. Regular external HR benchmarking comparisons were undertaken by companies such as Hackett and EP first Saratoga. These comparisons placed BTHR amongst the upper quartile of its peers. As part of the 2003 challenge to improve its own operational cost base further, HR was benchmarked by Hackett to establish its opening and subsequent closing position 2 years later. By 2005, its costs per employee were found to have improved to a level which placed it on a par with the HR costs per employee of companies in Hackett's 'quartile 1' profile.

Self-assessment of its operational readiness, however, suggested that it could further improve its efficiency and effectiveness. For example, there was evidence of duplication, overlaps, double handling, complexity, data capture gaps, and functional fragmentation leading to misinformation and misunderstanding. These generated failure costs that could be eradicated. The lack of a cohesive, jointly owned HR systems strategy contributed to this situation, and work began in late 2002 to define one.

HR also foresaw a need to refresh many of its own professional skills. To reinforce its standing as the 'people experts at the heart of change', it needed to strengthen IT literacy, commercial contract management, and relationship management skills. Building on already strong bonds with the finance community, HR established equally strong links with the legal and procurement teams. It also developed extremely close ties with the IT systems community in BT. All of these allies were to prove enormously important in the delivery of the strategic transformation plans for people, HR, and HR systems over the following 3 years.

Given this context, the challenge for HR was to make their policies, processes, and people management tools and practices intuitive and inviting to use. As a senior HR leadership team, we believed that excellent people management required the managers of people to be pro-active, objective, self-sufficient, and self-assured. It was important they saw that any change in the way they would be asked to fulfill their people management responsibilities would help them to achieve their own objectives and support their accountability for their people. Within HR itself, the HR function needed to ensure that they remained flexible, responsive, and agile, capable of rapidly deploying limited resources to optimize strategic and tactical contributions to the business's results. To achieve these goals, it was clear that policy, process, and practice needed to be aligned with each other. They also needed to be straightforward and easy to implement.

Flexible working practices and globalization meant that many teams were geographically dispersed. BT people were increasingly mobile and an increasing number of them were home-based. Against this backdrop and in line with the business strategy, HR needed to be customer-centric, cost-efficient and 'network enabled' with self-service capability available 24/7, globally. BT was promoting the idea of a global, digital, and networked economy to its customers, so it was important that it adopted the same principles and technology inside the company. Thus one of HR's key challenges was to help turn that rhetoric into reality across the company.

Using technology to transform the way people are managed

The vision and systems design parameters

As indicated above, underlying the new BT people system was BT's vision for its customers: 'connecting people with information, processes, and solutions'. Like BT's advertising, this internal program drew on the concept of 'more power to you!', in this case by delivering self-service capability to people, managers, and HR professionals. The aim was to deliver a single, easy-to-use, web-based, standard operating environment. The system was designed to become the recognized database for BT people and the first place to go for guidance and advice on people-related matters. Thus any future system would need to be both secure and readily accessible on a global 24/7 basis. The provision of access would need to cater for the varying needs of the diverse user population, offering access via the desktop, wi-fi, dial up, telephone, and post. The prime focus, however, was on-line employee and manager self-service. A critical output was to be the creation of one master source of corporate BT people and organizational data. A further output was to be the harmonization of people-related policies, procedures, and automated process workflows whilst complying with country-specific employment and data protection legislation.

A decision on a new system presented an opportunity to 'e-enable' effective decision-making about people and their needs. HR and managers needed to receive both standard and ad-hoc management information reports, as well as being able to view their team's business-related data. Fast, direct access to a single source of relevant information, instructions, or advice would aid analysis, speed up decision-making, and ensure consistency of outcomes; it was also hoped it would eradicate the 'not-invented-here, I need my own spreadsheet' culture that had grown up in the past and become a regular source of dispute in terms of data accuracy.

The new system was also required to support streamlined, workflow-driven processes and allow for future process improvement or enhanced functionality, opening up the opportunity to refresh the way people were managed across BT. In driving for high performance, managers were expected to have greater control and ownership of the task in hand. Thus, the ability to raise, manage, and close people/HR cases and track progress of workflow-driven activities was a necessary condition of the new system design.

Finally, the new system was required to be attractive, engage users, and to integrate with existing systems. To make it intuitive to use, it would need to be supported by the same tools and applications in use at the time to the customer-facing suite of systems used across BT, such as relationship management, comprehensive natural language search, and self-help training applications. It would also need to be available in multiple languages in order to support the business drive to 'do it once – do it right'. Individuals would be able to view and update their own personal data at a place and time convenient to them via an attractive 'one-stop-shop' people portal. There would be less opportunity for error or oversight. Together these features were intended to make employee self-service transactions and query resolution easier and faster. The single system was expected to create cohesion, comply with data protection legislation, and increase consistency in information, advice, and outcomes, improving the overall HR customer experience.

This vision and design parameters presented significant challenges to HR, which took a bold decision in recognizing that it had to simplify the company's people and HR policies and then radically re-engineer the associated processes to make them clear and easier to automate before implementing technology solutions. In e-enabling a simpler way of working, the business would realize benefits in efficiency and effectiveness across the HR supply chain. This would be evident in ease of access, reduced errors, the avoidance of double handling or duplication, faster processing times, and fewer calls to HR for simple queries, advice, or progress chasing.

With the design approach determined, HR took a further, key decision. To avoid delays in benefit realization through scope creep or specification variations, the new system would need to be designed and rolled out fast. HR accepted that the finished product would not necessarily be a perfect fit in every respect but achieving of 85–95% user acceptability on launch of the new e-enabled processes would be a treated as a success, given the scope, reach, and complexity of the task itself. Once the standard framework processes were bedded in and the single platform and global deployment was complete, HR gave a further commitment to enhance/fine tune specific aspects of system functionality.

The system requirements

The aim was to provide a single HR system platform. In previous years, this would have run counter to BT's culture and ways of working, which had emphasized de-centralization of many aspects of business and management, including its ICT budgets. However, there was a more receptive context for change: the timing for introducing BT's new HR system was right as the business was beginning to realize that there were key areas in which this decentralized approach added cost without adding the looked-for agility or flexibility. Adopting a 'one-BT' approach here would create a standard operating environment aligned with the company's systems simplification strategy. It would also unify the company's approach to people reporting and e-enable world class people management practices. The new system had to interface with multiple non-HR systems, operate globally, and allow for continuous process improvement, future organizational change, and technological advancement. Moreover time was short. The new system had to be ready in time to support planned policy changes, the forecast growth in user/geographical demand, strategic HR milestones, and the commercial realities of a refreshed outsourcing agreement.

The senior HR team saw advantages in creating a distinctive 'people portal' to channel access to a shared pool of HR expertise, personal learning, and various activities to do with people. Access rights were to be determined by an individual's role within BT, which would set the parameters for individual access and amend rights. In addition, the portal was designed to:

- Enable the organization to harvest collective 'know-how' because all people and HR content or refreshed information would be supplied from a managed, single source;
- Offer enhanced, web-based, self-service facilities including workflow management and automated e-mail capabilities;
- Provide self-help tools and natural language search capabilities to deliver direct 'point-and-click' access to relevant information and advice;

■ Capture immediate feedback on the helpfulness, relevance, and ease of use of the automated tools and system content.

Alongside the platform and the portal, the system had to provide an integrated data warehouse with data mining and diagnostic capabilities. These would supply the 'one-truth' view of people and organizational information, and over time would be developed to offer the managers of people and HR professionals real-time, online access to data, information, and reports.

From an HR perspective, the system was required to connect and integrate global and subsidiary entities, records, and data with the HR core. It was to facilitate reductions in operating and systems support costs across HR. The system was required to eradicate duplication or overlaps; minimize the need for manual interventions, 'policing', or HR approvals; and reduce administration or processing times across the end-to-end HR supply chain.

Implementing the systems strategy

During 2003, a long, hard look was taken at the existing suite of HR system capabilities within the company to see if they were fit for purpose, or capable of upgrading or expansion. There was a simultaneous review of the existing (and complex) BT-wide system infrastructure. Approximately 300 custom interfaces were found to exist between the two systems areas. The bulk of the UK HR administration activity ran on a legacy PeopleSoft 7 (PS7) platform owned and managed by a third party HR outsourcing provider. Over the years, this had been very heavily, albeit cleverly, customized to meet the administrators' operational needs. There were estimated to be about 9000 custom changes made to the original in 2003. From a technology perspective, heavy customization is a significant barrier to automated system upgrades; the legacy system was not web-enabled and was technologically obsolescent having been replaced by the PeopleSoft 8 (PS8) series.

Several studies began to examine the major differences between the old PS7 and the latest version of PS8. Research pointed to PS8's advantages in terms of cost; geographical operability and functionality. These can be summarized as follows:

- Cost
  - PS8 would be cheaper to maintain than the heavily customized PS7;
  - PS8 is web-based, needing only a browser for access, saving cost on user software installation;
  - Customized bolt-ons would no longer be required–simple transactions were already included, e.g. changing personal details or organizational unit codes (OUCs), saving maintenance/development costs.
- Global
  - PS8 could administer different currencies, local country requirements;
  - PS8 had multiple language capabilities
- Functionality
  - PS8 provided self-service capability and built-in workforce analytical tools;
  - The out-of-the-box 'vanilla'* PS8 already included much functionality.

It was apparent that the existing UK PS7 platform was not able to accommodate global expansion; it would also be unable to deliver the web-based changes and simpler automated workflows envisioned by the new strategic agenda for people and HR. Inaccessible to the line managers, and many BT HR professionals, BT's outsourced UK version of PS7 was neither user friendly nor visually attractive. Reporting was slow, expensive, and manually intensive. In striking contrast, outside of the UK, there were multiple, discrete HR systems, or in some cases no systems at all, supporting the various global offices. These separate systems also supported some UK-based subsidiaries.

Fortunately, the drive to re-establish BT's Global Services business had triggered a decision to invest in a country-specific, basic version of PS8. This decision provided first-hand experience of the new system capabilities, deployment decisions,

---

* By Vanilla it is meant the standard system without modification or aut>omization.

upgrading demands, and technical requirements. This decision had also paved the way for the creation of an ideal test-bed/trial capability. Given its absence of legacy ways of working, unfamiliarity with outsourced shared services and a uniquely diverse, open-minded, non-UK centric start-up perspective, the Global Services business presented an ideal environment in which to pilot new ways of working.

Global Services was deploying instances of PS8 in phases, providing an opportunity to test whether this solution could be adopted as the basis of a larger, holistic, company-wide solution. To do so, the Global Services systems plan would require rationalization and consolidation onto one single platform, involving expansion to incorporate the UK. It would also need to be enhanced to create an integrated standard operating environment that was capable of supporting a framework of consistent company policies and simple processes, modified only to comply with country-specific employment or data protection legislation.

The HR team drew upon the insights from BT Global Services' experiences and the expertise and advice of BT's IT team. As well as BT's existing plans for HR system investment, there were also other strategic system developments which could be exploited. Based on all of this, the HR community found that it was able to capitalize creatively on advances in systems technology, the explosion in 'off-the-shelf' applications, and the integration of e-enabled tools and techniques.

The technology decision tree

These design decisions, changes, and experiments led to a set of critical technology decisions, all of which contributed directly to the success of the project:

- There would be a single system across the entire business, which meant abandoning multiple smaller systems and replacing the heavily customized UK system;
- Investment in alternate, stand-alone people management systems would be stopped;
- The system would be purchased rather than built;
- The system would be configured rather than customized, i.e. a near 'vanilla' deployment;

- The system would be the master source of people and organizational information for BT;
- The system would exploit other planned system programs in BT, despite introducing additional risk to the program;
- In order to meet pressing timelines, the priority would be to agree an achievable scope;
- Change requests would be tightly controlled; all requests to undergo cost–benefit analysis;
- The system design would start from the end-user experience perspective (the employee and his/her line manager) not the HR administrator or policy maker;
- The change management implications would be resourced by dedicated professional resources to run in parallel with the technology team, ensuring that every opportunity was taken to involve and engage the users in determining the technological solution.

Further technology-related decisions were important, some of which naturally followed from the above decisions, including:

- The system's in-built functionality would be augmented by the integration of other modules, e.g. SPRO for supplier management related to people sourcing (internal/external);
- The system would sit within BT's firewall (this required development to allow third parties access to administer transactional processes and answer queries);
- Employee access would be through a single sign-on capability to the BT intranet (this already provided portals for online ordering and financial self-services);
- BT's infrastructure was being upgraded. Once delivered, a meta-directory hub would be the bridge and feeder system for people-related data to the user and other systems;
- The systems rules definitions, data directory definitions, configuration drivers, and the process redesign would be closely linked to optimize benefits and gains;
- A limited number of niche players with innovative application technologies would be bought in to

deliver and integrate essential operational functionality/interconnectivity;

■ Connectivity would require controlled access and interfaces 'sans frontiers';

■ Agreement to change would be restricted as effort would focus on delivery of the base platform and migration of the whole company, and shared services provider(s);

■ Functional upgrades, agreed customizations, newly acquired legal entities, smaller geographies, improved content or 'smart' applications would all come later;

■ System security and data compliance would need dedicated resource;

■ Formal technical testing, especially around data conversion, customization, integration, interface, and alignment triggers would require significant resource (given the scale and complexity of the deployment, and the interdependency with other systems);

■ There would be deliberate early releases of deliverables to prove the concepts, provide early feedback, and to build confidence and buy-in.

All such decisions had also to ensure that existing HR services would not be adversely impacted by the delivery of the program. Some of these decisions would need to be fine-tuned or adjusted as the program rolled out but they provided a very successful overall framework within which to start work. Later, critical success factors would also include acceptance testing by both policy owners and the wider user community, operational readiness testing, and extensive training, awareness, and communications activities.

Implementing the program

Getting business buy-in

For the program to be successful, employees, line managers, and HR professionals would have to adopt and use the system extensively. In addition, the solution involved the integration of multiple technologies and applications, and the buy-in of multiple vested interests within BT and beyond. Securing buy-in and acceptance of a standard framework for people processes and data capture alone would take a considerable investment in time, energy, and money, as well as extensive stakeholder management.

The key messages were simple and transparent from the outset, which were set out as follows in internal communications.

'We are not stopping urgent or critical requirements from moving forward.'

'We are enforcing mature dialogue and discipline regarding IT spend/costs.'

'We are channeling limited resources for common good.'

'We are ensuring alignment, synergies, and simplification.'

'We are establishing common definitions and protocols.'

The risks were equally transparent and significant; these included:

- Insufficient commitment to a 'near vanilla' deployment and resentment of 'vanilla first' approach;
- Too much functionality compromised in order to deliver 'vanilla' product;
- Scope creep, i.e. unable to maintain strict priorities and phasing in the face of business demands;
- Individual business units might not wait before commissioning local mission-critical solutions;
- Lack of HR, manager, or employee buy-in/support;
- End-user experience turned out to be insufficiently intuitive or speedy;
- Dependence on other major IT projects not directly under HR control, e.g. meta-directory, single sign-on;
- BT complexity would make it difficult to uncover all the local or niche systems/processes which had to be to be drawn into the solution;

- Inability to resolve ownership/timing issues around related topics, such as skills capture, asset management, new employee identification schemes, new organization unit coding standards;
- HR business partners/line managers fail to adapt to and adopt new ways of working;
- The business pays insufficient attention to/devotes inadequate time and resource to change;
- Data inaccuracy and failure to comply with data protection legislation around the world;
- Unexpected requirements from new commercial contracts, such as operability with significant off-shoring, could impact the program deliverables, timelines, and cost structure.

The first step taken to mitigate the risks was to identify key stakeholder groups (see Fig. 12.1), define their roles/ responsibilities, build relationships, and identify owners for

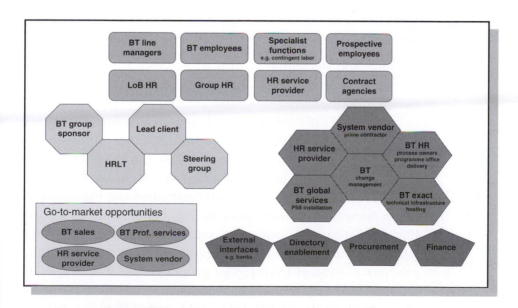

Figure 12.1
The BT stakeholder communities
Notes: HR, human resources; HRLT, human resource leadership team;
LOB, Line of Business.

contingency action planning and dispute resolution. The stake-holders were both internal and external to the business and could be categorized as the user, buyer, supplier, advisor, and future 'go-to-market' communities.

Certain stakeholders appeared in more than one category; for example, one company was represented in both the HR outsourcing provider and the system manufacturer categories (since they had taken ownership of BT's original UK PS7 system). Each group displayed specific characteristics: for example, on the one hand, the external community was looking for a win–win commercial outcome in which they could all share the prize of future business; on the other hand, the internal community had to commit to work for the greater good of the whole of BT, occasionally giving up short-term gain for the part of the organization they represented. This latter solution was not always easy when faced with their tough operational and commercial targets.

Managing the program

Creating and sustaining critical BT internal sponsor support, especially at stress points or points of tension/conflict was essential. Robust links were also created between the systems delivery program team and the commercial contract renewal team to ensure alignment in terms of future compatibility and capability. Formal governance structures were created (Fig. 12.2) to steer the overall program to ensure that funds were neither used inappropriately nor unwisely; that requirements were delivered to specification, budget, and time; and that all stakeholder groups were actively engaged and fairly represented in all decisions. A program office was set up and the program was called INUIT. The program core team was small but supplemented by a larger virtual team, including the seven companies, professionals, and lay end-users; HR policy owners, business partners, and administrators; technologists; and trainers. Maintaining momentum and sustaining alignment was a major achievement.

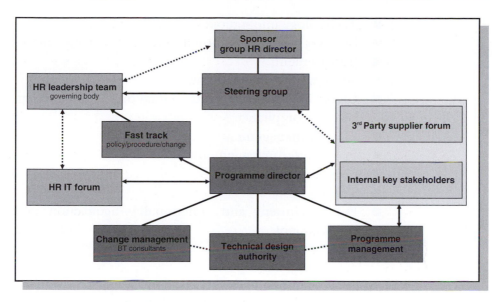

Figure 12.2
Program governance
Notes: HR, human resources.

The core plan managed the standard stages of system design and development, which were as follows:

- Requirements capture;
- Fit/gap analysis;
- System design;
- Configuration;
- Testing;
- Transition;
- Deployment.

Two parallel streams were designed to run in tandem because of the complex nature of the program: a technical stream and an implementation/change management stream. Figure 12.3 shows the outline plan.

There were also detailed plans addressing related deliverables such as:

- Policy simplification;
- Business process re-engineering;

- Technology integration;
- Business case preparation and financial management;
- Procurement;
- Security and role profiling;
- Global deployment including data protection and legislation compliance;
- Change management;
- Stakeholder management;
- Communications;
- Training;
- Future content and functionality acquisition and development.

Each of these plans had to dovetail and deliver specific outputs for the overall program plan to succeed. A series of weekly conference calls and specific weekly and monthly meetings were

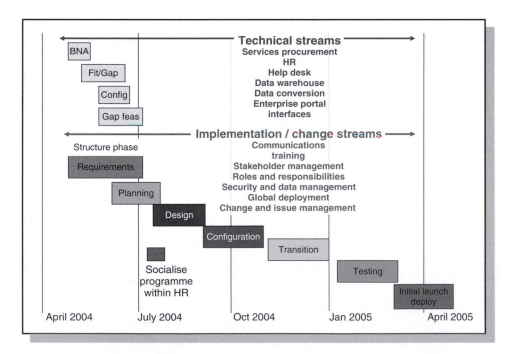

Figure 12.3
Phases of the program plan
Note: BNA, Business Needs Analysis; HR, human resources.

introduced with various cross-sections of the virtual program team to ensure that individual work stream leaders were kept up-to-date and stayed connected. They also enabled decision making and made it easier to resolve issues. An example of a work stream plan is shown in Figure 12.4.

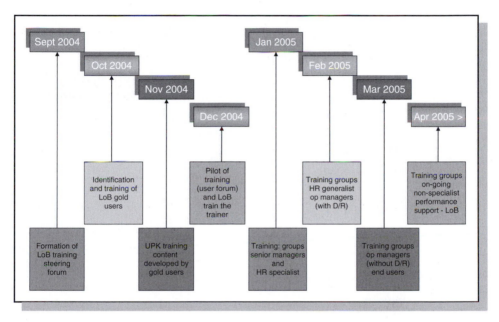

Figure 12.4
Example plan – training
Note: D/R, direct reports; LoB, Lines of Business.

HR Transformation: change management in practice

The transformation of HR and people management practice went far beyond the technology aspects. It offered a real opportunity to challenge the way HR worked and to transform the way people management practices were viewed, owned, and executed. Nothing was to be sacred. There were to be no 'protection zones'. Fresh thinking and open minds were needed.

The program would stray into both organizational and cultural change territory, both in terms of the business line managers and the HR function itself.

Needing expertise in change management and in keeping with the ethos of 'use what we sell', HR drew on the in-house capability of the change management practice team from Global Services. Change, communications, and training had to be coordinated to ensure maximum impact from limited resources: it became clear that alignment and consistency of message would be crucial and that awareness sessions and training would need to be synchronized. Honest, constructive feedback would need to be collected to help deliver a significantly improved customer experience for the end-users. Figure 12.5 outlines the plan to engage with users of the new systems and processes.

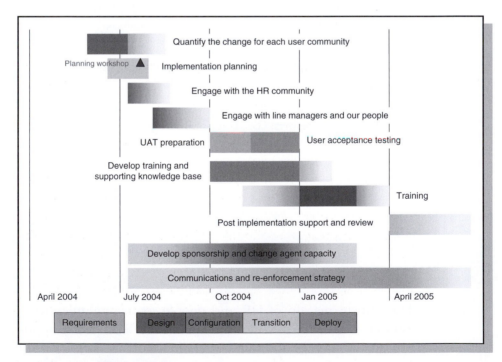

Figure 12.5
User engagement plan.
Note: UAT, user acceptance testing.

Changing the way HR works

The decision to overhaul and simplify HR policies and then to streamline and re-engineer processes was a painful one for the wider HR community. There were varying degrees of resistance as individuals came to terms with the implications of the planned changes for their jobs. Although significant time was spent communicating with and involving future users, local business pressures frequently overtook briefing opportunities and the cascading of information was not universally effective, making progress slower than hoped. To overcome this a series of web casts, conference calls, and awareness forums were designed to ensure that the HR community were informed before line managers. Joint awareness sessions with the HR provider teams were also intensified with members of the HR leadership team visiting the newly opened people service centers in Bangalore, India; Chicago, USA; and Bratislava, Slovakia.

HR process re-engineering

A key feature of the HR transformation story is that the project team devoted as much time to policy simplification and process re-engineering as they did to system design, development, and deployment. This investment and the soul-searching it entailed paid huge dividends in terms of cost-effective automation and the ability to introduce logical workflow management tools and techniques. Such a bold step is not for the faint-hearted. For example, Shrivastava and Shaw (2003) acknowledge that this is the higher-risk approach, demanding empowerment of re-engineering teams and highly effective change management. For BT, this meant that the process team leader had to work with multiple functional workstreams comprising of policy owners, departmental and transactional experts, and the systems designers to ensure that as far as was practicable the future 'to be' processes were simple to do and straightforward to follow.

The pressure on these functional policy owners and process leaders was intense. Most had busy day jobs and had to balance competing pressures for their time and effort between the need to work on the strategic initiatives and to service their everyday business demands. Despite busy work schedules, it was deemed crucial to drive the policy simplification and process re-engineering work so that the specification of the system requirements and new working practices could be completed within the demanding timescales of the program.

The purpose behind this challenging exercise was to ensure that processes related to BT people and HR all had the same 'look and feel'; that there was consistency in the standard of detail (to enable PS8 technical specifications to be defined); that process definitions were fit for purpose and, as far as possible, 'future-proofed'; and that the final definitions knitted together, creating seamless end-to-end processes

In this way, they would be able to highlight key interfaces and handoffs between the processes, identify common and/or shared inputs and outputs such as data reports, and decide how those connections would operate in practice.

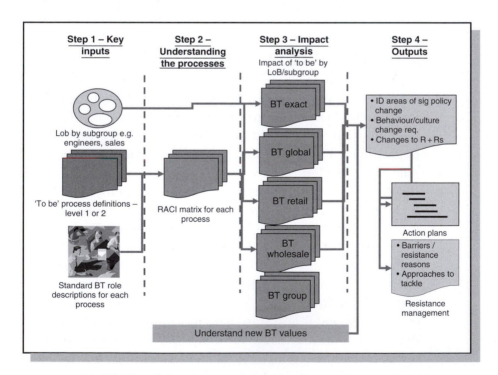

Figure 12.6
Process re-engineering.
Notes: ID, identify; req, required; R+Rs, Roles+ Responsibilities; RACI, Responsible Accountable Consulted Informed; sig, significant.

Figure 12.6 is indicative of the disciplined approach undertaken.

As a starting point, the 'as is' processes and any known process workarounds or exceptions were captured and catalogued, building on earlier work undertaken by an external process re-engineering consultancy. Following this stage, the people implications of the new business strategies (overall and for people and HR) were reviewed and applied to the 'as is' processes to see where steps were unnecessary, or where change or improvement was needed. Country-specific modifications were then applied to the standard process as appropriate.

The modified processes were then tested against the 'vanilla' capability of the new core HR administration system and capabilities such as the online help desk, automated workflows, interactive search engines, and data mining. This allowed the team to see how much more streamlined and intuitive they could become. The 'to be' processes were then shared with the wider HR communities and user groups to make sure they were fit for purpose, straightforward and logical. Wherever possible, enthusiasts or early adopters from other parts of the HR community were co-opted as change champions and system 'gold users'. Their help in testing the processes, spreading the word, and preparing the wider community was invaluable to the program delivery timetable.

In keeping with the original technology decisions described earlier, configuration of the system was the primary mechanism used to enhance critical functionality and to overcome some surprising basic system weaknesses. Customization was kept to an absolute minimum in an attempt to speed up the pan-BT deployment and ensure that future upgrades could be deployed automatically and at less cost. The default was that requests for customization were met with 'No', and a determined argument (with full lifetime cost–benefit analysis) was necessary to overcome the default response. The originator was also reminded that greater sophistication for a minority of super-users involving fine tuning or specific system change could be considered later after the initial platform had been deployed and all users loaded onto it.

The 'vanilla' approach was not an easy line to hold among managers and the HR teams. Fortunately, as a result of early awareness campaigns, many line managers saw the huge advantages of having immediate and direct access to basic guidance about people management issues. They too were quickly co-opted to help raise awareness further and to champion the change.

Innovative ideas for process design

In December 2003, the team organized a walk-through demonstration of the 'vanilla' PS8 system. Representatives in different communities of interest took the 'tour' during which they were shown the individual system modules that made up the whole suite. Around 200 people participated throughout the single day. These included groups of opinion formers, HR critics, and technical experts; groups of subject matter experts or functional process leads; and groups of end-users including union representatives. The system capability was demonstrated by the system provider, and a question and answer session with hands-on opportunity ended the tour. Each group was interviewed on the way in about what they wanted from a new HR system. They were also interviewed on their way out to capture their immediate reaction to the integrated capability of the 'vanilla' system. This innovative idea generated an openness of mind amongst the BT population and cemented an extremely positive and constructive relationship between the system supplier and the BT IT and HR systems communities that would help the program meet its objectives over the following 2 years.

The publicity material for PS8 system outlined the components of the new system. This provided the tour template, and is shown in Figure 12.7.

Two other innovative ideas were to prove equally important in terms of stimulating a fresh approach to process redesign. Each of these involved further investment in PS technology, adding capability to the basic system. These were chosen to simplify processes, since the new capabilities provided immediate help, ensured details were only entered once, removed the opportunity for error or confusion, and removed the need for HR monitoring of processes.

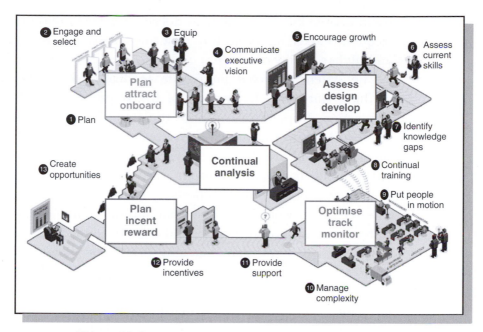

Figure 12.7
The PeopleSoft 'tour'.

The first additional investment was in the exploitation of the PS help desk application to give line managers and employees direct access to the People system via the portal to initiate, manage, or complete specific tasks such as recording sick absence or triggering disciplinary action. Similarly the investment in an integrated, natural language, query search engine tool, and automated web-based email capability facilitated the automatic handling of queries and questions through the portal drawing upon a single depository for responses to frequently asked questions.

The historic file of frequently asked questions collected over many years by the shared services administrator was updated and aligned with the new process designs and policy changes. Questions captured during process re-engineering, system development and general communication or awareness sessions were added and fed into this shared database. The content was assigned an owner from the BT policy or functional subject matter expert teams. It was their job to maintain the quality, accuracy, and validity of the standard responses and edit proposed changes in the future. Importantly, help desk and case-worker agents in the service centre were required to use the same knowledge base to deliver standard responses to frequently asked questions thus ensuring a consistent response and higher quality of advice.

The system collected immediate feedback from users as to the quality and effectiveness of the responses and where satisfaction dropped below 50%, the standard answers were referred back to the owner for refresh. The shared services provider would also be able to escalate responses that were either ineffective or inconsistent with their day-to-day experiences of processing transactions or assisting with casework. The BT owner would have the final authority on any change restoring control of style, tone, and content to the company.

Research had revealed that almost 80% of all telephone queries to the shared services center were satisfactorily answered at the first point of contact. By creating a single, constantly refreshed database that provided exactly the same response whether the query was made by telephone to the service centre or by an online query from the employee's desk meant that the advice was consistent, and the volume of unnecessary calls to the call centre could be reduced significantly.

When managers or employees encountered problems that could not be answered immediately from the database or involved a complex matter (a 'case') to progress, the help-desk application (allied with case workers behind the scenes) would allow them to start and then complete people-related cases such as triggering recruitment, occupational health referrals, or starting the disciplinary process with minimal delay. Users could track the progress of the cases they had submitted via the portal and could attach documentation to individual cases. Automated and agent-generated workflows ensured that cases were managed efficiently and effectively.

Figure 12.8 illustrates the concept behind the idea.

The third additional investment was the stand-alone PS user productivity tool (Figure 12.9). This was used to capture workflow and process steps, which could then be used to walk the user through the necessary actions to accomplish their task.

The fact that the workflow was captured in the system and could be tracked remotely also reduced some of the need for HR policing and authorization.

1. Click on Helpdesk

2. Complete details

3. Receive response

User contacts Helpdesk direct if they:
a) Cannot resolve their query via self-service
b) Have a query that requires looking at their personal history
c) Needs help to create a "case"

User completes personal details, details of the query/case and adds alternative and/or additional contacts as required.
Clicks submit

User receives confirmation 'pop up'with case ID & response times
plus
a) Email response or call from PeopleLine agent to resolve query or discuss further
or
b) Workflow email to initiate case management

Figure 12.8
User experience of the help desk.

- To deliver 90 – 95% of training

- The training content defined by dedicated functional experts

- Access via a web link–no special software needed on PC

- Sits on BT People System

- High quality 'walk' through each step of the process in 'real time'

- Choice of help levels and ability to test their own knowledge

- Provides training materials, performance support, contextual help, and glossaries

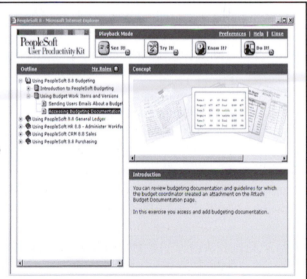

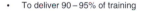

Figure 12.9
Self-help training tool.

Overall system

With these modules in place, the overall system outline is shown in Figure 12.10.

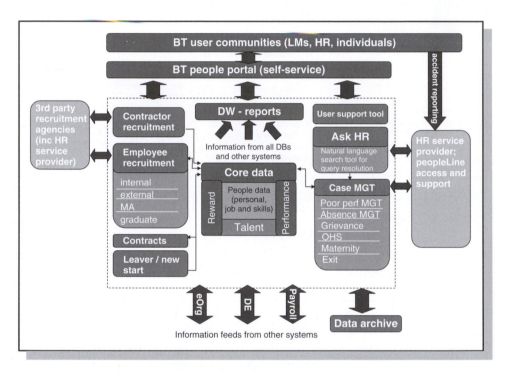

Figure 12.10

System schematic

Notes: (Bt's meta-directory hub) DBs, databases; DE, Directory Enablement; DW, data warehouse; eORG, eOrganisation (BT finance procurement system); HR, human resources; inc, including; LMs, Line Managers; MGT, management; OHS, Occupational Health Service; perf, performance.

Transition plans

These plans were both comprehensive and complicated: the transition had to release benefits into the business, and support the delivery of timely and accurate HR services to employees and future clients. The plan is outlined in Table 12.1.

Table 12.1

Transition plans.

Capability release	Description
Common policies	Audit, harmonize, and streamline HR policies
Common processes	Develop common processes that support an integrated HR service delivery model and standard operating environment internationally
Contact centers	Establish new HR contact centers, which exploit new technology, use workflow, and case management tools
Portal	Provide employees with a personalized view into self-help options, HR information, and company news
Global outsourced organization	Design, implement and support the transition to the new HR outsourced organizational model
Reporting	Consolidate people, HR, financial and 'soft' data in new data warehouse for online, real-time executive and management reporting
Recruitment and SPRO sourcing	Implement new e-recruitment module and on/off-boarding system, and a technology-enabled 'high-touch' candidate experience
Benefits integration	Integrate service delivery with third-party benefit administration providers
Employee queries and self-help	Introduce 'Ask HR' with natural query language and common search engine
Compensation	Provide system with flexibility to manage multiple compensation plans while using multiple payout formulas
HR technology architecture, infrastructure and support	Provide technical infrastructure, application hosting for new integrated BT people system
	Place workflow and manager self-service capability on desktop of 30 000 managers globally

Note: HR, human resources.

Deployment

Deployment was staggered for practical reasons. Management and HR users first experienced the change in April 2005 when the portal was turned on in the UK. This introduced them to the search and enquiry tools and the improved self-service capabilities. The HR outsourcing agreement with the shared services provider was signed in January 2005 but the service was not due to be introduced until August that year. To coincide with the launch, the UK systems data migrated from the outsourced PS7 platform to the PS8 platform. Specific functionality was turned on systematically, service line by service line, to allow for the completion of new working instructions, the opening of some of the new offshore facilities and the training of the shared services staff. Basic reporting followed. This phased approach allowed teething problems to be captured and resolved quickly. Transactional and business partner teams were able to prepare for and manage the transition well, and the end-users had time to grow in confidence and enthusiasm.

Global deployment was also staged. Each country went through an operational readiness audit before the full system capability was switched on. BT Ireland piloted the transformation; BT America followed proving it could operate equally well at scale. The pattern was followed with a phased deployment across Europe. First were English language user countries. BT Germany followed. Attention then turned to BT subsidiaries in France, Spain, and Italy. In this way the team was able to ensure that works councils' expectations and European data protection requirements were delivered to everyone's satisfaction. The Far East and Asia Pacific had specific challenges as there were fewer people spread over considerable distances. On cost grounds, systems deployment was regionalized and priority given to the English-speaking countries first. The global deployment is now nearing completion.

An evaluation: impacts on the business

So, how did the worlds of the various users change? Figures 12.11–12.13 summarize the hoped for changes, showing the series of promotional posters used prior to launch.

Though the system has yet to be systematically evaluated, initial feedback from representatives of the stakeholder groups has been highly positive, suggesting that many fundamental

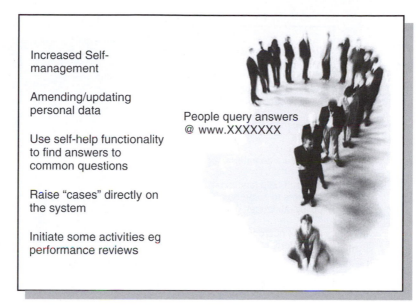

Increased Self-
management

Amending/updating
personal data

People query answers
@ www.XXXXXXX

Use self-help functionality
to find answers to
common questions

Raise "cases" directly on
the system

Initiate some activities eg
performance reviews

Figure 12.11
The impact on individuals.

objectives had been achieved and that users liked the system. Some comments from users included the following:

'I think this new system is intuitive and exciting.'

'Useful and easy. I have already passed this message onto my colleagues.'

'... found a huge amount of very useful information, which is easily accessed, quickly.'

'I had a look at the manager self service, again there is a huge amount of information, which would guide any manager, especially if they were new to BT.'

'It is useful to have one really good link to all HR items, rather than keep searching through the current A–Z, which at times seems to take forever!'

'I can see the new system will be well accepted I feel it is easy to navigate round the menus and find exactly what you need.'

Responsible for day-to-day people management

Advertise vacancy and select candidates for recruitment

Raise, manage and close people/HR "cases"

Operate automated people processes

Use self-help functionality to find answers to common questions or policy guidance

Access appropriate and pertinent management information

People solutions now online, anytime

Figure 12.12
The impact on managers.
Note: HR, human resources.

Be "Business"people -player/coaches

Become Human Capital Management masters

Focus on strategic agenda/HR specialisms

Drive transformational change and organisational development

Provide informed specialist advice, analysis and people consultancy to line management on skills, resource planning, total labour cost management, performance standards, employee engagement etc

Develop Manager people management capabilities

Design people products and solutions
Own HR service standards

Concur or approve some manager decisions in process workflows

Giving everyone a much clearer view soon

Figure 12.13
The impact on HR
Note: HR, human resources.

Lessons learned

So what were the keys to achieving this? We feel the following lessons arise from our case data:

- Managing stakeholders expectations and inputs. Early on, the program team identified critical partners and stakeholders within and beyond BT and established good working relationships.
- 'Vanilla' deployment. Learning from BT's past experience, a strong stance was taken to deploy the technology 'to be', with minimal customizations. Although a difficult line to hold, this did simplify decision-making in the program, and lays a foundation for future developments of the system and the processes it supports.
- Focus on process rather than technology. Although deploying 'vanilla' systems is labeled 'technology-focused' in the literature (e.g. Shrivastava and Shaw, 2003), BT used the program to undertake a major streamlining of its HR processes. It exploited the 'vanilla' stance (made primarily on timing and cost grounds) in order to simplify and align its own internal processes.
- Linkage with other strategic initiatives. Despite adding some risks to the program, the HR program team opted not to reinvent wheels but to work in partnership with other strategic IT programs, such as the meta-directory. This had benefits for both programs: HR regained mastery of people-related data and a sophisticated mechanism for distributing it to wherever it was needed in the business without incurring the full costs of such a development, while the directory infrastructure program gained a key ally and sponsor, always critical to the success of an infrastructure project.
- Identifying champions. The program team sought local champions wherever possible, both within the HR community ('gold users') and among line managers and employee end-users. This created local

expertise, which helped the new system to be accepted. It also ensured that there was a demand for the new system when resistance elsewhere had to be overcome. Importantly, the actual launch introduced users to the new BT PS rather than an HR system, aligning it more with the needs of the end-user.

■ Regular deliverables. Proving early and regular deliveries of capability to users created confidence in the system and allowed gradual familiarization with its features. Examples included the launch of computer training records which resolved a red flag issue for HR, the launch of contractor recruitment in the customer contact centers and a time and labor pilot in the USA. These quick wins brought increased commitment from stakeholders and users. For the program too, regular and early deliverables enabled project and readiness plans to be tested. They also allowed early feedback and correction, allowing users to see the program as responsive to their needs.

These lessons coincide with the critical success factors identified by Shrivastava and Shaw (2003):

■ Incremental delivery and creating early wins;
■ 'Vanilla' deployment, putting the onus on requesters to prove why 'vanilla' would not suffice;
■ Clear and candid communications, particularly about impacts and benefits;
■ HR taking the lead in the program, with support from senior management and fully engaging with the IT community (internal and suppliers);
■ Using employees as change agents;
■ Good training and an effective help desk.

Conclusions

Perhaps not surprisingly, BT's journey to simplification was complicated. In establishing a single global platform supporting end-to-end HR activities and a standard operating environment for people management practices in record time, it was also highly successful. Once roll-out is complete and the full functionality is turned on, the BT Group will have a unique, comprehensive global digital networked people management system with simple workflow-supported people processes, tools and techniques, and a single source of all organizational and people information.

Line managers will be able to carry out their responsibilities for their people, working smarter not harder. Since less time will need to be spent collecting data or finding information, greater time can be devoted to balanced decision-making and those all-important adult-to-adult conversations that underpin successful relationships and drive high performance and engagement.

HR too will have achieved its goals to improve efficiency and effectiveness, reduce its operational cost base; and create a standard operating environment on a global scale. It can focus on the strategic people agenda and work with the shared service provider to make the line manager and employee end-user experience of people management activities a very satisfying one.

Reference

Shrivastava, S. and Shaw, J.B. (2003) Liberating HR through technology. *Hum. Resource Manage.* 42, 201–22.

CHAPTER 13

Building a Road Map for e-HR at the London Stock Exchange

Andy Field

Introduction

This chapter focuses on developing a technology road map for an electronic human resources (e-HR) implementation as a precursor to creating a full business case. The concepts in this chapter have been based on lessons learnt from e-HR implementations in the London Stock Exchange (LSE). The LSE is the world's premier international equity exchanges and a leading provider of services that facilitate the raising of capital and the trading of shares. By the end of November 2006, the market capitalization of UK and international companies on the LSE's markets amounted to £4.2 trillion, with $6.1 trillion of equity business transacted over the year.

The programme was designed to modernize the human resource (HR) department and to alter the nature of the services from a reactive 'personnel' style to a strategic partner within the business. The program's specific objectives at the outset were to:

- Support the transition to a business partner model;
- Increase the range and quality of services;
- Reduce overall cost of HR to the business;
- Allow the existing HR resource to engage in 'value add' work;

- Create the tools for managers and employees to take responsibility for HR related employment life cycle events;
- Better allocate HR resource;
- Develop commercially focused management information.

In both examples the first stage in the programs was the creation of a long-term vision for the future of HR. This 'road map' provided a layout of how the program would deliver these aims directly or in support of other strategic objectives.

The e-HR road map

The e-HR road map is the template used to describe the aims of an e-HR implementation, with the main elements of this description being as follows:

- Scope. The scope of the implementation – linking e-HR with business and HR strategy;
- Technology. The technology used to deliver each of the elements;
- Sequence and timing. When the different e-HR elements of the road map will be delivered;
- Architecting the overall solution. How the elements are pieced together to work as a single entity;
- Implementation plans. Understanding the benefits, change issues and project plans.

This next section explores these elements in more detail and shows how the LSE road map was put together.

Scope – determining the e-HR strategy

The received wisdom is that any HR transformation and e-HR program should be driven ultimately by the business strategy. Key to the goals of the HR program will be the direction of the business, and more importantly how the HR function is interpreting the part they have to play in delivering the business strategy. An e-HR program can play a part in this delivery at two distinct levels: as a direct deliverable of the HR strategy and as a mechanism for delivering a broader HR program of change. The e-HR program at the LSE contained both of these elements within its scope (see Figure 13.1):

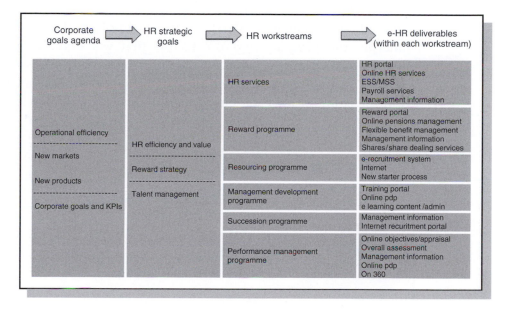

Figure 13.1
Translating corporate strategy into HR deliverables.
Note: The workstreams in Figure 13.1 highlight the e-HR deliverables only. Each workstream had other deliverables that were not impacted on, or by, the e-HR program. ESS, employee self-service; MSS, management support system; PDP, personal development planning.

As a direct response to the strategic goals of the organization, the HR function developed their own goals to impact the corporate agenda. The HR strategic goals were then broken down into workstreams, in turn which were further broken down into specific deliverables. Figure 13.1 shows the deliverables for each of the workstreams that were then specifically designated as 'e-HR deliverable'. This analytical approach was an important step as it ensured that the aims of the e-HR program were integrated into all the strategic HR initiatives (as well as ensuring the individual workstreams could integrate with each other). This process was an important step to understanding the full scope (road map) of the e-HR program.

Technology – delivering the e-HR elements

Once a basic understanding of the objectives has been achieved, it is vital to understand the technology that will underpin the program and the factors that will determine the architecture and functionality of the systems and process. Figure 13.2 highlights the factors that influence the overall technical solution for each element of the e-HR deliverables.

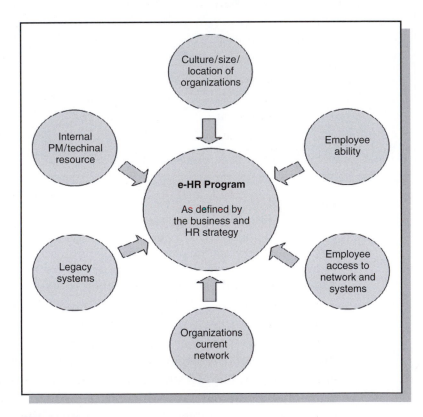

Figure 13.2
Factors that drive the technical approach to e-HR.
Notes: HR, human resources; PM.

How each factor impacts on the various elements of the program depends on the importance that an organization applies to each. However, all these factors will have a significant impact on the overall cost of the program. For example, legacy systems could be used 'as is', 'upgraded' or even 'replaced' by newer, more advanced systems. These decisions depend on factors such as the abilities of the legacy systems, the nature and scope of existing contracts with third parties, and the expected functionality required in the long term. Each choice will have a cost and benefit which has to be weighed against the desired outcomes.

Once the program has identified the elements required, the final decision prior to creating the first pass road map is to understand the architecture of the completed program.

Essentially, there are four options:

- Option 1. HR Core system with integral modules that can be 'switched on and configured' to create a 'single' HRIS;
- Option 2. HR Core system with modules bought, configured and hosted separately (still on internal networks) and connected back to the core system;
- Option 3. HR Core system with modules hosted and managed externally and connected back over the web to a core system – also known as application service provision (ASP);
- Option 4. Outsource of all systems including the Core HRIS.

The benefits and disadvantages of these options are briefly outlined in Figure 13.3. The decision on which option to take is the most important one that the program manager will make because it affects the complexity of the build, architecture and the all consuming question of the end cost.

Note: it is possible to have a combination of options 2 and 3 where some modules are outsourced and others are hosted internally.

It is important to understand that any e-HR implementation requires a 'core' HR system that drives all of the fundamental data required by all e-HR modules. This 'core' information

	Benefits	**Disadvantages**
Option 1		
Company system	■ Predefined process ■ Low complexity of data connectivity between modules ■ Relatively low level of internal IT support for implementation and operation required ■ Ease of upgrades and regression testing over system ■ Similar user functionality across all modules ■ Ease of reporting across modules ■ Organization management and work flow engines span all modules	■ High cost of implementation and licensing ■ Rigid process structure leads to system driving process re-engineering rather than system adopting best fit for organization ■ Difficult to configure beyond basic look and feel ■ Some modules are not necessarily 'best of breed' ■ Can require constant external operational support it there are low levels of IT skills within the organization
Option 2		
Separate internal modules and core HRIS	■ Allows 'best in breed' purchase of each HR module ■ Potentially allows for a 'cheaper' option than the core HR system ■ Ability to negotiate better prices for each module ■ Allows system configuration for each module to match company processes better	■ Complex connectivity issues between individual modules and core system ■ Higher levels of support required for each separate system ■ User interfaces have to be configured more heavily to ensure consistency in the user portal ■ Workflow and organization management and reporting become more complex to manage across different systems

Figure 13.3
Benefits and disadvantages of each of the main technical options.

	Benefits	Disadvantages
Option 3 Internal Core HRIS with ASP modules	■ Managed services require less internal HR and IR skills ■ Particularly good for complex HR modules that require a high degree of skill, e.g. Benefits management and pensions management ■ Less operational risk to HR. No requirements to keep on top of change, legislation and good practice ■ Reduced complexity in HR cost planning	■ More expensive for a managed service ■ HR has reduced control over delivery of services to the business ■ Complex connectivity issues with core internal HR systems ■ Increased configuration to ensure standard user interface ■ Increased complexity in managing work flow organization management and reporting ■ Increased complexity in security across the net, encryption and single sign on for users
Option 4 Outsource all systems	■ Reduces risk to the business ■ Reduces requirements for HR admin and IT skills in the business ■ Reduces complexity of cost planning and resourcing in HR ■ Fully managed and supported service ■ Contracts and SLAs to support required service levels ■ Economies of scale and ability to share good practice across all outsource clients	■ High cost ■ Long implementation time-table and detailed process mapping required ■ Complex contracts and services levels have to be agreed in advance ■ Rigid service delivery to the organization ■ Ad hoc and unforeseen services create high cost for the business ■ Lack of control over service provision ■ Loss of admin skills internally

Figure 13.3
Continued
Notes: ASP, application service provider; HR, human resources; HRIS, human resource information system; IR, ; IT, information technology; SLA, service level agreement.

must reside within the Human Resources Information System (HRIS) to ensure that all processes can be routed via a single entity and that this structure needs to be in place before the other non-core modules can be created.

Timing – planning the elements of the e-HR program

The timing and sequencing of the different elements of the e-HR vital to a successful implementation. To realize an integrated solution, it is important to understand the technical and data requirements for each stage of the development. Figure 13.4 highlights the underlying system architectural requirements within the context of a four stage e-HR road map. This sequencing of the development is equally important when considering the change and training requirements at the implementation stage of the program, for example, by introducing discreet levels of functionality into the business so as not to swamp the potential users with complex operations. Also, developing the e-HR service brand and not over-stretching

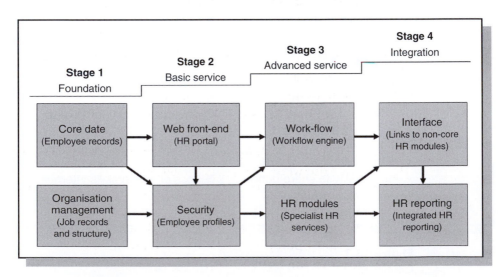

Figure 13.4
Underlying technical modules and their sequencing.
Note: HR, human resources.

HR's ability to support the systems will all become important criteria in the overall success of the programme.

Once the technical elements are identified, the next stage in defining the road map is classifying the e-HR workstreams that will be delivered by the underlying architecture. The classification of these workstreams (HR services) are defined by the strategy, cost and desired benefits.

The workstreams agreed for the LSE program were:

- Payroll and related services;
- HR Information, policy and guidance;
- HR administration and personnel records (this included employee and manager self-service and standard HR processes such as annual leave booking and sickness and absence recording);
- Organization management (the creation of a system based organization structure, in which positions, reporting lines and authorization rules are established in the core HRIS);
- Recruitment;
- Learning and development;
- Performance management;
- Reporting and management information;
- Benefits and reward.

Spending quality time in assessing the phasing of these work-streams allows for a far richer plan and a greater understanding of costs and benefits. The phasing of these work-streams within the overall implementation is subject to a series of factors:

- HR Strategy. Phasing the work-stream delivery to support the wider HR transformation;
- Dependencies. Work-streams which are dependent on the functionality or output of other work-streams;
- Complexity of service. The introduction of complexity of user operation as the e-HR brand develops;
- Cost of implementation. Spreading the development of the work-streams across a manageable timeframe;
- User and System support. The capability of HR to support the user community.

Once the phasing has been agreed the overall roadmap can be finalized.

Architecture – developing the e-HR road map

The cost–benefit analysis, when combined with an understanding of the timing and sequencing of the different e-HR elements, allows the HR function to articulate its vision for the program and forms the basis of a more detailed business case with which to persuade the organization to make the investment decision. This should address the following areas:

- Timing. When each workstream will be delivered and the ultimate length of the program;
- Program resources. The skills that will be required to deliver each of the workstreams, the underpinning technology and the transformational challenges that will lead to successful adoption by the organization;
- Cost. Technical architecture, the individual workstream applications, program resource costs and change plans;
- Benefits. The high-level benefits that the program will deliver to Human Resources and the organization.

The above items represent a distillation of the preparatory work described in previous sections and enable the construction of an informative road map that shows the nature and timing of each module of functionality. This plan has taken full regard for the various factors that influence the overall solution and is a major contributor to the creation of an issues and risks register that identifies factors that may impair the quality and cost of the implementation.

At this stage, it becomes apparent which modules must be delivered first to create a 'foundation layer' for the services that follow. Importantly, it provides a graphical illustration of investment that must be made 'upfront' with the prospect of minimal benefit until other modules are added or integrated to provide progressively more advanced services. In doing so, other vitally important insights into the e-HR program become evident:

- The 'technology challenge'. The level technology-related skills and capabilities
- The 'process challenge'. The level of HR process re-engineering skills and capabilities
- The 'transformation challenge'. The level of change management activities in the wider organization (see 'Change and Transformation' for more details)

The 'first-pass' road map for the LSE e-HR program is shown in Figure 13.5. It is important to recognize that for the initial

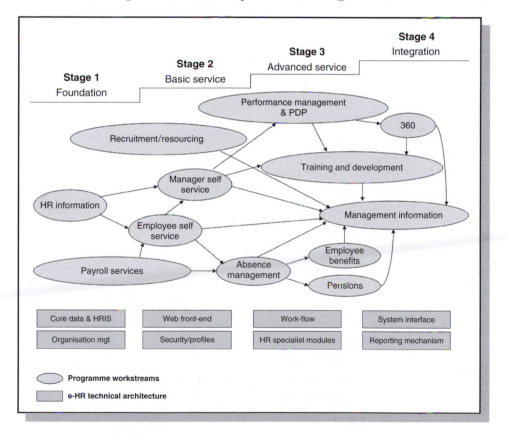

Figure 13.5
Road map with dependent workstreams and underlying technical architecture.
Notes: HR, human resources; HRIS, human resource information system; PDP, personal development planning.

exercise, which is seeking to create the e-HR road map, a confidence level of around 60% is necessary in terms of predicted costs and benefits. The final business case would expect to represent confidence levels of 90% plus, achieved through more rigorous examination of the different elements, including a detailed review of the processes associated with each one.

The road map is now at a stage that can be socialized with the senior management of HR and the wider business in order to gain support for the program. It would also be ready to pass any initial 'approval gates' in a company's investment program.

Beyond this point, a more detailed business case with full technical descriptions of the proposed architecture, detailed cost structures, timings, and benefits would be created, leading to implementation of the overall solution.

Implementation plans

Once an understanding has been reached as to the deliverables of the e-HR program, the next phase is to understand the cost–benefit characteristics of each element. At the LSE, a rigorous approach to the calculation of costs and benefits was undertaken. It was understood that the program would ultimately generate a range of potential benefits from each workstream, conveniently grouped under three headings, based on the work of Lepak and Snell (1998), namely:

- Operational. The ability to streamline processes and reduce the costs of HR in the organization
- Relational. Improvements in HR service quality, such as speedy access to accurate individual and team personnel data, better quality hires, an improved induction experience and so on. The development of a HR portal that allows convenient and intuitive access to on-line HR services
- Strategic/transformational. Moving the perception of HR from an administrative support function of the business to a strategic partner. HR commands respect at the most senior levels of the organization and influences wider business strategy. At this level, the e-HR

system allows the production of complex reporting and metrics to allow HR to apply commercial rigor to the management of human capital and become involved in wider strategic decision making.

Higher costs normally relate to higher complexity. This can be in terms of technical and process complexity, with considerations concerning the acquisition and configuration costs of system components, network upgrades, etc., and also, very importantly, the investment needed to manage successfully the changes to working practices and culture. Typical costs categories are set out below in Figure 13.6.

The initial cost benefit analysis on the exchanges program is shown in Figure 13.7. The low, medium, and high cost rating are a reflection on the cost of each workstream in relation to each other. The actual costs will be determined on the size of

Category	Description
Labor	Internal and external labor costs, including costs for workshops, testing and training
Content	Where applicable, the cost of development and maintenance of e-content (e.g. HR portal, learning modules, etc.)
Hardware	Server and associated support costs
Network	Costs of capacity to deliver e-HR to the desktop/laptop/mobile device
Desktop and other equipment	Providing sufficiently high specification devices to access e-HR functionality (including kiosks/hand held devices for remote workers)
Licenses	Software license costs
Support plus training	Help desk and business support (cost of collateral, training events and general support)
Operation	Post implementation costs – software upgrades, service centre support, outsource costs, etc.

Figure 13.6
Cost categories.
Source: Adapted from Reddington et al. (2005).
Note: HR, human resources.

Service module	Cost of service	Core module	Cost saving (O)	Service quality (R)	HR strategy (R)	Business strategy (T)	Delivery mechanism ASP/st and alone/core
HR portal	L	Y	L	H	M	L	Intranet/core
Payroll (absence/GLI/HR data)	M	Y	M	H	M	L	Core
HR admin 1 (ESS)	M	Y	H	H	M	L	Core
HR admin 2 (workflow processes)	M	Y	H	H	H	M	Core
HR admin 3 (team processes)	M	Y	L	H	M	M	Core
HR admin 4 (360)	M	Y	L	H	H	H	All
HR admin 5 (management information)	M	Y	L	H	H	H	Core
Organization management	M	Y	L	H	H	M	Core
Recruitment 1 (recruitment online)	M	Y	H	M	M	L	All

Recruitment 2 (internal/web enabled)	M	Y	M	M	H	H	All
Learning (administration/content)	H	N	H	H	H	H	All
Benefits management	M	N	L	H	M	L	All
Pension management	M	N	L	H	M	L	ASP
Performance management 1 (appraisal/PDP/objectives/assessment)	M/H	N	M	H	M	M	All
Management information (Dashboard)	M	N	L	L	H	H	Core/stand alone
Performance management 2	M	N	L	H	H	H	All

Fiugre 13.7

Model to assess impact of e-HR services at the LSE.

Notes: ASP, application service provider; core, module of a core; ESS, employee self-service; GLI, ; H, ; HR, human resources; HRIS, human resource information system; L, ; M, ; N, ; O, operational benefit; PDP, personal development planning; R, relational benefit; stand alone, host stand alone system on network and connect to core system; T, transformational benefits; Y,.

the organization, the technology, and the cost of internal and external resource.

The most public element of the program is the change and transformation plan.

The change plan has two objectives: operational and strategic.

Change and Transformation

The development of the road map highlights the main challenges of the change and transformation plan for both the e-HR programme and the wider HR strategy, the most public element of the programme. The change plan has two objectives, operational and strategic:

The operational objective is to ensure that the tools delivered by the program are adopted and used by the business in order for the process to work. Central to this strategy at the LSE was the online HR brand and the staging of the implementation.

At first, basic services were rolled out that were well branded and intuitive. These services focused on the individual and had the added benefit of driving data cleansing. These services were designed to be a standard bearer for more complex processes that followed. The rule of thumb with this implementation was that any services rolled out to all employees should be intuitive enough not to require formal training. In reality, the services that came later in the program could become more complex, as employees and managers became familiar with the brand, layout, and function and therefore still found these more complex services to be relatively intuitive to use.

The strategic objective of the program was the delivery of the wider strategic transformation objectives of HR. The focus here was to ensure that the operation and functionality of the service modules and the communications and training that formed the basis of the technical implementation were fully aligned to the wider transformational objectives of HR. An example within the exchanges program was the performance management workstream. In this instance the functionality of the system and process reflected the desire to ensure continuous reviews with flexible objectives. The training for employee and managers focused not only on the operation of the system but reinforced the messages that had been developed by the wider HR program.

The Exchanges' road map, therefore, not only allowed for the long-term planning of the technology implementation, but also drove a complicated implementation plan that created tangible entities to introduce wider strategic HR concepts.

Lessons learned from the e-HR program

It is important to understand that every organization is different – size, location, aspirations, values, culture, and politics. All of these factors will impact on the scope, design, and delivery of an e-HR implementation. In the case of the LSE programme, it became obvious very quickly that due to the size of the business, the benefits of automation would be small in terms of the savings achieved in the reduction of administration. (In a large company with highly resourced centralized administration units, even basic automation of individual processes can create significant saving.) To that end, it was even more important to visualize the integrated end product, as most of the hard savings in HR would only be realized once a number of the elements were delivered and integrated into the HR services.

Another important lesson learned from the program was the notion that a small organization could not drive enough benefit to justify the costs of implementation. This has been quite conclusively proved incorrect. Size may preclude some of the bigger well-known 'company' systems, due to high cost of licenses and configuration. However, as long as there is a stable core system on a robust platform, a combination of boutique style applications and managed ASP services can be channeled via a portal to provide an integrated service to the business at a relatively low cost.

Vitally important, of course, to the success of the program was the degree to which the organization embraced the new e-enabled services. Attention has already been drawn to the so-called transformation challenge and it is crucial that the status of this challenge is not subordinated to other considerations, such as technical architecture.

The road map provided the structure not only for the technology and process transformation, but also how these services should be implemented into the business.

The transformation plan therefore followed some simple principles which in turn had an effect on the overall road map:

- Functionality. Ensuring that the functionality offered to the users was intuitive and that there were discrete implementations that built a complexity of service over a period of time;
- Communications and branding. Ensuring that the services were instantly recognizable as part of the e-HR offering and the benefits of each new technology implementation were widely understood;
- Process and services. Ensuring that all HR processes and services replaced by the program functionality were removed in order to force traffic through the new offering;
- Benefits. Demonstrating the benefits to all levels of the business (from the convenience, speed and accuracy of service to integrated reporting and management information);
- HR transformation. Ensuring that the service implementations are delivered to coincide with the wider HR change programs. (This is mutually beneficial as it provides tangible deliverables to wider HR change initiatives whilst leveraging the transformational effort of the wider program.)

The viability of an e-HR program can be made without reference to the more intangible benefits that a program would naturally deliver. These intangible benefits (reputation, quality, etc.) are still excellent reasons, if used behind solid cost savings and services improvements that can be quantified. In conclusion, the creation of the roadmap will lead to a concise business case and a well planned implementation that is fully integrated with the wider HR strategy.

e-HR at the National Australia Bank

Neville Clement

Introduction

This chapter describes and evaluates the journey to transform and revitalize the National Australia Bank Ltd's (NAB) Human Resources (HR) function since the late 1990s, which is known internally as People & Organizational Development (POD). Central to the transformation is the introduction of electronically (*e*−) enabled employee and manager self-service (ESS and MSS). While other elements of the case will be featured, the major theme is the role played by information and communications technology on the HR function. Specifically, I will highlight early development of HR content of NAB's Intranet (NI), and how it was leveraged during the implementation of payroll and HR self-service software from SAP, a global provider of business software. The chapter highlights a vision of what NAB set out to achieve and how it went about executing that vision. The inevitable challenges are discussed, along with a commentary on how they were overcome. Finally, the chapter will critically evaluate our change program and outline some next steps, as NAB's POD function continues to search for greater efficiency and effectiveness using its *e*-HR capabilities.

About National Australia Bank Ltd

NAB's history traces back to 1858 when the National Bank of Australasia was established at the height of the Victorian gold rush. NAB's early growth was predominately based on gold and associated commercial activity but it was soon to expand throughout the farming and urban areas of the State of Victoria and later into the other Australian States.

In the course of its development NAB absorbed the Colonial Bank of Australasia (1918), the Bank of Queensland (1922), the Queensland National Bank (1948), and the Ballarat Banking Company (1955). In 1981 the National Bank of Australasia Limited and the Commercial Banking Company of Sydney Limited came together to form what is now National Australia Bank Ltd. Subsequently NAB acquired banks in the United Kingdom in 1987 and 1990 and the Bank of New Zealand in 1992.

Over this time, NAB has become much more than just a retail bank. NAB is an international financial services organization, providing a comprehensive range of financial products and services to consumers, businesses, community organizations, and governments.

NAB is organized around three regional businesses: Australia, United Kingdom, and New Zealand. It also has a global line of business known as Institutional Markets & Services, which provides institutions and corporate customers with debt, risk management, and investment products.

NAB's corporate goal is "To generate sustainable satisfactory returns for shareholders". NAB has recently undertaken a significant re-brand exercise under the banner of "We help our customers to fulfill their aspirations". In this, NAB strives to "back" its customers, not just "bank" them.

Key strategies include a focus on: quality customer processes - making it easy for customers to buy the financial products they need; becoming cost competitive; and bringing a vibrant, responsive, customer oriented brand to life in everything it does.

NAB's aspirational stakeholder measures for the next three years include:

- Stakeholders: double digit annual cash earnings rate; ROE 20%; Cost to Income ratio less than 45%
- Customers: satisfaction rate of above 80%
- People: employee satisfaction rate of above 80%
- Community: a trusted service and financial solutions provider

Key statistics as at 30 September 2006:

- More than 8.0 million retail and business banking customers and more than 2.3 million wealth management customers, globally
- Operations in United Kingdom (UK), Asia, Australia, New Zealand, and United States (USA)
- Net profit – $4,392 million
- Approximately 38,000 employees globally
- 1,258 branches and 2,642 ATMs globally
- Approximately 250 employees within POD Australia

The Early Stages of e-HR at NAB

During 1999, at the height of the dot-com boom, the organization was researching and evaluating options for introduction of *e*-technology in a range of business applications across many business units. POD - or HR as it was then known - was no exception.

NAB had recently introduced a global operating model. A major strategic question for the NAB was, as for many large organizations at the time, how to best leverage technology to support the model, primarily in the three larger regions of UK and Ireland (until 2004, NAB also operated in the Republic of Ireland), Australia, and New Zealand. The major attention was focused on the POD, Finance, and Procurement functions.

NAB embarked on a study comprising internal research, external consulting input, and site visits to a number of financial services and other organizations in various parts of the world. NAB's Executive Committee determined that an integrated enterprise resource management platform would be the key to the future.

Simultaneously, and in the knowledge of what the broader organization was looking to achieve, POD had been carrying out its own research, focusing on how to best leverage technology to transform and enhance the basis upon which its services were delivered. POD's research was conducted in similar fashion to that undertaken in other parts of NAB. That is, internal research, utilizing resources such as the Australian Human Resources Institute (AHRI), Corporate Executive Board, Gartner, and various HR related journals, as well as leveraging the external consulting input, and participation in the reference site visits.

Following vendor evaluation based upon the research undertaken, and in consideration of NAB's unique business requirements, a contract was signed with SAP for the purchase of software to enable an integrated POD, finance, and procurement platform. Functional executives leading these three areas were party to the final decision taken.

Implementation began in 2000. The initial plan was to run a pilot comprising a small number of SAP HR applications in NAB's UK and Ireland operations, located at the Glasgow based headquarters. Following the pilot, the intention was to implement the chosen HR, finance, and procurement components in the three major regions simultaneously. Implementation design was based upon a global framework of "standard SAP software", with customization to be contained to the minimum required to support regional legislative and regulatory requirements.

Learnings from the pilot led to a very different outcome from that initially envisaged. These were:

- NAB undertook more customization than was anticipated, to accommodate regional business, legislative, and regulatory requirements;
- the complexity of the legacy technology systems, coupled with the number of required interfaces to upstream and downstream applications, put the project timelines and costs under considerable pressure;
- the need for greater emphasis on securing local executive sponsorship and stakeholder support was evident;
- 'cleansing' and ongoing management of affected critical data was insufficient; and
- taking these factors into account, the implementation risk factors would need to be reassessed and profiled

As a result of the pilot and the invaluable learning that had ensued, NAB decided to rewrite the implementation plan, taking a region by region approach, beginning in New Zealand.

The New Zealand region of the NAB Group is represented by Bank of New Zealand (BNZ), acquired by NAB in 1993. BNZ had, since the acquisition, demonstrated its ability to successfully execute major projects. Given this capability, coupled with BNZ's smaller size relative to Australia, (around 5000 employees), the NAB Executive Committee decided to use BNZ as a platform to begin the regional roll-out, then to follow in Australia, and finally, return to the UK and Ireland to complete the roll-out plan.

In short, BNZ assembled a project team and during 2002 and 2003, successfully implemented SAP HR, finance, and procurement applications in three separate, but fully integrated releases. Anecdotal feedback from BNZ indicates that the level of integration SAP software offers across the HR, finance, and procurement functions has delivered streamlined processes, and more accurate and reliable data. Especially within POD, HR self-service has been a contributing factor in improving data reliability, through leveraging the visibility that employees and people leaders have to the data they are respectively responsible to maintain, and their ability to update it on-line. An additional benefit is the flexibility BNZ now has to recruit and deploy SAP technical skills across these functions whereas in the past, each legacy system required a specific, less-transferable skill base to be maintained.

During the BNZ implementation, a number of regulatory compliance requirements were emerging, such as the Basel II Accord, Sarbanes-Oxley Act, and International Financial Reporting Standards (IFRS). NAB found it needed to prioritize its labor and investment resources to meet these requirements, and as a result, the global ERP vision was halted during 2003. Instead, it was decided to continue only with HR and procurement in Australia. Implementation of the finance applications in Australia, and all functional applications for the UK and Ireland, was deferred indefinitely.

The remainder of this chapter will focus on the introduction of *e*-HR in Australia.

NAB HR, Australia

Once the contract with SAP was signed in 2000, the POD function in Australia began to turn its attention to getting ready for implementation of the HR software that was planned for 2003. The research referred to earlier in this chapter, had reinforced a number of common concepts which were clearly beginning to shape the future of successful HR functions. These included:

- a requirement for HR to demonstrate its capability to understand and influence business outcomes to secure a "seat at the executive table", that is, to be more "strategic" and less "operational";
- in order to demonstrate this shift along the "operational" to "strategic" continuum, HR needed to refresh and rebuild its internal processes and capabilities;
- a sense that many organizations wanted their HR functions to be "best practice", although quite what "best practice" meant and how to benchmark and assess this aspiration, was less clear;
- a view that line managers should take more direct responsibility for some aspects of people management, traditionally seen as the domain of HR, such as decisions to do with selection, development, pay, and exit;
- a call for HR functions to reduce costs, while maintaining or improving efficiency and effectiveness;
- most compellingly, HR "self-service" was seen to be a logical step to achieving cost efficiencies, through reduction in operational HR resourcing, and in enabling line managers to execute their responsibilities.

Armed with this research, and after much discussion and debate within the POD Leadership Team – which comprised the Global Executive General Manager (EGM) of POD and direct reports - a Transformation team, sponsored directly by the EGM, was formed. The team set out to rebuild, and transition to, a new operating model, which would be underpinned by the SAP software as an enabling system, thereby allowing POD to introduce *e*-HR. The Transformation team immediately developed a vision, and a set of success factors for the project.

POD Transformation Vision:

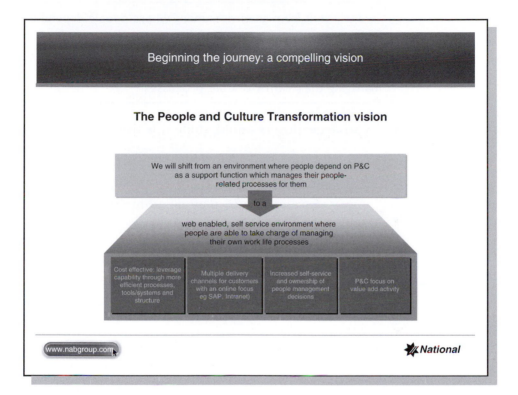

Figure 14.1
P&C transformation vision.
Notes: www.nabgroup.com.

This schematic illustrates the challenge the Transformation team was tasked with executing. The view of POD (then known as People & Culture) at the time was one of paternalism i.e, a function which had held onto the comfort of providing services to the business that, somewhat paradoxically, were appreciated throughout the organization, while considered low value. Needless to say, NAB's EXCO took little convincing that low value also translated to too costly.

POD's response to this, was to position the future vision as one in which people leaders would be enabled by self-service technology, and given accountability to manage a range of day to day "operational" HR processes, whilst employees would be empowered and expected to maintain a range of personal data and processes affecting their day to day life at work. Hence

> "we will shift from an environment where people depend on P&C as a support function which manages their people related processes for them, to a web enabled, self service environment where people are able to take charge of managing their own work life processes".

Four key strategic drivers would guide this vision:

1   Cost effectiveness: POD would look to leverage the capability and scale of efficient processes and technology systems to reduce manual administration, paper, and related costs;
2   Multiple channels: POD would explore moving from a predominantly hands-on service provided by HR Assistants in each business unit, to a multi-channel service offering, focusing on self-service via the NAB Intranet and SAP software supported by an employee call center, as a way to reduce the requirement for direct support of HR professionals;
3   Increased self-service: Through having the right tools, processes, and delivery channels in place, employees and people leaders would be both enabled, and compelled to take more accountability and ownership of day to day processes via self-service; and
4   POD focus on adding value: leveraging the impact of new channels would allow POD to reinvent its capabilities to step-change its focus away from high volume low value activity, to a more business oriented, or strategic value set.

From this point in 2000, the journey to introduce *e*-HR progressed in three stages:

Stage 1:   Stage 1: Leveraging the NAB Intranet
Stage 2:   Transitioning the Operating Model
Stage 3:   Introducing Self-Service

Preparing the Organization for Change

As with any change in a large organization, there are many stakeholders whose worlds are affected in different ways. The impact on the organization from what was to come from implementing e-HR was recognized early, and influenced the development of change management strategies. From this point forward, preparation of the organization for the evolution of the HR function was a continual focus and a structured change program was developed and implemented to support the key impacts of each stage of the journey.

Securing conceptual acceptance to the SAP and POD vision was seen by POD Executives as a critical first step. For the sake of simplicity, and while there were numerous stakeholder groups, this case study identifies four key groups and how POD set about to engage them:

The NAB Executive Committee

It was a given that members of EXCO had been exposed to the decision taken to introduce SAP software to NAB. For this group, it was essential for POD to outline the vision and how the implementation of SAP software would integrate with the new POD. This was achieved through a combination of leveraging relationships of the EGM of POD - a member of EXCO - and the business unit Heads of POD, who in turn, sat on the respective business unit leadership teams. These business teams generally comprised the member of EXCO who led the business unit, and their direct reports. In effect, this gave POD direct access to the first two levels of the organization. Formal leadership team briefings were supplemented by informal discussion with these key organizational leaders.

POD Population

Significant effort was expended in structuring and executing an engagement plan for the approximately 400 Australian employees of POD when the Transformation journey began. Members of the POD Leadership Team became responsible to share the vision and communicate progress with their respective teams. Formal team meetings and informal interaction within each of the P&C teams soon started to generate interest. This key communication channel was supplemented by the Transformation team's own activities such as:

- Coffee Club – each month, all members of the POD community were invited to an informal "coffee and muffin" session where a member of the Transformation team would outline progress, seek input and feedback into issues and challenges, and confirm next steps;
- Transformation Newsletter – issued monthly to reinforce key messages and invite feedback, either directly to the team, or via POD people leaders.

Business Unit Leadership Teams

Within a large organization such as NAB, ensuring senior leaders are first brought on board is essential to cascading positive and complete, contextual information about any organizational initiative. Done well, it is possible to reach large populations of employees relatively quickly and easily. Engagement of leadership teams was seen as a critical channel, and this was undertaken mainly via the business unit POD representatives, supported where required by a member of the Transformation team.

NAB Employees

Ultimately, an entire organization needs to be brought on board for any major change initiative to be successful. In the beginning, while the program was at a conceptual stage, this was less critical. As the program progressed, and tangible deliverables began to emerge, specific media and initiatives were adopted to target the delivery of information.

The key message here is that the team saw the need to develop a structured change program that would be executed in a combination of broad messages to continually prepare the organization, and specific event based messages, to support discrete deliverables in each of the three phases of the journey.

POD Transformation

Stage 1: Leveraging the NAB Intranet

NAB began to develop NAB Intranet (NI) during 2000. NI began with populating organizational information content, encouraging each business unit to contribute information about its operations, within a standard template. POD was one of the first business units to identify the benefits that could be realized from utilizing an intranet, particularly as a communication medium. Quickly, and deliberately, the POD Transformation team formed an alliance with the NI development team. This was formalized by cross representation on the respective POD Transformation and NI governance committees, whose role was to support, enable, and track the progress of the two initiatives.

Early in this alliance, an idea was hit upon to get some electronic processes up and running on NI, as a forerunner to the "self-service" that the SAP applications would bring. While NI was "pushing" organizational information to employees, it was felt that if it could be used to "pull" employees, to encourage them to use it as a day to day tool, then the introduction of the more extensive SAP self-service functionality could potentially be achieved easier. The question was, what would be the most appropriate processes to begin with?

Not surprisingly, NAB looked to payslips. NAB runs a fortnightly payroll for all employees and a paper payslip was delivered by mail to each employee's work location. Arguably, a payslip is one of the most eagerly anticipated and welcome pieces of communication between an employer and its employees. Apart from the anticipated willingness of employees to receive their payslip on-line, there would be added benefits for efficiency: reduced possibility of payslips being lost; reduction of paper through turning off hard-copy payslips; and the resulting cost reduction arising from less paper and manual distribution handling.

The on-line capability was developed, and payslips via NI was phased in across all business units during 2001. Feedback was generally very positive, and while there was the odd call to retain them, hard paper payslips were finally halted a number of months after all business units were live.

Riding the wave of this first success, NAB then introduced on-line leave applications and people leader leave approval. Apart from paper and associated cost reduction, NAB also achieved increased control over and accuracy of the recording of leave taken. Whereas paper based applications can go missing after approval, and therefore not be recorded – a direct cost to the organization - the recording and audit trail of electronic transactions is more certain.

Other applications electronically enabled in this way on NI, included internal job applications, and a staff directory.

Throughout the development and implementation of these initiatives, NAB continued its ongoing change and communication program. Some of the salient activities that supported the NI phase are now covered.

Securing Organizational Commitment

Importantly, NAB assembled a NAB Intranet Governance Committee. This was chaired by a member of EXCO and represented by senior leaders from each of POD (also representing the POD Transformation team), Technology, and, at appropriate stages, the business units who were either planning, or in the midst of, a NI application "go-live". As referenced earlier, this committee was formed to support, enable and track progress to plan. However, it was also the primary decision-making body with regard to project planning, including assessment of priorities (both what to do, and where best to extract greatest impact), costs, benefits, and risks. Clearly the Committee had a broader agenda than to support POD's Transformation; the key focus was on enabling business process value in as many business units as possible.

Harnessing Business Unit Support

The key target in securing business unit support was the Business Unit Leadership Teams. As described earlier, relationships forged between business leaders and the co-located POD business unit teams were leveraged to gain support and commitment to NI. As well, members of the NI team took every opportunity to get before business unit leadership teams, to position and discuss their ideas, gain feedback, and secure commitment and, where necessary, funding to proceed. While leadership teams were asked to cascade communication within their respective business units, this had mixed results.

"nab TV"

nab TV is an internal capability, complete with its own recording studio, used on a regular basis to communicate to all employees. Sessions go to air at a specified time and day each week, and are repeated regularly during the week. nab TV was used both to communicate specific messages around NI, and at various times, to communicate an integrated message in conjunction with POD Transformation, demonstrating the emerging use of NI as an enabler for people. Payslips on line was a good example of the collaborative approach to using NI.

"Sneaker Brigade" and "Scooter Campaign"

The NI team, themselves a mix of creative individuals, devised some rather unique approaches to generate interest and encourage employees to look for more news about what NI was doing. The Sneaker Brigade and Scooter Campaign were examples of the creation and use of metaphor. A Vespa Scooter used in the Scooter Campaign was subsequently given away as a prize in a competition for employees, aimed at collecting feedback on NI.

The following boxes describe the intent behind these two examples and how they were used. (Note: NI was initially known as the "Corporate Intranet")

Case: Scooter Campaign

Once the Corporate Intranet was ready it was essential to get as many people to visit as possible. The awareness marketing campaign was anchored on two images. First, a person because Corporate Intranet is about people. And second, a motor scooter as a metaphor for Corporate Intranet as "a new way of getting around the National". The awareness campaign was delivered via email with click button access to the Corporate Intranet and the Support group.

Campaign Images

With this campaign we took something that is highly intangible and made it real. We had images that said Corporate Intranet is all about people zipping around the organisation with ease.

What the Scooter Campaign did for us:

- Got people to visit the site

- Connected people with technology

- Made getting to the site and accessing support easy with click buttons

Case: The Sneaker Brigade

The Sneaker Brigade Logo

"The Sneaker Brigade", so called because they wear soft soled shoes and "run" around from PC to PC, are a great way to create a sense of fun around the connection experience. It also gives the organisation a baseline level of connectivity – all those PCs capable of connecting to the IP network are optimised to do so.

The Sneaker Brigade is a small group of technical support personnel, who visit people at their desktop and connect them to Corporate Intranet. If connection is not possible immediately then the user is told what the problems are and what is needed to fix them. The Sneaker Brigade are successful because they connect many people who were technically capable of connecting but never had the need. The Sneaker Brigade also provide a report on the connectivity status of business units as they go.

What The Sneaker Brigade did for us:

• made getting connected easy and fun

• allowed us to be seen to be helping people get connected

• gave the business unit a summary of what to do to get all their people connected

Overall, the thrust of the NI approach to change and communication was to attempt to create a novel and compelling message and excite and engage employees about an emerging new world – a world embracing technology to make their lives easier. Leveraging the NI phase was, for POD Transformation, an ideal opportunity to whet the appetite of 24,000 employees. Afterall, SAP was coming!

Stage 2: Transitioning the POD Operating Model 2000-2006

During 1998, NAB had implemented a global business model, centralizing a number of support functions in Australia. POD's response to this was to create a shared service function whose role was to develop frameworks, products, and services - in response to global and regional business needs - that would be implemented primarily by small, business unit HR teams left in each region. The teams within Global Shared Service included Recruitment and Selection, Performance Management, Remuneration and Benefits, Employee and Industrial Relations, Learning and Development, and Services (Payroll, Transaction Management, and HR Management Information).

POD has undergone a number of organizational changes since, starting from around 2000. Rather than track all of those changes, this segment highlights some of the changes introduced in conjunction with the emergence of *e*-HR, and again, emphasizes the critical importance of maintaining effective change and communications through the continuing evolution. Figure (14.2) illustrates the high level changes between 2000 and 2006.

Broadly, as a carry-over from the last major change in 1998, each business unit had resident HR Managers - an early variant of the role known in HR circles to day, as Business Partners - and were supported by HR Assistants. In the paper based environment of the day, the major contribution of these people was at an operational level. HR Assistants would, by necessity, shuffle paper and act as a conduit between business units and the Services segment of Shared Services. As noted above, Shared Services was a centralized group, containing the majority of

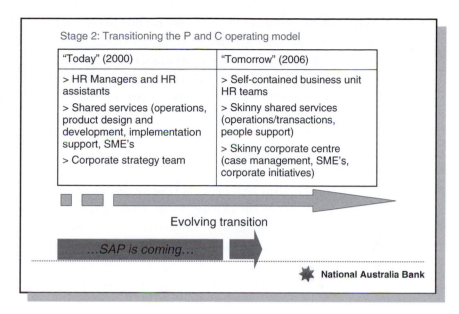

Figure 14.2
The journey – 2000 and beyond.
Notes: HR, human resource; P&C, People & Culture; SME, subject matter expert.

HR resources and capability, and was perhaps, in today's parlance, a "Centre of Excellence" comprising expertise across the entire employment cycle from joining, to exit. In addition, there was a central Corporate Strategy team who looked mainly across Group requirements, and supplemented Shared Services with thought leadership and topical research.

While POD was able to deliver many excellent outcomes, its efficiency was hampered by the high overheads of running paper-based, labor intensive manual transactions. Also, as with many HR organizations, and in NAB's case, particularly since capability was centralized away from business units, there was a tendency to design and build products and services seen through POD's eyes, rather than from the viewpoint of business value creation.

The organization of POD today, has – among other things - responded to both of these issues. First, the introduction of self-service has significantly changed the role of POD teams resident in the business units, through automating many processes, thereby allowing these teams to focus on more value accreting work; and second, a sound proportion of the Shared

Service, and Corporate Strategy teams has been decentralized, to give business units greater end to end management of their own priorities and HR resource management. To support these changes, in 2003, a "People Advisory Centre" (PAC) was introduced. Introduction of PAC enabled the removal of HR Assistants from within the business units. A further explanation of PAC follows in the next section.

Concomitant with this, the Corporate Strategy team has also been largely decentralized and now forms an integral segment of the Business Unit POD teams. Those remaining in the Corporate Center focus on driving value from a small number of region-wide, cross business unit initiatives such as recruitment, talent management, and learning including compliance based learning.

Meanwhile, communication of the evolving changes across the four stakeholder groups described earlier in this chapter, continued. During the period from 2000, to 2003, special emphasis was given to preparing the region for the introduction of SAP software, including periodic updates on the progress of the implementation across the Tasman Sea, in Bank of New Zealand.

Stage 3: Introducing SAP Software, and Extending Self-Service

For Australia, the SAP software roll-out began in 2003. Readers will recall that NAB had already begun to introduce some elements of self-service to the delivery of P&C services, via NI which, by then, was generally accepted as an everyday tool of trade. The SAP software roll-out introduced Payroll management, replacing a 25 year-old internally developed legacy system. In addition, SAP added or substituted an extensive array of integrated HR Management functionality. SAP applications included:

- Leave Management: employee online application and workflow approval to people leaders
- Limited Performance Management: Role Purpose Statements for all roles; Qualifications and Skills repository for completion by employees (in progress, 2006)

- Salary Packaging: ability for all employees to restructure benefits within package limits
- Salary Reviews: ability for people leaders to update salary levels and incentive targets, and perform ad hoc salary increases, on-line
- Transaction Management: centralized management of hires, moves, exits, promotions
- Organization and Position Management: NAB implemented a "position reports to" organizational structure, designed to facilitate workflow management
- Time Recording: individual work schedules are recorded for every employee. Recording of exception time by employees initiates auto-calculation of time based penalty payments such as overtime, and meal money
- Employee Self-Service (ESS) and Manager Self-Service (MSS) enabling the above functions

NI provides the front end for these SAP applications. However, NAB self-service does not just include SAP applications. A number of additional POD applications are accessed directly via NI. These comprise some home grown, mainly lotus notes or access database built applications, and some proprietary "off the shelf" purchased applications. Most, but not all are web-enabled, facilitating remote access. While NAB would like to consolidate more applications within the SAP software portfolio, the applications available on the currently installed version of SAP software (SAP R/3, 4.6C) do not sufficiently provide the business solutions sought. Clearly, consolidation within SAP software would provide better integration of functionality, and potentially reduce operating and maintenance costs incurred by having to run multiple alternative applications. Later versions of SAP software provide greater flexibility and functionality and if in future NAB upgrades from version 4.6C, it will re-assess whether new applications could be added.

As mentioned earlier, self-service is supported by PAC, an employee call center which operates on a combination of voice and data (e-mail). Average daily contacts to PAC are around 700, with a split of 60% voice, and 40% email.

Figure (14.3) summarizes NAB's POD *e*-HR or self-service model.

NAB Intranet	■ Provides front-end access to all POD applications including SAP MSS and ESS, non-SAP applications including Learning Campus, (compliance and role-based learning), half-yearly performance data capture, and remuneration reviews. ■ Universal access for all employees – first line of support ■ Contains all policy, process descriptions and maps, and procedure ■ Information is organized for employees via a drop-down "People Tool Bar" which is structured around key areas, eg Health & Safety, Careers, Performance & Rewards ■ Specific information for people leaders is organized via a "People Leader" page ■ All POD content is centrally maintained by subject matter experts (SME's) in POD
People Advisory Centre (PAC)	■ Call center support for all POD related needs ■ Second level of support; self-service is considered first level ■ Advisers coach employees on how to navigate NI content and self-service applications ■ All contacts are logged and tracked in a Content Management System ■ Aims for 85% "one and done" resolution; the remaining 15% of contacts are referred to Case Management, process specialists, or Systems Support ■ Quality management processes including call and email monitoring are embedded, and monthly user feedback is sought on all PAC Advisers

Figure 14.3

Bringing employees on the journey

The introduction of SAP applications changed the work lives of some 25,000 employees in Australia. This was not without challenges and a number of principles guided the roll-out. These included:

- The implementation of SAP software was positioned as a "business initiative". Although the SAP project team had a relatively visible profile, managing a successful project was secondary to ensuring the primary purpose of delivering a business solution to the POD business unit.
- Highly committed sponsorship. Sponsors were at executive level and generally self-appointed rather than organizationally "encouraged". The benefit speaks for itself: people who put themselves forward for assignments generally do so because they believe in a cause, and are therefore more likely to engage. Apart from being enthusiastic champions, the sponsors provided guidance and strategic direction on broad organizational matters, and assisted in the removal of barriers, and provision of resources
- Strong and active governance. Governance overview was evident all the way to Board level. Understandably, given the experience of the UK and Ireland pilot, the Board and EXCO were determined that due learning had been captured, and that the Australian roll-out would follow Bank of New Zealand's much more successful lead. Project Governance was therefore rigorous, and at a practical level, managed by a Steering Committee of senior leaders who in turn, would report to EXCO and Board. The Steering Committee was provided with regular reporting under a framework driven by the Charter and project plan, with special emphasis on milestones and agreed deliverables. In return, the somewhat intimate nature of the governance framework generated a high level of understanding and acknowledgment of the risks and complexities faced by the project, and this assisted in enabling timely sign-offs and go/no-go decisions. The Steering Committee also approved funding under a stage-gate arrangement, and had oversight of the commissioning of periodic reviews. These were conducted

by externally sourced independent consultants, as well as the SAP software Vendor. Furthermore, NAB's internal audit division gave full-time commitment to the project.

■ Rather than a revolution, the SAP self-service roll-out was seen as a natural extension of the introduction of NI

■ A talented and committed project team was assembled, including where possible, members who had previously been involved in UK and Ireland, and New Zealand. The team was led by visible, respected and connected leaders

■ In view of the size of the Australian business, coupled with the complexity of the business model and technology landscape, it was decided to begin with a small pilot. SAP software was first rolled-out – with reduced functional scope - in November 2003 to approximately 300 executives, board directors, and pensioners. Apart from proving the efficacy of the project execution, NAB felt this would be a great way to enlist some very senior change champions by giving them first hand, advance experience of using SAP applications!

■ Enormous emphasis was placed on anticipating, mitigating, and communicating expected changes. This was effected by inclusion of a small but dedicated, specialist change and communications team, within the project

■ Following the very successfully pilot, NAB then rolled out full functionality to approximately 25,000 employees, in four deployments, throughout 2004. Figure (14.4), which is an extract from a post implementation review conducted by an external management consulting company, bears testament to the success of the roll-out.

■ After each release, all who had contributed were invited to attend a celebration hosted by the project, thereby further strengthening the basis for teamwork and collaboration across many parts of the organization

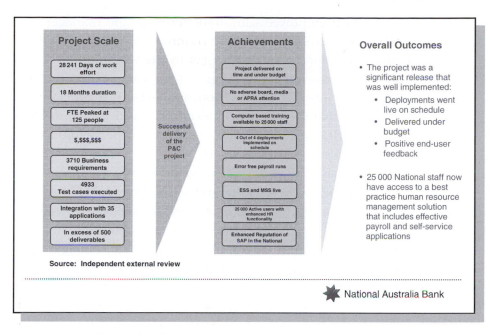

Figure 14.4
Some project outcomes.
Notes: APRA, Australian Prudential Regulatory Authority; ESS, employee self-service; MSS, manager self-service; P&C, People & Culture.
Source: Independent external review.

How did the changes affect the NAB population?

Notwithstanding the planning and preparation that preceded the rollout, the changes nonetheless had an impact across three major groups as briefly described below:

Changes to the People Leader role

Within the NAB, it was understood that, by nature of the role, a manager, or people leader, has a significant impact on the productivity of his or her people. Supporting this notion is the view that an employee's loyalty is often to the manager, not to the organization. And where positive relationships are built between employees and managers in the workplace, this can lead to a positive impact on tangible costs, for instance, through reduced turnover. Logically, this implies that managers should be accountable for people management, and be empowered with the authority, tools and support to properly fulfill their responsibilities.

The introduction of MSS has allowed for key decisions which have traditionally been seen within the domain of the POD function, to be given over to managers. These include decisions with respect to recruitment and selection, development, promotion, pay, exit etc. Giving greater control to managers, not only for the decisions they take, but the means to execute them quickly and efficiently, is a tangible step in strengthening the direct relationships with their employees, thereby increasing the potential to generate higher employee satisfaction, engagement, and productivity.

Changes experienced by employees

The introduction of *e*-HR has introduced a number of changes for employees. These include:

- Employees now have ownership of and the ability to update personal data on-line, including work location and contact details, home address and contact details (optional), mail address preference, emergency contacts, spouse and dependant details (optional). Employees are able to see and track the changes on their desk-top. Before the introduction of SAP applications, these data would have been updated by sending paper forms to central POD; delivery was not always reliable, accuracy of data input not guaranteed, and employees would have little or no visibility of whether or not the requested change had been effected until physically tested, for instance whether an expected piece of mail were received.

- The provision of on-line role support. For instance, every employee now has access to, and responsibility - in conjunction with their people leader - to maintain a Role Purpose Statement on-line. Roles are grouped into generic "families" and customized according to the unique requirements of specific positions, and to keep pace with organizational changes. Thus, maintenance of Role Purpose Statements has been made easier than the historic individual hard copy job descriptions, and has proven useful in ensuring ongoing role clarity throughout times of organizational change, together with providing ready access to job-sizing and internal market-match data for salary review purposes. Employees also have access via NI to up to date policy, process and procedure information. Dispensing with traditional paper based manuals has not only made this information easier and quicker to find for employees, it has significantly enhanced the ease by which the content can be centrally updated and distributed.

- On-line transactions including leave applications, viewing and printing payslips, and recording exception time. Since every employee has an individual work schedule recorded within SAP, recording of exception time initiates automatic calculation and payment of any award related allowances. This has removed the requirement for employees to separately apply for any meal money, overtime, stand-by, and call-out allowances that may apply. Furthermore, these transactions would previously have required a separate paper form to be completed and sent to central POD. Completion of transactions on-line has removed paper, as well as solving the inevitable problem of forms being lost in the mail. Whilst not quantified, NAB is confident that as a result, employee downtime has reduced, and productivity therefore improved.

- Real-time access to organization and business unit communication. Use of NI is used as a key communication medium that affords all employees immediate desk-top visibility of important messages. Although intended to supplement rather than displace face to face and other communication channels, NI has the benefit of being able to ensure key points are consistent across the entire organization. Employee feedback confirms that NAB's efforts in improving openness and transparency of communication using NI and nab TV have had a positive impact. Additionally, NI provides a straightforward means to provide feedback, whether ad hoc on any topic, or targeted to a specific organizational request. The visible manner in which this feedback can be provided places accountability on NAB leaders to respond, thereby demonstrating a commitment to listen to employee's ideas and opinions.

A shift in role for POD

For the P&C teams within the business units, since the Transformation journey began in 2000, there has been a marked shift from high-touch operational, to a deeper involvement in business driven people strategy. This has been aided by the removal of HR Assistants, and the introduction of PAC, coupled with the decentralizing of higher capability subject matter experts from the old Shared Service unit and Strategy Team, to business units. The primary purpose of the business unit POD teams today, is to "assist line managers to define, develop, and implement strategic business solutions". Feedback within POD suggests that some people have found the continual shifting sands over the past 6 years difficult. Conversely, the changes have opened up new and exciting development opportunities for many others.

Centrally for POD, there has been a significant reduction in paper based, manual transactions; the removal of some 80,000 pieces of paper annually. The introduction of PAC has largely been a success; the main theme of employee feedback gained through quality monitoring, is that while sometimes the call wait times are too long, the quality of advice given is generally of a very high standard.

Redeploying the majority of subject matter capability into the business units has seen a corresponding decrease in the number of corporate driven initiatives built. This, in turn has given business units a greater sense of ownership and influence over people strategy and development.

Collectively, POD has become a smaller, more efficient unit, although the journey is by no means complete.

e-HR was a significant initiative and presented NAB with some challenges and learning opportunities

Figure (14.5) outlines some of the more significant challenges and considerations faced by NAB, together with a flavor of how NAB managed and learned from them. In some instances, these relate to the entire Transformation journey. Given the size and significance of the SAP software rollout, others relate specifically to the implementation phase and are noted accordingly.

Integrated planning and execution:	
■ bringing together the various pieces and people. ■ engagement and co-operation between the various projects, and the core POD business function	■ The journey over a six-year period has traversed three main stages: Leveraging NI; Transitioning the Operating Model; and Introducing Self-Service via SAP applications. At various times, these have been discrete projects. Critically, at points of cross-over, NAB ensured integration through cross-governance representation eg POD represented on the NI Governance Committee and likewise, NI representation on the POD Transformation team. Similarly, the SAP project was sponsored by and represented by the POD business unit. This approach was instrumental in generating and maintaining a sense of shared ownership and commitment to joint success.

Figure 14.5

<table>
<tr><td></td><td>■ Also with respect to the SAP project, co-location of the entire core team, peaking at around 125 including POD SME's, Technology Development support, Testing, Change, Communications and Training specialists, added a further sense of camaraderie and belonging
■ All roles in all phases were clearly defined, agreed and documented
■ Executive Sponsorship from within POD "set the scene"
■ A number of POD individuals who would be affected by the changes were selected onto the project teams. This generated greater understanding of why the changes were occurring, and helped to reduce the prospect of personal anxiety</td></tr>
<tr><td>Minimizing organizational disruption from the rollout of SAP applications and self-service</td><td>■ Breaking the release into 4 deployments reduced the risk of stopping the entire organization, and made the change more manageable for the business units, POD and the project itself
■ The Change and Communications team produced and managed a Stakeholder Impact Assessment, and a Business Relationship Plan, together with a Communication Strategy
■ Significant process reengineering took place within POD in advance of the SAP applications rollout to ensure effective integration and interface between SAP software and business process, thereby minimizing process impact. This was of particular importance given the "standard SAP software" ideal adopted
■ Risk was further mitigated through the use of an extensive test program. Adoption of a low risk test program for Australia, as it had been in New Zealand, was seen as particularly prudent, given learning from the UK and Ireland pilot.</td></tr>
</table>

Figure 14.5
Continued

Introducing SAP software within a complex legacy technology environment	■ Full engagement with and commitment of the NAB Technology department. ■ All interfaces to the legacy payroll had to be mapped and analyzed for upstream and downstream impacts. This extended to End User Computing applications to determine whether or not each should be regarded as in, or out of scope ■ NAB took a "standard" approach to implementing SAP software, recognizing that customization requires additional effort (and cost) in initial development, ongoing maintenance, and eventual upgrade stages. Customization was therefore generally restricted to employment and compliance regulatory and legislative requirements, although some additional changes were made at the request of POD's process owners. With hindsight, NAB would have chosen to do less customization, instead placing more emphasis on challenging and re-engineering internal business processes
Assessing Organizational Readiness for SAP software and self-service roll-out	■ A business unit by business unit assessment, including identification of key risks was undertaken against a set of pre-defined criteria ■ Business Advocates were appointed in each business unit, with direct access to business unit leadership teams. These people played a two-way role in ensuring the respective business units had given attention to critical steps such as organizational data lock-downs and cleansing, while representing the project in two-way communications and feedback ■ The governing Steering Committee required evidence of business unit sign-off before approving a deployment. This was facilitated via the Business Advocates

Figure 14.5
Continued

Resistance from Stakeholder groups for SAP software and self-service roll-out	■ The Stakeholder Impact Assessments provided input into where resistance may come from and for what reason. This fed into the Business Relationship Plan which was managed primarily through active management of the Business Advocates. Where necessary, objection clinics were run, encouraging participants to "vent". This data was in turn used to update the risk register and inform the communication plan. ■ One of the main objections stemmed from a perception that line managers and employees were being asked to take over POD's work. It was common to hear that "we don't have time to do HR work". NAB response - in paraphrase - was that it was the same work but would be completed in a different and more efficient way. NAB noted that objections of this nature were more likely to come from Corporate Center functions rather than the front-line business units
Communication	■ As noted throughout this chapter, communication received significant attention throughout each phase. ■ Referring specifically to the SAP software rollout, a specific Communication plan was tailored for each business unit, within the broad framework of the project Communication Strategy. To reinforce the "business" perspective of SAP, most of the communication was signed by the POD executive sponsor.
Training Development and Delivery for SAP software and self-service roll-out	■ NAB contracted a professional Training service provider to develop and deliver training. Again, this support was co-located with the Project team.

Figure 14.5
Continued

	■ MSS and ESS training was delivered on-line and made available to all users. Trainees were invited to give feedback on content and usefulness. While the feedback received was excellent, the take-up was somewhat disappointing.
	■ Some elements of the central POD population, including the PAC Advisers, were given extensive class-room training
Delivering the SAP project on-time and within budget	■ Selection of the right people to lead and work on the project paid enormous dividends
	■ NAB adopted SAP's own project methodology (ASAP). NAB took an uncompromising approach to applying the methodology, adhering steadfastly to the project Charter, while accepting that business requirements can and do change.
	■ A scope review process was put in place, ensuring clear review criteria, a prioritization process, and cost/benefit analysis for mooted changes. A "drop-dead" scope finalization date was established and purposefully communicated to ensure project go-live was not unduly compromised
	■ Risks and Issues were openly raised early and assigned ownership for active resolution.
	■ The Project Director encouraged open and objective "no surprises" project management reporting, utilizing a simple but effective process based upon green, amber or red "traffic lights"
	■ Critically, the Project Director was not prepared to move go-live dates, and this reinforced the requirement for effective project management

Figure 14.5

Continued

Notes: NI, NAB's intranet, ESS, employee self-service; MSS, manager self service; NAB, National Australia Bank; POD, people & organizational development; SME, subject matter expert.

Taking Stock: What has been achieved to-date and where to from here?

NAB's POD function looks considerably different today than when the Transformation journey began in 2000. Efficiency and effectiveness improvements have been evident. On the efficiency side, process re-engineering, the removal of paper and the implementation of *e*-enabled processes contributed an initial saving in transactional costs of around 20%. Collectively, the introduction of NI, SAP applications, the evolution of the POD operating model, and a more prudent, business driven approach to how POD work is planned, prioritized, and delivered, has resulted in a reduction of core direct operating costs of around 40%.

As a measure of effectiveness, a survey of POD's internal users demonstrated an increase in satisfaction between 2001 and 2004, from 20% "satisfied with POD support", to 90%. (NAB ceased using a formal survey of internal customer satisfaction after 2004.)

NAB continues to work on improvements including:

- Continual process improvement – a number of POD employees have been trained in Six Sigma and this is beginning to show potential for some significant further process improvements. In addition, POD employees with responsibility for transaction management have been empowered and encouraged to keep finding ways to make POD "easy to do business with". While end to end processes within the POD function itself have been improved over time and are operating generally well, attention is now turning to improving the employee interface to POD, i.e. improving the look, feel and user friendliness of the self-service processes
- Productivity improvement – attention is also turning to how better to benchmark and measure the efficiency and effectiveness of POD's transactional operations
- Technology improvements are in progress, including a refresh of NI content and search facility. A recent

survey indicates users often have difficult navigating and making sense of the vast information contained in NI. The intent is to improve this, leading to a reduction in the number of PAC contacts. Reducing contacts made to PAC, in favor of increasing the usage of NI is expected to lead to further cost reduction on the grounds that data channels are less expensive than voice (figure 14.6 adapted from Corporate Leadership Council research). NAB is also looking to integrate as many POD applications as possible through use of a single portal and central security sign-on

■ Data management proves to be an ongoing challenge. Some elements of self-service adopted by NAB require employees and line managers to keep data up to date. Failure to do so can have serious impacts: for instance, workflow is affected if organization structures are not maintained; mail is incorrectly delivered if workplace locations are wrong. NAB is currently working

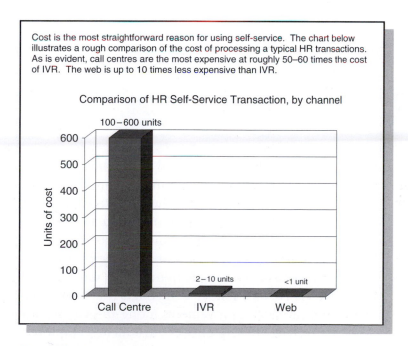

Figure 14.6
The web as a significantly cheaper channel.
Source: Adapted from Corporate Leadership Council.

through an ongoing process to instill greater education for users, and strengthen governance around data management

■ Communication. The requirement for communication never ceases. POD must maintain a continued marketing presence to ensure fundamental understanding of what it delivers, to whom, how etc. Clearly the operating model is integral to this; as the operating model changes, so too, must POD positively and effectively ring in the changes. As a case in point, some pockets of resistance to self-service still remain. This is generally pointed toward MSS responsibilities in the Corporate Center and is one of the contributors to the data management challenge. In hindsight, making training on SAP applications compulsory may have helped MSS users to better understand the importance of their self-service responsibilities. NAB, is now considering a self-service communication refresh program, and the question of how to ensure ongoing education and training for users, including an introduction to self-service for new entrants.

Summary, insights, and conclusion

This chapter has described a number of elements of NAB's introduction of *e*-HR to its Australian workforce. A major concept is the well-planned manner in which NAB approached this. Importantly, *e*-HR was not seen as an end in itself. Moreover, NAB set out to transform its HR function, developing a vision, and relentlessly and methodically driving toward it. Choosing to implement *e*-HR was seen as an enabler for employees and line managers; achieving cost-efficiencies and process improvements along the way were natural, albeit expected, consequences. Introducing employees to the concept of self-service through NI, whilst planning for the implementation of SAP applications, was a useful tactic. Sensing that applications such as payslips on-line and leave management would be very much top of mind for all employees, seemed to hit the mark. Whilst the introduction of SAP software as the core self-service platform had its challenges, it is generally operating effectively, with remaining issues having more to do with ongoing training and education, than with the platform itself.

Throughout the journey, having executive sponsorship and a clear governance structure was of immense value. Among other things, this ensured visibility of POD's vision, thereby encouraging commitment and accountability from within POD, to deliver on stated goals. Furthermore, the change management approach adopted was essential for POD to be able to demonstrate genuine concern for, and understanding of, the many stakeholder impacts identified. NAB learned not to underestimate the impact of change: the early UK & Ireland pilot in 2000, was a case in point. Whether directly or indirectly, the implementation of e-HR meant change for literally every employee. Sharing and validating the vision with stakeholders at appropriate points, together with helping to prepare the business for change, anticipating and dealing with inevitable resistance along the way, was part and parcel of the journey. Needing to have the right people engaged at the right time was also understood, from selecting the right stakeholders, to identifying and managing the right people within project teams. To say that communication was critical, whilst trite, is also understated. Anyone who has experienced almost any type of organizational change will know this!

NAB started the POD transformation journey, understanding where it was at, and with a clear vision of where it needed to re-invent. At face value, the time journey has at times been slow. However, this has been somewhat deliberate, and reflects the manner in which the evolving nature of the POD function has been integrated with other initiatives, both in organizational design, and NAB's global timetable for the SAP software implementation. Along the way, POD has attempted to measure the impact of the changes adopted, and most importantly, strived to continually improve its processes and business delivery focus. Critically, POD has understood that re-inventing itself has been about a great deal more than cost reductions, and the efficiency gains from implementing e-HR.

Through this chapter, NAB has shared its experiences in the context of its own unique circumstances. There is no one right answer; those wishing to follow a similar path will need to confront many questions and issues according to their own business needs.

Reference

Corporate Executive Council (2000), "Unlocking the Potential of Universal Web Access".

CHAPTER 15

Using Technology to Transform HR at Surrey County Council

Graham White with Martin Reddington

Introduction

This chapter takes the form of an extended, thought-provoking set of interviews conducted during May 2007 by Martin Reddington (MR) with Graham White (GW), who is head of human resources (HR) and organizational development (OD) at Surrey County Council. Graham is a well-known speaker on the UK HR practitioner circuit for his opinions on HR, based on many years of making changes in the HR functions of a number of organizations, the most recent of which is in local government. Here, he gives his provocative views on HR transformation, e-HR, and the future of the HR function. Graham is well-known in the UK to have made the predictions of a virtual HR function a near reality and by doing so, made it a more strategic and efficient function.

MR: What factors helped shape your thinking about the changes you have made at Surrey County Council?

GW: It was Confucius who once said 'Only the wisest and stupidest of men never change'. Far be it from me to replace my thinking with his but I dare to suggest he may have been only half right. In my experience I have found too many occasions that only certain HR professionals and the stupidest of men never change. Since the inception of the HR function, our profession has been on a mission to halt growth and development of our contribution. It has taken just over a century to drag us from welfare officers to personnel management and from human resources to human capital management. Whilst the world cruised through the industrial revolution and into the century of technology, we have clung to the edges of organizational management on an almost unchanged agenda. On a daily basis our colleagues leading industry, commerce and government have faced the unknown, the unexpected and unimagined whilst we held strong to the philosophy that there was no need for electric light, since the oil lamp did just as well.

In the midst of the most exciting century of the world's existence, when innovation and technology has revolutionized the revolutionaries, HR continues to squawk like parrots, defending itself again criticism of its inertia by suggesting that the elaborate and detailed process developed by HR experts for career succession planning is there to 'protect the organization when no-one is attracted to work here.'

If HR were to write a vision statement to sum up how it ended the 1990s it might have read – 'we burned that bridge when we got to it.'

Whilst the great support functions of industry and commerce have learned to present their bosses with answers and solutions, we instead seek questions and problems. By adopting this approach and sticking to certain tried and tested strategies we end up becoming counterproductive, producing coping mechanisms and ultimately moving backwards, rather than forwards. For example, we might try to:

- Increase control through centralization and bureaucracy;
- Escape into 'busyness';
- Rely on metrics;
- Look to scapegoats.

Following a very varied, exciting and challenging career in Human Resources where so many before have attempted to predict the future of our profession, I have reached a conclusion. In this new twenty-first century, e-HR technology and the availability of human capital information, the like of which we have never seen before, are the most critical elements that will define the future role and purpose for HR. I now believe that perfecting our e-HR strategies is no longer an option or an alternative; it is the only way we can ensure HR emerges into the second decade of this new century. It is the only certain guarantee that we will continue to have a purpose and make a credible contribution to commerce and industry. It is time that we as HR professionals open our eyes to the reality of our profession's future in a twenty-first century that will be full of new technology, new values and a new ways of working.

Try this simple exercise in mental arithmetic with some of your HR colleagues:

- Add 1000 and 10;
- Add another 1000;
- Add 40;
- Add another 1000;
- Add 40;
- Have you got that number in your head? Now add 10;
- What have you got?
- Most of your colleagues will say 4000!
- And of course they are absolutely WRONG.

It is a trait of many to allow predetermined assumptions to cloud reality. In HR we fall into this trap on an almost daily basis. Our own outlook and perception of the future of HR is nothing more than a little bit different from what we have now. We have become slaves to evolutionary change, believing it is the only certain means of success.

MR: What were your initial impressions at Surrey County Council?

GW: In my current role as head of HR and OD at Surrey County Council, we began the review of our contribution against a backdrop of general criticism and lack of appreciation. We looked again at what our purpose was. We asked questions such as:

- What do we do?
- Does it add value?

- What would happen if we were not here?
- How are we seen by other parts of the organization?

The answers for Surrey County Council were very revealing. The county had very large and very professional HR teams located in a myriad of locations. Almost 400 people had roles that were identified as HR or HR related. They were spread throughout the organization and had a range of reporting lines, structures and accountabilities. This meant that their delivery methodologies and practices were very varied and there was evidence of conflicting priorities depending on the reporting lines and managing arrangements. Whilst there was a corporate HR team, its operational approach was based on giving best advice but allowing individual delegation and interpretation depending on the reporting lines and managing arrangements. This meant, in reality, that individual HR teams operated independently and consequently services chose when, and when not, to take HR advice. Looking back, we found hundreds of different types of contracts and over 1000 different iterations. We had a range of interpretations of our reward structures; differing services considered and dealt with grievances in a very unilateral fashion. Career succession planning was not evident and talent management boarded on patronage. Policy interpretation had become an art not a science, and generally there was a lack of understanding by both 'users' and 'deliverers' as to what our actual purpose was.

It was my second day, 5 October 2002. I had arrived a day earlier and was shown into a cupboard where I thought I was to hang my coat. It was only after this it was explained to me that it was also my office. With just enough room for two chairs, my CE arrived and managed to get into the other chair and suggested my office was 'smart and bijou' and the last time he had been in it was to see the doctor! Following a few more pleasantries, I plucked up the courage to ask him what his evaluation of his HR service was. Remember, this was my second day. The room went silent and he considered his position very carefully and then declared that he thought HR in the Council was 'absolutely crap!' There followed one of those moments when you wish it was 2 days earlier. And then I took stock and considered that what I was facing was in fact the best challenge of my career.

For all of us in HR, the following questions fundamentally strike at the heart of traditional HR values:

- What do we do?
- Does it add value?
- What would happen if we were not here?
- How are we seen by other parts of the organization?

We are compelled to revisit what we thought was important and we arrive at the cross roads all HR departments need to encounter: do we continue to be a bureaucratic collector of data, processor of information, creator of rules and nanny to others, or do we embrace the HR powerhouse that has remained dormant in our organizations for so long? Do we discover the power and influence of e-HR? Then and there I accepted the unspoken challenge every HR professional accepts when faced with the cynical and the doubting. Without saying a word, my new CE and I looked at each other and realized we had agreed the problem and I had accepted the challenge.

This wasn't the first time I had been here. It was a cool April morning when I began my first day as the head of HR for a division of a leading financial institution. As part of my induction I was to meet the CE. As I sat outside his office, I was taken by the size of the waiting area; we could have put four desks in the seating area alone.

Finally, I was called into the longest office I have ever seen – you could have played a doubles match of badminton and still had room for the spectators! It appeared to be in three sections: at the far end the CE sat at a desk the size of a Nimitz- class aircraft carrier; the middle section was made up of a double suite of leather furniture and two round coffee tables; and finally, there was the conference table. If this desk was made from real wood they must have chopped down a redwood tree from Canada, as I have never seen something so beautiful. As I sat at the conference table, the CE was finishing a phone call. I was a little anxious that I might be disturbing him but I need not have been. He was so far away from me, I would have needed semaphore to communicate with him. Then the call ended and he bellowed out loudly, 'Welcome, Graham!'

Then he began walking towards me; the journey would take a few minutes. As he left area one (the desk) and entered area 2 (the suite) he called out, 'I don't know why we employed you!' This really lifted my confidence on my first morning. Then as he entered area 3 (the conference table) he explained in just as loud a voice, 'What we should have done was bought an answering machine that said, 'HELLO, HR HERE.....NO!!'

It transpired that the organization's view of HR was all we ever said, did or wished to do, was to say, 'No'. After a short silence, as I brought my heart rate back to below 175, I assured him from that day forward HR would never say 'no' again. Instead, we would transform the support, advice, and contribution of HR into a powerful and influential HR Management Service that supported management through an e-HR strategy that creates an environment where HR and managers alike were informed, equipped, and empowered to create trend patterns and predictions to ensure workforce contribution.

MR: How did you begin to assimilate a way forward?

GW: Back in Surrey County Council stage one of my plan had now begun. I needed to do three things very quickly:

■ Understand the size and ability of my team;
■ Discover what our businesses really needed – not wanted;
■ Begin to deliver a professional, unified HR service.

There was some initial disagreement from my colleagues in HR and the organization. The organization wanted an added-value HR service that was cost-effective, efficient, and able to deliver everything expected of it the day after I arrived! Many years before this, as a young training officer, I was in the presence of the head of Training when he told me: 'Information is power. The more I know and the less you know, the more powerful I am.'

If ever a man was wrong it was that day. Information is power, but only if you give it away. Information is power, but only if it's shared. Information is power, but only if it is analyzed. Information is power, but only if you use it.

Until I knew what I had and what I needed to do, I remained blind and without information. I needed to become the most informed person within the organization regarding people issues and the County's approach to managing its human resources.

Charles Steinmetz was once called out of retirement by General Electric to help them locate a problem in their new power station near New York. They had two huge generators – one humming, the other not. Having spent no more than 15 minutes looking, listening, and feeling, he finally placed a chalk-marked 'X' on a small component in one machine. General Electric's engineers promptly examined the component, and were amazed to find the defect in the precise location of Steinmetz's mark.

Some time later, General Electric received an invoice from the wily engineer for $10,000.

The MD [managing director] exclaimed, '20 minutes work for $10,000! Incredulous!' They protested the bill and challenged him to itemize it. A few days later, a letter arrived from Steinmetz in which he wrote, 'Making one chalk mark: $1. Knowing where to place it: $9999.'

For me, back in the County Council, my first 6 months were spent bringing together all the HR staff into one service. This meant creating a structure with a single head of HR, and a simple structure of reporting. This was followed by a full audit of the skills, abilities, and expertise of my HR colleagues. At the same time, I needed to force open the seven different baronies within the county. I needed to discover what their priorities were and how they saw HR helping to achieve them. And finally, I had to establish the contribution of HR as a professional service that deserved to be acknowledged and respected; and to do this, I needed information and I needed it to be accurate and well distributed.

I do add one word of caution, though. Share information widely but interpret it wisely; misinformation holds many consequences. It is not just about estimation; for it to add value, it must hold the power of credible prediction. In 1975, there were 150 Elvis Presley impersonators registered in the USA. They looked like Elvis, they dressed like Elvis, they moved like Elvis, and they sang like Elvis. In 2004, it was found that there were over 2000 registered Elvis impersonators. To the ill informed one might ask, 'Does this mean in 2023, every third American will be a registered Elvis impersonator?' I doubt it......

Whilst enjoying a recent newspaper article on the train to Surbiton [UK], I read that it suggested that the stresses of life in the twenty-first century have created a situation where one in four people in the UK are mentally unstable. I then looked up and got a little worried when I realized the three people nearest me looked very sensible!

This was a very significant moment for my team and me. Here I was, sitting on a precipice, looking back with nowhere to return. We had been found out, and questions were being asked! Looking ahead, we could see only virgin soil and uncharted ground. It was then I remembered words I had read on a card sent to me from a friend, as I was leaving college and heading out into the real world. The card read: 'Don't just go along a well beaten track; go instead where there is no path and leave a trail.'

MR: What were the main obstacles to progress?

GW: Easy, the function itself. Right then, I realized didn't have much optimism for the future of HR and that position hasn't changed much. In my opinion, if we continue down this current road, the HR function is reducing itself to three things: resourcing, rewarding, and releasing – all of which can be done by others smarter, quicker and more cheaply. If we fail to realize this then I predict that by the end of the decade HR, as we know it today, will have all the potential of the dodo and be on the final road to extinction.

In their book, *Funky Business*, Jonas Ridderstrale and Kjell Nordstrom describe peoples' approach to change as either 'tourist' or 'refugee'. They say they are either embracing it, wanting to know all they can, or they are trying to escape it...

When I talk of the future of HR to colleague HR professionals, I find the situation not dissimilar. For those who want to be refugees and escape, the message is not good and they don't want to receive it. Trying to introduce change to your HR team can all too easily become like managing a cemetery – lots of people under you but no-one listening.

For me, my wake up call began just over 10 years ago in 1995. Tom Stewart (a member of the board of editors of *Fortune Magazine*) began it all when he wrote in *Fortune Magazine* his now famous 'modest proposal'.

'Nestling warm and sleepy in your company, like the asp in Cleopatra's bosom, is a department whose employees spend 80% of their time on routine administrative tasks. Nearly every function of this department can be performed more expertly for less by others.'

And what was he talking about? 'I am describing, of course, your human resources department, and I have a modest proposal: Why not blow the sucker up? I mean abolish it. Deep-six it. Rub it out; eliminate, toss, obliterate, nuke it; give it the old heave-ho...'

And if companies didn't accept his advice, his second suggestion was to CEs. He told them:

'You should compel your HR departments to outsource all those activities that are not strategic. And then in good HR fashion, you should tell HR Staff that they are not capable of being put in charge of anything and so face termination.'

Less than 3 years later, in 1998, Randal Schuler (*Professor of Human Resource International Management in the Department of Human Resource Management at the School of Management and Labor Relations, Rutgers University [NJ, USA]*) issued another warning to human resource professionals, saying:

'If HR didn't change, it would be dissolved, with its activities shared out among the finance and legal departments, outside consultants, and line managers.'

In the year 2000, in a leading international HR conference in Geneva, the keynote speaker, a leading CE of a global blue chip company said:

> 'I and many of my colleagues believed that HR is on the wrong track. It is failing to get involved in shaping top management's view of the future direction of their corporation.'

And what did we do with this enlightening information? We started to listen to HR gurus and so called HR experts, who claimed that if we followed their guidance and complied with their direction as outlined in their latest book (£19.99 on Amazon – reductions if you buy 10 for the rest of your HR team) you will solve the problem of the age and make HR an added-value service.

Tell me something. How many of us have come into work on a Monday and met our financial director bouncing down the corridor with a smile on his face, saying, 'I have just read a new book and I intend completely changing the way we do our accounts. I am going to turn financial forecasting on its head. I want to change the language of profit and loss…' How many of us? NONE. And yet with indecent haste, we see ourselves being compelled to do HR differently every time someone writes a book. We listen to anyone and believe they are telling the truth

There's an African river that starts in a mountain range in Namibia. The river is called the Okavango – Kalahari. Everyone knows where it starts – it's a huge river and it flows all the way to the Kalahari Desert. But that's the problem; no-one really knows where it finishes, it just sort of fades away.

The vast majority of what HR starts or gets involved in does exactly the same.

Big starts – fanfares; senior management wheeled out on road shows; events over subscribed. Go back in 6 months time, and it just sort of faded away.

Back to my plan and stage one; I was adamant this was not going to happen to my colleagues or myself in the County Council. I had got the answers to my initial questions. I now had

all of HR staff reporting into a structure that I held accountability for. I know knew the size, make up, and abilities of my
team and we held a very substantive skills audit for all of them.
I had successfully collated the expectations of my colleagues in
the services, this was both varied and at times a little circum-
spect, but at least I had a base line from which to begin. But
most important of all, we were beginning to focus on delivering professional services. So now we were ready to enter stage
two of my plan.

Knowledge management pioneer, Larry Prusak (founder
and executive director of the Institute for Knowledge Management; IKM) claimed in 2003 that HR was on a countdown and
that if we in HR do nothing more than we have always done,
then the future is certain death.

By illustration, Larry told his audience that at the start of
the last century [1900s] every major company had a director
of electricity. He said it was new, people didn't understand it,
and so it was necessary to have a department to help managers
come to terms with the role managers would be required to
undertake.

Today's new job applicant enters employment with a whole
new set of expectations and today's new manager enters
that same arena with new inherent engagement skills that
guarantee only one thing for sure; if we don't change, if
HR doesn't change, we will become obsolete and ultimately
extinct.

Twenty-first century organizations are already seeing the new
line managers and their staff engaging in such a way as to give
effect to their philosophy of unlocking the value contained in
their organizations. It is that thinking that has underpinned
and given substance to modern organizational change strategies. It's not HR that's doing that.

The paradigm shift in the psychological contract from one of
a 'coercive relationship' to that of 'partner' is being attempted
without us. And rightly so – this contract is between the
employee and their manager.

We had too many people in HR doing too many things
that did not require professional expertise. We were working on activities that did not support managers or assist
their engagement with their staff. What we were doing was

allowing managers to abdicate their responsibilities and put all management of staff onto HR, thus negating their own requirements to engage their workforce. To make matters worse, HR seemed not only to accept this position but also to promote it actively. This is called 'survival by activity' or in simple terms, 'the busier I am, the more important my role must be'.

All around, I see the mobilization of workforces around a commonly understood, accepted and agreed intent, and if HR sits and lets it happen, our belief that we can influence the future becomes nothing more than myth and pipe dream.

I am not a guru. I don't write books (well, except for this chapter) and I do not intend trying to convince anyone to do anything different from what they believe but I tell you this: I believe that HR is being presented with an opportunity to become either a significant player in our organizations – or an 'also-ran' heading for oblivion.

It is an offer of the keys of the kingdom or the nails of our coffin.

MR: What happened then? Were there any significant results of your changes?

GW: Back in Surrey County Council, stage two meant reviewing the size and shape of the HR team. Although we did not want to admit it, we had too many HR staff doing too many transactional activities that added little in professional contribution; and this had to change and change quickly. The HR team underwent its second reorganization. All non-added-value work was transferred to an internal shared service center. The tactical HR support for education was outsourced to a third party provider and the internal team was reduced to 150 HR professionals.

The challenge that befell us then is one faced by all in the HR profession. We need to decide if we are we going to take advantage of this opportunity or let it pass us by once again. How many of us remember Smith Corona? That's right, they made typewriters. In fact, they were one of the most successful makers of typewriters ever. And their success was down to one thing – listening to the customer. They produced it in pink because users asked for it; they made it quiet because typists wanted it; and they changed its shape to make it look softer. Anything the customer wanted they got but whilst Smith Corona spent all this time listening to the customers, no-one was watching elsewhere; no-one was predicting or looking to the future and suddenly nobody wanted typewriters – not even quiet, pink, shapely ones. They wanted word processors.

We in HR have our own delusions. And like the typewriter we need to be on our guard – use it, don't lose it. Randal Schuler elaborated on his earlier comments, when he said:

> '*The human resource department is being presented with an opportunity to become either a significant player on the management team – or an also-ran heading for oblivion.*'

What have we done when faced with the choice of 'use it or lose it'? I find that many HR colleagues in HR departments still remain focused on issues involving administrative expertise rather than business strategy. They would rather redesign a form than remove an unnecessary process.

Ten years ago, we were being told that our future contribution required a repositioning of our HR departments – with the formation of new roles, new competencies, new relationships, and new ways of operating for both HR and line managers. Its now 2007 – 10 years on and HR's opportunities to assist line managers in managing the business in today's competitive environment are still teetering on an unlimited opportunity, or a huge failure to engage.

We have to consider what this opportunity is:

- We have to know our business;
- We have to have the ability to predict;
- We have to see into the future and tell the organization what is ahead;
- We have to have the right information at our fingertips;
- We have to have good, meaningful analysis within easy grasp;
- We have to have the confidence to direct our colleagues.

And so back in Surrey County Council we entered stage three. In an early meeting with my HR colleagues, I asked them to suggest which animal best described our HR department. I got lots of weird and wonderful suggestions – everything from a tiger to a weasel. Most people hadn't really thought through why they picked the animal, other than they either liked it or were afraid of it. But one knowledgeable-looking, young HR officer called out 'Labrador!' I was so taken by her enthusiasm, if not volume, that I asked her to explain her choice. She was new into the organization and had come from a different industry. She replied,

---

'because in my short time in the County I have found that HR is seen as helpful, it comes when it is called, and it never bites.'

How insightful she was.

With a much reduced but more highly qualified and respected team we entered stage three of our conversion with the business. We were now ready to declare that:

- We knew our business;
- We could predict its needs;
- We could share what we believed the future held;
- We had detailed and reliable information at our finger tips;
- We had finally begun to earn the respect and confidence of our service colleagues.

This was a period of great satisfaction for all concerned. I found that my senior team in HR was invited to become members of service management teams; we were no longer simply called in when things had faltered. We were in from the beginning, if not before. The County's senior team sought advice and proposals from HR and regularly accepted papers for consideration. But was this enough? Had we reached the end of our journey? I believe we had not. There were at least two more steps necessary to ensure our survival.

My career in HR is now in its twentieth year. In that time, we have moved from personnel officers to HR consultants to business partners but try as we may, HR as a profession remains remarkably complacent about coming to grips with the expectations of our organizations and what new roles HR should be playing. Whether we want to believe it or not the future for HR, as we know it, looks bleak. Personnel, HR consultants, business partners; the names change but it's still only a few years to extinction unless...

The future is no longer a mere tactical or operational one; it no longer fits even the latest concept of being a business partner. I believe that if we are serious about HR moving forward, serious about HR advancing and serious about taking Randal Schuler's words to heart, then HR has to move beyond even David Ulrich's philosophy of being business partners and finally become STRATEGIC PLAYERS.

And so to stage four of our plan in the County Council – the transformation to 'strategic players' of a service that my former CE had once described as 'absolutely crap!'

For the past 20 years [since the mid-1980s], I have seen personnel bungling the opportunities to monitor and manage the uncontrolled growth and expansion of organizational design and structures. Even as long ago as the 1980s, personnel could have objected more forcefully when organizations added layers of unnecessary staff and line managers to already lengthy chains of command. When we could have migrated to a new position we decided instead to hibernate while empire building ran rampant.

I watched as an insignificant personnel officer working in a major textile factory in Northern Ireland whilst middle management was created with the full blessing, if not support, of my personnel manager. These managers put themselves between top management and the operating people and contributed nothing but the stifling of innovative thought and entrepreneurial spirit. And HR sat there and did nothing.

At the same time, HR staff firmly believed that they were upholding the conscience of the organization in terms of doing the right things ('being strategic') and doing things right ('being tactical). We filled our time either supporting or implementing programs for sensitivity training, productivity enhancement, and optimum worker output.

I was working in a textile organization that had historically lost lots of money. A new financial director was appointed and with the personnel manager they created between them the *PROFIT CREATION PLAN*. HR developed the rules for this plan:

1   Don't spend any money....

After a year of draconian measures, we made a very slight profit and so the two strategic minds (finance and HR) got together again and came up with the new PROFIT CREATION PLAN. HR again offered to develop a set of rules for this plan; their offer was accepted and after much soul searching and closed debate, a new set of rules were developed:

1   Don't spend any money....

Okay, I accept HR provided a number of management practices to assist managers to work more effectively in a bureaucratic environment; but what they didn't do and what they could have done was recommend a course of action to deal with issues of organizational ineptness.

The opportunity was there even then – HR could have played a more strategic and decisive role when organizations finally began to dismantle structures in a hurry, often without much analysis and foresight.

But HR didn't step forward when it could have done, when the organization was overwhelmed by an onslaught of management and organizational fads that promised a variety of recipes to boost shareholder value. We had: quality first; right first time; just in time; continuous improvement and many more. Indeed, like many HR departments before us, with a few notable exceptions, we not only didn't help we actually contributed to quick-fix thinking with ludicrous suggestions that completely ignored the critical people issues, which resulted in a de-motivated and anxious workforce.

In that textile factory, in the lovely town of Donaghadee, a dire situation had been reached. Closure and transfer of production out of the UK was only months away and was only ultimately avoided by the appointment of a new site director.

A man who saw the value of people and wanted to inspire the HR team to put in place a new environment where HR took on a critical and exciting new role. Even in the early days of computing, he inspired HR along with the rest of the departments to begin collating, reviewing and monitoring trends and patterns, to help build the talent within the organization. For HR, it was a whole new world; a time to contribute analysis and support line managers with credible and accurate information, analysis, interpretation, and prediction.

What he knew then is only recently being discovered more broadly – he took our organization to a new plain where we realized that managing a restructured, flat, chopped-up organization is difficult and creates a multitude of people and structural challenges that HR must be aware of if they want to contribute to corporate success. We discovered a number of fundamental facts:

- If we wanted to support a flat, downsized organization it would require a different kind of information that focuses on different ways of measuring and predicting employment and performance trends;
- We would need to develop, test, and implement new measurements of capability and performance to support the workforce skills base;
- We had to discover ways to carry out detailed analysis of past trends and future forecasts to aid the building of innovative reward, recognition, and incentive schemes;
- We needed detailed exit analysis, staff advocacy, customer satisfaction matrix, and workforce planning tools.

We were 20 years ahead of our time. We had no e-HR architecture, no PowerPoint, our computer server took up a whole room and produced reports that were both bigger than '*War and Peace*' [L.N. Tolstoy] and even more difficult to understand. So we spent many hours with calculators and note pads but it worked. At a time when the majority of the industry moved their operations off-shore, the factory survived for a further 15 years, bringing jobs, and millions of pounds of income into the local community. A columnist who writes in the *Orlando Sentinel*, said,

---

'HR was once the calm eye at the center of the downsizing storm; untouched because it was seen as a support service, rather than a business process.'

The problem was that we in HR saw ourselves as support services and as keepers of the rules, policies, and procedures. Therefore, we lost credibility with line management when they needed us most, and in the process, we lost a sense of identity, purpose, and direction.

I have gradually come to a conclusion that whilst it was Tom Stewart's words that shook me into action, the idea that the HR function is heading for extinction probably began in earnest even earlier when consultants started to make money from business process reengineering. We did have a go at supporting but the problem was that we were preparing to leave the twentieth century with HR thinking designed during the nineteenth century. We had the opportunity to reposition ourselves into a new and different environment, unencumbered with the baggage of size or power, but missed it again. I am not sure how many more chances we will have.

So we are doing it now. Stage four sees the HR team reduce again. We started at 400, scaled down to 150, and now we've reached 40.

One current school of thought suggests that HR should now play an important role as process consultants, whose role is to connect the processes of other functions such as marketing, finance, R&D, and manufacturing.

Another argues that HR should be responsible for shaping the organization and its culture; for determining required competencies; for acquiring and developing people with the necessary capabilities, skills, and behavioral characteristics; for retaining those who perform; and for getting rid of those who fail.

And of course there is the proverbial third group of leading HR thinkers who disagree with the notion that HR should be responsible for anything. They claim that the primary responsibility rests with line management – HR should play the role of facilitator; that is, a business consultant or partner who will assist the line manager in making the right decisions.

I am beginning to feel a little like the Decca Recording Company who in 1962 decided that they didn't like the sound of the latest band auditioning for them. They said groups with guitars were on the way out. So they let an unknown band calling themselves The Beatles walk out of their offices.

The big question I find myself arriving at is: is it too late to stop the process of dismantling HR?' I think not – technology has given us another opportunity. We have the opportunity to reposition ourselves into a new and different environment, unencumbered with the baggage of size or power. A reduced and altered HR presence still has all the potential to play a crucial role.

But the real difference is that we will be armed with the information and resources to ensure that people and organizational decisions are informed with real and credible analysis and research. We will be able to prove or disprove the alignment of future planning with the business plan to keep the other players coordinated and focused.

Future strategy for staff growth and development will be based on credible predictions of growth patterns and analytical measurement.

This new HR executive will take on the role of a tough but fair-minded keeper of the corporate conscience and provide in-depth predictions that will inform strong direction on all people related issues, including selection, career management, development and training, performance management, remuneration, employee relations, and the overall direction of the organization. But we can only do this if we have the information in the first place.

MR: When did you introduce e-HR and what was its impact?

GW: Finally, we reached stage five. In Surrey County Council we have not become fortune-tellers – we do not predict the unpredictable but because we are properly equipped and take advantage of modern e-HR architecture we have become informed and with this information our HR strategic players are in the business, forecasting the future based on business intelligence.

Finding, developing, measuring, and rewarding talent has become part of a line manager's job with policy coming from HR, good on-line support, and a very effective shared service center.

Most or all of HR administration, including compensation and benefits, are now outside of HR. And the same will happen everywhere else. A few HR professionals will become experts in brand management.

The majority of us will head up service centers or become line managers.

And the remaining few of us will evolve into a new and very different HR role.

We will be: fountains of information, analysts of future business shape and design, predictors of corporate resourcing, and guardians of business heritage.

The future of our organizations will be in our hands. BUT ONLY IF WE GET IT RIGHT!

What we don't need now is another set of gimmicks to fix what is obviously not working. We need professional e-HR information and we need to become STRATEGIC PLAYERS.

At the end of the last century [1900s], people like Ulrich were telling us our future contribution required a repositioning of our HR departments: new roles, new competencies, new relationships, and new ways of operating for both HR and line managers. It's now 2007 – 7 years on and HR's opportunities to assist line managers in managing the business in today's competitive environment are still teetering on an unlimited opportunity. But we have to reconsider what that opportunity is and how to harness the power of e-HR. This means that we will need to know our business and have the ability to predict its future direction. We will need to have the guts to direct our colleagues and to say, 'absolutely 'yes' or absolutely 'no", if they are about to foul things up in the people and organizational area because of lack of information and lack of interpretation...

MR: How would you characterize the outcomes of your time in office?

GW: So stage five in the County Council sees us with a HR staff to council staff ratio of about 1:600. HR has moved to a new role of 'strategic player' working very closely with service management, ensuring best advice is given and uniformity of approach is retained.

When the circus came to New York in 1978, the publicity posters carried the question: 'Can aerialist Tito Goano – spinning at 75 miles an hour – accomplish the most difficult acrobatic feat of the twentieth century?'

The answer was, 'NO'.

Every night for 9 months, Tito attempted the first ever quadruple somersault in mid-air from a flying trapeze 60 feet above the ground. Every night for 9 months, he got part way through, missed his catcher, and plunged into the safety net. At Madison Square Gardens, he sustained a whole season of magnificent failure. Asked if he had ever got it right, Tito replied: 'Yes, once at rehearsals and no-one saw me.'

Will anybody see us in the future, or is this just a rehearsal? Surrey County Council has saved £9 million with a 90% cut in HR. We have saved more than £9 million in the past 4 years [since 2003] by dramatically slashing the number of professional jobs in our HR department from 400 to just 40.

Whilst seen by many as a massed cull it was part of a very well-planned organizational restructure that I had the privilege to spearhead. The five stages of the plan have seen general HR administration transferred to an internal shared-services center, and most of the HR support service for education outsourced.

The restructure led to the removal of over 300 posts across HR. The final part of the process was completed in May 2006 as part of the Council's business delivery review. I believe reductions have not affected HR services, despite the ratio of HR people to employees dropping from 1:80 to 1:600. The new ratio is still very credible, even in today's climate.

The HR function has completely changed its profile within the council as a result of the shake-up. I set about to change the view of a CE who told me my service was 'absolutely crap' and I have done this. I raised the game of HR, to move beyond being a large bureaucracy into a dynamic, strategic player in our organization.

And what of the CE and his views of HR. He moved on about 18 months ago, during the move from stage three to stage four of my strategy. In his final months, I called him and asked for

10 minutes of his very busy time to update me on his views of my service. What happened next was quite amazing. He said, 'Let's not just have a few minutes – let me take you out for lunch.' If you knew me (or could see my picture) you would know I never give up chances for meals, especially when they are free. But on this occasion, I could predict a sudden loss of appetite, as I envisaged sitting across the table from such an esteemed leader.

But I went and we ate and he told me a story I will never forget. He said that many other parts of the corporate center were seeking to become strategic, just like HR. He told me he decided to remain open-minded by each of our efforts but 3 years later he saw only one corporate service that could truly claim success – and it was HR.

I just had to ask him how he had come to this conclusion. 'Simple,' he said. 'Property Services were one of the other corporate services that sought strategic status but my window still rattles and my radiator leaks. In HR you fixed the things that were causing us the most problems and you kept fixing until we had little to complain about and before we knew it you had become a critical advisor to the organization.

In 1996, Kenny Rogers, the famous singer, found himself discussing his career with his manager, Ken Kragen. 'Careers are like small airplanes,' Kragen explained. 'If you get up to a certain height, even if you turn the engine off, you glide for a long time. Kenny, you won't hit the ground in your own lifetime.' There was a long silence. 'Ken,' Rogers finally replied, 'I think I'm planning to live a lot longer than you think.'

I think in many cases HR's engine has been off for some time and gliding has been all that could be achieved. It's time to get that engine going again because I don't know about others but I plan to make sure wherever I am, HR is planning to live a lot longer than you think.

Reference

Ridderstrale, J. and Nordstrom, K. (1999) *Funky Business*. Stockholm: Book House Publishing.

CHAPTER 16

HRM, Technology and Strategic Roles: Considering the Social Implications

Anne Keegan and Helen Francis

Introduction

Human resources (HR) functions are facing unprecedented change as they are under pressure to become more 'strategic' and to use technology in ways that make them more efficient and effective. It has been argued that the traditional HR function is disappearing as new forms of organization and delivery emerge supported by developments in information systems (Losey et al., 2005; CIPD, 2005a). As we have heard in a number of chapters, these involve moves towards a three-legged functional design based on shared services, centers of expertise, and the creation of HR business partners in line with Ulrich's (1997) modeling of HR. Key benefits claimed for what is commonly referred to as the shared services model include reduction in transaction costs, achievement of more efficient and better quality HR services, and allowing the function to focus on more strategic 'performance-enhancing' activities (Reddington et al., 2005; Roberts, 2005; Chapter 1: Technology, Outsourcing, and HR Transformation: an Introduction).

Determining the nature and impact of new forms of HR in terms of the functions' relationship with the organization is a key area of investigation amongst a growing body of HR practitioners and academics frustrated with what has been described as a 'fixation' with Ulrich's (1997) business partnering model. A key concern is the minimal attention paid to ensuring that HR structures vary in ways that better 'reflect the business [the organization] is in and what business customers want' (Chartered Institute of Personnel and Development (CIPD) 2006a, p. 5).

In this chapter we examine current debate about the changing 'anatomy' of the HR function as it seeks to transform itself, acknowledging that this focus on structure is deeply connected to the roles HR practitioners have and the functions' relationships with different stakeholders (CIPD, 2006a; Morley et al., 2006). We do this by structuring our chapter into six sections. In section one, we discuss the uptake of the language of business partnering by the CIPD and others, locating this within a changing business context within which HR functions are finding themselves. In section two, we discuss the evolving remits of line managers as they are expected to assume responsibility for an increasing range of HR tasks. In section three we examine structural changes and point to what we refer to as the 'strategic amplification' of HR work, noting the significance of the shift from labor-intensive to technology-intensive HR service delivery, or 'e-enabled HR' (Florkowski and Olivas-Luján, 2006; Reddington and Martin, 2006).

In section four we explain our research design and then present our findings. Here, we show how changes in HR are seen in the eyes of our respondents to be largely driven by a focus on the strategic role, and e-enabled HR services, and the potential impact of these upon the function's relationship with employees, employee wellbeing, and the career paths of HR professionals. In the final section, we conclude by asking, is the framing of HR roles and activities around the notion of business partner/strategic partner damaging the function's potential to facilitate more critically reflective HR practice on broader issues of employee wellbeing?

Emergent models and the evolution of HR

Debate about new forms of HR tends to be more prescriptive than descriptive and there is a lack of empirical evidence about how new roles are being played out or how technology is influencing structural change within the function (Caldwell, 2003; Hoobler and Johnson, 2004; Valverde et al., 2006). Having said that, insights into the potential tensions arising from the re-engineering of HR functions along the lines proposed by Ulrich lines are beginning to emerge from empirical studies that identify, for example, the distancing of HR from employees and their front-line managers, segmentation of HR roles, and an imbalance emerging between people-oriented and business-oriented HR roles (Hope-Hailey et al., 2005; CIPD, 2006b; Francis and Keegan, 2006).

These trends can be set in the broader context of the long-running debate on the roles of HR managers (Ulrich, 1997; Purcell et al., 2003; Marchington and Wilkinson, 2005). In the UK context, Legge (1978) produced one of the most influential models of HR which identified two strategies through which personnel managers could gain power and influence within the organization – conformist innovator and the deviant innovator. The conformist innovator attempts to relate his/her work clearly to the dominant values and norms in the organization aiming simply to satisfy the requirements of senior management. The deviant innovator subscribes to a quite different set of norms, gaining credibility and support for ideas driven by social values rather than strict economic criteria (Marchington and Wilkinson, 2005, p. 131).

Alternative classifications include one constructed by Tyson and Fell (1986), which drew on a building industry metaphor to identify three distinct 'types' or models of HR practice. These ranged from a basic administrative model (clerk of works) to a sophisticated, industrial-relations model (contracts manager) and a business-oriented, strategically aware function, which designed the employment relationship (the architect; Tyson, 1995, p. 22) and Storey (1992) who proposed a four-fold typology of HR roles, based on two dimensions, strategic/ tactical and interventionary/non-interventionary: 'advisers', 'handmaidens', 'regulators', and 'changemakers'.

These models construct how the HR function can best contribute to improved employee and organizational performance and therefore create expectations about effective HR practice. Increasingly, they have focused on a split between strategic and non-strategic roles played by HR practitioners (Boxall and Purcell, 2003; Purcell et al., 2003) and links between human resource management (HRM) and firm financial performance have become more prominent in recent years (Huselid, 1995; Pfeffer, 1998). The business partner modeling of HR originally developed by Ulrich in 1997 has become particularly influential in this context (Caldwell, 2003), and is informed by recent debate about how ICT can help free up HR professionals to play a strategic role (CIPD, 2007).

In Ulrich's model HR practitioners engage in a set of proactive roles defined along two axes: strategy versus operations, and process versus people. The four key roles emerging from this framework are strategic partner, administrative expert, employee champion, and change agent. The strategic partner role is one in which HR professionals partner with line managers to help them reach their goals through effective strategy formulation and strategy execution. Change agents are responsible for the delivery of organizational transformation and culture change. Administrative experts constantly improve organizational efficiency by re-engineering the HR function and other work processes such as introducing 'shared services' (Ulrich and Brockbank, 2005).

The employee champion is a particularly interesting role. It is most closely associated with responsibility for employees but differs from previous conceptualizations of employee facing roles such as the 'consensus negotiator' of Torrington and Hall (2005), the 'regulator' of Storey (1992), or 'contracts manager' of Tyson (1995). These other roles recognize the inherent plurality in managing the employment relationship and acknowledge the inevitability of trade-offs between employee needs and goals and organizational objectives. The occupiers of these roles are recognized as being caught in 'a precarious balancing act' between management and labor, whereas the employee champion appears to be closely identified with management as a partner in delivering value (Caldwell, 2003, p. 997) in a pattern typically reminiscent of Legge's (1978) 'conformist innovator'.

The positioning of the HR function as a key organizational player is proving very attractive to HR professionals and, as CIPD research shows (Caldwell, 2003; Brown et al., 2004), the concept of the business partner is often used as a synonym for strategic partner, which in turn is proving the most attractive of Ulrich's original four roles for most HR people. Given the uptake of the business partner model by the CIPD and others, this framing of the business partner as strategic partner has consequences for the other roles originally conceptualized by Ulrich, especially the employee champion role. The way the employee champion is perceived by HR practitioners is an area particularly worth considering when we address employee wellbeing, an issue we return to later in the chapter.

Bearing in mind the history of HR practitioner's struggles for acceptance as key organizational players (Watson, 1977; Legge, 1978; Guest and King, 2004), it is hardly surprising that a way of modeling HR practice, constituting HR as 'hard', 'business driven', and 'strategic', has become so popular. According to some commentators demand for business partners has increased by 30% in the UK in 2004 alone and there is evidence of substantial increases in salaries (Beckett, 2005). In this context, the CIPD acknowledge that the focus amongst HR professionals on the strategic role 'might be achieved at the expense of the employee champion role' (CIPD, 2005a, p. 54), a point emphasized by Ulrich and Brockbank (2005) in their discussion of trends in the UK and who call for practitioners not to lose sight of the employee champion role.

One aim of Ulrich and Brockbank (2005) in reformulating their vision of the changing HR function, and typology of roles, is to re-emphasize the importance of an employee-facing HR function. They make a distinction between the role of 'human capital developer' and 'employee advocate' and draw attention to the need for employees to be treated fairly and with dignity. Kochan (2004, p. 132) also argues that HR has a role in advocating employee interests, stating that,

> 'HRM professionals will need to redefine their role and professional identity to advocate and support a better balance between employer and employee interests at work.'

While stressing the importance of employee advocacy, like their earlier modeling of business partnership, Ulrich and Brockbank's arguments remain underpinned by a strong notion of mutuality between different stakeholders, guided by the belief that managers, employees, consultants, and HR professionals will all work collaboratively towards a common goal of efficiency and high-performance levels. These arguments fail to address in any depth, what HR professionals actually do as opposed to what they should do. Questions remain about the real problems they face in seeking to achieve a balance between competing stakeholder interests and values, nor why so many firms still operate with a financial rather than people-driven approach (Brown, 2005).

Line-manager accountability for HR

The development of a HR business partnership, the style of which we have described above is of critical importance not only to HR but also to line managers who play a pivotal role in enabling such a development (CIPD, 2006a). While there is a dearth of research into employee perceptions about business partnering and shared services there is a growing body of research into devolution of HR to line managers (Hutchinson and Purcell, 2003; Reddington et al., 2005; McConville, 2006). Opinions on the advisability of devolving HR responsibilities to the line vary. Based on an empirical study of the devolution of HR responsibilities to line managers in a large food service organization, Whitaker and Marchington (2003) summarize opposing views on the advisability of devolving HR to the line.

On the one hand, there is a case to be made that HR is best left to those people directly responsible for supervising staff who are primarily responsible for manufacturing products, selling goods, and equipment or providing a public or customer service (Cunningham and Hyman, 1999; Cooper, 2001). On the other hand, there are concerns about allowing line managers to take on HR tasks when their 'primary responsibilities lie elsewhere, namely in meeting service or production goals' and while it is perceived they 'have scant regard for learning how to find ways to get the best out of their staff' (Whitaker and Marchington, 2003, p. 245).

The authors conclude that in devolving HR tasks and activities to the line, line managers are likely to need significant ongoing support from HR if costly errors are to be avoided (Earnshaw et al., 2000; Renwick, 2003; Marchington and Wilkinson, 2005). Renwick's (2003) review of line-managers' experiences for example also indicates that line managers may well lack the capability and responsibility to deal with some HR work or may not want this responsibility. More recent survey evidence by Hales (2005) indicates that the issue of competing priorities experienced by front-line managers remains strong. Based on a survey of 135 organizations, Hales findings paint a picture of 'a stable, consistent Front Line Management (FLM) role where a common performance-oriented supervisory core is surrounded by a penumbra of additional managerial responsibilities relating to stewardship, translating strategy into operations, unit management, and, exceptionally, business management' (Hales, 2005, p. 501). Not surprisingly therefore, where managers are taking ownership of HR, this can add to what is already a substantial workload, leading to job strain and tension (McConville, 2006) while at the same time it is not clear that line managers are motivated or trained to take on these HR roles and activities. Most of the research evidence to-date suggests that devolving HR to the line is likely to be more costly and less straightforward than normative treatments of the move to business partnership often imply.

Structural change and strategic amplification of HR work

As various commentators have advocated the adoption of HR shared service provision and role specialization (Beer, 1997; Ulrich, 1997; Ulrich and Brockbank, 2005), a new delivery model of HR is emerging which we referred to in our introduction as the three-legged functional design of shared service centers (SSCs) together with business partners and centers of expertise (CIPD, 2006b, p. 2). Described as the 'shared service' model (Ulrich and Brockbank, 2005) this 'new' structure is replacing traditional HR structures characterized by integrated teams that executed all HR activities from administration to strategy (Beer, 1997; Tamkin et al., 2006). Business partners are typically treated as being similar to the 'strategic partner' noted in Ulrich's typology (CIPD, 2003).

Service centers generally offer a common service provision in routine HR administration across business units to achieve economies of scale, and may include provision of additional professional expertise. Beer (1997) describes this, and wider developments:

'Companies are creating geographically decentralized human resource service centers responsible for providing traditional administrative services. Unlike the strategic human resource professionals, typically called 'human resource partners,' HR specialists in these centers are not affiliated with a particular business unit, branch, or plant. Enabled by information technology and telephone eight hundred numbers, these centers provide services to geographically dispersed sub-units of the corporation. Administrative service centers do not have to reside within the HR function, however; a more radical, and probably superior solution, is to transfer these centers to a corporate service organization which will provide HR services for a fee.' (Beer, 1997, p. 51/52)

Centers of excellence may include small teams of HR experts with specialist knowledge in areas such as resourcing, employee relations, and so on and who give professional support to business partners, often developing detailed policy for corporate HR and acting as a reference point for shared service agents dealing with complex issues raised by clients (Tamkin et al., 2006). Beer describes a situation in which:

> 'The corporate human resource staff will be composed of a few key subject matter experts in disciplines such as compensation, management development, diversity, and organization effectiveness.' (Beer, 1997, p. 53)

The advent of increasingly sophisticated HR information technologies has been an important influence on the uptake of the shared services model and SSCs are now almost synonymously linked with 'e-HRM' (Paauwe and Farndale, 2007). While there is a growing amount of research in this field reflected in the first European academic workshop on e-HRM hosted at Twente University (Enschede, the Netherlands) in the autumn of 2006, the role and impact of e-HR in transformation of the function remains under-theorized in the management literature (Florkowski and Olivas-Luján, 2006; Martin et al., 2006).

Florkowski and Olivas-Luján (2006, p. 706) argue that as technology becomes an 'increasingly vital component of HR service delivery, researchers must expand their efforts to understand the opportunities and threats that it fosters'. They suggest that HR information technologies may play a key role in allowing HR professionals to 'successfully balance' Ulrich's four competing roles, but that there is also a risk that large investments in IT will not lead to an improvement in satisfaction of HR customers, or render the function more efficient. A key issue emerging in our own research examined below is an apparent imbalance in the execution of these roles, with emphasis placed on business-facing strategic partner role and far less on employee-facing champion role.

Finally, the outsourcing of HR activities is also attracting increasing attention in the academic literature even if from a low base (Cooke, 2005). Commentators argue that the HR function is increasingly under siege from external consultants (Redman and Wilkinson, 2001; CIPD, 2005c) which produces pressure to reorganize its activities and compete with external service providers. It would seem clear HR outsourcing is increasing (Woodall et al., 2002; Morgan, 2006) with many HR managers turning toward outsourcing as a way of meeting the demands to engage in more strategic, value-adding HR activities (Lepak et al., 2005).

Much like the turn to the shared service models, discussions on outsourcing are largely centered on issues such as cost and efficiency and the freeing up of HR practitioners for strategic activities while little attention is given to the effects of outsourcing on employees, on HR careers or on the effects of such configurations of service delivery on traditional and evolving roles of HR professionals (Kessler et al., 1999; Cooke, 2005).

Research methods

Our chapter dovetails with other work discussed above addressing the changing roles of the HR function. We direct our attention to the emergence of the 'thinking performer' concept, a concept that represents an attempt by the CIPD to shape the debate about what constitutes effective HR practice. The study reported here was designed to identify the meanings respondents attach to the concept of the thinking performer and how it relates to changing role of HRM. Our research started with a systematic review of the literature, CIPD professional standards and in-depth conversations with a purposive sample of respondents whom we believed likely to have rich insights into the emergence of the thinking performer, and how the thinking performer is being traced into practice (Patton, 2002). To that end, all but one of our respondents are linked to the CIPD and included:

■ Members of the CIPD 'executive' (10 members of the membership and professional development committee and the professional knowledge and information departments);

■ Examiners (two PDS);

■ Professional Development Scheme (PDS) course leaders (seven);

■ HR practitioners (51) including HR assistants, HR advisors, HR managers, HR directors, HR business partners, HR recruitment consultants;

■ Members of national upgrading panel (three);

■ Students working towards graduate membership of CIPD (11);

■ Regional (Scottish) secretary of the general municipal boilermakers union.

Our interviews were initially semi-structured around a list of questions pertaining to changes in the nature of the HR function including HR roles and HR service delivery in respondent's organizations and their recognition and understanding of the thinking performer concept. As the interviews progressed, the theme of HR business partnership and specifically the model of four HR roles from Ulrich's (1997) '*HR Champions*' book came up regularly. Consistent with accepted exploratory research practice, we adapted our semi-structured questionnaire to take account of this emerging pattern and incorporated questions to explore this issue in relation to changing HR roles and HR service delivery (Cresswell, 1998).

All interviews were tape-recorded and transcribed producing approximately 1500 pages of transcripts. A 'start list' of analyst-constructed (Patton, 2002) codes was drawn up prior to the interviews reflecting initial themes drawn from the extant literature on changing HR roles and service delivery and the literature on the *Thinking Performer* published by the CIPD. These codes included: familiarity, uptake, and usage of the thinking performer concept; structure, process, and practice in HR work; configuration of HR service delivery and range of activities of HR undertaken within and outside the organization; current and aspirational HR roles; and key concepts, expressions, and beliefs associated with the thinking performer and HR practice.

When the first interviews had been conducted, we drew up some more specific indigenous codes closer to respondents emergent categories, for example, codes relating to the emerging theme of 'business partnership'. All transcripts were coded for these emergent issues. Coded material was summarized and outlines of these placed into partially ordered matrix displays (Miles and Huberman, 1994) designed to impose minimal conceptual structure on the material displayed. As textual summaries evolved, the following themes emerged: framing of HR policy and practice; structural changes and devolution of HR tasks to the line; shrinking employee champion role and costs to employee wellbeing; and finally loss of employee trust and confidence. In the next section we discuss each of these themes in turn.

Findings

The framing of HR policy and practice

Earlier we noted that exploring the changing role and function of HR has been identified as a major research theme by the CIPD. This indicates a deep-seated concern at the emphasis typically placed on transactional rather than strategic and 'transformational' issues amongst HR practitioners, and the need for them to engage in value-adding activities (Whittaker and Johns, 2004; CIPD, 2006b). This focus is encapsulated in the term 'the thinking performer' used by the CIPD to frame the vision for its professional standards, described as someone:

> 'who 'makes the move' to becoming a business partner and (...) 'is an HR professional who applies a critically thoughtful approach to their own job so as to make a contribution to organisational survival, profitability and to meeting its vision and strategic goals.' (Whittaker and Johns, 2004, p. 32)

The values propounded here, are similar to those underpinning the business partner modeling of HR as developed by

Ulrich (1997), which has been trumpeted as the practitioner paradigm towards which the profession should aspire (Caldwell, 2003, p. 988), and recently described as a 'dominant influence' on structural changes taking place within HR (CIPD, 2005a; 2006b).

Indeed, a recent CIPD report on HR within the UK public sector suggests that the presence of these new ideas about the re-configuration of the HR function have been as strong a driver for change as the oft cited business or service delivery imperatives shaping practice within the sector (CIPD, 2005a). HR professionals are increasingly recruited from other sectors 'to provide fresh perspectives on the way HR operates'. They offer 'a more business-oriented view in which a partnership approach is taken as understood' (CIPD, 2005a, p. 9).

In this context it is perhaps not surprising that at the start of our study, the concept of business partner emerged naturally and unprompted in interviews as people spoke about their roles, changes in the delivery of HR services, and where the function is going generally. As noted in our methodology, in latter interviews we subsequently added questions to address recognition and application of Ulrich's model of business partnership.

The role of business partner appeared to offer great appeal to practitioners seeking to raise their influence and credibility and secure their identities as professionals. In this context, our analysis of the language they used to describe and explain HR work showed that it is framed by a strategy discourse that effectively closes off discussion about more employee focused, operational issues.

On considering Ulrich's roles, consistent with CIPD research noted earlier, our analysis suggests a trend towards people either describing themselves as strategic partners and using the term synonymously with business partner, or discussing their career aspirations in terms of movement towards strategic partner status. There is far less emphasis on the other three roles. According to one senior CIPD advisor we interviewed who has carried out extensive research in many public and private and public sector organizations experimenting with 'progressive' HR systems;

> 'Everybody claims to be strategic partner, people struggle with the change agent, everybody likes to be the administrative expert, and nobody wants to be the employee champion.'

In a similar vein, one of our respondents who is a HR business partner described the situation in his company as follows:

> 'The emphasis is definitely on being a strategic partner, change agent as well. Depending on what you are doing at the time, some background admin, knowledge, and virtually zero on the employee champion role.' (business partner)

Clearly, at the heart of business partnering there is a concern with business focused strategic activity. As one senior recruitment consultant for the HR profession remarks,

> 'Most HR professionals will now have 'value added' stamped on their foreheads, because they are being asked always to think in terms of the business objectives and how what they do supports the business objectives and the business plan.'

In this sense, HR work has thus become more focused on delivering business needs and HR practitioners must become more adept at measuring their effectiveness in terms of business competitiveness rather than employee comfort (Ulrich, 1998). These findings are consistent with a recent review of how recruitment consultants view an ideal candidate for business partner,

> 'Success in the role will have more to do with producing business metrics, than dishing out tea and sympathy' (…). The desire and ability to be an intrinsic part of the management team is a must. It's the new element of commercialism that excites yet eludes recruiters (…). Language is often a better indicator of aptitude than a list of qualifications or competencies.' (Beckett, 2005)

The emphasis respondents place on business and strategy as the foundation for HR ideals, practice, and values suggests that they are locked into business 'speak'. While business language sensitizes HR practitioners to the importance of value added HR activities, our analysis of respondents accounts' indicates that the same language closes off possibilities for understanding and dealing with inevitable tensions in meeting employee needs and aspirations and business objectives. The priority in HR work is becoming the delivery of strategic HR solutions. Operational activities, including both administrative expertise and employee championship in terms of Ulrich's original typology, are targeted for decentralization to SSCs, corporate service organizations (Beer, 1997), outsourcing, or trade union representatives. Regarding the latter, Reilly and Williams (2006) regard it as impossible and undesirable that HR practitioners take on an employee champion role because it places them in an impossible situation as members of the management team. Purcell (2006) also argues that the employee champion role is emphatically not part of HR's brief, that employees need their own representatives as advocates to argue their case. Indeed, one of our respondents noted that trade unions were expected to 'fill the gap' as HR became less involved in the day-to-day aspects of HR work and expressed concern about losing his position in being able to advocate employee interests:

'It's a strange word but I don't think there's anybody got permission to be an employee champion in our sort of set up really... the unions see it as their role for the employees to come to them to tell them about their problems, not HR.'

Structural changes and devolution of HR tasks to the line

While administrative expertise is seen as something that is essential to get right, it is no longer the heart of HR activity. Some commentators, like Beer (1997) advocate the complete separation of HR strategy and consultancy work from administrative activities that were HR's traditional base of expertise. Although these visions of HR may have seemed exaggerated a few short years ago, our respondents typically report far-reaching structural changes to manage this aspect of the HR function linked to the e-enablement of HR. This includes the creation of HR service centers enabled by call-center technology and which have become line managers' prime source of HR expertise. These tend to operate to a set of agreed service-level targets consistent with recent research evidence of the 'widespread acceptance of self-service as 'the' way to manage HR, for both employees and managers' (Martin, 2005; CIPD, 2006a).

On describing the creation of new service centers respondents in our study talked of significant reductions in numbers of on-site HR staff and higher ratios of employees to HR specialists, ranging from 1:100 to 1:300. This trend works hand in hand with ongoing devolution of 'HR tasks' to the line, including absence management, grievance handling, management of discipline, coaching, and counseling employees.

Consistent with extant research noted earlier, our respondents noted that line management involvement in HR work of this kind is not without its difficulties. The issue of competing priorities experienced by front-line managers was a key theme raised by respondents in our study, together with concerns about the lack of priority line managers were prepared to give to people management issues, exacerbated by inadequate training and the need for selection procedures that focus on people-oriented and not just technical skills.

'... sometimes you wonder have they been selected because they did well in sales?'
    '... I don't think that a 1-day training course is going to make a manager into an HR manager!'

In this context, it might be naïve to assume that line managers have the time, the training, or the interest to give employee wellbeing the kind of priority it deserves, especially when it appears to have increasingly less priority amongst HR professionals themselves.

Changing HR careers: shrinking employee champion role

The strategic amplification of HR work noted by our respondents seems to have an effect that the employee champion role is not perceived to be a potential career route for HR practitioners, and in the face of a perceived contraction of this role, some respondents expressed concern about their career options. Those who were originally attracted to the profession because of the promise of fulfilling the long-standing ethical agenda at the heart of HR work talk of facing a bleak future. For example, one junior practitioner working in a global electronics firm, which had recently siphoned HR services off into a call center remarked;

'We lost that human contact, we were at the end of a telephone, we weren't allowed to go out and see people anymore, to give advise to people face-to-face … We are losing what HR's about.'

He goes on to talk about feeling 'let down' by the failure of the profession to realize how important the employee champion is to a fully rounded HR function:

'I want to be an employee champion working directly with people and I can't. I can see that avenue being closed off fairly soon and it makes me uncertain about whether or not I want to stay in HR.'

Linked with the above, our findings reveal that the employee champion role is not seen as a viable career move for ambitious HR practitioners, a finding that dovetails with the CIPD (2003) survey noted earlier, which shows that the employee champion role is least favored by respondents. Furthermore, while Jarvis and Robinson (2005) cite survey evidence to indicate that HR directors have currently worked in the profession for an average of 20 years, there is a concern amongst some of our respondents that a gulf is beginning to emerge between those at the top and lower rungs of the HR career ladder as people are perceived to be parachuting into top HR jobs from outside the profession:

'... business and strategic partners and people at the lower end of the scale like administrators and lower line who are beginning to feel like they have been cut off. It's almost a two-tier system. Strategic partner are the important guys, but that's not how it should be.' (HR Advisor)

At a more senior level, HR directors in our study also expressed concern about the profession losing sight of its distinctive employee champion role. One HR director responded by moving to a smaller organization where he had an opportunity to carve out a form of business partnership 'with attitude', which proactively embraces the employee agenda (see Francis and Keegan, 2005 for case example).

Our findings resonate with current debate within the HR literature in which it is argued that that while the traditional 'linear' model of career progression remains in evidence, significant alterations in the shape of HR careers are emerging as organizations move towards the shared services model (Hiltrop, 1998; Caldwell, 2003; CIPD, 2006c). As integrated teams are restructured into a central SSC, business partners, and centers of expertise, career progression is expected to become more 'crab-like', and demarcations between transactional and strategic HR activities become more marked as segmentation between roles deepens (CIPD, 2006c, p. ix).

As a result, graduates seeking careers in HR are likely to experience difficulties finding entry-level jobs with the kind of built-in opportunities for development and progression typical of more traditional functional structures. It is within this context that those junior practitioners within our study who

felt increasingly 'cut off' from business and strategic partners talked about a disconnection between administrative and
'strategic' HR activities and a lack of attention being given to
day-to-day employee concerns.

'I don't think there's a strong enough link between who's
actually designing (the vision) and seeing the business into
the future, and what's actually happening. … especially with
the strategic partner, if you like, some of the things that
come out at that level, and you think 'have they actually
been down in the front here', you know, to find out what's
going on?'

Loss of employee trust and confidence

Our study suggests that the devolution of transactional HR
work to the line combined with its relocation to service centers,
and largely strategic orientation of business partners, means
employees are increasingly losing day-to-day contact with HR
specialists and relying on line managers who may have neither the time nor the training to give HR work the priority it
needs. In this context, one HR manager who had worked in
the profession for several years reflected on what she described
as increasing divisions at the workplace that were leading to
significant changes in levels of trust between employees/their
representatives and HR professionals:

'When I first started in HR I felt quite comfortable with my
role in HR and I'd say now I'm sort of starting to feel like
there's a definite divide between employees and
management, and although there's been lots of talk and
everything about, you know, partnership agreement and
working partnership, there's something not quite right
there, there's something that's stopping that happening,
there's no trust. I mean there doesn't seem to be any trust
from our unions. I've got a meeting with them tomorrow

> actually to try and do some relationship building with them but, em, they don't trust us in HR. They've said to me quite bluntly... we support the business but we don't support the employees, no matter what we say.'

The nature and impact of the potentially growing alienation of HR service from employees remains under researched (Reddington et al., 2005) and raises questions about the lack of basic social and infrastructural support for employees, a point emphasized by Harry Donaldson, regional (Scottish) secretary of the GMB Union:

> 'If business partnering becomes too much driven by team leaders and line managers, and the only place that you can contact HR is to actually go through a PC, or 'phone a call center, then employees will question whether their employer really cares about them and are serious about the maxim that they are the company's most valued assets. It seems to me that the role of employee champion will become the sole preserve of the trade union.'

Discussion: strategic amplification and costs to employee wellbeing

What are the consequences of the strategic amplification of HR work noted by our respondents and found in much of the literature about e-enabled HR and performance? Peccei (2004) argues that the heavy emphasis being placed within the HR literature on the achievement of business-oriented performance outcomes has obscured the importance of employee wellbeing in its own right, and that there is a dearth of research investigating what HR practices help to sustain and underpin 'happy workplaces'. Similarly, Grant and Shields (2002) argue that the emphasis typically placed on the business case

for HR suggests a one-sided focus on organizational outcomes at the expense of employees, resonating with Winstanley
and Woodall's (2000) assertions that employee wellbeing and
ethics within the unfolding field of HRM remain contentious,
and that:

'... the ethical dimension of HR policy and practice has been
almost ignored in recent texts on HRM, where the focus
has shifted to 'strategic fit' and 'best practice' approaches.'
   (Winstanley and Woodall, 2000, p. 6)

Ulrich himself argues that a high degree of alignment
between HR employee champions and management can lead
to extreme alienation of employees from both HR and management, which has obvious implications for employee wellbeing. This dynamic can be avoided, he argues, if HR professionals effectively 'represent both employee needs and implement management agendas' (Ulrich, 1997, p. 5). The real
possibility of value-role conflict is not addressed here, perhaps
because Ulrich's conception of the employee champion (and
of employee advocate) seems to take for granted one of the
central nostrums of normative models of HR, that employee
wellbeing and organizational goals can always be aligned, for
example through the creation of high-commitment or high-
performance work practices (Tyson, 1995; Purcell et al., 2003).
The inherent 'duality' in HR work described by writers like
Legge (1978) and Keenoy (1997; 1999) is not recognized in
this modeling of HR nor in current 'talk' about what HR is
doing and where it is heading (Dunn, 1990; Hart, 1993).

Making sense of the possible trade-offs in HR policy and
practice, between the pursuit of high performance working
and employee wellbeing is made difficult by the fact that the
latter construct has been conceived broadly by researchers, and
'often not in a way that is intuitively actionable for managers
and employees' (Harter et al., 2003, p. 208). The impact of HR
practices on employee outcomes is thought to be considerably
more complex than that normally assumed in the HR literature, and there remain serious questions about the nature and

effects of high performance work practices on employee well-being (Peccei, 2004, p. 12). Moreover little is known regarding the 'time lag' effect this will have on employees (Hope-Hailey et al., 2005) and there is a clear need for longitudinal research into employee perceptions of HR transformations over time.

Conceptualizing HRM in ways that acknowledge these complexities and tensions seems to us an essential goal which could be facilitated by a critically reflective framing of HR practice. This could provide a critical response to what Legge (1999) notes as a trend to represent employees primarily in terms of market-based rhetoric and Renwick (2003) observes as the 'gambling' by HR practitioners with employee wellbeing in their efforts to gain strategic influence.

Efforts to pursue constructive dialogue on the employee-facing role in HR work is hampered by an unfortunate tendency to use phrases like 'tea and sympathy' to describe what employee champions (should) do, and to suggest that strategic business partnership is the 'future', and that any attempt to reclaim a space for talking about employee wellbeing is tantamount to dragging the profession back into the dark ages of 'welfare work' (Beckett, 2005; Keegan and Francis, 2006). These attitudes miss the point, as both are essential to the future of HR. We hope that our chapter can contribute to more critical dialogue that helps reclaim a space for talking and thinking about the transformation of HR and the role of ICT-enabled technology in terms of employee needs and not just the business case.

References

Beckett, H. (2005) Perfect partners. *People Manage.* 1 April, 16–23.

Beer, M. (1997) The transformation of the human resource function: resolving the tension between a traditional administrative role and a new strategic role. *Hum. Resource Manage.* 36, 49–56.

Boxall, P. and Purcell, J. (2003) *Strategy and Human Resource Management.* Basingstoke and New York: Palgrave Macmillan.

Brown, D. (2005) Are you a people person? *People Manage.* 27 October, 9.

Brown, D., Caldwell, R., White, K., Atkinson, H., Tansley, T., Goodge, P, and Emmott, M. (2004) *Business Partnering, a New Direction for HR*. London: CIPD.

Caldwell, R. (2003) The changing roles of personnel managers: old ambiguities, new uncertainties. *J. Manage. Stud.* 40, 983–1004.

Chartered Institute of Personnel and Development HR Report (2003) HR Survey: *Where We Are and Where We Are Going?* Available online at:www.cipd.co.uk/subjects/hrpract/hrtrends/hrsurvey.htm?IsSrchRes=1 (last accessed 23 September 2007).

Chartered Institute of Personnel and Development Report (2005a) *Fit for Business, Building a Strategic HR Function in the Public Sector.* London: CIPD.

Chartered Institute of Personnel and Development Report (2005c) *HR Outsourcing: the Key Decisions.* London: CIPD.

Chartered Institute of Personnel and Development Report (2006a) *The HR Function, Today's Challenges, Tomorrow's Direction.* Available online at: www.cipd.co.uk/subjects/hrpract/general/_hrfunctn.htm (last accessed 23 September 2007).

Chartered Institute of Personnel and Development Report (2006b) The *Changing HR Function, Key Questions to Ask.* Available online at: www.cipd.co.uk/NR/rdonlyres/ACD1E019-8D4F-4F82-AF7A-2022C2322BDE/0/changhrfunc.pdf (last accessed 23 September 2007).

Chartered Institute of Personnel and Development Report (2006c) *Managing and Developing HR Careers, Emerging Trends and Issues.* London: CIPD.

Chartered Institute of Personnel and Development Report (2007) *HR and Technology: Impact and Advantages.* London: CIPD.

Cooke, F., Shen, J. and McBride, A. (2005). Outsourcing HR as a Competitive strategy? A literature review and an Assessment of implications. *Hum. Resource Manage.* Vol. 44, 413–432.

Cooper, C. (2001) Win by a canvas. *People Manage.* 25, January.

Cresswell, J. (1998) *Qualitative Inquiry and Research Design: Choosing Among Five Traditions,* Thousand Oaks, CA: Sage Publications.

Cunningham, I. and Hyman, J. (1999) Devolving human resource responsibilities to the line, Beginning of the end or a new beginning for personnel? *Pers. Rev.* 28, 1–13.

Dunn, S. (1990) Root metaphor in the old and new industrial relations. *Br. J. Indust. Relat.* 28, 1–31.

Earnshaw, J., Marchington, M., and Goodman, J. (2000) Unfair to whom? Discipline and dismissed in small establishments. *Indust. Relat. J.* 31, 62–73.

Florkowski, G.M. and Olivas-Luján, M.R. (2006) The diffusion of human-resource information-technology innovations in US and non-US firms. *Pers. Rev.* 35, 684–710.

Francis, H. and Keegan, A. (2005) Slippery slope. *People Manage.* 30 June, 26–31.

Francis, H. and Keegan, A. (2006) The changing face of HR: in search of balance. *Hum. Resource Manage. J.* 13, 231–49.

Grant, D. and Shields, J. (2002) In search of the subject: researching employee reactions to human resource management. *J. Indust. Relat.* 44, 313–34.

Guest, D. and King, Z. (2004) Power, innovation and problem-solving: the personnel managers' three steps to heaven? *J. Manage. Stud.* 41, 401–23.

Hales, C. (2005) Rooted in supervision, branching into management: continuity and change in the role of first-line manager. *J. Manage. Stud.* 42, 471–506.

Hart, T.J. (1993) Human resource management: time to exorcize the militant tendency. *Empl. Relat.* 15, 29–36.

Harter, J.K., Schmidt, F.L., and Keyes, C.L.M. (2003) Well-being in the workplace and its relationship to business outcomes, a review of the Gallup studies. In *Flourishing: The Positive Person and the Good Life* (C.L.M. Keyes and J. Haidt, eds.) Washington, DC: American Psychological Association.

Hiltrop, J.M. (1998) Preparing people for the future: the next agenda for HRM. *Euro. Manage. J.* Vol. 15, 70–8.

Hoobler, J. and Johnson N. (2004) An analysis of current human resource management publications. *Pers. Rev.* Vol. 33, (6) p. 665–676.

Hope-Hailey, V., Farndale, E., and Truss, C. (2005) The HR department's role in organisational performance. *Hum. Resource Manage. J.* 15, 49–66.

Huselid, M. (1995) The impact of human resource management practices on turnover, productivity, and corporate financial performance. *Acad. Manage. J.* 38, 635–72.

Hutchinson, S. and Purcell, J. (2003). *Bringing Policies to Life: The Vital Role of Front Line Managers in People Management.* London: CIPD.

Jarvis, J. and Robinson, D. (2005) Watch your step. *People Manage.* 27 October, 31–5.

Keegan, A. and Boselie P. (2006) The lack of impact of dissensus inspired analysis on developments in the field of HRM. *J. Manage. Stud.* 43, 1491–511.

Keegan, A. and Francis, H. (2006) Facing facts. *People Manage.* 23 February, 9.

Keenoy, T. (1997) Review article: HRMism and the languages of re-presentation. *J. Manage. Stud.* 34, 825–41.

Keenoy, T. (1999) As hologram: a polemic. *J. Manage. Stud.* 36, 1–23.

Kessler, I., Coyle-Shapiro, J., and Purcell, J. (1999). Outsourcing and the employee perspective. *Hum. Resource Manage. J.* 9, 5–19.

Kochan, T. (2004) Restoring trust in the human resource manage-ment profession. *Asia Pacific J. Hum. Resour.* 42, 132–46.

Legge, K. (1978) *Power, Innovation and Problem-Solving in Personnel Management.* London: McGraw-Hill.

Legge, K. (1999). Representing people at work. *Organization,* 6: 2, 247–264.

Lepak, D., Bartol, K., and Erhardt, N. (2005). A contingency frame-work for the delivery of HR practices. *Hum. Resource Manage. Rev.* 15, 139–59.

Losey, M. Meisinger, S.R., and Ulrich, D. (2005) Conclusion: reality, impact and professionalism. *Hum. Resource Manage.* 44, 201–6.

Marchington, M. and Wilkinson, A. (2005) *Human Resource Manage-ment at Work.* (3rdedn.), London: CIPD.

Martin, G. (2005) *Technology and People Management, the Opportunity and the Challenge, Research Report.* London: CIPD.

Martin, G., Wood, G., and Colling, D. (2006) Institutions, HR strate-gies and the Adoption of e-HR. *Proceedings of the First European Academic Workshop on Electronic Human Resource, University of Twente, 25–26 October.*

McConville (2006) Devolved HRM responsibilities, middle-managers and role dissonance. *Pers. Rev.* 35, 637–53.

Miles, B.M. and Huberman, A.M. (1994) *Qualitative Data Analysis: an Expanded Source Book.* London: Sage Publications.

Morgan, D. (2006) Relocation, outsourcing and the interim market: the latest facts. *Human Resourcefulness.* January. Available online at: www.digbymorgannewsletter.co.uk/story3_HR_11_05.html (last accessed 23 September 2007).

Morley, M.J., Gunnigle, P., O'Sullivan, M., and Collings, D.G. (2006) New directions in the roles and responsibilities of the HRM function. *Pers. Rev.* 35, 609–17.

Paauwe, J., and Farndale, E. (2007). HR shared services centers in Nederland. Ervaringen, Verwachtingen en lessen voor de toekomst. *Tijdschrift voor HRM,* 10, 7–31.

Patton, M. (2002). *Qualitative Research and Evaluation Methods.* (3rd edn.), Thousand Oaks, CA: Sage Publications.

Peccei, R. (2004) *Human Resource Management and the Search for the Happy Workplace, Inaugural Address.* Erasmus University Rotterdam: Erasmus Research Institute of Management.

Pfeffer, J. (1998) *The Human Equation; Building Profits by Putting People First.* Boston: Harvard Business School Press.

Purcell, J. (2006) cited in Tamkin, P., Reilly, P., and Strebler, M. (2006) *The Changing HR Function: the Key Questions.* CIPD Research Report, London: CIPD.

Purcell, J., Kinnie, N., Hutchinson, S., Rayton, B., and Swart, J. (2003) *Understanding the People and Performance Link: Unlocking the Black Box, Research Report.* London: CIPD.

Reddington, M. and Martin, G. (2006) Theorizing the Links Between e-HR and Strategic HRM: a Framework, Case Illustrations and Some Reflections, *Proceedings of the First European Academic Workshop on Electronic Human Resource Management,* Vrije Universiteit, Amsterdam.

Redman, T. and Wilkinson, A. (2001). *Contemporary Human Resource Management,* Upper Saddle River, NJ: Prentice Hall.

Reddington, M., Williamson, M., and Withers, M. (2005) *Transforming HR: Creating Value through People.* Oxford: Butterworth-Heinemann/Elsevier.

Reilly, P. and Williams, T. (2006) *Strategic HR building the capability to deliver.* London: Gower.

Renwick, D. (2003) HR managers, guardians of employee wellbeing? *Pers. Rev.* 32, 341–59.

Roberts, J. (2005) 'Throw away the rulebook', HR urged. *People Manage.* 11, 12.

Storey, J. (1992) *Developments in the Management of Human Resources.* Oxford: Blackwell.

Tamkin, P., Reilly, P., and Hirsh, W. (2006) Managing and Developing HR Careers: Emerging Trends and Issues. CIPD Research Report, London: CIPD.

Tamkin, P., Reilly, P., and Hirsh, W. (2006) *Managing and Developing HR Careers: Emerging Trends and Issues.* CIPD Research Report, London: CIPD.

Torrington, D., Hall, L., and Taylor, S. (2005) Ethics and corporate social responsibility. In *Human Resource Management.* (6th edn.), (D. Torrington, L. Hall, and S. Taylor, eds.), Harlow, FT/Prentice Hall, 715–734.

Tyson, S. (1995) *Human Resource Strategy.* London: FT/Prentice Hall.

Tyson, S. and Fell, A. (1986) *Evaluating the personnel function.* London: Hutchinson.

Ulrich, D. (1997) *HR Champions.* Boston, MA: Harvard Business School Press.

Ulrich, D. (1998). A new mandate for Human Resources. *Harvard Business Review,* Jan/Feb 1998, Vol. 76, p124–134.

Ulrich, D. and Brockbank, W. (2005) *The HR Value Proposition.* Boston, MA: Harvard Business School Press.

Valverde, M., Ryan, G., and Sloer, C. (2006) Distributing HRM responsibilities: a classification of organizations. *Pers. Rev.* 35, 618–36.

Watson, T. (1977). *The Personnel Managers.* London: Routledge and Kegan Paul.

Whittaker, J. and Johns, T. (2004) Standards deliver. *People Manage.* June, 32–6.

Whittaker, S. and Marchington, M. (2003) Devolving HR responsibility to the line: threat opportunity or partnership? *Empl. Relat.* 25, 245–61.

Winstanley, D. and Woodall, J. (2000) The ethical dimension of human resource management. *Hum. Resource Manage. J.* 10, 5–20.

Woodall, J., Gourlay, S.N., and Short, D. (2002) Trends in outsourcing HRD in the UK: the implications for strategic HRD. *Int. J. Hum. Resource. Dev. Manage.* 2, 50–63.

Further reading

CIPD (2004) Professional Standards. Available online at: www.cipd.co.uk/mandq/standards/ professionalstandardsfulllversion.htm?IsSrchRes=1.

CIPD Report (2005b) HR, *where is your career heading.* Available online at: www.cipd.co.uk/NR/rdonlyres/7D4E95C3-706E-4224-957B-534F9D7B2E61/0/hrsr1005.pdf (last accessed 23 September 2007).

Cooke, F.L., Shen, J., and Mcbride, A. (2005) Outsourcing HR as a competitive strategy? A literature review and an assessment of implications. *Hum. Resource Manage.* 44, 413–32.

Legge, K. (1995) *Human Resource Management, Rhetorics and Realities.* London: Macmillan Press.

Townley, B. (2004) Managerial technologies, ethics and managing. *J. Manage. Stud.* 41, 425–45.

Watson, T. (2004) HRM and critical social science analysis. *J. Manage. Stud.* 41, 447–67.

Abbreviations

AHRI	Australian Human Resources Institute
ASP	application service provider
ATM	automatic teller machine
BBC	British Broadcasting Corporation
BNZ	Bank of New Zealand
BPO	business process outsourcing
BTHR	BT Human Resources
CEO	chief executive officer
Ci	corporate intranet
CIPD	Chartered Institute of Personnel and Development
CRM	customer relationship management
CSR	Corporate Social Responsibility
CT	computerized tomography
CV	curriculum vitae
DIF	droit individuel à la formation (legislation in France)
DOI	diffusion of innovations
EEO	equal employment opportunity
EGM	executive general manager
EPM	electronic performance management
ERP	enterprise resource planning
ESS	employee self-service
FTE	full-time equivalent
GP	general practitioner
GUI	graphical user interface
HQ	head quarters
HR	human resource

HR-ICT	human resource information and communication technology
HRIS	human resource information system
HRM	human resource management
HRMS	human resource management system
HRO	human resource outsourcing
ICT	information and communication technology
IES	Institute of Employment
IHRIM	International Association for Human Resource Information Management
IPCM	individual performance and career management
IPDS	Integrated Personnel Development System
IQPC	International Quality and Productivity Council
IS	information systems
IT	information technology
ITC	information technology communication
IVR	interactive voice response
JAS	job announcement system
JV	joint venture
KSAOs	knowledge, skills, abilities, and other job requirements
LAN	local area network
LoB	Line of Business
LSE	London Stock Exchange
MIS	managing information strategy
MSS	management support system
NAB	National Australia Bank
NAO	National Audit Office
NOS	national occupational standards
NPfIT	National Programme for Information Technology
OD	organizational development
OSP	outside service provider
OUC	organizational unit code
P&C	People & Culture
P&OD	planning and organizational development
PAC	people advisory center
PASO	Panel Survey of Organizations
PDM	personal development manager
PDP	personal development planning
PDR	personal development record

PEO	professional employer organization
PSS	people success system
R&D	research and development
RBV	resource-based view
SHRM	Society for Human Resource Management
SLA	service level agreement
SME	small-to-medium enterprise
SME	subject matter expert
SP	service provider
SSC	shared service center
SSN	social security numbers
TCT	transaction cost theory
TEC	Techology Evaluation Center

PSO

PSS people support system

R&D research and development

RBV resource-based view

SHRM Society for Human Resource Management

SVA shareholder value added

VC virtual service system

WBS global account managers

TCE transaction cost theory

TQM Total Quality Management

Index